D0530956

Child Abuse

AN EVIDENCE BASE FOR CONFIDENT PRACTICE

4th edition

Brian Corby, David Shemmings and David Wilkins

Open University Press

Open University Press
McGraw-Hill Education
McGraw-Hill House
Shoppenhangers Road
Maidenhead
Berkshire
England
SL6 2QL

email: enquiries@openup.co.uk
world wide web: www.openup.co.uk

and Two Penn Plaza, New York, NY 10121–2289, USA

First published 1993
Second edition 2000
Third edition 2006
First published in this fourth edition 2012

A catalogue record of this book is available from the British Library

ISBN-13: 978-0-33-524509-3
ISBN-10: 0-33-524509-9
eISBN: 978-0-33-524510-9

Library of Congress Cataloging-in-Publication Data
CIP data applied for

Typesetting and e-book compilations by RefineCatch Limited, Bungay, Suffolk
Printed in the Great Britain by CPI Antony Rowe, Chippenham, Wiltshire

*The **McGraw·Hill** Companies*

'This is a timely and much welcome new edition of Brian Corby's highly respected work. It retains the excellent historical focus of the previous editions, but has been substantially updated to take account of the debates about the reform and reprofessionalistion of social work in the wake of the death of (Baby) Peter Connelly.'

Sue White, Professor of Social Work, University of Birmingham, UK

'This core text surveys the global landscape, recognising that cultural contexts shape definitions of and responses to child abuse and neglect ... The revised edition takes account of new directions in policy and practice in the aftermath of the Munro review in England, notably the need for systemic and therapeutic approaches to practice.'

Dr Caroline Humphrey, Senior Lecturer in Social Work, University of Hull, UK.

'This text stands out in the field [due to] its comprehensiveness. While it makes a conventional bow to the necessity for up-to-date research and evidence-based practice, it is unusual in its insistence that to be fully understood these issues must also be seen in both a historic and a cross-cultural perspective. This updated edition should prove invaluable to students, academics, policy makers and professionals across many jurisdictions.'

Helen Buckley, Associate Professor and Co-ordinator, Postgraduate Diploma in Child Protection and Welfare, Trinity College Dublin, Ireland

'There are many valuable Child Abuse or Child Protection texts available on the market, however very few successfully provide a comprehensive resource to support both. Not only does this book provide an excellent insight into the subject of Child Abuse, but it also explores the current difficulties within Safeguarding Children and Child Protection practice, with clear explanation of legislative changes and the modern challenges faced.'

Amy Dopson, Child Branch Leader Professional Preparation Nursing, University of Surrey, UK

Dedicated to the memory of the late Brian Corby and to the thousands of child protection professionals committed to keeping children safe

Contents

Acknowledgements

We would like to thank the following people for their contributions and their help, without which this book would not have been written: Yvonne Shemmings and Hayley Wilkins for their remarkable patience and unwavering support, Janet Wilkins for her studious reading of draft chapters and helpful feedback, and, not least, Alex Clabburn and Richard Townrow from McGraw-Hill, who guided us through the writing process with skill and expertise. Finally, we thank Jon Ingoldby for his editing, Claire Munce for overseeing the production of the book, and Denise Tucker for preparing the index.

Introduction

The late Brian Corby

The three previous editions of this book were written by Brian Corby (1946–2007), one of the best known and most respected experts in the field of child protection. The need for a fourth edition of his work is now evident, given the myriad changes in the policy and context of child protection since 2005, and as new authors to this text, we – Professor David Shemmings and David Wilkins – feel privileged to be able to keep Brian's work alive and contemporary. Our aims remain philosophically the same as those of the previous three editions. Given Brian's expertise in this field and the popularity of the previous editions, this book will seek to retain the uniqueness of his approach and to build on, rather than radically alter, his work.

Providing a practitioner knowledge base

It was noted in the Introduction to the first edition of this book that it 'is important that practitioners are fully conversant with what is known about child abuse and that they are able to weigh up the strengths and weaknesses of that knowledge'. This remains the case with this fourth edition. None of the editions of the book to date have attempted to provide a 'how to' guide to child protection and this again remains the case with this edition. Rather, the target audience is that of the relatively autonomous practitioner developing her/his judgement about child abuse issues based on knowledge derived not only from academic research and evaluation of practice interventions but also from studies on the history, politics and social construction of the subject.

So what has changed since the last edition?

Central government policy and child protection

Since 1993 the task of protecting children has become more and more determined by central government policy and guidelines. This trend was also in evidence at the time of the second and third editions of this book, published in 2000 and 2006 respectively. The 1990s witnessed a considerable shift in thinking about how best to organise for and respond to child protection concerns. First, serious child abuse was seen to be a relatively rare occurrence among all the referrals made about child care concerns, and, second, by placing all its focus on such serious abuse, state intervention to support families with children in need was being neglected. A third issue was that the intrusive style and nature of child protection interventions was leading to an alienation of families and, therefore, to less trust on their part in state services to provide support and help. These findings and concerns led to considerable policy changes and a shift in emphasis towards the idea of 'safeguarding' children by focusing on needs-led work with children and their families. The comprehensive assessment framework, introduced in 2000, set out how this could be achieved (Department of Health 2000a).

More recently, this trend has intensified through the *Every Child Matters* (Department of Health 2003b) agenda and in reports such as those from Professor Eileen Munro on the state of child protection in England. These sources highlighted the importance of early, effective help being given to children who may otherwise require a more expensive and more intrusive form of intervention later on. How these types of report translate into policy and practice will likely be an area of some interest over the coming years.

Victoria Climbié and Peter Connelly

In the introduction to the third edition, the death of 8-year-old Victoria Climbié was discussed. Following Victoria's death at the hands of her great-aunt and her partner, the Laming Report (2003) emphasised the failings of the whole child protection system. As a consequence, Laming's main recommendations – closer management of professionals who work directly with families, greater accountability throughout all agencies with child protection responsibilities and the strengthening of inter-agency recording and information-sharing by electronic technology – were mostly concerned with establishing procedures and protocols rather than with developing the expertise of practitioners. Laming's findings were incorporated into legislation via the 2004 Children Act.

In 2007, 17-month-old Peter Connelly ('Baby P') died. In the intense public scrutiny that followed, one could not help but notice similarities with the death of Victoria. They both died at the hands of adults who were meant to be caring for them and they were both well known to professionals and services tasked with protecting children. Following Peter's death, a number of inquiries took place, including a further report by Lord Laming (2009) and a review of child protection in England by Professor Eileen Munro (see below). The second Laming Report argued that the necessary reforms were already in place and that child protection practitioners simply needed to 'get on with it'. However, Laming also found that child protection services were underfunded, too focused on process and targets at the expense of keeping children safe, that progress was being hindered by the lack of a nationwide computer system and that an over-complicated assessment process encouraged practitioners to complete tasks while losing sight of the child's overall experience.

The Munro Review of Child Protection

In contrast, *The Munro Review of Child Protection* (Munro 2010, 2011a, 2011b) sought to understand why previous reviews and inquiries had failed to produce the much sought-after improvements in practice. Munro argued that to understand what happens in child protection, especially how and why things go wrong, we need to understand what motivates the behaviour of professionals as well as how the systems in place to protect children often result in unintended consequences. The review set out a thorough and analytical overview of the state of child protection in England. Munro was careful to say that previous reviews and inquiries had been well meaning but also noted that the processes and procedures which developed as a result and over time had reduced significantly the amount of contact professionals were able to have with children.

Knowledge and procedures

At the time of writing, the changes envisaged by the Munro Report are only just beginning to be implemented by the government and only time will tell what impact these changes will have. Whatever the outcome, it remains the case that even in circumstances where professionals have increased autonomy, this does not entirely remove the need for procedures to guide practice. A study of the implementation of the child assessment framework shows how social workers can use their knowledge, skills and understanding to good effect even when required to follow procedures (Millar and Corby 2006). As Brian Corby argued in the previous edition, it is important for professionals who work directly with families to have a sound knowledge base when working within systems and protocols, because of the dangers of assuming that systems can replace, rather than enhance, judgement. However, we also feel strongly that it is no less important for practitioners who work directly with families to have a good knowledge base when, as envisaged by the Munro Report, they are to be asked to take on even more responsibility for exercising professional judgements regarding children who may be at risk of harm.

Aims and objectives

We will focus on a broad range of sources of knowledge about the mistreatment of children, drawing on a variety of research and thinking carried out in a variety of professional and academic disciplines: social work, medicine, history, sociology, philosophy, social policy and psychology. We intend to achieve this by presenting up-to-date research-based knowledge in a critical way, evaluating its strengths and weaknesses, and giving particular attention to how the values and beliefs of researchers influence their findings.

The changing knowledge base

The scope of child protection work has increased and developed dramatically since the publication of the first edition of this book in 1993. At that time the main concerns were with intra-familial neglect and abuse and the main forms of abuse were physical, sexual and emotional. The early 1990s saw increased concern about organised abuse and a rise and fall in concerns about ritual abuse. Throughout the 1990s and into the new millennium, the abuse of children in institutional settings was a constant concern. Bullying of children has been another issue that has come onto the agenda, as has their commercial sexual exploitation. Concerns about the effects on children of parental drug and alcohol misuse, parental mental health and domestic violence (the 'toxic trio'; Brandon et al. 2009) have also become more central and in the late twentieth and early twenty-first centuries there have been major issues raised about paedophiles and child murder. In general terms, there was a shift in emphasis onto extra-familial abuse during this period and away from intra-familial abuse. Arguably, there has subsequently been an increase again in concerns about intra-familial abuse but without necessarily a reduction in concern about extra-familiar abuse. Other emerging concerns – such as child abuse and neglect in an international context, the treatment of child asylum seekers in Britain, abuse of children on the internet and Fabricated or Induced Illness (FII) (previously known as Munchausen's syndrome by proxy) – are discussed further and with a view to developing a more international feel to this edition.

The field of study of child abuse and neglect is such a diverse and fast-changing one that it is not easy to maintain coherence. In order to do this, however, we have decided to adhere to the format of the third edition as far as possible and to incorporate new information and topics within that format. To a large extent, decisions as to what information and research to include or omit must be left to the authors' judgements. However, as a guide to this, it should be noted that material from key British and international journals for 1999 to 2012 has been researched together with relevant British and American books and government reports and publications. Material adding new or strengthening information has been included. Some older references have been discarded where their findings have been replicated by newer studies. All government statistics used have been replaced by the latest figures.

The extent of child abuse and neglect

In order to maintain the historical overview of child protection policy and practice in Chapters 1 and 2, it has been necessary to adjust the chapter structure of the book. The most significant statistics in the extent of child abuse and neglect in the UK, previously found in Chapter 5 of the third edition, are now included here. Estimates of the prevalence and incidence of child maltreatment may not have direct relevance for fieldwork but they are crucial in the wider allocation of resources and in the development of policy. This information also gives a sense of the size of the problem and of how numbers of children felt to be at risk have changed over time. There are two main sources of statistical knowledge. The first, drawn largely from government departments, measures the incidence of child abuse as reported, recorded or registered by official agencies. The second, deriving from a broader research base, measures the incidence and prevalence of abuse in a given sample of people.[1] As a result, official statistics tell us more about the way in which child abuse is defined in practice and responded to over time, whereas research studies tell us more about the 'hidden' problem, about abuse that does not come to the attention of official authorities.

We will look first at official statistics. Figure I.1 has been devised using figures from the National Society for the Prevention of Cruelty to Children (NSPCC) and from relevant government departments. A significant change took place in 2010 in that from then onwards, figures have been collected via the Children in Need census. As such, the figures from 2010 were not endorsed by the Office for National Statistics (ONS) and remain 'experimental statistics', subject to further testing and validation. While there are many problems associated with the interpretation of these sets of statistics because of variations in practice between local authorities (Corby 1990), and changes in categories over time, they nevertheless provide at least a basis from which to assess and monitor trends of practice in general terms.

As can be seen, there was a sharp decline in numbers on the register between 1991 and 1992. This followed the elimination of the 'grave concern' category, as a result of which there was need for more specificity about the causes of concern before registration could be completed.[2] Throughout the 1990s, there was a more gradual decline in numbers, so that by 1999 the rate was just under 3 per 1,000. The decline in numbers reached its lowest point so far in 2002. In 2004 the rate per 1,000 children on child protection registers was approximately 2.5. However, there has since been a notable increase of over 50 per cent since 2006, rising to a peak in 2010, when the highest number of children in England were subject to child protection plans since

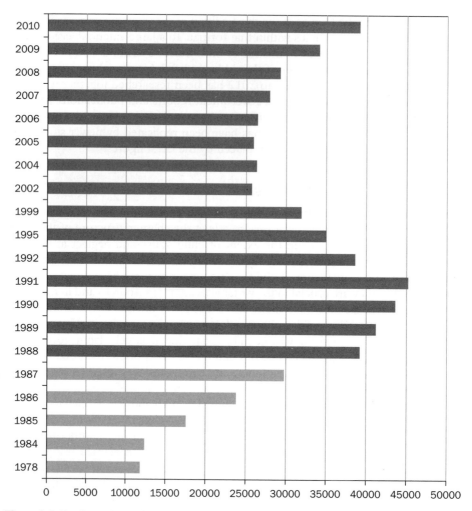

Figure I.1 Total numbers of children subject to child protection plans in Wales and England for selected years between 1978 and 1987 and in England only for selected years between 1988 and 2010
Sources: 1978–86 Creighton (1984, 1985, 1986); 1987 Association of the Directors of Social Services (1988); 1988–2002 Department of Health (1989, 1990, 1991c, 1992, 1993, 1996, 2000b, 2003a); 2004–6 Department for Education and Skills (2004a, 2005, 2006); 2007–9 Department for Children, Schools and Families (2007, 2008a, 2009a); 2010 Department for Education (2010)

1991. The most likely explanation for much of the increase is the media reporting of the case of Peter Connelly, which led to a substantial increase in referral rates from late 2008 onwards, although 12 per cent of the increase took place before this time, demonstrating that other factors were already having an impact.

When looking at these figures, it appears that child protection concerns diminished considerably between 1991 and 2005–6 before increasing again from 2007 onwards. However, if one looks at the number of registrations per year (see Figure I.2), a different picture emerges. The number of registrations per annum rose by a third between 1988 and 1995 and then stayed at about the same level until 2008, when they started to increase. In the period 1988–95, the number of de-registrations increased by 40 per cent, and in 2004 there were more de-registrations than registrations. In 2008 and 2010, the numbers of registrations increased again. Thus the impression of a decline in child protection activity in the 1990s given by Figure I.1 is not borne out by the figures in Figure I.2. In terms of registration numbers per year, child protection work has been on the increase since 1990 (although there was a small drop in 2002). It was the concomitant rise in de-registrations between 1988 and 2004 that contributed to the lowering of the overall totals in this time frame and it is the widening gap between registrations and de-registrations from 2008 onwards that accounts for the overall growth in this time frame.

A breakdown of the numbers of children subject to child protection plans according to different categories of abuse (see Table I.1) provides more detail about the nature of the development of official child protection work in Britain over the same period.

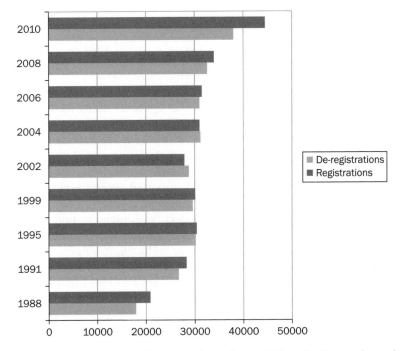

Figure I.2 Registrations to and de-registrations from child protection registers/children subject to child protection plans for selected years ending 31 March 1988–2010
Sources: 1978–86 Creighton (1984, 1985, 1986); 1987 Association of the Directors of Social Services (1988); 1988–2002 Department of Health (1989, 1990, 1991c, 1992, 1993, 1996, 2000b, 2003a); 2004–6 Department for Education and Skills (2004a, 2005, 2006); 2007–9 Department for Children, Schools and Families (2007, 2008a, 2009a); 2010 Department for Education (2010)

Table I.1 Breakdown of the numbers of children subject to child protection plans according to different categories of abuse

Category of abuse	1986	1988	1991	1995	1999	2002	2004	2008	2010
Physical abuse	10,422	11,100	9,000	12,300	9,100	4,200	4,100	3,400	4,700
Neglect	1,888	4,900	5,600	9,200	13,900	10,100	11,000	13,400	17,200
Sexual abuse	5,922	5,800	5,600	7,200	6,600	2,800	2,500	2,000	2,200
Emotional abuse	455	1,700	2,600	3,800	5,400	4,500	5,100	7,900	11,400
Grave concern	5,133	14,400	21,100	–	–	–	–	–	–
Joint categories	–	1,300	1,300	2,500	–	4,100	3,600	2,500	3,400
Total	23,820	39,200	45,200	35,000	31,900	25,700	26,300	29,200	39,100

Note: The figures in the categories for 1999 exceed the total by 3,100. This is because between 1998 and 2001 the Department of Health included mixed categories in each of the separate categories and thus there is an element of double counting. Figures for 1988–99 are for England only.

The alternative method for investigating the extent of child abuse is via the broader research base. Generally speaking, this approach finds far higher levels of child abuse and neglect than is recorded in official statistics. In one such study on behalf of the NSPCC, in which 2,869 young adults aged 18–24 were surveyed about their childhood experiences, Cawson et al. (2000) found that 7 per cent reported serious physical abuse in childhood, 1 per cent reported serious sexual abuse, 11 per cent reported serious neglect and 6 per cent reported serious emotional abuse. In total, the study found that 16 per cent of the sample considered themselves to have been seriously abused or neglected in childhood (with many respondents reporting multiple types of maltreatment). This equates to around 1 in 6 children in England, and if intermediate levels of maltreatment were included, this figure would rise to 1 in 3. In a follow-up study, again on behalf of the NSPCC, Radford et al. (2011) interviewed adults (aged 18–24) and children (aged 11 to 17); 1 in 4 adults reported having been seriously maltreated in childhood and around 1 in 5 of the children reported serious levels of maltreatment (see Figure I.3 for a comparison).

As can be seen, these two studies (one reporting in 1998–9 and one in 2009) show a drop in the levels of verbal abuse, physical punishment, coercive sex, physical abuse and problems with care. Levels of neglect were found to be similar (9.4 per cent of respondents reporting some form of neglect in 1998 compared with 9.9 per cent in 2009). If accurate, this is clearly a good thing. Nevertheless, although there are clear difficulties with official statistics, in that they can only ever capture child abuse or neglect which comes to the attention of the appropriate authorities, self-report studies of the type employed by the NSPCC also have difficulties, such as inaccurate

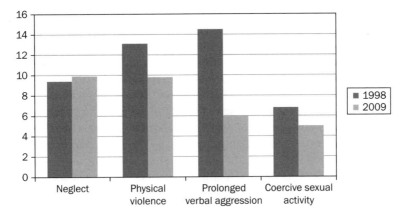

Figure I.3 A comparison of self-reported rates of neglect and physical, emotional and sexual abuse between 1998 and 2009
Source: Radford et al. (2011)

recollection of childhood experiences and embarrassment on the part of the respondent, which can prevent complete disclosures and biases such as the respondent's feelings at the time of the research or specific biases such as social desirability bias (a motivation to respond in the manner likely to be viewed as favourable by others).

In conclusion, we feel it is highly likely, if not proven, that child abuse and neglect is more widespread than official statistics can demonstrate but that by its very nature the phenomenon of child abuse and neglect is one of the more difficult issues to study, and that a complete and accurate knowledge of the likely prevalence and incidence is unlikely to be established.

Outline of the remaining chapters

In Chapter 1 the focus is on how, throughout history, there have been different constructions and understandings of what constitutes childhood and child abuse and neglect. It is argued that careful analysis of historical research can help in the understanding of the present.

Chapters 2 and 3 concentrate on the recent history of child protection policy and practice from 1870 up to the present time. Detailed consideration is given to how social and political forces have shaped the way in which we respond to child abuse allegations today. The aim is to help those currently involved in this field of activity to understand the reasons for the complex and often contradictory nature of that response.

Chapter 4 considers the issue of child abuse and neglect definitions, and the impact of different definitions on policy, practice and research.

Chapter 5 looks critically at the question of the likely perpetrators of child abuse and in what circumstances child abuse is more likely to occur. This is an area of considerable development since the previous edition.

Chapter 6 considers a range of social and psychological theories and ideologies that have been applied to child abuse and neglect to explain why it happens. This chapter also includes a consideration of the increasingly important concept of disorganised attachment as well as the 'explanatory mechanisms' likely to lead to it (Shemmings and Shemmings 2011).

Chapter 7 reviews research into the consequences and aftermath of the abuse and neglect of children, with implications for both practice and policy in ongoing child protection work.

Chapter 8 describes empirical research into child protection practice, examining key studies which demonstrate the effectiveness of different forms of intervention and the perspective of service users. The impact of research on policy and practice is particularly emphasised.

Chapter 9 considers global and cultural perspectives on child abuse and how these areas relate to practice in the UK – for example, the issues of trafficked children and forced marriages.

Finally, Chapter 10 aims to bring together the main themes from preceding chapters and identify key issues for the future.

1

Childhood, child abuse and history

Introduction

The activities and concerns of the helping professions are, by and large, very present-oriented. They are committed to tackling current social, health, educational and personal problems and to finding useful and pragmatic tools to support them in this endeavour. Indeed, such is their determination to discover new solutions to such problems that they tend to ignore what has gone before and to demonstrate a lack of enthusiasm for understanding how similar concerns have been constructed and responded to in earlier times. Yet there is much that can be learned from an examination of the way in which our own and other societies have tackled the same sort of problems and concerns in the past, provided that this is done with care and awareness of the fact that the issues, though similar, are being played out in different contexts.

If we consider the specific field of child protection work, this ignorance of the past is all too evident. Many accounts of the background to child protection work begin with Henry Kempe and his 'discovery' of the child battering syndrome in the early 1960s (Kempe et al. 1962), as if the problem either did not exist before this or had somehow lain dormant. Similarly, sexual abuse is often described as having been discovered in Britain at the beginning of the 1980s. However, to take just one example, accounts of the child protection movement in the late nineteenth and early twentieth centuries, such as those by Behlmer (1982), Rose (1986, 1991) and Ferguson (1990, 2004), demonstrate that very similar things were taking place in this field then as have been happening in Britain at the end of the twentieth and beginning of the twenty-first centuries. Infant life protection protagonists, the National Society for the Prevention of Cruelty to Children (NSPCC) officials and various other philanthropic agents were then emphasising the widespread nature of child abuse and seeking to convince the public of the need for a change in attitude towards the care and treatment of children. They too were decrying the fact that the law and procedures were deficient in dealing with the problem and arguing vehemently that children should be more adequately protected. The experiences of these late Victorians, considered in more detail in Chapter 2, in fact provide us with a rich source of useful material for evaluating recent responses to child protection issues. As we shall see, however, in order to benefit from this type of approach, we have to interpret the historian's word as critically and as objectively as possible.

Interpreting history

Historians themselves are well aware of the difficulties of learning from the past:

> The study of past attitudes, of modes of thought and feeling is one of the most difficult branches of historiography. Not only is evidence patchy and often indirect, particularly where intimate family matters or the mentality of the inarticulate or the illiterate are concerned, but the interpretation of such evidence requires an empathy, a feeling for nuances, and above all an objectivity, a deliberate attempt to set aside one's own cultural assumptions that is not easy to attain . . . Huge generalisations have been hoisted on the slenderest foundations, evidence

that is not congenial has been ignored or brushed aside, while other testimony has been crudely or carelessly misinterpreted. All of which suggests the need for a reminder that bad history can still mislead the 'general public' as well as other scholars and students.

(Wilson 1984: 198)

All historical writing is inevitably selective. The range of sources available is often vast. Historians have their favoured viewpoints and theories, which influence the way in which they interpret data, and these result in emphasis on certain types of evidence and lack of attention to others. For instance, historical writing varies considerably with regard to the attention paid to the different forms of structural oppression, such as race, class, gender and age, and their impact on attitudes and behaviours. Currently there is considerable reassessment of the past through these filters, particularly in the case of race and gender.

When history is used as a means of casting light on present issues, there seem to be two mainstream perspectives. The first views the present as an inevitable improvement on the past. Adherents of this viewpoint draw comfort from the ignorance and mistakes (as they see them) of previous generations. Those favouring the second perspective paint a rosy picture of yesteryear and see the present not as progress from the past, but as retrogressive. The first perspective views the past as barbaric, the second as a golden age. It is important to be aware of and to understand different viewpoints of this kind in order to maximise the usefulness of historical material.

Childhood and history

The issues of childhood and child abuse are closely linked. Views about the status and rights of children have considerable influence on the way in which they are treated by adults and, therefore, determine to some extent what is considered to be mistreatment. For the purposes of analysis, however, they will be treated separately. In what follows we will consider what historians have to tell us about childhood.

While historically informed awareness of the socially constructed nature of childhood may not solve the immediate question – whether professionals at a child protection conference should recommend an application for an emergency protection order in the case of a young child left alone and unprotected, or how a community mental health team should advise an abused teenage girl experiencing suicidal thoughts – nevertheless such awareness can enable social workers to reflect more fully on the social and political underpinnings to these situations and may ultimately inform the decisions that are finally reached in these and other cases. As one historian puts it:

One possible spin-off of a historical approach is that it can prevent us from taking any particular set of attitudes or behaviours as 'natural' or 'normal'. By examining the historical variety of the position of children and of ideas about childhood and by tracing back some of the steps by which we arrived at our present situation, we can achieve a more dispassionate analysis.

(Jordanova 1989: 4–5)

To the lay person the notion of childhood is self-evident. We all 'know' a child when we see one. Of course it becomes a little more difficult in the case of adolescents. Nevertheless, most people consider childhood to be an age-related phenomenon. This is reflected in British law, which prescribes a series of legal rights and responsibilities that takes effect at different ages. These statutes provide protection for children, place duties on their parents, impose prohibitions on certain activities and later lift them.

There are all sorts of anomalies. For instance, in the UK a 16-year-old is deemed responsible enough to marry (with parental consent) and have children, but not responsible enough to buy an alcoholic drink in a public house or to watch a category 18 film. Following the passing of the Sexual Offences Act (Amendment) 2000 and the Sexual Offences Act 2003, the age of sexual consent in England, Wales and Scotland was set at 16 regardless of sexual orientation. In 2008, the age of sexual consent was lowered from 17 to 16 in Northern Ireland in order to bring the law in line with the rest of the UK. However, other countries set different ages – for example, 18 in Egypt, 15 in France, 14 in Germany and 13 in Spain. While the age of 18 is generally thought to be the beginning of adulthood in the UK, there are still prohibitions that last until the age of 21. Only then can a person stand as a councillor or Member of Parliament, apply for a licence to sell alcohol, have a heavy goods vehicle licence or apply to adopt a child. Such is the power of chronological age.

Despite these tightly age-related demarcations, we know that children develop and mature, both physically and psychologically, at different rates. We also know that in societies other than our own, childhood is construed differently. In many of the world's poorer countries, childhood is mostly shorter, particularly if a child is poor, black and female (Ennew 1986). Children generally assume what we would term adult responsibilities at an earlier age in these societies than in richer industrially developed countries – they are more likely to fend for themselves on the streets (Panter-Brick 2002) and work for a living (UNICEF 2011). In richer societies, childhood, in the sense of being free from such demands, has tended to be extended to higher and higher ages. The trend is to keep young people in education longer, because of the reduced demand for manual labour and the increased demand for a better-trained workforce as technology and markets develop and become more complex.

Historians seem to have paid far more attention to children and the concept of childhood since the 1960s than ever before. This may well reflect the apparent growth in concerns about children and childhood in contemporary society during this period. Even here, however, we need to be careful in our interpretations, because there is evidence, even in the earliest societies, of child-centred concerns on the part of parents. Sommerville (1982) notes that in Mesopotamia, in 1800 BC, parents were expressing the same sort of worries about their children as parents are now, that they were not obedient and not working hard enough at school. Concerns about children, therefore, seem to be perennial ones. Nevertheless, it is true that, since the 1960s, we do have a great deal more historical material to draw upon than before.

Philippe Ariès and childhood

The most influential work on childhood of this period has been that of Philippe Ariès, a French social historian. Along with Lloyd de Mause, an American psycho-historian whose work is considered later, he is probably the most often quoted historian in child care and child protection textbooks. The popular view put forward about Ariès' ideas in these texts (with one notable exception – Frost and Stein 1989) is that the notion of childhood is a relatively recent one (a product of the sixteenth and seventeenth centuries). This is usually used to show that we have become more sensitive to children and their needs than was true in the past. Strangely this is almost a total misreading of what Ariès was arguing. In *Centuries of Childhood*, he wrote:

> In medieval society the idea of childhood did not exist: this is not to suggest that children were neglected, forsaken or despised. The idea of childhood is not to be confused with affection for children: it corresponds to an awareness of the particular nature of childhood, that particular nature which distinguishes the child from the adult, even the young adult. In medieval society this awareness was lacking.
>
> (Ariès 1962: 125)

Indeed, even the normally meticulous social commentator Bill Bryson gets him wrong in his populist book *At Home* when he wryly quotes Ariès as stating, 'The idea of childhood did not exist' (2011: 566). Bryson goes on to say that following Ariès, historians began to claim that children were viewed with something akin to indifference or even dislike. However, Ariès did not see the absence of the concept of childhood as detrimental to children. Indeed he thought the opposite to be true. During the Middle Ages, according to him, children mingled with adults as soon as that was physically possible. They spent much of their time together in both work and play. It was only gradually in the sixteenth and seventeenth centuries with the advent of formal education dominated by religion-based morality that children became separated from adults in the way that we understand it today. This increasing differentiation of children from adults in the public sphere was seen by Ariès as a backward step; that is, it served to place greater restrictions on children in their formative years. The concept of childhood is not seen by him as improving children's status, but as a limiting force placing children more at the mercy of adults than had previously been the case. Ariès can be seen, therefore, in some respects as a child liberationist. He would have liked to undo the chains imposed by this modern concept of childhood and return to a more varied, open and liberated past.

Many historians, however, have found Ariès' account of the development of childhood to be implausible (Pollock 1983; Hanawalt 1995). Pollock (1983) summarises the criticisms of his work in her excellent study, *Forgotten Children*. Her main argument is that Ariès' sources of evidence are not sufficient to back his wide-ranging claims. First, he placed heavy reliance on paintings that could have been analysed in a variety of ways, although he interpreted them only in ways that supported his views. His second main source was Heroard's diary of the early years of the future Louis XIII of France. He used this work, which shows Louis to have been regarded and reared as a little man from a very early age, particularly in terms of sexuality, to demonstrate his general thesis of the non-existence of childhood at that time. Pollock's (1983) view is that this case is atypical and tells us very little about how children in general were viewed and treated at this time. This seems to be a reasonable criticism: consider what impression the diary of Queen Elizabeth II's nanny would give of child-rearing practices in the early twentieth century to readers in the twenty-fourth century (Crawford 2003). Pollock (1983) is critical of Ariès rather rosy view of family life in the Middle Ages, which suggests full integration of children and adults into an idealised communal life. She also points out that Ariès has nothing to say about the care of children who are still physically dependent on their parents. He gives the impression that until children are aged 7 they do not count (it is almost as if they have no existence at all) and that once they reach this age they are fully mature and are assimilated into adult life without any problems. The views of another historian, Barbara Hanawalt, support this critique:

> For children to survive, they need not only to be nursed, fed and kept warm (biology), but also to be played with and talked to (culture), or they cannot be socialized. It matters not whether a mother or her surrogate perform these basic tasks or whether or not a sentimental attitude toward a childish state is present; it is simply that these activities must take place for the child to survive. Likewise it is very difficult to set children of seven to skilled labor such as smelting, plowing or carpentry.
>
> (Hanawalt 1995: 9)

The disputes over Ariès' work highlight the potential benefits and dangers of a historical perspective on children's issues. He clearly sensitises us to the fact that childhood is a social construction and that the 'problems' of childhood can be socially created. However, he is deficient in terms of explaining why this happens and makes rather sweeping statements on the basis of limited sources. As Wilson points out: 'Unfortunately, Ariès expressed himself more categorically than he might have done, and he attracted followers, rather than critics, initially' (Wilson 1984: 183). Archard accuses Ariès of 'presentism', i.e. judging the past by the standards of the present. He argues that:

> Ariès judged that the past lacked a concept of childhood. In fact what the past lacked was our concept of childhood. Previous society did not fail to think of children as different from adults; it merely thought about the difference in a different way from ours.
>
> (Archard 2004: 22–3)

The barbaric past perspective

Many historians have used Ariès' argument that childhood did not exist until the sixteenth century to show that in fact children have been subject to, at the least, detached emotional upbringings and, at the most, severe abuse including infanticide (de Mause 1976; Shorter 1976; Stone 1977). De Mause in particular makes this claim. His argument is that the more remote the period of history being examined, the more cruel the treatment of children becomes.

The history of childhood is a nightmare from which we have only recently begun to awaken. The further back in history one goes, the lower the level of child care, and the more likely children are to be killed, abandoned, beaten, terrorised and sexually abused.

(de Mause 1976: 1)

De Mause therefore shares with Ariès the belief that childhood is a product of relatively recent times, but there the similarity of view ends. Whereas Ariès sees the development of the concept of childhood as repressive, de Mause sees it as highly progressive. For him, childhood has evolved from the dark ages to the golden present. He outlines seven evolutionary stages ranging from what he terms the infanticidal mode, which existed until the fourth century, to the helping mode, which commenced in the middle of the twentieth century. Gradually, over generations of evolution, we have progressed, according to de Mause, from a state where parents were unable to see their children as separate beings with any particular needs, to one where they regard them as distinct, different and deserving of a special set of rights that emphasise respect for them as full human beings. Stone (1977), focusing on the 1500–1800 period, provides some support for this type of thesis. He argues that affection and love between spouses and for their children were impossible before the eighteenth century because of the material conditions of pre-industrial life. Adults did not invest emotionally in children because it was not considered to be worthwhile. Child mortality rates were so high that 'to preserve their mental stability, parents were obliged to limit the degree of their psychological involvement with their infant children' (Stone 1977: 70). It was only in the nineteenth century, in his view, that children were first seen as individuals with special needs because of their vulnerability. This change in perception stemmed initially from the upper and middle classes, who had acquired more leisure time to devote to child care concerns, and was gradually filtered down to the poorer classes.

These and similar views have been heavily criticised by other historians. Demos (1986) is critical of de Mause for the selectivity of his material and the fact that he seems to ignore the context totally and, therefore, the meaning of the behaviours that he is condemning. Macfarlane's (1979) review of Stone's work is particularly telling. He quotes many examples of parents expressing love and affection for their children before the eighteenth century. In particular, Macfarlane (1970) refers to the diary of a seventeenth-century Puritan vicar, Ralph Josselin, and to the grief that he expresses at the death of his 8-year-old daughter, Mary.[1] Macfarlane (1979) argues that Stone (1977) ignores evidence from poorer modern societies and from social anthropological studies that demonstrate considerable evidence of close child-adult emotional ties despite gross material poverty and high rates of child mortality. Macfarlane does not accept Stone's neat evolutionary scheme and is unconvinced by his belief that affective relationships are determined totally by economics.

There is a growing body of evidence to suggest that the concept of childhood as a status eliciting a form of response and treatment different to that of adults has always existed. Boswell, in his study of abandonment of children in antiquity, argues: 'It is clear, however, that there was no general absence of tender feeling for children as special beings among any pre-modern European peoples' (Boswell 1990: 37).

Hanawalt's description of fifteenth-century family life based on city records and literary sources dispels notions of parental detachment and lack of child-centredness (Hanawalt 1995). Pollock (1983), drawing from a study of 496 published diaries and autobiographies written between 1500 and 1900, argues that the concept of child-hood changed and developed during this period, but certainly existed throughout. The sources that she considered all demonstrated a certain amount of ambivalence towards their children. All saw them as a mixture of good and bad or of innocence and depravity. All demonstrated human concern and a sense of responsibility, as well as finding their children wearisome and exasperating. In particular, the diaries she examined showed that the death of a child created the same heartfelt reactions throughout the centuries studied. It must be concluded, therefore, that although there is no doubt that children in former times were expected to work and become what we today would consider to be adult at an earlier age than our own children, claims regarding the non-existence of the notion of childhood, as we perceive it now, are grossly exaggerated. It seems likely that children have always had a separate status, particularly early on when they are more physically dependent. As societies develop economically, there is a tendency for childhood, as we know it, to be extended and to gain more attention as a separate category, a process that is testified to by the growth of child protective legislation.

A major flaw in many historical analyses of childhood is that they tend to generalise about the way in which children are perceived (and, therefore, behave and are treated), as if all children's experiences are similar at a particular time. It is highly likely that this is far from true. Children of different classes, genders, races and abilities are likely to have widely different experiences in every period of history. A good example of this variation in experience is provided by the period of industrialisation in Britain in the nineteenth century, during which the development of greater sensitivity and sentiment towards middle-class childhood coincided with appalling working conditions for children of the labouring classes in mills, factories and on the street (Davin 1990).

A similar modern-day example can be seen in India, albeit with gender rather than class variations. Since a 1997 UNICEF report (http://www.unicef.org/pon97/) which, basing its calculations on male:female ratios in other countries, estimated that as many as 50 million women and girls were missing from the population of India, the ratio of male:female children has risen even further. Indian census figures for 2011 indicate that there are 7 million fewer girls aged 5 or under than boys and a study on behalf of the Centre for Global Health Research (Prabhat et al. 2006) found a sharp drop in the number of girls born per 1,000 boys between 1990 and 2005 (962 in 1981, 945 in 1991 and 927 in 2001). Both UNICEF and the Centre for Global Health Research argued that the selective abortion of female foetuses makes a large contribution to these figures, with the latter study estimating that up to 10 million female foetuses have been aborted over the past two decades, the majority between 2000 and 2005. In a potentially significant shift, the UNICEF report stated that fewer girls were born in rural areas than urban areas, perhaps because females were seen to be less economically productive than males and to be a financial burden as a result of traditional dowry systems. However, the Centre for Global Health Research study found that there were fewer girls in urban areas and argued that families in wealthier, urban areas were more likely to have access to ultrasound equipment and medical services (although they acknowledge that ultrasound equipment is also in widespread usage in rural areas), and that wealthier families have more reason to be concerned about having to share their wealth as a result of their daughter marrying into another family.

Child abuse and history

What do historians tell us about child abuse? The existence of child mistreatment in history (infanticide, abandonment, severe physical chastisement, child prostitution and harsh labour) is indisputable. However, the extent of such mistreatment and the interpretation of it within the societies where it took place are issues of greater contention. As we shall see, some historians consider that the vast majority of children in the past were callously treated and that this was seen as relatively normal because there was little sense of childhood as a protected status. Other historians take the view that extreme ill-treatment of children was not as common in recorded history as argued by the above. They argue that although living conditions and general standards of care for children were far lower than those of today, and although far greater expectations were placed on most children in terms of hard labour, this was largely a consequence of harsh economic conditions and that gross maltreatment was never accepted as normal. A distinction should be drawn between harsh living conditions and cruel treatment. From this point of view it is argued that within the prevailing standards of each age there have been cruel and loving parents and those children who had cruel parents were likely to be abused, but society did not necessarily condone or accept such abuse.

Cruel treatment of children in antiquity

De Mause (1976) placed the Roman empire in his infanticide mode. Infanticide was not legally a crime there until AD 318 (made punishable by death in AD 374). De Mause concludes from this that it was not only common practice but also evidence of the cruelty of the times. Boswell, whose study *The Kindness of Strangers* (1990) is concerned with abandonment rather than infanticide, a distinction he is keen to maintain, is far less critical of the mores of this period. Whereas de Mause (1976) judges the Romans by the standards of the late twentieth century (using psychoanalytic theory as his baseline), Boswell (1990) takes into account the meaning of forms of behaviour that, on the face of it, seem barbaric but are more understandable under closer scrutiny. Undoubtedly, the Romans practised infanticide. However, seen in the light of the fact that there were no adequate contraceptive techniques and the medical knowledge needed for abortion did not exist, it becomes clear that much (not all) infanticide was a crude, though somewhat callous, means of controlling family size. Abandoning a child was another method of achieving this. Boswell (1990) demonstrates that abandonment was many times more popular than infanticide for two reasons. First, the average Roman probably took no more pleasure in killing new-born babies than any other morally sound and empathic person would. Second, abandonment, which was usually carried out in a public place, frequently led to a child being rescued and looked after by someone else. This was in most cases a desired and intended outcome.[2] Boswell's (1990) sympathetic account of the process of abandonment contrasts sharply with the more lurid views of de Mause (1976):

> Parents abandoned their offspring in desperation when they were unable to support them, due to poverty or disaster; in shame when they were unwilling to keep them because of their physical condition or ancestry (e.g. illegitimate or incestuous); in self interest or the interest of another child, when inheritance or domestic resources would be compromised by another mouth; in hope, when they believed that someone of greater means or higher standing might find them and bring them up in better circumstances; in resignation, when a child was of unwelcome gender or ominous auspices; or in callousness, if they simply could not be bothered with parenthood.
>
> (Boswell 1990: 428)

Child cruelty in the Middle Ages

Boswell's study goes through to the Renaissance period. He argues that abandonment continued to be a common practice throughout Europe, never openly approved of but never officially outlawed. Gradually the Church became more involved and began to organise and regulate the activity. Monasteries provided havens for unwanted children through the practice of oblation. In the early thirteenth century, foundling homes were established and the process of abandonment became centralised around these institutions. However, what are seen as progressive developments do not always achieve their intended goals. Boswell (1990) argued that the death rate through disease in these places was probably higher than that resulting from the previous practice of abandonment.

How common infanticide was during this period is uncertain. Although it was prohibited by ecclesiastical law in most European societies at this time, there is much evidence to show that it was a not uncommon occurrence. Shahar (1990) comments:

> The scope of the phenomenon cannot be gauged, but the number of cases was certainly too great for all of them to be attributed to murderous impulses resulting from post partum depression or other grave mental disturbances (although these factors were certainly involved in some cases).
>
> (Shahar 1990: 127)

There can be little doubt that infanticide/exposure of children continued to be a crude means of disposing of unwanted babies and that Church authorities pursued it with different levels of rigour at different times in history. Sharpe (1984) points out that by the sixteenth century infanticide was singled out for severe punishment by most European states and comments that: 'The infanticide wave in England at least may have resulted in more executions than the more familiar witch craze' (Sharpe 1984: 61). The issue of infanticide and child abandonment persisted as a relatively common occurrence right through to the early twentieth century in England and there was much ambivalence about whether offenders should be punished or pitied. Both are now relatively rare events, although it is notable that there are approximately 50 baby abandonments per year and still a good deal of uncertainty as how best to respond (Sher and Hackman 2002).

Reverting back to the Middle Ages, another concern was that of child deaths in the home, ostensibly as a result of accidents. Hanawalt (1977) refers to synodal legislation of the thirteenth century that warns parents not to sleep with their children and not to leave them alone or unattended near fires. It is fairly clear that parents were viewed with considerable suspicion in cases where children did die as a consequence of these activities. Langer (1974), drawing on ecclesiastical court records across Europe, shows that a common response to such deaths was to require the mothers of the dead infants to do penance. Shahar (1990) notes, however, that once children had achieved greater measures of independence their security was far more assured – according to her research, murder of children other than new-borns was very rare during the Middle Age period.

Sexual abuse of children in antiquity and the Middle Ages

There is little clear evidence about sexual abuse of children in antiquity and medieval times. Again de Mause is unequivocal about the former: the child in antiquity lived his earliest years in an atmosphere of sexual abuse. Growing up in Greece or Rome often included being sexually used by older men (de Mause 1976: 43). Wiedemann (1989) is equally unequivocal in holding a contrary position:

> Nor for that matter do the occasional references to the sexual exploitation of children by perverts prove that Roman society as a whole was imbued either with a psychotic hatred of childhood, or with a degree of sexual freedom to put modern California to shame.
>
> (Wiedemann 1989: 30)

He points out that pederasty was not acceptable to the Romans and that if it involved a boy of citizen status it was apparently a criminal offence.[3]

Turning to intra-familial abuse, it is clear that the Greeks and Romans operated a strict incest taboo. Sophocles' *Oedipus Rex* displays the horrors that accompanied unwitting incest. Boswell's (1990) study of abandonment was inspired by an inscription he read which warned men that by going to brothels they might be committing incest with children whom they had abandoned years before. Such fears and anxieties demonstrate how deep-seated the taboo really was. However, we simply do not know to what extent sexual abuse of children either within or outside families was a feature in ancient societies. This is hardly surprising. As we shall see in Chapter 2, it is only since the 1980s that there has been a concerted attempt to focus on intra-familial sexual abuse in Britain and the USA and to try to measure its true extent.

Similarly, therefore, and no doubt for the same reasons, there is also very little information on the subject of sexual abuse during the Middle Ages. Incest did not become a legal offence in England until the twentieth century (except for a brief period during the regency of Cromwell). However, it should not be assumed that the absence of legislation meant a lack of concern about or acceptance of such behaviour. Prior to this more secular century, the Church played a lead role in policing sexuality in England for nearly two millennia through the pulpit, the confessional and ultimately the ecclesiastical courts (see Gagnon and Parker 1995). In Scotland, by contrast, incest was made a crime punishable by death in 1757. However it was policed, it is clear that the incest taboo persisted throughout Europe in this period.

Child abuse from the Middle Ages to Victorian times

Evidence for this period is as scanty as that for earlier ages. Demos (1986) carried out a study of court records in New England in the seventeenth century and found a conspicuous absence of child abuse cases. Such a finding is usually attributed to the belief that cruelty to children in this period of history was so much the norm that court action was a rarity. Demos argues that this could not have been the case, because he also found several instances of master-servant violence, which resulted in action being taken to prevent its continuation. He comes to the conclusion that child abuse was probably less prevalent in New England village communities at this time than it is generally in the USA today. He attributes this to the fact that families were larger and less introverted and intense, children's labour value was high, filial duty was greater and there was more communal oversight.[4] This study runs counter to the generally held belief, put forward by de Mause (1976) and others, that child abuse inevitably declines with social progress.

Pollock (1983) demonstrated that public concern about cruelty to children in Britain existed well before the time it is generally thought to have been discovered, that is, in the last three decades of the nineteenth century. She carried out a study of child cruelty reports in *The Times* between 1785 and 1860 and found 385 tried cases of child neglect, physical and sexual abuse, of which only 27 (7 per cent) were found not guilty. She commented:

> The manner in which the cases were reported by the newspaper provides an indication of the attitudes of the time to cruelty to children. The fact that the majority of the cases were also found guilty meant that law and society condemned child abuse long before the specific Prevention of Cruelty to Children Act in 1889. Parents who abused their offspring were generally considered 'unnatural' and the cruelty as 'horrific' or 'barbaric'.

> (Pollock 1983: 93)

However, there can be little doubt that the lot of the large numbers of children of the very poor in the seventeenth, eighteenth and early nineteenth centuries was a harsh one by present-day standards, even though the cruelty was not inflicted by the parents. The accounts of the opening of the London Foundling Hospital in 1741 (McClure 1981) and of the conditions for children in workhouses at the end of the eighteenth century (Cunningham 1991) are just two reminders of the harsh reality of life for these generations of deprived children.

Concluding comments

This brief excursion into the early history of child abuse can prove nothing definitely. However, it should dispel at least two commonly held beliefs: first, the notion that the further one goes back in history the worse the treatment of children; second, that it is only in recent times that societies such as ours have taken concerted steps to deal with the problem.

With regard to the first point, there is no doubt that there was much harsh treatment of children in previous eras that would not be tolerated now. Nor is there any doubt that present-day children as a whole are much more likely to survive infancy and enjoy far better health than their predecessors as a result of medical, hygienic and material advances. On the other hand, there is evidence that children in every era have been valued, cared for and nurtured. There can be no doubt that, as was stressed at the start of this chapter, many historians and other writers have underestimated the degree of concern that parents of previous generations have shown for their children. Also, there is ample evidence of official concern and state action to protect children from abuse by their parents provided by historians such as Boswell (1990), Hanawalt (1977) and Demos (1986). However, this evidence seems to go unnoticed. This blindness to the efforts of previous generations to regulate cruelty to children by their parents is perhaps explained by the fact that each new generation needs to think that it is improving on the past.

Careful analysis of the history of child abuse can serve to dispel myths and to put current problems into perspective. What emerges is that every society has taken some steps to deal with the issue of the care of its young and has devised some means of intervention into family life to ensure this. These efforts have been influenced by the cultures, material circumstances, technologies and politics impinging on those societies. Examining these efforts with due regard to these contextual factors can enhance our understanding of current approaches to the problem.

Recommended reading

Ariès, P. (1962) *Centuries of Childhood*. Harmondsworth: Penguin.

Boswell, J. (1990) *The Kindness of Strangers: The Abandonment of Children in Western Europe from Late Antiquity to the Renaissance*. New York: Vintage.

Cunningham, H. (2005) *Children and Childhood in Western Society Since 1500*, 2nd edn. Harlow: Pearson.

de Mause, L. (ed.) (1976) *The History of Childhood*. London: Souvenir Press.

Heywood, C. (2001) *A History of Childhood: Children and Childhood in the West from Medieval to Modern Times*. Cambridge: Polity Press.

Pollock, L. (1983) *Forgotten Children: Parent-Child Relations from 1500 to 1900*. Cambridge: Cambridge University Press.

Shahar, S. (1990) *Childhood in the Middle Ages*. London: Routledge.

Woodhead, M. and Montgomery, H. (2003) *Understanding Childhood – An Interdisciplinary Approach*. Chichester: Wiley.

2

A history of child abuse and neglect 1870–2000

Introduction

As we saw in Chapter 1, child abuse is not a new phenomenon, nor is public or state concern about it. The focus of this chapter is on how society has responded to child abuse and neglect between 1870 and 2000, from Victorian- and Edwardian-era responses to the formation of the sophisticated, modern systems for monitoring child welfare that we now see. We shall consider how these responses are often shaped by wider social, economic and political factors but also how responses are often overtly reactive to individual events such as the well-publicised death of a child. The year 1870 has been selected as the starting date because of the clear thread between the social organisation around the problem of child abuse that started at that time and has continued until now, rather than to suggest that there was no response to child abuse before this time. The decade since 2000 is considered in the next chapter.

Late Victorian and Edwardian responses to child abuse

The late Victorian age saw a flurry of activity around the issue of child protection of a similar degree and nature to that which has taken place in modern times since the early 1970s.

Socio-economic factors

Throughout the nineteenth century there were dramatic changes in terms of population growth, industrialisation and urbanisation in Britain. Between 1801 and 1861 the population doubled to a total of 20 million, of whom 7 million were under the age of 15. By 1901 the population was 32.5 million, of whom 10.5 million were under the age of 15. Children formed one-third of the population throughout most of this period compared with one-fifth at the present time. Even so, infant mortality rates were around 15 per cent throughout most of the nineteenth century. Rose tells us: 'Even as late as 1895 half the children up to 5 would die in the worst slums, compared with 19 per cent in a healthy district like Dulwich' (Rose 1991: 2). Until the passing of the 1880 Education Act, when schooling became compulsory for children up to the age of 10, the children of the poor were likely to spend more time labouring than being educated. The 1861 census showed that one-third of all children aged 5 to 9 and nearly 50 per cent of 10- to 14-year-olds were working. Figures for working-class children alone, had they been collated, would have been much higher.

By any measure, the nineteenth century was a time of great upheaval and traumatic change for poor families and their children. These demographic changes, created largely by the demands of new technologies, led to new problems and concerns about the upbringing of children and new forms of state intervention into family life.

Child care concerns up to 1870

There had been four categories of children causing concern to the state up to the end of the 1860s: children of the street (termed as vagabonds, beggars or street traders), young offenders, children at work and children looked after in Poor Law authority institutions. The main pattern of response had been for issues to be initially taken up by philanthropic societies of different religious persuasions acting as pressure groups, followed by government intervention and state legislation (Dingwall et al. 1984).

None of these child care issues involved direct intervention in the internal workings of the family. Although there was considerable concern to control the unruliness of children on the street (prompted by public order anxieties) and to influence the nature and amount of work that children were expected to undertake (prompted by concerns about exposure to immorality as well as by concerns about exploitation), there was little thought given at this time to more direct state intervention into family life to protect children from ill-treatment by their parents. Behlmer argued that the prevailing view was that to 'patrol industry on behalf of the young was England's Christian duty. To patrol the home was a sacrilege' (Behlmer 1982: 9). While this analysis is generally correct, it is important to note that the sacrosanctity of domestic privacy to which Behlmer refers had always been more applicable to wealthier families than to those of the poor. In the pre-industrialised period, the latter were subject to Church and community controls. The breakdown in these mechanisms that accompanied industrialisation created the need for new ways of maintaining moral and social order among poor families, which is where the philanthropists came in. The issue for them and the state was how best to establish this new form of intervention without undermining parents' responsibility for their children.

Baby farming

In the late 1860s and early 1870s this new form of state intervention into family affairs began tentatively, with its focus on the issue of baby farming (see *The Ghost of Lily Painter* – Davies 2011 – for a fictionalised but informative account of this period). This term was used to describe the then common practice of paying for babies to be nursed and reared by substitute parents – the forerunner of today's private foster parents. The practice was widespread because of the absence of adequate contraceptive devices, the illegality and risks associated with abortion, the stigma attached to illegitimacy and the need for poorer unmarried women to be free to work. The trade was created by unwanted pregnancies. It was a free-market enterprise uncontrolled by state surveillance. While many of the women who undertook this work may have been honest and trustworthy, there were several infamous cases of babies being murdered by their 'carers', which created widespread public concern (Rose 1986).

In 1870 the Infant Life Protection Society was established with a view to controlling the practice of baby farming by means of a system of registration and inspection. By 1872, this pressure group had succeeded in pushing through the Infant Life Protection Act, which required any adult who 'fostered' more than one child under the age of 1 year to register with the local authority and to meet certain required standards. In practice this Act proved ineffective as the resources needed to police it were not made available. London County Council was one authority viewed as taking this issue more seriously and even they appointed only one inspector in 1878 to cover the whole of the metropolitan area. Further Acts dealing with this issue followed: the 1897 Infant Life Protection Act, the 1908 Children Act and the 1933 Children and Young Persons Act. The main developments were that registration was required for the first child placed, the protected age was raised to 9, and inspection, largely by health visitors, was made more thorough and comprehensive (Hendrick 1994).

The Infant Life Protection Society's concern with baby farming, though seen by some as unnecessary state interference into domestic arrangements, did not meet massive resistance from the establishment. The reason for this is that it was seen as an issue that was only marginal to family life.

The formation of the NSPCC

It was not to be long, however, before the so-called bastions of the family were to be more directly assaulted. In 1881, Thomas Agnew, a banker from Liverpool, travelled to New York where he visited the New York Society for the Prevention of Cruelty to Children. Agnew was deeply impressed with what he saw and when he returned to the UK he set up the Liverpool Society for the Prevention of Cruelty to Children (SPCC). In 1884, the London SPCC was established and by 1889 the London Society had opened 32 branches or aid committees across England, Wales and Scotland. In the same year, the name of the organisation was changed to the National Society for the Prevention of Cruelty to Children (NSPCC). While other philanthropic societies, such as Dr Barnardo's, had been 'rescuing' children living outside their families, the NSPCC's concern was to 'rescue' children living in their own homes.

The early NSPCC protagonists considered existing arrangements for the reporting of child ill-treatment and neglect and the subsequent impeachment of parents to be something of a lottery. They argued that there were no statutory means of protecting children before cases of parental cruelty were tried and no means of ensuring continued protection once convicted parents had served their sentences.[1]

The following steps were taken to remedy this situation. Inspectors, initially very few in number, were appointed to seek out and report to the police instances of abuse and neglect, even though, until the passing of legislation in 1889, they had no legal authority or mandate to carry out this task. Shelters were established to provide places of safety for children pending prosecutions. They too were not backed by the force of law until later. Shocking cases of child mistreatment were publicised in order to influence public opinion and generate resources. Parliamentary lobbying to change the law regarding cruelty to children was relentlessly pursued.

The outcome of all this pressure was the 1889 Prevention of Cruelty to Children Act. This Act defined specific parental misdemeanours against children and created penalties for wilful ill-treatment or neglect leading to unnecessary suffering or injury to health. It empowered the police to arrest anyone found to be ill-treating a child and obtain warrants to enter the homes of children who might be in danger. The Act also legalised the removal of children to places of safety and enabled 'fit person' orders (the forerunners of care orders) to be imposed on children whose parents had been convicted of offences against them.

Further Acts followed in 1894, 1904 and 1908, the effects of which were to consolidate and extend the original Act. By 1908 the main components of child protection law that exist today were in place. As Dingwall et al. put it:

> there have been virtually no fundamental changes in the categories of children covered by the interventionist legislation since 1894. Subsequent legislation has consolidated the Victorian statutes and occasionally modernised their wording. It has introduced a few new types of disposition and redistributed enforcement duties. Nevertheless, the issues of principle were mostly settled in Victorian times.
>
> (Dingwall et al. 1984: 220)

The foundations were set even then for much of the form and style of current intervention practices in child protection work, according to Ferguson (1990). In his lucid account of an NSPCC case in the north-east of England in 1898, he depicts an inspector grappling with the same contradictions and complexities as present-day social workers. Even at this early stage, there was much emphasis on providing advice, support and material help, and court action was viewed as a last resort. This style of intervention developed as a result of two main factors. First, NSPCC inspectors had to gain acceptance in communities if they were to be effective. Second, their ultimate concern and that of the state was to inculcate a sense of responsibility in parents without undermining them. Advice, persuasion and the threat of prosecution were methods more in tune with these twin goals.

By 1914 the NSPCC had established itself as a national institution. Its officers, together with its Scottish counterparts, covered the whole of the British Isles. Despite being feared in many communities, the NSPCC was respected and this was reflected in the high percentage of its referrals that came from neighbours and relatives. According to Behlmer (1982), 58 per cent of the 23,124 cases reported to the NSPCC in 1986–7 emanated from the general public.

Returning to Bill Bryson (2011), he notes that the Royal Society for the Protection of Animals, the RSPCA, predates the NSPCC by some 60 years; and he adds that, ironically, unlike the RSPCA, the NSPCC has never been 'royally blessed'.

Responding to sexual abuse

During this era, child sexual abuse within the family, previously ignored as an issue, was also being tackled by the NSPCC. Behlmer (1982: 70) notes that the London SPCC in its first year dealt with 95 cases involving 'domestic victims', of which 12 concerned 'an evil which is altogether too unmentionable' (sexual assault or incest). However, despite this awareness and recognition, the NSPCC did not bring child sexual abuse to public attention in the same way as it had publicised physical abuse and neglect. This response reflected the general attitude to the issue, which was akin to a conspiracy of silence.

In contrast to this, child prostitution received far more public attention. Following a series of articles published in the *Pall Mall Gazette* in 1885, exposing a child prostitution ring that lured young English girls to brothels in Belgium, legislation was introduced to raise the age of lawful consent to intercourse for girls from 13 to 16 – a response that Gorham (1978) viewed as inappropriate, but typical of the romanticised view of childhood held by middle-class Victorians, and of the ignorance of the material conditions and pressures experienced by working-class female children.

The issue of intra-familial abuse or incest meanwhile continued to receive little public attention or recognition. Where it was acknowledged, it was seen as linked to low intelligence and as a product of the overcrowded sleeping conditions of the poorer classes (Wohl 1978). Arguably, it was Sigmund Freud, rather than organisations such as the NSPCC, who can be credited with much of the effort in presenting childhood sexual abuse as one potent source of adult psychological difficulties. Although Freud later recanted his seduction theory – which claimed that a repressed memory of child sexual abuse was a necessary precondition for later hysterical or obsessional symptoms – it is nevertheless the case that he did much to publicise not only the prevalence of child maltreatment in general and child sexual abuse in particular, but also the harm these behaviours were causing to individuals and to society.

Following Freud's work, it become more common for specialist organisations to demonstrate a willingness to discuss and publicise the problem of sexual abuse, if not for wider society as a whole, and this led to the NSPCC, along with the National Vigilance Association (formed in 1885) to press for a law to criminalise incest, which was not a specific category of crime at this time. This pressure resulted in the passing of the 1908 Incest Act. Although the impact of this Act was very limited, incest was now officially recognised as a crime and this in turn at least created the potential for more effective intervention.

Protecting children within the family

As can be seen, there were considerable shifts in thinking about state intervention into family life between 1870 and 1914. We have focused on the child protection aspects, but one could look at a range of other areas, such as education, working conditions and health, and see similar developments taking place. Parton sees this era as one characterised by the emergence of the 'social question' resulting from a failure of liberal economics to provide an adequate basis for a broadly functioning society:

In the last quarter of the nineteenth century the political debate increasingly focused on the need to address a growing number of social problems, such as crime, vagrancy and disease without imposing a strong (sovereign) state on the wishes and activities of individuals.

(Parton 2005: 11)

While these problems could be dealt with to some degree in ways external to families, by means of legislation to restrict child labour, public hygiene measures and the introduction of schooling, it was increasingly apparent that the family was a crucially important area for intervention and influence.

This development in political thinking created the conditions in which the NSPCC operated at this time. As noted above, NSPCC inspectors tried to protect children by working with parents to educate them and help them modify their ways. There is no doubt, however, that child protection proved to be a particularly problematic part of the social modernisation exercise, in that it called into question parental behaviour inside the family home. The NSPCC workers of this time faced the dilemma that social agencies still face: how to influence the family without undermining its independence (see Behlmer 1982 and Gordon 1989). The goal was to change the internal behaviour of the family in order to ensure child protection, but without disrupting the order of things. Similarities between the late Victorian approach and that of the present response to child abuse abound.

Between the two world wars

A shift in focus

In contrast to the amount of change and degree of concern that characterised child protection work, particularly in the first three decades of the 1870–1914 period, there was a definite shift in focus away from this issue between the two world wars. Early on in this period there was a sense that a corner had been turned. The 1923 Home Office report on the work of the Children's Branch pointed out that, despite the fact that the 1908 Children Act had broadened the grounds for neglect proceedings, the number of prosecutions of parents had dropped from 4,106 in 1900 to 2,052 by 1921 (Home Office 1923). The work of the NSPCC reflected these changes. In 1913–14 the NSPCC dealt with 54,772 cases. However, the number of prosecutions resulting from these investigations was only 2,349 (approximately 4 per cent compared with a prosecution rate of 10 per cent in 1895–6). Why had this shift in emphasis taken place?

Several reasons have been put forward. The 1923 Home Office report attributed the change to improved standards of parenting:

The children of the poorer classes are better cared for than they used to be, and it is now unusual to see dirty and ragged children in the streets of our great cities. Cases of extreme brutality which were all too common not so many years ago are now becoming less frequent.

(Home Office 1923: 69–70)

These improved parenting standards were seen to be the result of better welfare provision (for example, school meals, health and child maternity services), changes in working-class habits (such as reduced alcohol consumption) and the work of agencies like the NSPCC.

However, one cannot ignore the fact that average living standards were also improving during this period, despite the recession which struck in the 1930s and primarily affected the north and west of the country. Despite this economic setback, by 1939 the average family in the UK was better fed, better housed and healthier than they had been two decades before. The sharp increase in car ownership and in the popularity of leisure activities such as travel and sporting events also indicates a growing sense of prosperity (Stevenson and Cook 1977).[2] These factors point to the likelihood of less abuse taking place but also to the possibility that the kind of abject poverty noted in the Home Office report in 1923 ('dirty and ragged children') may have reduced not as a consequence of improved parenting standards but as a natural byproduct of a reduction in the extent of gross material deprivation.

Rose (1991) attributed the perceived reduction in child abuse to the decline in the birth rate. He pointed out that the average number of children born to families in 1915 was 2.5 compared with 6 in the 1860s, and commented: 'One may conclude, therefore, that children being born in the Edwardian period were more "expected" and therefore on the whole more wanted than before' (Rose 1991: 243).

Ferguson (2004) uses the term 'sequestration' to describe what was happening during this period. The NSPCC and others in this field were carrying out their work relatively free from scrutiny and criticism. Child deaths from neglect and abuse had reduced considerably since before the First World War. Ill-treatment of children was, therefore, seen to be a containable problem and left to the professionals. In his view, this process persisted right through to the rediscovery of child abuse in the 1960s and 1970s (see below).

Dingwall et al. (1984) argued that child protection in itself had never been a major concern of the state, except in the 1880–1900 period. Its real worry was the threat provided by the inadequate moral socialisation of children and the mainte-nance of social order. Neglect was seen as a cause of delinquency and was considered to be an important target of intervention for that reason, not because of concern for the well-being of individual children.[3]

Gordon (1989), drawing from the North American scene, argued that the amount and type of child abuse did not differ significantly during the period 1880–1960 but the response to it did. She linked societal concerns about child abuse and other forms of family violence to the strength of feminist thinking, arguing that when women have a strong voice, as they had in the late Victorian and early Edwardian eras, the effect is to create a tougher response to the issue (although she did not argue that this meant the agencies established to deal with the problem employed a feminist analysis). Her explanation, therefore, of the lack of overt focus on child abuse in the Depression period in the USA is as follows:

One of the major characteristics of depression-era social work was a policy of defending the 'conventional' nuclear family . . . A sympathy arose for the unem-ployed husband, the stress and role-conflict that frequently engendered his violence; remarkably less sympathy was mustered for the situation of mothers doing double shifts – at home and at work – in attempts to hold the family together ... Indeed violence altogether was de-emphasized, and the SPCCs devoted themselves almost exclusively to child neglect, now conceived primarily in terms of economic neglect, such as malnutrition or inadequate medical care.

(Gordon 1989: 22–3)

This argument seems to have as good an explanatory value for the British situation as for that in the USA at this time. Certainly, between the two world wars, the government's focus was predictably on national security, on the increasing and potentially violent threat to the country from the Soviet Union and Nazi Germany and therefore, as Gordon argues, its focus on 'women's issues', such as childrearing and the family, or on the violence of men at home, became less important and, as a result, less attention was given to it.

All the foregoing explanations have some validity. There is no way of knowing for certain whether the incidence of child abuse during this era reduced or not. However, it is clear that there was a much less evangelical approach to the problem than in the previous era and a probability that a good deal of abuse went unnoticed. During this era much of the work of the NSPCC was focused more on general neglect among poor families than on particular instances of abuse (see Ferguson 2004).

Sexual abuse

Gordon (1989) provides one of the few accounts of official responses to child sexual abuse during this period. The case records she studied show that such abuse persisted throughout the period 1880 to 1960. The 1880–1910 records showed that the SPCC workers of that time more readily accepted allegations of sexual abuse and that they judged sexual abusers of children as socially and morally inferior beings. From 1910 onwards there was a much less direct, more tentative approach to this issue, with far greater emphasis on abuse by strangers, on girls' sexual delinquency and a good deal of victim-blaming. The problem of child sexual abuse, as Gordon (1989) saw it, though never high on the agenda, went underground for much of this time. Nevertheless, the number of prosecutions for incest under the 1908 Incest Act gradually increased over time, reaching 100 a year by the beginning of the Second World War, and there is clear evidence of the vigorous pursuit of child sexual abuse cases in some NSPCC accounts (Housden 1955).[4] It therefore seems reasonable to conclude that while there was little general acceptance of the existence of child sexual abuse, appropriate agencies did take action where there was clear enough evidence of it occurring.

1945–74: the rise of the children's departments and rediscovery of child abuse

The Curtis Committee

There was an upsurge of interest in the welfare of deprived children after the Second World War. The report of the Curtis Committee, set up to inquire into the conditions of children 'deprived of a normal home life with their own parents and relatives' (Curtis 1946: 5), provided a comprehensive and thoughtful account of the child care concerns of the day. However, it is again notable that child neglect is referred to more because of its link with subsequent delinquent behaviour than for any concern about harm to the child. This despite the fact that one of the catalysts for concern about children cared for by the state at the time was the death of a 12-year-old child, Dennis O'Neill, killed by his foster father (Home Office 1945).

Child care work under the 1948 Children Act

The 1948 Children Act was greatly influenced by the findings of the Curtis Committee and paid little attention specifically to child abuse. However, in 1950 a joint circular was issued to local authorities, proposing the setting up of coordinating committees for overseeing 'problem family' cases that were being visited by a wide range of departments (Home Office 1950). Under the 1952 Children and Young Persons (Amendment) Act, children's departments' powers to intervene were broadened. This Act also empowered authorities to seek fit person orders on children without the requirement that parents first be prosecuted for cruelty or neglect. This change enabled authorities to protect children more easily and further reduced the need to prosecute parents, which was in tune with the less punitive approach towards families that characterised this period.

The other major development was the push for a preventive approach. This notion was attractive to a wide variety of constituencies. Child care officers understood that admissions to care were preventable, given sufficient levels of support before a crisis point was reached. Central government departments, concerned by a dramatic rise in the number of children in care following the implementation of the 1948 Act, saw it as a cost-effective option. In addition they were concerned about the link between neglect and delinquency and the need to do something about the latter. There was also support from research for a change of emphasis. Bowlby's study of institutional care for children and his theories about the deleterious effects of maternal deprivation were prominent in this respect (Bowlby 1951; Bowlby et al. 1965).

Packman (1975) has shown how in practice throughout the 1950s child care officers had spent more and more of their time working with families to prevent receptions into care. Such work received legal backing with the passing of the 1963 Children and Young Persons Act, Section 1 of which empowered local authorities to provide material and financial assistance to keep children at home where it was thought to be in their best interests.

The main concern for the remainder of the 1960s continued to be delinquency, the cause of which was seen to be neglect, and the solution, increased support for the family. The 1969 Children and Young Persons Act reflected this concern. Neglected children were treated by the law in the same way as children beyond control, children in moral danger, children refusing to go to school and children committing offences. In the mid-1970s, when attention switched more directly to the ill-treatment of children by their parents, this legislation proved to be inadequate in many respects.

With regard to the professional response, there was a move towards a less specialised approach to child care work and to a broader family problem perspective.

Deprived children were seen to be the products of deprived families, and a family-based service was felt to be essential, but with a broader remit and more powers than before. It was within this context that the Seebohm report of 1968 recommended the formation of new unified social services departments comprising the former health and welfare and children's departments. These new departments were to be set up to 'meet the social needs of individuals, families, and communities' (Seebohm 1968: 43). These recommendations were made law and implemented in 1971.

The 'rediscovery' of child abuse in the USA

In the USA, child abuse was formally rediscovered in 1962 when Henry Kempe, a paediatrician, and his associates coined the term 'the battered child syndrome', which described and explained the process that led to parents (primarily mothers) physically assaulting their babies and young children (Kempe et al. 1962). Although paediatric radiologists had already recognised this problem (Pfohl 1977), Kempe and his colleagues were the first to confidently attribute children's injuries to deliberate mistreatment rather than to the outcome of accident or disease. Kempe argued that abuse of children was far more widespread than anyone had previously considered and that professionals (doctors in particular) had been ignoring it. Kempe's original thinking also stressed the psychological aspects of child abuse. Essentially his view was that child abuse resulted from the parent's emotional or psychological problems, which in turn stemmed from their own emotionally depriving childhood experiences. This view was far more in keeping with prevailing social mores, seeing child abuse as being the result of parental psychological problems rather than due to cruelty, poverty or ignorance. Kempe argued that parents needed psychological treatment or therapy, that their children needed temporary protection and that in most cases rehabilitation should be possible. The main exceptions to this rule were parents diagnosed as having psychotic illnesses.

This model of child abuse was remarkably influential throughout the USA in the 1970s and 1980s. Thanks to the tireless campaigning of Kempe and others, physical abuse of children became a major social issue, attracting national publicity and massive funding (Nelson 1984). As early as 1967, every state in the USA had mandatory reporting laws and the Children's Bureau was spending considerable amounts of money on research into the problem.

It is hard to pinpoint the reasons for the re-emergence of this age-old problem at this time. Certainly, technological developments, such as the use of X-rays, played a part. However, Pfohl (1977) attributed much to the professional aspirations of paediatricians, who in an era of better physical health among children were in search of a new role. Nevertheless, broader social factors need to be taken into account as well. The climate was right for greater focus on the care and upbringing of children. The relative affluence of the 1960s created the conditions for people to pay greater attention to the psychological needs of children and to the quality of parent-child relationships. By giving child abuse a medical label and seeing it as treatable, new forms of intervention into family life were not seen as threatening the independence of families in general because they were aimed only at the families that had 'the illness'.

The re-emergence of child abuse as a problem in Britain

Parton (1979, 1981, 1985) provided a detailed account of the development of child abuse as a social problem in Britain in the late 1960s and the 1970s. The pattern of development was similar to (and greatly influenced by) that in the USA. He saw the growth of the problem as very closely linked to professional aspirations and to the politics of the family and the state.

There were two main professional groupings involved in the 1960s: medical doctors (notably paediatricians) and the NSPCC. In 1963, Griffiths and Moynihan, two orthopaedic surgeons, used the term 'battered baby syndrome' in an influential article in the *British Medical Journal* (Griffiths and Moynihan 1963). The amount of medical literature devoted to this topic developed steadily throughout the 1960s but the problem was not responded to at a wider level at this stage.

The NSPCC was facing an identity crisis at this time. Throughout the 1950s and 1960s, the new children's departments grew in size and stature and there was considerable overlap between their responsibilities and those of the NSPCC. Both were tackling similar problems in similar ways, but the children's departments were better resourced and had a broader statutory mandate. The emergence of a direct focus on physical child mistreatment offered the NSPCC the opportunity of developing a more specialist and separate role. Contact was made with Henry Kempe and his associates and as a result a project was established in London to provide specialist casework help for families referred for child abuse at a centre named Denver House (see Baher et al. 1976). During this period the NSPCC was prolific in its publications on the subject of child abuse and was highly influential in placing it firmly on the social problem agenda (see Parton 1985).

Summary

On the face of it, the period between 1945 and 1974 was one in which family policy in general and the response to neglectful families in particular were relatively benign. The policy style of the time was unequivocally family-oriented and family-sympathetic. Families were identified as being at risk and families expected to be the recipients of help (Ingleby 1960). Whether such a policy served the interests of the children and women in these families is an open question. Gordon's (1989) account of the US situation is instructive, given the dearth of British studies of child protection during this period. She characterised the 1940–60 period as follows:

> The defend-the-conventional-family policy in social work continued through the 1940s and 1950s. These decades represented the low point in public awareness of family-violence problems and in the status of child protection work within the social-work profession.
>
> (Gordon 1989: 23)

She also described the increasing influence of psychoanalysis on social workers' understanding of family violence. In Britain, the influence of psychoanalytical theory has always been much less than in the USA (Yelloly 1980) but there can be little doubt that the work of Bowlby (1951) helped to focus attention on the emotional qualities of parenting and emphasised the need to bolster families with advice, support and casework. Far less direct attention was paid to violence to children and to women within those families.

Sexual abuse, as we now perceive it, continued to receive limited focus. The main forms of perceived sexual abuse at this time were either incest, seen as a rare and pathological phenomenon, or girls in moral danger because of insufficient controls being exerted by their parents (Greenland 1958; Allen and Morton 1961).

Thus from a feminist perspective, policy responses to child abuse during this period were deficient in terms of protecting women and children from male violence. However, this period has been viewed by other commentators as one of some enlightenment with regard to child care issues. For instance, Parton (1985) and Holman (1988) both consider the child protection practices of the period 1947 to 1990 to be retrogressive and over-intrusive into family life in comparison with this one; they are critical of the decline in state support for the family and the loss of emphasis on preventive work. Although broad social, economic and political factors influence responses to child abuse, individual tragic cases exert a huge influence of their own and the shift from a 'family support' model to a focus on 'child protection' which occurred after this period can be attributed substantially, if not entirely, to the death of (and subsequent public inquiry into) one child: Maria Colwell.

1974–90: the 'first era' of child protection practice

Maria Colwell

Maria Colwell, aged 7, was killed by her stepfather in 1973 (Department of Health and Social Security 1974). She had been in the care of East Sussex County Council for five years following a period of general neglect and low standards of care, and for nearly all of this time she had been looked after by her aunt. Her mother had mean-while remarried and had given birth to three children. In 1971, she was determined to have Maria back home. East Sussex County Council agreed to a plan of rehabilita-tion and supported Maria's mother's application to discharge the care order. Maria, who had been very resistant to returning to her mother, died 13 months later, grossly under-nourished and severely beaten by her step-father. This was despite the fact that throughout this period there had been many health and welfare workers involved in the oversight of her development who had failed to 'see' the neglect and ill-treatment that took place over some considerable time.

How the Maria Colwell case came to have such an impact was carefully analysed by Parton (1979). He argued that her death did not immediately cause a great deal of national concern. The key factor was the decision of the then minister of the Department of Health and Social Security, Sir Keith Joseph, to hold a public inquiry into what happened. Parton pinpointed the influence of a group called the Tunbridge Wells Study Group, consisting of paediatricians, lawyers and social workers, as a key factor acting on Joseph to make his decision. Joseph himself was very much in tune with the ideas of this group, as he was promulgating a more general thesis about cycles of deprivation among poor families and the need for such families to be targeted for specialist intervention (Joseph 1972).

The resulting inquiry – the first of its kind – aided by media reporting, arrested the attention of the public. The inquiry established a precedent for many subsequent public inquiries into child deaths and focused on the individual failure of professionals and not on wider issues of child abuse. Diane Lees, Maria's social worker, was particularly vilified. The social work profession was considered to be too soft and permissive. The more benign family approach to child neglect issues, prevalent since 1948, was called into question. In addition, the professional autonomy afforded to those working with children for over half a century was now forfeited– in this new era, child protection was to become public property (Ferguson 2004).

The establishment of a system for dealing with child abuse

As a consequence of the Maria Colwell inquiry report, the Department of Health and Social Security, by means of a series of circulars and letters, laid the foundations of the system that currently exists for protecting children. The aims of the changes were to raise awareness of child abuse, to ensure that allegations of abuse were promptly responded to, to improve inter-agency cooperation and put in place more thorough systems for monitoring children considered to be at risk. The mechanisms for achieving these aims were:

- area review committees, consisting of higher and middle managers from all agencies with a role to play in the protection of children, whose function was to coordinate and oversee all work in this area
- case conferences involving all frontdoor professionals, whose function was to assess new cases and to review ongoing casework
- registers of all children considered to be abused or at risk of abuse.

Intervention into families with children considered to be at risk thus became, at least in form, more focused and intrusive. The concerns of the previous era – to avoid the separation of parents and children and to support the family as a whole – were now officially called into question. The 1975 Children Act, largely concerned with more general child care issues, reflected the mood of the times. Drawing on a study of children in long-term care (Rowe and Lambert 1973), it emphasised the needs of children as distinct from parents. The Act also made two major changes to child protection practice. First, it allowed for care proceedings to be issued when a child was or might be living in the same household as a person who had committed violent or indecent (Schedule 1) offences under the 1933 Children and Young Persons Act. This particular response was a direct result of the death of another child, Susan Auckland, at the hands of her father, previously convicted for the manslaughter of another of his children (Department of Health and Social Security 1975). Second, it required the appointment of guardians *ad litem* to act exclusively on behalf of the child in legal proceedings. This change was made out of concern for cases such as Maria Colwell's, where parents sought to discharge legal orders and the local authority was not opposing them. In other words, to ensure the views and voice of the child could be represented in court. These changes reflected the new emphasis on abuse of children and the deficiencies of the 1969 Children and Young Persons Act for the purpose of protecting children.

Child abuse work 1975–85

For the remainder of the 1970s the pressure to create more effective detection, investigation and monitoring systems for child abuse continued. From 1973 to 1981 there were 26 inquiries into the deaths and serious abuse of children in Britain caused by their carers (Corby et al. 2001). In almost all cases, various health and welfare agencies were involved, often in a statutory capacity (Department of Health and Social Security 1982). By means of further advice and circulars from the Department of Health and Social Security, considerable effort was made to incorporate lessons from these inquiries into practice. From relatively small beginnings, child abuse work developed into a major preoccupation of social services departments.

The definition of child abuse broadened over time. This is well demonstrated by the changes in terminology. By 1980, the term 'child abuse' had replaced 'baby battering' and the subsequent term 'non-accidental injury'. The 1980 Department of Health and Social Security circular entitled *Child Abuse: Central Register Systems* outlined four categories of abuse or risk of abuse: physical injury; physical neglect; failure to thrive incorporated with emotional abuse; and living in the same household as someone convicted of Schedule 1 offences of the 1933 Children and Young Persons Act (Department of Health and Social Security 1980). It is notable that the sexual abuse of children was not considered as a category for registration.

In the first half of the 1980s there was some relaxation in the drive to establish better systems for responding to child abuse. There were fewer public inquiries (six in the three years from the beginning of 1982 to the end of 1984) (Corby et al. 2001) and a general consolidation of the rash of changes that had taken place in the 1970s. By this time, social services departments were firmly in the lead role in this field, despite official concern to emphasise inter-professional aspects.

Intrusive social work practice?

Therefore, between 1970 and 1985 state intervention into families to protect children had become more systematic, but whether it had become more intrusive is open to question. The most comprehensive research into practice during this period was that of Dingwall et al. (1983). They argued that the 'new' response to child abuse was tougher in aspect than in practice. They tried to demonstrate that, despite greater concerns for children at risk, social workers were still operating in a relatively benign way with families (similar to the practices of the pre-Colwell era). They identified a 'rule of optimism' in operation, whereby social workers were expected to make the best interpretation of an allegation of abuse. This 'rule', they argued, was not one of social workers' own making, but reflected prevailing liberal views about the respective roles of the state and the family: namely that while the state has a legitimate role in intervening into families to ensure the protection of children, this should be done only with due regard to the rights of parents as well as to the needs of children. Thus the liberal approach they identified being adopted by social workers was in line with the general requirements of the state.

Parton (1985) argued that an increase in the use of place of safety orders in the 1970s and the gross numbers of children in care was evidence of a more intrusive approach towards families.

Corby (1987) found that intervention into families suspected of abusing their children was, from the parents' viewpoint, punitive and severe. Parents suspected of abusing their children were at first treated with great suspicion, poorly informed of what was happening and had no rights of attendance at case conferences. However, after the initial stages of intervention, this highly proceduralised and apparently punitive approach gave way to a more sympathetic and helpful response in many cases. Relatively few cases resulted in court action and there was evidence to support Dingwall et al.'s (1983) view that, overall, intervention was characterised by a cautious optimism.

Arguably, therefore, it can be concluded that increased state intrusion into family life between 1975 and 1985, while being officially encouraged, was in practice being tentatively implemented. The focus was still on working cooperatively and supportively with families as far as possible.

Developments in the general child care field

At the same time, there were counter-concerns being put forward about the dangers of over-intrusive, heavy-handed practice in the general child care field. Parton (1991) dated these concerns from 1978. First, a series of studies was commissioned by the DHSS, resulting in a number of publications summarised in a report entitled *Social Work Decisions in Child Care* (Department of Health and Social Security 1985a). These studies, while not directly focused on child abuse, came to the general conclusion that not enough attention was being paid to the needs of families (Packman 1986). Second, the House of Commons Social Services Committee chaired by Renée Short undertook an inquiry into children in care and reported in 1984 (House of Commons 1984). It took as its major concern the perennial problem of the relationship between the state, children and the family, namely how the state can best protect children without undermining the independence of the family. In particular it was vexed by the relative weight to be given to professional discretionary powers (especially those of social workers) and to a legally enforced rights-based approach, and came to the conclusion that there should be a shift towards the latter (see Parton 1991). The report recommended the establishment of a working party on child care law, whose report in 1985 (Department of Health and Social Security 1985b) laid the foundation for the 1989 Children Act.

The Jasmine Beckford inquiry, 1985

However, against this backdrop of reports and parliamentary focus, as with Maria Colwell and Susan Auckland, it was the death of Jasmine Beckford and the subsequent public inquiry (Brent 1985) that arguably had the most significant impact of this period. Jasmine, aged 4, died in July 1984, emaciated and horrifically beaten over an extended period of time by her step-father, Morris Beckford. Jasmine and her younger sister, Louise, had both suffered severe injuries in 1981, for which Morris Beckford was given a suspended sentence. The children were committed to the care of Brent Borough Council and lived with foster carers for six months. They were returned on a trial basis to the care of their parents. The social services department supported the family somewhat sporadically over the next two years and Jasmine was seen only once by her social worker in the last 10 months of her life. The judge at the trial of Morris Beckford and Jasmine's mother described the social worker as being 'naive beyond belief'.

The inquiry into Jasmine's death found that the social worker had regarded Jasmine's parents as the primary clients and that Jasmine's parents' explanations of why she could not be seen had been uncritically accepted. The final report of the inquiry made 68 recommendations, aimed primarily at combating the over-optimism of social workers. Dingwall et al.'s (1983) 'rule of optimism' was mistakenly interpreted to support this view. The report stressed that too much emphasis was placed on the rehabilitation of Jasmine and her sister to their parents, and that evidence to suggest the likelihood of further abuse was ignored. The report was unequivocal that the primary task of social work must be the protection of children and that, where necessary, the full force of the law should be employed.

The findings of the Beckford inquiry had an immediate impact on policy and practice. The Department of Health and Social Security (1986) published draft guidelines setting out recommendations for improving inter-professional coordination in child abuse work. The main proposed changes consisted of reframing child abuse work as child protection work, emphasising the statutory obligation placed on local authorities to act primarily on behalf of children at risk. It was also proposed that area review committees be renamed joint child abuse committees (but in the final guidelines issued in 1988 they were in fact renamed area child protection committees). Social services departments were allocated the main responsibility for coordinating a protection plan for children whose names appeared on the child protection register. Among other changes, it is notable that parental attendance at formal case conferences was felt to be inappropriate, despite a range of professionals feeling the opposite (Brown and Waters 1985), although they could attend informal meetings with key professionals. The tone and message of this document focused attention on the protection of children first and the consideration of the needs and rights of parents second.

The effects of the Beckford inquiry report were immediate. Statistics regarding child protection (see the introductory chapter) show a massive rise in the numbers of children assessed as being at risk. The number of place of safety orders increased dramatically in 1986 and 1987 after nine years at roughly the same level, and there was a significant rise in the number of children coming into care as a result of child abuse and neglect.

Between 1985 and 1989 there were a further 12 inquiries following child deaths (Department of Health 1991a; Corby et al. 2001). All of the physical abuse inquiries of this period were at pains to emphasise the need for a child-focused approach, with much more emphasis on assessing families for potential risk.

Child sexual abuse

Support for those in favour of a return to a more family-focused approach was augmented from an unlikely source. In the summer of 1987, newspapers reported a child sexual abuse scandal in Cleveland. Over a period of six months, 121 children had been brought into care on the recommendation of two paediatricians who, using a physical test pioneered in Leeds (see Hobbs and Wynne 1986), diagnosed the majority of them as having been sexually abused (by anal penetration). The parents of these children were in uproar and had attracted the attention of the local Labour MP, Stuart Bell, to their cause. He raised the matter in Parliament and the outcome was the establishment of another, but this time very different, public inquiry.

Up to this time the issue of child sexual abuse had been a relatively minor concern for child protection agencies in Britain. As with physical abuse, concerns about the sexual abuse of children originally stemmed from experience in the USA. The main protagonists there were survivors of sexual abuse (Armstrong 1978; Brady 1979; Angelou 1983), feminist writers such as Rush (1980) who saw such abuse as symptomatic of gender power inequalities, and the medical profession. Among the latter, Kempe and his associates were again prominent (Kempe and Kempe 1978).

Another approach to the problem was developed by Giaretto et al. (1978). Giaretto's work was a major influence on the British scene and on the work of child psychiatrists, psychologists and social workers at Great Ormond Street Hospital (see Bentovim et al. 1988; Furniss 1991). Their approach, which will also be considered in more detail in Chapters 6 and 8, was to develop a method of intervention based on family therapy principles. In addition they developed techniques (again pioneered in the USA) for helping children disclose the fact that they had been sexually abused, using drawings, play, anatomically correct dolls and video-recordings. These techniques were adapted by social workers in several statutory agencies and employed in Cleveland.

By 1987 child sexual abuse was beginning to feature in the official child protection agenda, although responses to the problem throughout Britain were patchy and variable. A MORI poll survey commissioned by Channel 4 television demonstrated that 1 in 10 children had experienced some form of sexual abuse by the age of 15 and in half of these cases the abuse had been committed by either a family member or somebody known and previously trusted by the child (Baker and Duncan 1985). As already noted, paediatricians developed the reflex anal dilatation test (Hobbs and Wynne 1986) which was seen as a breakthrough in terms of providing definite physical evidence of sexual abuse, which up to this time had proved difficult to evidence in court.

The Cleveland inquiry

These developments set the scene for what happened in Cleveland. The rash of child sexual abuse diagnoses and the subsequent removal of children into statutory care can be attributed to a combination of factors. First, there was heightened awareness of the possible extent of sexual abuse of children among key social services personnel and community paediatricians. Second, the paediatricians were aware of the newly developed reflex anal dilatation test, convinced of its validity and determined to use it. Third, other agencies, particularly the police and police surgeons, were more traditional in their approach and did not accept the new thinking, thus creating a major split in the inter-professional approach. Fourth, the social services department had recently reorganised its child protection system in response to the findings of the Beckford inquiry (Brent 1985). The result of this cocktail of factors was that the paediatricians diagnosed far more cases of sexual abuse than had previously been the norm, the social services department acted swiftly and authoritatively to remove the children, and the police, who would usually have been closely involved in gathering evidence, dissociated themselves completely from what was happening.

As a result, large numbers of children were committed to care. Although all the children had been diagnosed as being abused, it was not clear who had abused them. Social workers, using the techniques developed at Great Ormond Street Hospital (Bentovim et al. 1988), held a series of interviews to try to establish the facts, and in the meantime, parents were denied access to their children in order to ensure that they did not influence their evidence.

The main findings of the Cleveland inquiry report (Butler-Sloss 1988) confirmed that child sexual abuse was a more widespread phenomenon than had previously been thought to be the case. The chair of the inquiry, Lord Justice Elizabeth Butler-Sloss, was at pains to stress that child sexual abuse must remain on the social policy agenda. However, the report criticised individuals from every agency and profession for not working together more cooperatively as well as the specific use of the reflex anal dilatation test without supporting social evidence.

Social workers were singled out for particular criticism, judged as they were to have rushed in overzealously to rescue abused children. The more zealous approach that had been encouraged in the case of physical abuse was seen as inappropriate with regard to sexual abuse. Those concerned with more general child care matters were of the view that social workers had been inappropriately intrusive into families where such an approach was not required, and lobbied for more legal rights for parents and more legal control over social workers. Campbell (1988) has argued that the extent of child sexual abuse by males, to which events at Cleveland pointed, was perceived as threatening to men, and the response was to defend the family against perceived attacks from outside. The Cleveland report broadly agreed with the need for parental rights to be given a firmer footing and that parents should be fully informed of decision-making, particularly with regard to medical examinations (some children at Cleveland were examined on four or more occasions).[5]

Although the Cleveland inquiry added momentum to the growing view that a more family-supportive approach was needed, other sources, such as the Short report (House of Commons 1984), had already been advocating such a change. Other social changes – beyond that of child abuse – taking place in the 1980s were also viewed with concern by politicians. The traditional family had been under threat throughout this period as a result of recession and unemployment, high divorce rates and the growth of lone-parent families. It was estimated that by the early 1990s there were 3 million children living in poverty (Kumar 1993). Concerns about teenage pregnancy and violent teenagers also came to the fore in the 1990s. Factors such as these contributed to questioning a perceived obsession in some quarters with intra-familial child abuse and as evidence of the need for a change in direction.

The draft *Working Together* guidelines issued in 1986 were hastily amended to incorporate the recommendations of the Cleveland report (Department of Health and Social Security 1988), some of which created a complete U-turn in policy, notably relating to parental participation at case conferences. Whereas the 1986 draft had stated that it was inappropriate for parents to attend, the 1988 view was that they should be invited where practicable, unless their presence would impact negatively on the child's best interests. These guidelines placed greater emphasis on careful inter-disciplinary consultation before intervention in sexual abuse cases and recommended joint police and social services department investigations as the norm.

The 1989 Children Act

The Cleveland report also impacted on the passage of the 1989 Children Act through Parliament. This Act, for the most part implemented on 14 October 1991, remains fundamental to the practice of child protection. The key concepts of the Act include parental responsibility, the welfare of the child and partnership working between parents and professionals as well as between local authorities, the National Health Service (NHS) and other agencies having contact with children. The key tensions of the time can be seen in the way the Act attempts to ensure the provision of necessary levels of support to enable children to remain with their families but also to ensure that children at risk are identified and protected, if necessary by removing them from their families. The Act also aims to consolidate all child care law, public and private, under one piece of legislation as well as attempting to address various other concerns, such as the need to increase the use of voluntary care arrangements, making them less punitive and more supportive of families (see Lowe 1989).

Amendments were made in light of the events in Cleveland, such as empowering children to refuse to undergo medical assessments if they so wished (Sec. 44(7)) and enabling local authorities to provide or pay for accommodation for alleged abusers so that children could remain at home during investigations (Schedule 2, para. 5). The legal rights of parents were also strengthened and the discretionary powers of professionals reduced. These rights included making provision for parents to have contact with children in care. All of these changes – emphasising increased parental participation, more voluntary approaches and greater control over professional discretion – were reinforced by events in Cleveland.

However, the implementation of the Children Act was also affected by case law, in some instances by case law preceding 1989. For example, the case of *Gillick* v. *West Norfolk and Wisbech Area Health Authority and another* (1986) established the notion of 'Gillick' competence, which set out the parameters for deciding when a child (i.e. below 16 years) is able to consent to medical treatment without the need for parental consent or knowledge. The judgment also established the broader principle that parental power over a child exists for the benefit of the child and not for the benefit of the parent(s). The Children Act 1989 is more concerned with setting out parental responsibility rather than power, but clearly the two are interrelated. This can be seen in the case of *Re M (Minors) (Residence Order: Jurisdiction)* (1993) which separated the right of a parent to determine where the child should live from their responsibility to provide a decent home for the child. In other words, parental power does not extend to being able to accommodate the child in clearly unsuitable accommodation and neither can the parent choose to provide no accommodation at all because the responsibility of the parent intersects and overrides this power.

1991–2000: the 'second era' of child protection practice

Following the implementation of the 1989 Children Act, the practice of child protection entered a new era, underpinned by the new powers and duties given to local authorities and the new concept of parental responsibility. However, very quickly the new framework was subjected to an unexpected 'stress test' in the form of concerns about 'satanic' and 'institutional' abuse of children.[6]

Concerns over satanic abuse

Interest in satanic abuse originated in the USA where a series of allegations and publications about the phenomenon arose in the 1980s (Smith and Prader 1980; Spencer 1989). Social workers in the UK, when faced with very disturbing and strange accounts of child abuse, took note of these publications, and several major investigations took place in the 1990s into cases of suspected satanic abuse in Congleton, Rochdale, Manchester, Liverpool and Nottingham among many others. The shared features of these cases were accounts by young children of being involved in rituals with adults dressed in cloaks and various black magic paraphernalia and being subjected to (or witnessing) acts of sexual indecency and physical cruelty. Often, social workers and the police responded by removing the children and interviewing them about their experiences. At first, the considerable public interest in these cases was quite supportive of the child protection professionals and praised them for their bravery. However, in all of the cases, this support quickly turned to criticism regarding the nature and quality of the interventions.

Matters came to a head following a case in the Orkneys in 1991. A number of children were suspected to have been involved in ritualistic sexual abuse and were removed by police and social services from their families in dawn raids. The children were moved to mainland Scotland and placed into foster care where they were subjected to intensive interviewing and denied any contact with their parents.[7] Six weeks later, a decision was reached that the legal proceedings were incompetent and the children were ordered to return home.

The subsequent public inquiry (Clyde 1992), as with the Cleveland inquiry, did not make a judgement as to whether abuse had taken place or not, but did examine whether the actions of professionals could be deemed reasonable in light of the information they had available at the time. The overall findings were consistent with those of Cleveland; Lord Clyde was particularly critical of the style and quantity of the interviewing of children (it was considered to be insufficiently objective and far too frequent and intense), the manner of the removal of the children from their homes and the ban on contact between parents and children (it was considered to be traumatic for both and unnecessary for the protection of the children). The net outcome of this inquiry was to confirm the need for a less intrusive style of intervention into child abuse cases.

Following the Orkney case, the spate of concerns about satanist abuse disappeared almost as suddenly as it had started. The Department of Health commissioned research into all 84 cases of alleged ritual abuse from 1987 to 1992 and found no hard evidence in any of them to support the notion that satanic cults were torturing or killing children. However, there was evidence of sexual abuse of children in a large number of these cases, often by multiple perpetrators either from the extended family networks or in a few instances by organised paedophile rings (La Fontaine 1994). La Fontaine explained the rise and fall of concerns about satanist abuse as stemming from a unique combination of circumstances involving Christian fundamentalism, the influence of North American writing about such abuse and the readiness of professionals to take literally what La Fontaine (1998) clearly thought were the fantasies of disturbed and deprived children, many of whom were being subjected to appalling sexual (but not satanist) abuse. There was a considerable backlash against those who did believe that children were being abused as part of satanist rituals and they have subsequently been vilified in the press (Corby and Cox 1998). A similar set of experiences took place in response to ritual abuse allegations in Oude Pekela, a small town in the Netherlands (Jonker and Jonker-Bakker 1997).

Concerns over institutional abuse

The 1990s also saw a massive growth in concern about the abuse of children in settings other than their own homes, including those in the care of local authorities and in day nurseries. Between 1991 and 2000 there were at least 12 public inquiries into abuse in institutional settings, outstripping the number of inquiries of abuse of children in their own homes (Corby et al. 2001). This was in stark contrast to the 1970s and 1980s when there were three inquiries into institutional abuse in Lewisham in 1985, in Belfast in 1985 and in Greenwich in 1987, compared with nearly 50 into abuse by family members.

One notable example related to a system known as 'Pindown', in use at the time in children's homes in Staffordshire (Staffordshire County Council 1991). Pindown was a crude method of controlling children in care (and some on the verge of care) who were considered to be challenging in their behaviours. Pindown was essentially a form of solitary confinement based very loosely on sensory deprivation principles. Children were kept in poorly furnished rooms, not spoken to by staff, and given tedious and repetitive tasks to complete. This system operated in some institutions for over six years with the tacit approval of the management of Staffordshire Social Services Department. A total of 132 children were subjected to the Pindown regime, including one 9-year-old. Another child was kept under this regime for 84 continuous days. Not surprisingly, the subsequent inquiry report found the Pindown regime to be abusive in the extreme (Staffordshire County Council 1991).

In the immediate aftermath, a series of other concerns were raised about regimes in Southwark, Brentwood, Bradford, Lincolnshire, Kirklees, North Wales, Islington, Sheffield, Lambeth and Chepstow, indicating that events in Staffordshire were not isolated examples. Inquiries were also started in Leicestershire and Gwent regarding the sexual abuse of children in residential care.[8]

The Department of Health responded to this flurry of concern by commissioning a general inquiry into the state of residential children's services in England (Utting 1991; Warner 1992), with similar inquiries taking place in Wales and Scotland (Social Services Inspectorate, Wales, and Social Information Systems 1991; Skinner 1992). The Utting report provided an overview of the strengths and weaknesses of residential care at the time, reaffirming the low status of such care, the low levels of qualified staff, the impact of a decline in the use of residential care and its usage as a choice of last resort for children and young people with particular problems and difficulties (Utting 1991). With regard to abuse, the report seemed satisfied that changes in the 1989 Children Act, particularly those relating to making representations (Sec. 26), carrying out inspections and appointing independent visitors for children in care were sufficient to prevent the sort of ill-treatment that had been in evidence.

These initiatives, however, did not stem the flow of new concerns about abuse of children in residential settings. Allegations of sexual abuse and physical mistreatment of children resulted in inquiries into the Shieldfield day nursery in Newcastle (Hunt 1994) and at a residential boarding school for children with learning difficulties in Northumbria (Kilgallon 1995), as well as wide-scale police investigations into almost all children's homes in Merseyside, Cheshire, Clwyd and Gwynedd. In response to these increased concerns, the Department of Health commissioned a further inquiry into the situation of all children living away from home, including children in long-term hospitals, residential schools and foster care (Utting 1997). The main message of the report was to reaffirm the need for considerable vigilance, but it also stressed that measures were being put into place to ensure greater safety for children not living in their own homes.

A particular set of concerns about institutional abuse in North Wales eventually led to the establishment of a tribunal of inquiry. This type of inquiry was the most formidable means of carrying out quasi-judicial investigations into matters of national concern and had never previously been used in connection with child abuse. The tribunal was set up following a series of allegations regarding the widespread sexual abuse of children in residential homes in North Wales, possibly involving senior figures and a large-scale cover-up. Its establishment undoubtedly reflected not only the need to examine events in North Wales but also the extent of the concern that abuse of children in care generally had raised in society.

The inquiry commenced in 1996 and reported in 2000 (Waterhouse 2000). It examined all allegations of abuse taking place in 84 statutory, voluntary and private residential settings between 1974 and 1996, as well as those arising from foster care placements. It eventually focused on 29 children's homes and 15 foster homes. The tribunal found evidence of widespread sexual and physical abuse of boys and girls in Clwyd during this period and evidence of some physical abuse in Gwynedd. However, contrary to the views of many, the tribunal found no evidence of a paedophile ring operating in Clwyd or in Bryn Estyn (but said it had very little evidence to go on).

Despite these findings, the tribunal did not have a great effect on policy and practice developments in residential care for children, largely because by the time it came to report, new initiatives had been or were already being introduced. These included the Quality Protects programme established in 1998 (Department of Health 1998b) to tackle issues relating to the health, educational and social development of children in care, the passing of the Leaving Care Act 2000, to provide better follow-up services and support for children formally in care, and of the Care Standards Act 2000, aimed at achieving a greater element of independence in residential care inspection. However, the tribunal has been influential in highlighting the poor standard of residential children's care in the 1970s and 1980s and the poor outcomes of care provision (evidenced by high rates of unemployment and imprisonment of ex-care residents). Finally, it exposed the vulnerability to abuse of children in residential care because of the lack of adequate procedures for making complaints (particularly prior to the 1989 Children Act), poor support for staff who wished to raise concerns and ineffective inspection arrangements.

Working Together guidelines 1991 and the *Memorandum of Good Practice* 1992

In response to Cleveland and some of the other concerns about child abuse discussed above, new child protection guidelines were produced in 1991 outlining the need for more measured, planned and coordinated interventions (Department of Health 1991b). This guidance revised and updated the previous *Working Together* guidelines, issued in 1988, and aimed primarily at striking a balance between the kind of over-zealous intervention seen in Cleveland and the far too limited intervention seen in the cases of Maria Colwell, Jasmine Beckford and others. It aimed to do this by promoting inter-agency working, setting out how to manage child protection services at a strategic level but also giving guidance for practice in individual cases. In particular, it was made a requirement that social workers and the police should conduct joint investigations into all serious cases of physical abuse and into all allegations of sexual abuse. In 1992, guidelines were issued setting out in detail the requirements for videoed joint interviews, which, following the recommendations of the Pigot Committee, were to be allowed as evidence-in-chief at the criminal trials of alleged abusers in order to ease the pains for child witnesses in court (Home Office/Department of Health 1992). For the first time, serious case reviews (or 'Part 8' reviews, referring to the relevant section of *Working Together*)[9] were introduced in order to help local authorities and other agencies learn from instances of death or serious injury to a child. These guidelines were updated in 1999 following the publication of *Child Protection: Messages from Research* in 1995 (Department of Health 1995).

Organised abuse, paedophiles, the commercial sexual exploitation of children and child abuse via the internet

Other extra-familial abuse concerns that figured largely in the 1990s were organised abuse, abuse by paedophiles, commercial exploitation of children by means of prostitution and pornography, and abuse via the internet. It could be argued that there are linkages between all these areas of concern. If so, then it is the notion of the paedophile that provides the link and, most certainly, since the late 1990s, this has been the key issue for the public.

'Organised abuse' was defined in the 1991 *Working Together* guidelines (Department of Health 1991b) as 'a generic term which covers abuse which may involve a number of abusers, a number of abused children and young people and often encompasses different forms of abuse. It involves to a greater or lesser extent an element of organization'. A good deal of the abuse of this nature took place within extended families, whereas the popular image of organised abuse is that of paedophile rings in which children are systematically passed around by strangers to be sexually abused or to be coerced into the production of pornographic material (or both). Such rings are also associated with child murder – the Jason Swift case is a classic example of this type of abuse.[10] They are also often considered to be in operation in institutional abuse, although no evidence of the operation of such rings has been found in any of the inquiries into residential abuse. There is good reason to believe, therefore, that children exposed to multiple abuse, particularly those at the younger end of the age spectrum, are most at risk from within their own extended families even though they may be exposed to abuse from extra-familial abusers as well.

The notion of a large network of evil people preying on vulnerable children outside the family does not, therefore, bear scrutiny. Nevertheless the public perception and fear of 'the paedophile' remained strong in the public mind in the 1990s and was influential in bringing about important changes in policy and practice during this time. Starting with the Jason Swift case in the 1980s (see Note 10) and the murders committed by Fred and Rosemary West (Bridge 1995), fears about stranger assault escalated. In response to this public anxiety, two pieces of legislation were enacted in the late 1990s (see Parton 2005). The 1997 Sex Offenders Act made it a requirement that convicted offenders register with the police and keep them informed of their whereabouts for varying lengths of time, depending on the seriousness of their offence, and the 1998 Crime and Disorder Act empowered the police to apply for sex offender orders, allowing the police to register and prescribe restrictions in the movement of offenders not covered by the 1997 Act requirements. Police and probation services throughout the country were also involved in setting up protocols for assessing and managing the risk that such offenders posed to the public.[11]

The murder of Sarah Payne in July 2000 in Sussex created an outbreak of public anxiety about the risks to children from sex offenders. Fuelled by a campaign organised by the now-defunct *News of the World* tabloid newspaper, there followed a demand for the presence and location of all sex offenders in communities to be made known to residents, drawing on the model of 'Megan's Law', introduced across the USA in 1996 following the rape and murder of 7-year-old Megan Kanka in New Jersey by a neighbour with a history of sexual assaults. However, rather than implement a UK version of Megan's Law, the government introduced the Criminal Justice and Court Services Act 2000, making it a requirement for agencies to work together to assess and monitor released prisoners thought to pose a risk to the public. These tasks were to be carried out by multi-agency public protection panels, consisting largely of police and probation officers as well as other relevant agencies. They are required to ensure that risk assessments are carried out on all serious offenders released from custody, to classify the levels of risk they pose, and to agree on planned management of that risk. Thus, although the American model has not been followed, there has been considerable development in the measures aimed at protecting children from so-called paedophiles (Lovell 2001). The pressure for maintaining and increasing these measures continued following the murders of two 11-year-old girls, Jessica Chapman and Holly Wells, by their school caretaker, Ian Huntley, in Soham in 2002. At Huntley's trial, it was revealed that he had been investigated by police on several occasions between 1995 and 1999 following allegations of rape, indecent assault and having sexual intercourse with girls under the legal age of consent. However, none of this information was properly recorded or shared when Huntley was appointed to his post as a school caretaker in 2001. The Bichard inquiry, set up to investigate these matters, argued for better electronic systems of record-keeping and clear protocols for the sharing of information between relevant agencies (Bichard 2004), and in 2011 a national police database was set up to allow regional police forces to share data on convicted criminals, suspects and victims of crime, as well as the details of people questioned but not charged by police. Concerns about disclosure of information and civil liberty issues were seen as irrelevant where protection of children is a concern.

While many of these shifts towards improved information-sharing and assessment of risk are understandable in the light of the tragic deaths involved, there are potential dysfunctions. The first is that there is likely to be much less emphasis on understanding and differentiating between the reasons for paedophile activities and the motives for abuse and, therefore, on treating the problem (Colton and Vanstone 1996; Featherstone and Lancaster 1997). Second, there is a danger that abuse becomes associated with individual pathology which can lead to overlooking other explanations. Third, there is a danger that concern with extra-familial abuse may lead to less attention being paid to abuse of children within families.

Commercial sexual exploitation of children (which includes child prostitution and child pornography) is another issue that came onto the child abuse agenda in the 1990s. Much of the campaigning work in relation to child prostitution has been carried out by voluntary agencies such as Barnardo's and the Children's Society (Lee and O'Brien 1995; Swann 1998). They present a model of children being groomed for prostitution by male pimps frequently posing as boyfriends. The image created is one of victimisation and exploitation and has had a powerful effect on policy development in Britain. In 2000, the Department of Health and other government departments produced new guidance requiring children involved in prostitution to be treated as victims of child abuse rather than as offenders and pointed to the need for law enforcement measures to be targeted on those exploiting them (Department of Health/Home Office/Department of Education and Employment/National Assembly for Wales 2000). It was noted earlier in the chapter that the late Victorian reformers made unhelpful assumptions about the lives of working-class children in order to rescue them from prostitution and it was not particularly successful. In modern-day times, while decriminalisation and supportive help are a major step forward, these provide no guarantee in themselves of solving the problem. Cusick (2002) demonstrates the importance of taking into account social as well as psychological factors in the causation of commercial sexual exploitation of children, such as poverty, homelessness, family breakdown, leaving care and running away. She also notes the importance of listening to children's accounts and respecting their wishes and views. Clearly, solving the problem of child prostitution is a complex and comprehensive task requiring carefully thought-through aims and tactics (Shaw and Butler 1998).

The issue of commercial sexual exploitation of children has also taken on a global perspective with public concern raised about sexual tourism in South-East Asia (Munir and Yasin 1997) and the trafficking of children, particularly from eastern European countries (Manion 2002) (see Chapter 9).

The 1990s also saw a rise in concerns about the use of child pornography. While this is being considered under an extra-familial abuse heading, Itzin (1997) demonstrates that the use of child pornography and involvement of children in the production of pornography frequently commences within the family, thus rendering the distinction invalid. She also demonstrates the links between child pornography and organised abuse, prostitution and sexual offending against children. Both child pornography and child abuse on the internet are listed as forms of abuse in the 1999 *Working Together to Safeguard Children* guidelines (Department of Health 1999) and there has also been a large increase in the prosecution of adults who access child pornography sites on the internet (Calder 2004). It has long been suspected that there is a link between viewing child pornography and direct sexual abuse of children, and in 2009 Bourke and Hernandez published the results of their study of 155 offenders sentenced for the possession of child abuse images, the majority of whom claimed to have had committed no previous acts of direct sexual abuse. After an 18-month programme, the researchers established that 131 of the 155 offenders had in fact committed direct sexual abuse (with a 2,369 per cent increase in the number of admitted offences).

The range of concerns about abuse of children outside the family and the measures taken to combat them were wide-ranging and extensive. Some concerns – such as 'satanic abuse' – have subsided while others (especially in respect of 'stranger' paedophilia) continue to concern child protection professionals. An emphasis on external risks may, however, deflect attention and focus from intra-familial abuse (although, as has been seen in relation to child sexual abuse, it is important not to assume that the two are *not* interlinked). The next two sections consider how, despite these concerns, the pressure in the late 1990s was for a return to a 'family support' model of responding to child abuse allegations.

Messages from Research 1995

In 1995, the research projects set up by the Department of Health following the Cleveland inquiry report were published individually (20 in all). They were also summarised in *Child Protection: Messages from Research* (Department of Health 1995) and implications for child protection policy and practice were distilled from their findings.

The main findings of these research projects were as follows:

- The child protection system acted like a giant sieve, taking in a broad spectrum of referrals about the care of children, ranging from concerns about the demeanour of toddlers in nurseries through to allegations of incest. In all, 24 per cent of these referrals resulted in child protection conferences and, at just over half of these, recommendations were made for placement on the child protection register (see Gibbons et al. 1995a).

- Most of the 85 per cent of families not registered received minimal intervention and service provision. Services were centred on children and their families who had been placed on the child protection register (Gibbons et al. 1995b).
- Nearly all families that were subject to initial child protection investigations were poor, had experienced problems such as death, divorces, accidents and illnesses (physical and mental) and had previously been referred to social services departments or were current service users. The children in most of these families were in need as defined by the 1989 Children Act (Farmer and Owen 1995).
- Parents at the receiving end of child protection investigations experienced them as difficult and stigmatic forms of intervention. Many parents felt that they were being unfairly labelled as child abusers. To their mind, child abuse was equated with serious physical assaults and sexual abuse, not with problems with parenting (Farmer and Owen 1995).
- There were too few attempts to engage parents in the child protection process either by giving adequate information or by enabling participation at child protection conferences. There was little evidence of working in partnership with parents (Thoburn et al. 1995).
- In terms of child protection, there was overall a 70 per cent success rate, using incidence of re-abuse as an indicator.

These findings were supported from another source, that of the Audit Commission (1994), whose remit was to assess the efficiency of the use of public money. It found that spending on child protection work was poorly planned and that its concentration on a relatively small number of families meant that obligations to provide resources for children in need under Section 17 of the Children Act were not being met.

The general picture created by these two influential sources was that child protection work had become too bureaucratised, too proceduralised and over-focused on overt incidents of child abuse, such as bruising or sexual abuse allegations. As a consequence of this, broader family problems and, in particular, the issue of general neglect, were tending to be overlooked. If more obvious forms of abuse were not present it seemed likely families would receive little attention, even though a broader assessment might have identified many unmet needs as far as the children in these families were concerned. The summarising document, *Child Protection: Messages from Research* (Department of Health 1995), also focused on research that indicated children living in generally neglectful situations suffered worse long-term consequences in terms of personal, social and economic development and success than the majority of those who were physically and sexually abused (see Egeland et al. 1983). The point was that standards of care in neglectful families tended to persist throughout childhood, whereas other forms of abuse might be isolated or spasmodic. The emphasis was on the psychological impact of such abuse. It was deemed that children living in persistently adverse conditions, possibly experiencing the most psychologically damaging effects, were the least likely to receive supportive services.

Refocusing from child protection to family support 1995–2000

As stressed at the beginning of this chapter, the early 1990s saw social workers and other professionals in the child protection field operating with a much greater degree of uncertainty than before in relation to issues of physical and sexual abuse and neglect within the family. In the first two years after the implementation of the 1989 Children Act, the numbers of care proceedings and applications for emergency care orders reduced considerably. There was a fair degree of tentativeness in pursuing allegations of sexual abuse within the family following the fall-out from Cleveland (Corby 1998). Greater attempts were made to work more closely with families in this period. Parental participation at conferences became more common, as did professional-parental consultations in the period following initial interventions. While there were those that queried the nature of this more partnership-focused approach (Corby et al. 1996), it cannot be denied that the introduction of the Children Act and the new *Working Together* guidelines (Department of Health 1991b) were having some impact on practice.

What was needed, therefore, in child protection work, was a refocus in thinking about working with families and a shift in the allocation and delivery of services. The response from the then Conservative Health Secretary, John Bovis, was a recommendation that practitioners develop a 'lighter touch' approach in their work with children and families, but there was little guidance forthcoming at this time on how best to achieve this, and the responses of many social workers in particular was to play safe and retain focus on what they saw as the most serious and concerning cases (Platt 2001; Spratt 2001). A second series of Department of Health-sponsored research projects which had been examining child care practice in the mid-1990s reached similar findings and was at pains to show that much of the child protection focus was not particularly productive (Department of Health 2001).

Despite this early slow progress, the Department of Health was intent on bringing about the changes to which its research was pointing, and it pressed ahead with the development of a new framework which could achieve both an assessment of children in need and of their safety. Indeed, the underlying philosophy of the framework was that in all but the most extreme cases these were in fact one and the same thing, so that by achieving a full assessment of children's needs (provided the required resources were there to meet them) children were at the same time being safeguarded. What was needed was to think more flexibly about dealing with safeguarding concerns than before. A particular gain of the new approach was seen to be the fact that families where long-term neglect rather than abuse was occurring (situations that, as has been seen, were being identified by research as having the worst longer-term effects of all forms of abuse on children's development) were likely to receive more effective support than before. Such families might include those where parents were substance misusers or had mental health or domestic violence problems (Cleaver et al. 1999).

The incoming Labour government (1997–2010) concurred with much of this analysis and supported the development of what was to be entitled the *Framework for the Assessment of Children in Need and Their Families* when it was implemented in April 2001 (Department of Health 2000a). However, as has been seen in earlier sections of this chapter, there were at this time many pressing concerns about children in care coming out of the North Wales tribunal of inquiry, and concerns about child protection work in the community continued to arise, with highly publicised Part 8 review reports into the death of Ricki Neave in Cambridgeshire in 1997 (Bridge 1997) and the gross neglect of young children in a family in Caerphilly in Wales in 1998 (Bridge 1998a).

The government's response to events such as these was to lengthen general training of social workers, to introduce specialised post-qualifying child care programmes, to produce new guidelines for safeguarding children (Department of Health 1999) and to introduce the Quality Protects programme (Department of Health 1998b). It also brought in a range of legislation to improve leaving care standards and the inspection of children's homes. However, the main concern of the Labour administration was to improve the circumstances of a much wider range of children than those defined as in need. One of the cornerstones of New Labour policy was its stated determination to tackle the legacy of child poverty left by the outgoing Conservative administration, and in order to achieve this it introduced a range of community-based projects and services, initially targeted on poorer districts, but with a view to universal coverage in the future. These projects, Sure Start, Children's Fund and the Connexions Service, covered the age range from 0 to 18. More recent initiatives have included improved nursery and after-school provision and the introduction of tax credits to promote greater opportunity for mothers to work. Other key goals of the New Labour project for children and families have been to tackle youth crime and to reduce teenage pregnancy.

Many of these goals are set out in the government Green Paper *Every Child Matters* (Department of Health 2003b), which was the precursor to the 2004 Children Act. We will return to these developments in the next chapter. However, also included in the Green Paper were further concerns about child protection, following on from the Victoria Climbié inquiry which reported earlier in 2003 (see below). Thus, despite all the attempts to situate serious child abuse in a broader context of family problems and issues, and despite the emphasis on extra-familial abuse which seemed to dominate the 1990s and the early years of the new millennium, child deaths by abuse within the family continued to arouse widespread public and professional concern.

The Victoria Climbié inquiry

The first two years of the millennium witnessed three deaths by child abuse which were widely reported on in the national press. The first of these was that of 8-year-old Victoria Climbié in 2000 which resulted in a statutory inquiry ordered by the Secretary of State for Health (Laming 2003). The other two deaths were responded to by serious case reviews, later made available for publication.

The Climbié case was unlike many others inquired into, in that there was no consistent ongoing involvement with Victoria and her 'family' on the part of health, social care and police agencies based on agreed concern about her safety. To some degree this was a result of Victoria's unusual family circumstances. She was born in the Ivory Coast and in 1998, aged 7, sent by her parents to live with her great-aunt in the suburbs of Paris (for her educational betterment). However, her great-aunt, Marie Therese Kouao, was experiencing considerable domestic and financial difficulties,

and she departed for London early in 1999, accompanied by Victoria, to seek employment and a new life. Much of her and Victoria's early contact with care agencies was
concerned with securing accommodation. Mrs Kouao eventually solved this herself
by moving in to live with Carl Manning, whom she met when he was driving a bus on
which she and Victoria were travelling. With the knowledge that was subsequently
available to the inquiry, it was clear that physical abuse, including beatings, burns and
hot water scalding were inflicted on Victoria not long after moving into Manning's
flat. However, there were really only three contacts between health and social care
professionals and Victoria from then until the time of her death (approximately eight
months later). The first two (in July 1999) involved her being taken to two different
hospitals with, first, scabs and cuts on her face and head, and second, scald marks
(also on face and head). At the first of these two referrals, Victoria was diagnosed as
having scabies. At the second Mrs Kouao alleged that Victoria had poured hot water
over herself to reduce the itching pain caused by the scabies. While there was more
suspicion about what was happening to Victoria after this second referral, there was
no definite assessment carried out and no proper follow-up. The third point of contact
was in November when Mrs Kouao alleged that Canning had sexually abused Victoria,
perhaps prompted by a belief that this would result in her getting help with her
housing difficulties. However, she subsequently withdrew this allegation and, once
again, it was not followed up. There was no further contact until Victoria died in
February 2000 as a result of beatings, hypothermia and gross neglect.

The Climbié inquiry, chaired by Lord Laming, who had a distinguished career in
social services management and inspection, came to similar conclusions to those of
many other inquiries, namely how poor communication between agencies, lack of
attention paid to children in their own right and failure to follow up concerns can lead
to disastrous consequences. However, what was different from previous inquiries was
the complete condemnation of the way in which child protection work was organised
and conducted at all levels. Lord Laming was at pains not to point the finger just at
frontdoor workers but also at senior managers, councillors and to bodies such as area
child protection committees. He also pointed to the shortcomings of central government for failing to establish clear lines of accountability up to the highest levels of
administration. Laming was also critical of standards of training, and of the lack of
effective systems for sharing information. The report made 108 recommendations,
of which the key ones are as follows:

1   The establishment of a children's commissioner post backed by a National
    Agency for Children and Families to act as a champion for children in terms of
    needs, safeguarding and rights.
2   The establishment of direct lines of accountability for safeguarding children from
    central government downwards headed by a minister for children and families.
3   The replacement of area child protection committees with safeguarding children
    boards (SCBs).
4   The introduction of computerised cross-agency recording systems in relation to
    children in need at local levels, and the establishment of a national data bank of
    all children up to the age of 16.

5   Increased managerial scrutiny of (and accountability for) the work of frontdoor workers with child protection responsibilities.

6   Greater emphasis on joint child protection training.

Concluding comments

There are a variety of reasons for the somewhat bewildering developments between the publication of the Jasmine Beckford inquiry report, the passing of the 1989 Children Act and the Victoria Climbié inquiry, which followed Victoria's death in 2000. They can best be understood by reference to the way in which the issue of child abuse was responded to in earlier years.

Throughout the whole of the period reviewed in this chapter, and continuing today, there was and is ambivalence and uncertainty about the best way for the state to intervene in families to ensure that children are properly socialised and not ill-treated. Preserving the independence of the family and the rights of parents has always had to be balanced against the welfare of children and their rights to be protected by those sanctioned to carry out child protection work. For many years this task was left to the judgement of the NSPCC and later to child care officers in children's depart-ments, with backing from the courts as and when required. This approach was deemed to be working well as long as support for the family remained the major goal.

The rediscovery of child abuse challenged this consensus position, just as it did in the late Victorian era. Social workers and others were increasingly pressed to inter-vene more authoritatively into families in light of an understanding that abuse of children by their parents was more widespread than had previously been imagined.

Looking back across the period considered in this chapter, there have been times when specific focus on child protection has been the main concern (the late Victorian era and 1970 to the present) and times when a broader family-supportive approach to child care issues has predominated (from 1914 through to the end of the 1960s). Events at Cleveland and changes to family structure and cohesion created the basis of a shift back to more family-supportive approaches in the 1990s. This shift was re-inforced under the 1997–2010 Labour administration's focus on early intervention. However, events in the preceding 20 years had created an awareness of the fact that families could be dangerous and distressing places for many children and there was to be no simple U-turn. Chapter 3 will look at how these conflicting demands and ways of thinking have impacted on child protection work from 2000 up to the present time.

Child abuse: a historical time-line 1800–2000

1800–70   State concern with
   • children of the streets
   • children at work
   • young offenders
   • Poor Law children

1861	Offences Against the Person Act
1872	Baby farming and the Infant Life Protection Act
1887	Formation of the NSPCC
1889	Prevention of Cruelty to Children Act
1908	Children Act and Incest Act
1933	Children and Young Persons Act
1945	Dennis O'Neill inquiry
1946	Curtis Committee
1948	Children Act and the formation of children's departments
1950	Coordinating committees (cruelty and neglect)
1962	Henry Kempe and the battered child syndrome
1974	Maria Colwell inquiry. Formation of the child abuse prevention system Area Child Protection Committees established
1975	Susan Auckland inquiry and Children Act
1974–80	Seventeen public inquiries into child abuse deaths
1980	Broadening of concerns (child abuse)
1981–5	Fifteen public inquiries into child abuse deaths
1984	Short report
1985	Jasmine Beckford inquiry MORI poll survey into child sexual abuse
1986–91	Twelve public inquiries into child abuse deaths
1986	Draft *Working Together* guidelines (child protection)
1987	Kimberley Carlile and Tyra Henry inquiries
1988	Cleveland inquiry and new *Working Together* guidelines
1989	Children Act
1991	New *Working Together* guidelines
1995	Children (Scotland) Act
1999	Protection of Children Act
2000	*Framework for the Assessment of Children in Need and Their Families* Death of Victoria Climbié

Recommended reading

Ferguson, H. (2004) *Protecting Children in Time: Child Abuse, Child Protection and the Consequences of Modernity*. Basingstoke: Palgrave Macmillan.

Gordon, L. (1989) *Heroes of Their Own Lives: The Politics and History of Family Violence, Boston 1880–1960*. London: Virago.

Hendrick, H. (1994) *Child Welfare: England 1872–1989*. London: Routledge.

Parton, N. (1985) *The Politics of Child Abuse*. London: Macmillan.

Parton, N. (1991) *Governing the Family: Child Care, Child Protection and the State*. London: Macmillan.

Reder, P., Duncan, S. and Gray, M. (1993) *Beyond Blame: Child Abuse Tragedies Revisited*. London: Routledge.

Rose, L. (1991) *The Erosion of Childhood: Child Oppression in Britain 1860–1918*. London: Routledge.

3

Protecting children and young people from harm: contemporary perspectives

Introduction

The years from 2000 to 2011 saw, if anything, an increased focus on child care, child welfare and child protection compared to the two preceding decades. As in other areas, such as health and education, the newly elected Labour administration (1997–2010) seemed determined to demonstrate its commitment to the public sector by, on the one hand, increased funding, but on the other hand by enacting a series of reforms.

The new approach in the latter part of the 1990s and the early twenty-first century was an attempt to find middle ground between under-reacting to child abuse and over-reacting. The Labour government especially sought to do this by improving universal services for all children, and trying to intervene much earlier in families and thus prevent future difficulties from arising. This approach can also be seen as a way of trying to 'normalise' the involvement of state agencies in family life and thus avoid stigmatising particular 'problem' families.

With the general election of May 2010 and the formation of the Conservative-Liberal Democrat coalition government, another shift in thinking took place. Prompted by an economic desire to cut government spending and a political ambition to empower local decision-making, the new administration sought to discover ways in which child protection could be reformed to enable more local flexibility but without incurring significantly increased costs – indeed, if anything, the desire was to 'do more, with less'. However, as happened in previous eras, notable cases of child protection have also had a resounding influence on contemporary child protection practice. This chapter will examine the period following the Climbié inquiry up to 2012.

Legislative and policy changes following the Climbié inquiry

Following the publication of the report of the Climbié inquiry, the government published a Green Paper entitled *Every Child Matters* (Department of Health 2003b). This document identified five outcomes for all children in the country:[1]

1 Being healthy.
2 Staying safe.
3 Enjoying and achieving.
4 Making a positive contribution.
5 Achieving economic well-being.

According to some commentators, this Green Paper was one of the most significant changes for children's services of the past 20–30 years (Lownsbrough and O'Leary 2005).

In a further response to Laming's recommendations, the government also proposed to establish a nationwide database of all children in England, to introduce children's trusts in every local area to bring together health, education and social services, to replace area child protection committees with local safeguarding children's boards (LSCBs) and for local authorities to appoint directors of children's services to oversee services and establish clear lines of accountability. In 2003, responsibility for children's services was transferred from the Department of Health to the Department for Education and Skills (renamed the Department for Education in 2010). In 2004, the Children Act placed these reforms on a statutory footing. Children's commissioner posts were also established in England, Northern Ireland, Scotland and Wales and Margaret Hodge MP was appointed as the first children's minister.

In September 2006, the 'Every Disabled Child Matters' (EDCM) campaign was launched and in March 2007 the government published a policy document entitled *Every Parent Matters* (Department for Education and Skills 2007a). Both were clearly influenced by the *Every Child Matters* agenda. The EDCM campaign was a joint venture between Contact a Family, the Council for Disabled Children, Mencap and the Special Educational Consortium. The aims of this campaign were to raise the profile of disabled children and ensure that this vulnerable group was not overlooked. The impact of the EDCM campaign could clearly be seen in the launch of the government's 'Aiming High for Disabled Children' agenda in May 2007. As part of Aiming High, additional funds were provided to pay for short breaks for disabled children (such as overnight care, youth activities or holiday play schemes). Additional money was eventually given to all local authorities, the initiative having first been trialled in 35 'pathfinder' areas (such as the London Borough of Enfield and by Suffolk County Council).[2]

The *Every Parent Matters* document set out how all parents and carers were to be supported, from 'early years' intervention, through school and into their child's adulthood. Four pieces of legislation have also been passed since 1995 to support carers. The Carers (Recognition and Services) Act 1995 gave new rights and a legal status to carers, including the right to request an assessment from the local authority. The Carers and Disabled Children Act 2000 applied to all carers aged 16 and over and placed a duty on local authorities to provide direct services to them, following an assessment of need. The Carers (Equal Opportunities) Act 2004 placed a duty on local authorities to inform carers of their rights and required carers' assessments to take account of whether carers wished to work, undertake training or education, or engage in leisure activities. Finally, the Work and Families Act 2004 gave carers the right to request flexible working arrangements, if certain criteria were met.

These ambitious developments need to be understood as part of the wider government agenda aimed at taking 'all children out of poverty by 2020' as well as to 'develop the potential of all children'. Neither the 2003 *Every Child Matters* Green Paper nor the 2004 Children Act focused specifically on safeguarding to any great degree, despite the concerns raised by the Climbié inquiry. The main emphasis was on prevention, tackling poor parenting via early intervention and linking families with young children into a wide range of universal services.

The *Working Together to Safeguard Children* guidelines were also updated and re-issued in light of these developments, in 2006 and 2010. The government sought to emphasise the wider responsibilities of all agencies to promote the welfare of children and to safeguard them. The guidance also set out in extraordinary detail how individual cases should be managed, with, for example, a flowchart of how to respond to children involved in forced marriages. Such prescription was later criticised by the

Munro report on child protection (Munro 2011a), which noted that *Working Together* was now 55 times longer than the comparative guidance issued in 1974.

Despite the laudable aims of *Every Child Matters* and associated programmes, there were concerns that the drive to establish universal provision for all children inevitably meant that the needs of the most deprived and vulnerable children were overlooked. Nevertheless, it is undoubtedly difficult for any government to raise universal standards and at the same time maintain a strong focus on children at risk.

Serious case reviews

LSCBs are required to consider undertaking a serious case review (SCR) whenever a child dies and when abuse or neglect are known or suspected factors. SCRs may also be undertaken when a child receives a serious injury or health impairment as a result of abuse or neglect, when a child is subject to serious sexual assault or abuse, when a child's main carer has been murdered, when a child is killed by a carer with mental health difficulties, or where there are concerns about the way in which agencies have worked together in terms of child protection. The aim of SCRs was to enable professionals to learn lessons and improve future practice. To aid this process, every two years the Department for Education (or previous equivalent) commissions an analysis of every SCR in the country (see Brandon et al. 2008a, 2009, 2010). The most recent of these – and the fifth overall – was published in 2010 and covered all 268 SCRs between 2007 and 2009. Of these, 152 involved a child death and 166 involved serious harm or injury. Between 2005 and 2007, 189 SCRs were held and between 2003 and 2005, 161. Despite this significant increase, the characteristics of the children's families remained fairly consistent, as did the proportion of the children known to children's social care and the number who had been subject to child protection plans. The major themes of the report were as follows:

- there has been an increase in the number of SCRs undertaken
- themes and trends remained very similar across many of the SCRs
- not all cases of serious injury led to an SCR being held, even if the criteria set out in *Working Together* appear to have been met
- around half of children killed or seriously harmed have not been known to children's social care, confirming that 'safeguarding is everyone's responsibility'
- the particular vulnerability of babies, especially babies born prematurely
- the tendency for the needs of 'hard to help' teenagers to be overlooked by services (around 25 per cent of SCRs involved adolescents)
- a 'toxic trio' of family characteristics (parental substance misuse, family violence and mental health problems), compounded by poverty, frequent home moves and evictions can present serious risks to children, although they do not act as predictors for serious harm or death in individual cases (see Chapter 5)
- the importance of building strong relationships with children and their families
- patterns of cooperation or non-cooperation are significant – patterns of non-attendance or non-cooperation, even hostility, are not necessarily permanent and

should not be used as reasons for closing cases (see the case of Khyra Ishaq, below)

- the dangers of 'start again' syndrome, when new workers are allocated to a case and overlook knowledge of the past and decide to focus only on the present – this is especially prevalent in cases of neglect
- the chaos and low expectations of families can lead to professionals feeling overwhelmed and losing focus on the child and his or her needs
- the 'rule of optimism' is still in evidence in the way many professionals are reluctant to make negative judgements about parents
- children and young people continue to be 'missing' in cases – young people may rarely be spoken to, siblings are not regularly seen and disabled children especially are overlooked.

There are clearly powerful lessons to be learned from SCRs, although it must be acknowledged that such cases may not be reflective of wider practice. In the most recent analyses, the authors note that, with the publication and general government acceptance of the Munro report, policy-makers do seem more understanding of the complexity of child protection work and to accept the need to more effectively support professionals.

Notable child protection cases

Despite attempts to increase the universal provision of services and to improve outcomes for all children, it was perhaps inevitable that shocking cases of child abuse would still come to light and, at times, dominate the agenda of child protection. We have selected three cases which we feel illustrate the complexity of the contemporary field of child protection: the death of Peter Connelly, the 'kidnapping' of Shannon Matthews and the death of Khyra Ishaq.

Peter Connelly

The death of Peter Connelly in 2007 was viewed as being in some ways similar to the death of Victoria Climbié seven years earlier, partly because both children died in the London Borough of Haringey but also because they were both killed by their 'carers' and they both suffered unimaginable cruelty and physical injury. However, the death of Peter was viewed as even more damning for child protection professionals, given the amount of contact they had had with him prior to his death. In the case of Victoria, very little attention had been given her by professionals; in the case of Peter, he received of a lot of attention without a resultant improved level of protection. It was simply not the fact of Peter's death and the horror of his treatment that made this case notable – after all, in the two years after Peter's death, 30 children were killed by their carers and/or by familiar adults without anything like the same media or political attention. The difference in Peter's case was the inability of professionals to protect him, despite having frequent contact with him and knowing a great deal of worrying information about him (*Observer* 2009).

Peter was born in 2006 and lived with his mother, Tracey Connelly, her partner Steven Barker and his brother, Jason Owen, previously called Jason Barker (although neither males were thought by professionals at the time to be involved in Tracey's life). Peter's father left the family home when Peter was 4 months of age. After Peter's death, it became evident that Steven Barker had moved into the family home at the end of 2006 and by July 2007 Jason Owen had also moved in, together with his 15-year-old girlfriend and his children from a previous relationship.

In December 2006, Peter was seen by his general practitioner (GP) because of a head injury. He was subsequently examined at the Whittington Hospital in Islington, where bruising and scratches were observed on his body. This prompted the arrest of Peter's mother and maternal grandmother and Peter's name was added to Haringey's child protection register. Peter was discharged from hospital and accommodated with a family friend and his mother was released on bail in January 2007, after which Peter soon returned to her care. In April, Peter attended North Middlesex Hospital in Enfield, where staff observed further bruising and scratches. Peter was seen at the same hospital in June and 12 areas of bruising were seen on his face and body. In July, a social worker visited Peter at home and noted that he had chocolate and antibacterial cream on his face and head. Subsequently, it became clear that these had been deliberately mixed together and applied in order to prevent the social worker from seeing bruises and other marks. The home environment was observed to be disorganised, smelly and dirty, and weapons, animal faeces, fleas, lice and Nazi paraphernalia were also seen. In total, Peter had contact with professionals on 60 separate occasions, not including hospital attendances. On 1 August 2007, two days before he died, Peter was examined at St Anne's Hospital in Haringey, by which time his back was broken. Mrs Connelly was able to prevent a thorough examination taking place by claiming Peter was too 'grouchy'.

It was only following a post-mortem that the full extent of Peter's injuries became known, including a broken back, head injuries, fractured bones, a torn ear and missing fingernails. In November 2008, Barker and Owen were found guilty of causing or allowing the death of a child and Tracey Connelly pleaded guilty to the same offence. It remains unclear exactly who killed Peter or which injuries were attributable to whom.

Several local inquiries, a national task force and a national inquiry were all held following Peter's death. An SCR in Haringey was criticised by the government and found by the Office for Standards in Education (Ofsted) to be inadequate. An independent review of Haringey's child protection services reported to the government on 1 December 2008 and found that they were 'wholly inadequate'. A second SCR was completed in May 2009 and found that Peter's death was preventable and that further abuse could have been prevented had sufficient action been taken following his first examination at the Whittington Hospital in December 2006.

In addition, the government set up the Social Work Task Force in 2009, tasked with undertaking a national, comprehensive review of frontdoor social work practice. The final report of the Task Force is discussed in more detail below, as is *The Protection of Children in England: A Progress Report* (Laming 2009) and *The Munro Review of Child Protection* (Munro 2010, 2011a, 2011b). These three reports were commissioned mostly in response to the Peter Connelly case and, therefore, the impact of his death is likely to have a significant and long-term impact on the practice of child protection in the UK.

Shannon Matthews

Unlike Peter Connelly, Shannon Matthews was not killed, but in February 2008 she disappeared, prompting the police to launch a major missing person operation. Prior to her disappearance, Shannon lived with her mother, Karen Matthews, and her mother's partner, Craig Meehan. The police hunt for Shannon was, by any measure, huge: 1,500 motorists were questioned and 3,000 homes were searched. A total of 250 officers and 60 detectives were assigned to the case as well as over half of the UK's victim recovery dogs (*Huddersfield Daily Examiner* 2008; *Yorkshire Evening Post* 2008a, 2008b). Twenty-four days after her disappearance, Shannon was found concealed in the flat of Michael Donovan, Craig Meehan's uncle. Shannon was made subject to police protection and placed into the care of the local authority.

Following an investigation and court process, Donovan and Matthews were found guilty of kidnapping, false imprisonment and perverting the course of justice; Meehan was earlier found guilty of possessing indecent images of children. It became evident that Matthews' plan had been for Shannon to be released by Donovan and then 'found' by him soon after, enabling them to claim and share the £50,000 reward offered for information leading to her safe return (BBC 2008).

An SCR was held by Kirklees SCB and found that Shannon's kidnapping could not have been reasonably anticipated and that the only course of action that could have protected her – removing her from home via a care order prior to the 'kidnapping' – would not have been possible based on the evidence available at the time. The family were known to children's services prior to these events and concerns had been noted about the family's care of their children. The SCR was not particularly critical of how agencies had responded to the family. We selected this case as a good example of the complexity of contemporary child protection work and the often impossible positions that professionals can find themselves in.

Khyra Ishaq

The series of events that lead to Khyra's death, aged 7, on 17 May 2008, began in December 2007 when her mother, Angela Gordon, removed her from school in order, she claimed, to educate her at home. Over the next 17 months, the family had sporadic contact with child protection services due to reported concerns about Khyra. In December 2008, the deputy head of Khyra's former school contacted social services to report concerns and although a social worker visited the home she was not allowed in. A further home visit was attempted in January 2008 but no one answered the door. An educational social worker visited in February 2008 but also failed to see Khyra. A further home visit took place in February, this time by two social workers who did manage to see Khyra, although they were not allowed to enter the home – she was brought to the front door to see them. This was the last time Khyra was seen by any professional. Another unsuccessful home visit took place in April following a report by a neighbour saying that Khyra was looking 'abnormally thin' – on this occasion, there was no answer at the door. At the time of her death from starvation, Khyra weighed just 16.8kg and her body mass index was so low it could not be recorded on the medical chart. Two other children living in the home were found to be suffering from malnutrition. Following Khyra's death, her mother and her mother's partner, Junaid Abuhamza, were arrested – both admitted manslaughter on the grounds of diminished responsibility. In addition to malnutrition, Khyra was found to have over 60 injuries on her body. The SCR into Khyra's death found that it had been preventable. Safeguarding procedures were not followed, most obviously the failure of professionals to see the child. The reluctance of professionals to complete a thorough assessment was explained partly by Gordon's previous complaint of harassment against the social worker who visited the home in February 2008 – this led to professionals being fearful of repercussions if they acted more forthrightly over entering the home. It also became apparent that the home contained plentiful food but the children were simply not allowed to eat it.

The government's reaction to this was to consider changing the rules governing home education. An earlier report had found that, proportionally, home educated children are more likely to be known to social services than other school-age children (Badman 2009). However, previous attempts by the Labour government to ensure home educated children register with local authorities were fiercely resisted by advocacy groups for home educating parents, who argued that this would result in home education becoming subject to Ofsted inspection – at the time of writing, the law remains unchanged. As with other examples, it is often the high-profile death of a child, raising a particular concern or a gap in legislation, that leads to new procedures being developed. Although it recommended changes in the arrangements for home educated children, the SCR into the Ishaq case also found that if child protection professionals had followed the procedures *already* in place, her death could have been avoided. But as Munro articulates in her final report (2011b), we need to understand why procedures are not followed, rather than simply exhorting professionals to 'do better' next time.

The Social Work Task Force, Lord Laming and the Munro report

The Social Work Task Force

As indicated above, three significant reports into child protection were commissioned between 2009 and 2010. The first of these, the Social Work Task Force, was a joint venture between the Department of Health and the Department for Children, Schools and Families, set up in 2008 in the wake of the Peter Connelly case. The Task Force focused on four areas: recruitment and retention, training, quality and leadership. It was envisaged that the report of the Task Force would identify ways to make improvements in all of these areas. Early proposals were for a recognised post-qualifying year to be introduced for social workers, to include a more manageable caseload and enhanced supervision, greater inspection of training courses, a programme to identify 'future leaders' in social work, a high-profile marketing campaign to raise the status of the social work profession and extra pay for the best social workers to ensure they work directly with parents and children.

The interim report of the Task Force identified the main obstacles to social work becoming a more effective and confident profession, including its poor public image, ineffective training and education, a career structure that encourages the best social workers to move away from practice, an over-emphasis on process and a loss of skill with regard to supervision, reflection and analysis. The final report of the Social Work Task Force – *Building a Safe, Confident Future* – (Social Work Task Force 2009), made a number of recommendations:

Education and training

- Stronger criteria governing the calibre of entrants to social work education and training
- Overhaul the content and delivery of social work degree courses
- New arrangements for high-quality practice placements for all social work students
- Assessed and supported year in employment as final stage in becoming a social worker
- More transparent and effective regulation of education and training
- Time, resources and support
- Clear national standards for employers of social workers
- Establish national requirements for supervision
- Dedicated programmes of training and support for managers of practitioners working directly with family members

Professional development and career progression

- Set up a national framework for continuing professional development
- Create a single nationally recognised career structure

Leadership

- Establish an independent national college of social work
- Public value and understanding
- Programme of action on public understanding of social work

A cohesive and purposeful system

- The development of a 'licence to practise' for social workers
- A new system for forecasting supply and demand
- A single national reform programme for social work

The Labour government accepted all of these recommendations in full and in January 2010 the Social Work Reform Board (SWRB) was created in order to oversee their implementation. The Board was commissioned to advise the government and coordinate the work of educators, employers, professional associations and the new College of Social Work. In March 2010, an implementation plan – *Building a Safe and Confident Future: Implementing the Recommendations of the Social Work Task Force* – was published by the Department of Health, the Department for Children, Schools and Families and the Department for Business, Innovation and Skills (2010). This document committed an additional £200 million of funding in 2010–11, in order to support recruitment, student bursaries and workforce development, to improve information technology systems in children's social care, to pilot new career structures and to support employers through the first year of reform. The document recognised that it would take an extended period of time to implement the recommendations of the Task Force and set out the following timetable:

- from September 2012, strengthen entry requirements for social work degree courses
- a new master's degree in social work practice to be piloted from September 2011
- new arrangements for the curriculum of social work education and changes to practice placements to be in place by September 2012
- an assessed year in employment model for newly qualified social workers to be piloted from 2012 and to be fully in place by 2016
- standards for employers, including national standards for supervision, to be implemented by all relevant employers by April 2011
- to establish a College of Social Work by April 2011
- the General Social Care Council (GSCC) to make its regulation of higher education more transparent and a new regulatory framework to be in place for initial social work education from September 2012
- the GSCC to work with government to develop the 'licence to practise' for social workers.

In December 2010, the Social Work Task Force published a review of its activity over the previous year – *Building a Safe and Confident Future: One Year on – Detailed Proposals from the Social Work Reform Board*. This document indicated that progress had been made in many areas, with many other areas still undergoing development. However, the overall impression from the report is that much has been proposed, very ambitiously in the authors' opinions, but that any changes will take a long time to filter through to the practice of social work, a fact openly acknowledged by the Board.

Interestingly, there were two attempts to establish a national college of social work. Firstly, in early 2011, the British Association of Social Workers (BASW), the largest professional association of social workers in the UK, renamed itself 'BASW – The College of Social Work'. Secondly, the official College of Social Work was launched in January 2012. Prior to this, BASW and the College of Social Work held discussions about forming just one college but these were not successful.

Two notable events have had an impact on the process described above. Firstly, in May 2010, the new coalition government was formed and secondly, the final Munro report was published in May 2011. Neither of these events were foreseen when the Social Work Task Force was commissioned in 2008 and although the new government continues to support the work of the SWRB, it is also clear that the way in which the reforms will be implemented has changed. For example, there will now be no role for the GSCC in regulating social work education (neither qualifying nor post-qualification degrees or awards) as the coalition administration has announced that the GSCC will be abolished by 2014–15. The impact of the Munro report is considered in more detail below.

Lord Laming

Even before the Munro inquiry was planned, another response to the Connelly case had taken place, in the form of a second report from Lord Laming. This report – *The Protection of Children in England: A Progress Report* – published in March 2009, was commissioned to examine what had been achieved since the first Laming report, what barriers remained to effective safeguarding work and what actions could be taken by the government to overcome these barriers. In total, Laming made 58 recommendations, which the government at the time accepted in full. One of the most radical was for every referral from a professional to lead to an initial assessment, including direct contact with the child and their family. Although the government initially accepted this recommendation and suggested it would be included as part of an updated version of *Working Together* in 2009, research by Loughborough University estimated that it would lead to an increase in the number of initial assessments by between 4 and 479 per cent, depending on the authority (this is not a typographical error – the range really was this great), with an average increase across the country of 91 per cent. This would require the services of an additional 2,000 social workers, costing around £116 million (Holmes et al. 2010). Once this became clear, the government indicated it could no longer accept this recommendation.

In May 2009, the government published *The Protection of Children in England: Action Plan – The Government's Response to Lord Laming*, which set out specific actions the government did intend to take, such as appointing a chief adviser on the safety of children, broadening Ofsted's role regarding the review of SCRs and making good on the delivery of ContactPoint, a national database of all children in England (Department for Children, Schools and Families 2009b). However, with the formation of the new coalition government, this document no longer reflects current policy and many of the actions in the report have been reversed. For example, Sir Roger Singleton, who was appointed as the first chief adviser on the safety of children, resigned in June 2010, following the abolition of the National Safeguarding Delivery Unit, whose work he partly oversaw. Sir Roger cited the forthcoming Munro report as the reason for his resignation, indicating that this would likely lead to a much wider change in circumstances. In addition, the national ContactPoint database was discontinued in June 2010,[3] and the Munro report would later recommend that Ofsted be relieved of its responsibility for evaluating SCRs. Therefore, Laming's second report has very much been superseded by the more wide-ranging and in-depth Munro report.

The Munro report

Important though both of the above reports have been, the most significant report since Climbié in 2003 is undoubtedly *The Munro Review of Child Protection*. As we saw in the Introduction, this review, published in three parts, attempted to take a different approach, and did so not only by making recommendations to improve practice, but by basing these recommendations on a thorough understanding of why previous attempts at improvement had not had the desired outcome or had also had unintended consequences.

The first part of the report – *A Systems Analysis* – was published in 2010 (Munro 2010) and was the result of an extensive 'listening exercise', which considered the views of children, families, carers, social workers and other professionals. This report set out the systems approach employed in order to gain a fuller understanding of the whole of the child protection system, rather than focus on smaller parts in isolation which, by implication, Munro felt other reports had done. The report identified one particular dominant theme, in that the priorities of professionals could become skewed by well-meaning attempts to improve outcomes via the implementation of more and more complex policies and procedures. Munro gave the example of timescales for assessments, arguing they were introduced to prevent 'drift' but had the unintended consequence of an over-preoccupation with meeting national perform-ance indicators for timeliness and a reduced focus on the inherent *quality* of assessments and their impact on the safety of children. Munro argued that profes-sionals were too focused on compliance with rules and regulations, that the exercise of professional judgement was stymied by a culture of targets and that children's needs were not being put first.

The second part of the report – *The Child's Journey* – was published in February 2011 (Munro 2011a) and aimed to map the experience of children in moving through the system from needing to receiving protection from abuse and neglect. Part of the review involved working with five local authorities, who were piloting more flexible approaches. These included the London Borough of Tower Hamlets, which had sought permission from the secretary of state to suspend their need to adhere to assessment timescales in order to pilot a new assessment tool. Finally, the report gave notice of the likely areas that the final report would focus on, including the role of Ofsted and inspec-tions, the need to simplify *Working Together*, the role of national indicators, the role of early intervention and the need to focus on the quality of assessments. The final report, published in May 2011 (Munro 2011b) set out the following 15 recommendations:

- **Recommendation 1**: the government should revise *Working Together to Safeguard Children* and *The Framework for the Assessment of Children in Need and their Families*. This would include removing the distinction between initial and core assessments and the associated timescales. They should be replaced with a list of the decisions social workers need to make in order to understand families and make interventions.

- **Recommendation 2**: unannounced inspections should examine the effective-ness of the contributions of all local services, including health, education, police, probation and the justice system on child protection.

- **Recommendation 3**: the new inspection framework should examine the child's journey, how their wishes and experiences shape the provision of services and the effectiveness of the help provided to children, young people and their families.

- **Recommendation 4**: local authorities and partners should use a combination of nationally collected and locally published performance data to help benchmark performance. This would include information on social worker caseloads and how many social workers feel their caseloads are unmanageable. However, this should not be treated as an unambiguous measure of good or bad performance.

- **Recommendation 5**: each LSCB should submit an annual report to the chief executive and leader of the council, and (subject to legislation) to the local police and crime commissioner and the chair of the health and well-being board.

- **Recommendation 6**: LSCBs should assess the effectiveness of help being provided to children and families (including the effectiveness and value for money of early intervention services and multi-agency training).

- **Recommendation 7**: the role of the director of children's services and the lead member for children's services should be protected from any additional functions, unless there are exceptional circumstances.

- **Recommendation 8**: the government should work with the medical royal colleges and local authorities to research the impact of current health reforms on effective partnership arrangements around child protection.

- **Recommendation 9**: LSCBs should use a systems approach to SCRs and Ofsted's evaluation of SCRs should end.

- **Recommendation 10:** The government should place a duty on local authorities and statutory partners to provide sufficient early intervention services for those children and young people who do not meet child protection thresholds.

- **Recommendation 11:** the SWRB's Professional Capabilities Framework should also explicitly state those qualities needed in child and family social work. This framework should inform social work qualification training, postgraduate professional development and performance appraisal.

- **Recommendation 12:** employers and higher education institutions should work together so that social work students are better prepared for the challenges of child protection work.

- **Recommendation 13:** local authorities should review and redesign the ways in which child and family social work is delivered, drawing on evidence of effective interventions and helping social workers to use evidence-based practice.

- **Recommendation 14:** local authorities should designate a principal child and family social worker, a senior manager still actively involved in frontdoor practice who will have lead responsibility for practice within a council. They will feed back the views and experiences of the frontdoor to all levels of management.

- **Recommendation 15:** a chief social worker should be created in government, whose duties would include advising the government on social work practice. The chief social worker would also have a role to play, alongside the College of Social Work, in improving the media image of children's social work.

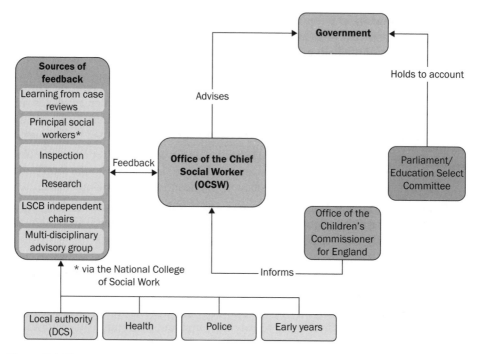

Figure 3.1 The new system of child protection, as proposed by the final report of the Munro review (2011b)

The report also set out a proposed new national system for child protection (see Figure 3.1). In July 2011, the government gave a formal response to the Munro report. They 'accepted' recommendations 1, 2, 3, 4, 5, 11, 12, 13 and 14, 'accepted in principle' recommendations 6, 7, 8, 10 and 15 and committed to 'considering further' recommendation 9 (Department for Education 2011). Practitioners working directly with families will already have experienced the first practical change with the removal of the distinction between initial and core assessments and the removal of perform-ance indicators related to their timely completion in December 2011.[4]

Safeguarding children within a network of family support

As we have seen above, the late 1990s and the first decade of the twenty-first century witnessed considerable developments in child protection policy and practice in the UK; if anything, more considerable than the developments of the 1980s and early 1990s. As we shall see in the next chapter, in both the UK and the USA there has also been a period of almost unparalleled growth of interest in, and broadening of the definitions of, child abuse. Both countries have as a result shifted their emphasis onto more preventive measures.

The European response has been quite different. The increased focus on child abuse which took place in Britain and the USA in the 1970s and 1980s did not happen in Europe to the same extent. Child protection systems of the kind developed in Britain and the USA (and also in Canada, Australia and New Zealand) have not been copied in Europe. Thus, these countries do not have child protection registers or systems of mandatory reporting. For example, the French system of child protection combines social welfare and judicial protection services, with the primary focus on supporting families, usually with their consent and approval. If families decline support and a child is felt to be in danger, a judicial protection service can intervene, a much more legalistic process than that of child protection plans and Section 47 inquiries in the UK. To some degree, there has been a questioning of this more indirect approach among European nations, and there is some admiration of the more direct approaches adopted in Britain (see Schweppe 2002).

Nevertheless, whether admired or not, by the early 1990s this direct approach in the UK was being re-thought, and, as a result of a combination of factors (most notably outcries against excessive state intervention, increased poverty and changing family structures), emphasis shifted back to working more supportively and preventatively with parents. This emphasis gathered pace with the *Every Child Matters* agenda. Although these developments were clearly family supportive, Parton (2005) argues that children have increasingly become the central concern and the direct focus of the state, with the parents (or parent) moving more to the background. Despite the publication of the *Every Parent Matters* policy in 2007 (Department for Education and Skills 2007a), this is still the case; policy with regard to parents seems to focus primarily on increasing the uptake of paid employment.[5]

However, this does not mean that child protection concerns disappeared. The persistence of child deaths through abuse ensured this, and it is clear from recent central government guidelines and the various proposals stemming from the case of Peter Connelly, that there is no diminution of concern, certainly about serious physical abuse. Thus, the recommendations of the Munro report (2011b) that child protection professionals should be enabled to exercise far more professional judgement do not represent a complete turn-round or reversion to the pre-Maria Colwell approaches.

What has changed more recently, especially following the increase in referrals that took place following the case of Peter Connelly, is that children's social care services have increased their 'thresholds' for referrals to the point that, unless a child is felt to be at a very high risk of significant harm, the support and intervention they receive is likely to be in place for only for a very time-limited period. According to the Violence Research Group at Cardiff University, there was a 20 per cent rise in the number of children aged 0 to 10 who needed emergency hospital treatment in 2010 compared with 2009 (Sivarajasingam et al. 2010). This increase might be attributable to the number of children being left for longer in at-risk homes.

If, as envisaged by the Munro report, social workers and other professionals are to exercise professional judgement far more extensively, this would appear unlikely to be successful without considerable retraining for social workers and other professionals, because it is likely to create uncertainties for individual practitioners who have developed ways of thinking and working in line with a procedurally governed philosophy (Platt 2001; Spratt 2001).

A more balanced approach also seems to have considerable implications for resources. Most of the families referred as a result of child care and child abuse concerns are living in poverty with considerable material problems and difficulties. Until the publication of the Field report into poverty in 2010 (Field 2010), there appeared to be little consideration of the cost implications of meeting the needs of these families in order to support them in the care of their children (see Tunstill and Aldgate 2000). The Labour government did have ambitious targets for reducing child poverty, centred – as noted above – on supporting wider parental employment but also via provision of tax credits and child care initiatives. The funding for such measures was reduced by the coalition government, indicating a change of focus again. In whichever way this type of support is provided, there are clear cost implications in providing the resources needed to meet the range of health, environmental, social and financial needs of families referred for support in caring for their children. The size of the problem is another important factor – as discussed in the Introduction, there were 607,000 referrals to social services departments in England in the year ending March 2010 (and 612,600 in the year ending March 2011, of which 440,800 led to initial assessments).[6]

Safeguarding children: spirit possession and witchcraft

From 2005 onwards, there has been an increased awareness of the need to safeguard and protect children believed to be 'possessed by spirits'. As already noted, *Working Together* (Department of Health 2006) was the first document of its type to include a specific section on this sort of abuse. This was prompted by the report of the Climbié inquiry, which noted that Victoria was believed by her 'carers' to be possessed by 'evil spirits'. In 2005, three adults were convicted for extreme cruelty towards a child, known only as Child B, who they believed was 'possessed'. These, and other cases, helped to highlight this previously overlooked problem and prompted the government, in 2007, to issue guidance – *Safeguarding Children from Abuse Linked to a Belief in Spirit Possession* (Department for Education and Skills 2007b). This guidance was based heavily on research by Stobart (2006), who found that although belief in possession and witchcraft was widespread in religious and faith communities, actual 'known' cases of abuse linked to these phenomena made up only 0.1 per cent of child protection inquiries in 2003/4. Both *Working Together* and *Safeguarding Children from Abuse Linked to a Belief in Spirit Possession* recognised that although the number of cases may be small, the harm caused to children by these types of belief could be substantial, as well as acknowledging that there could be a larger number of un-detected cases.

Clearly, there are complexities in defining a belief in 'possession' or 'witchcraft'. Many major religions, including Islam, Judaism and Christianity, include examples of 'spirit possession' in their holy texts as well as references to 'witchcraft', but in terms of child abuse, the government was concerned about a specific belief that an evil spirit had entered a child and was controlling him or her. The term 'witchcraft' referred to a belief that the child so possessed could cause harm to other people because of their 'possession'. Some religious communities may respond to these types of beliefs via exorcism, defined by the guidance as being 'an attempt to expel the evil spirit'. The guidance also distinguishes between a general belief in 'spirits', which it acknowledges is widespread in the population, and cases of abuse linked to such belief, which appear to be rare. A range of factors were found to make children more vulnerable to abuse because of these types of belief, including changes in family structure, a negative experience of migration and the carer's mental health.

In 2010, the Church of England's Churches' Child Protection Advisory Service (CCPAS) published a document on good practice for working with faith communities and places of worship, specifically related to the issue of 'spirit possession' and abuse. Unlike the government's guidance, which states that these beliefs are not confined to particular cultures, countries, religions or communities, the Church's document linked such beliefs to African cultural practices while also acknowledging that many faith communities, including the Church of England, may also use 'exorcism' and that this may or may not be abusive, depending on how it is undertaken.

Nevertheless, the number of identified cases of child abuse linked to 'spirit possession' and 'witchcraft' remains low. In an article in 2010, Davis argued that, with increasing migration into the UK from West Africa, there may be an increasing number of unidentified cases.

Children's rights, child abuse and neglect: the way forward

Much of the discussion about child abuse focuses on individuals and families. However, as discussed in Chapters 1 and 2, the broader societal context has a major influence on the way in which child abuse and neglect issues are responded to and understood. Changing that context can have a more profound impact on child protection work than changes in systems and procedures. In other words, thinking differently about children and their rights has, to some degree, brought about a diminution in child maltreatment but the potential to do more is considerable.

There have been notable developments over the past 15–20 years in relation to thinking about children's rights. Sociologists, for instance, have started to see children as subjects of study in their own right (Corsaro 2004), as opposed to seeing them as a group in relation to adults. The views of the child have more and more been sought in the design and completion of research (Fraser et al. 2004). In world terms, the 1989 *UN Convention on the Rights of the Child* was a key landmark. This document sets out basic rights for children for nation states to adhere to. It stresses that children should be free from abuse, that they should have rights to education, rights against labour exploitation and rights to live with their parents – rights that can only be curtailed by judicial means. Every member of the United Nations, except the USA and Somalia, are signatories to the Convention. Since 1991, Somalia has had no functioning central government and so it remains unratified for that reason; why the USA has not ratified the treaty is less clear, although some believe its non-adoption could be related to political and religious conservatism (Smolin 2006). Even the world's newest country, the Republic of South Sudan, which formally declared independence from Sudan on 9 July 2011, is a signatory and already has in place a Child Act (2009), requiring the government to recognise, respect and ensure the rights of children as enshrined in the Convention.

In Britain, the rights of children were considerably enhanced in legal terms by the 1989 Children Act. The main effects of these changes have been in relation to seeking children's views about key decisions made in relation to them. Thus, their wishes and feelings must be taken into account in court hearings, reviews and conferences and in relation to decisions about placements and medicals. However, there are limits imposed on these developments, most notably that the child's age and understanding have to be taken into consideration when making the various decisions. While to some extent the need to place some limits on self-determination seems reasonable, there are dangers. A clear example of this resides in the scepticism that surrounds accounts by younger children about sexual abuse.

The rights of disabled children are even more likely to be infringed than those of other children. Disabled children are more vulnerable to physical and sexual abuse, particularly in out-of-home settings, which they frequent more than other children. On the other hand, their abuse is less likely to come to light.

Nevertheless, efforts continue in this field. In 2008, UNICEF released a publication entitled *Handbook on Legislative Reform: Realising Children's Rights,* which sets out how the Committee on the Rights of the Child, the body responsible for monitoring the implementation of the Convention, has achieved notable successes by way of states enacting laws on previously unlegislated areas of child abuse, such as female genital mutilation and child trafficking.

In general terms, therefore, while there have been some important developments in relation to children's rights at the level of conventions and research, there is still much more to be done. Many professionals are still uneasy at relating to children and still tend to work largely through parents. This is despite reported exhortations in government guidance for child protection professionals to focus on the child. Giving children's voices the same degree of credence as those of adults in judicial and quasi-judicial proceedings is still a long way off, particularly in regard to children at the younger end of the range.

Gender issues, child abuse and neglect

Feminist ideas have had a major impact on how we think about, and understand, all forms of child abuse. Feminists have highlighted the emotionally abusive impact of domestic violence on children. They have also contributed to awareness of mental health issues among women and the links between these and family violence. Their contribution to the understanding of child sexual abuse both within and outside families continues to be important despite some recession in this area.

More recently, feminist thinking has shown how gender socialisation plays an important role in the aetiology of child abuse. This point of view argues that placing more emphasis on mothers as carers effectively absolves males from responsibility for caring and ill-equips them for it as well – physical abuse of children is sometimes a consequence. Male sexual socialisation – that is, with the expectation that they have stronger sexual needs than women and must be assertive and take control – helps create a climate in which child sexual abuse can happen.

There are clear lessons to take from both the above contributions. First, men can be seen to be a risk to children and it is important that professionals working directly with families remain aware of this. They must be careful not to assume shared values, concerns and interests between parents; in particular they need to be attuned to the possibility of male violence to their partners.

Second, there is much that could be done to reduce the risk of child abuse by tackling issues of gender socialisation. It seems important to engage fathers in child protection work, because, if the roots of violence to both children and women lie in male socialisation, then without men's involvement the logical target for change is being systematically missed (Scourfield 2003). There are some practical considerations too. For example, research suggests that a large number of children will live with a 'social father'. This term is increasingly being used to describe any father-figure who is not biologically related to the child he is caring for, including men who are married to or cohabiting with the child's mother and who may previously have been referred to as 'step-fathers'. In some contexts, especially when they are married to the child's mother, social fathers can exhibit significantly higher levels of cooperation in caregiving, take on more shared responsibility and be more engaged with the child than biological fathers (Berger et al. 2008).

However, engaging males in health and welfare interventions is a difficult task for a variety of reasons. There are barriers, such as a view of childrearing as female business, and the fact that in many cases males are most likely to be the abusive carer and/ or bear responsibility for family violence. Also, many of the families being worked with are headed by female lone parents and any males involved in such families are seen as peripheral figures. Other barriers stem from the element of fear on the part of a largely female workforce engaging with potentially violent males, and the upsurge of concern about paedophiles over the last 10 years.

In general terms, it is evident that structural feminism has been, and remains, an important means of raising awareness about child protection issues. Angelides (2004) has argued that concerns about sexual abuse of children come onto the policy agenda when feminism is strong and vice versa. Uncomfortable though the ideas of feminists may be for parts of mainstream society, nevertheless there can be little doubt that they haves been highly influential in reshaping thinking about sexual relationships and sexual abuse in Britain over the past 25 years.

On the other hand, at the micro level, feminist-informed thinking is being used to understand the processes taking place within families leading to abuse and violence – for example, by studying the overlap between violence against women and child abuse in the same family (Edleson 1999) as well as examining why violence against children and violence against women are, nevertheless, often treated decidedly differently (Messing 2011; see also Featherstone 1997; Featherstone and Trinder 1997).

Poverty and child protection

Most child abuse and neglect theoreticians attest to these issues being for individuals and families, and stress that the emotional and psychological impact of being neglected or ill-treated are the key factors for consideration; nevertheless, intervention takes place almost exclusively with poor families. What accounts for this and what are the implications of it for future policy and practice?

One account is that abuse occurs across all social classes but is more likely to be identified in poorer families because they are less able to deal with and contain their problems. Another account is that physical abuse and neglect are positively correlated poverty and poor families, i.e. child abuse and neglect are strongly related to harsh living standards and the stresses of living in them. Finally, drug and alcohol misuse are also much more common in poorer neighbourhoods. Living in such conditions impacts on parenting and the treatment and care of children.

Of course, the immediate riposte to these findings is that not all poor families ill-treat their children and this is clearly true. However, there are studies that show, unsurprisingly, that families most at risk within such poor environments are those that are exposed to multiple forms of disadvantage, including physical and mental illness, bereavements and disability (Brandon et al. 2010).

A third account linking child abuse and neglect to poverty is that which proposes a cyclical transmission of abuse and neglect, i.e. abuse and neglect go across generations in poor families. However, it poses another question – why do only 30 per cent of ill-treated children go on to become neglectful or abusive parents?

All these accounts have some explanatory value. However, it is important not to get into either/or debates within the poverty explanations or between them and other explanations. It is likely that child abuse is more closely associated with living in poverty, with the possible exception of child sexual abuse. It is also likely that abuse and neglect of children outside poorer families remain much more hidden from official notice. Finally, it is likely that poor standards of care and ill-treatment of children go across generations in a small number of highly deprived and disadvantaged families.

However, important though poverty is, there are many other factors that, in different combinations, contribute to the causation of child abuse and neglect along with poverty. This multi-dimensional explanation of child abuse and neglect is one that has long been adopted by the assessment framework, which emphasises the emotional security needs of the child, parenting capacity and environmental factors. We are also seeing concerted attempts to raise community standards in relation to combating crime and ensuring that facilities to maximise the potential for children are in place.

One example is the report by Frank Field MP, published in December 2010, having been commissioned by the prime minister, David Cameron. Field's report – *The Foundation Years: Preventing Poor Children Becoming Poor Adults* – was published at the same time as figures from the Joseph Rowntree Foundation indicated that the number of children living in poverty in working households had increased to its highest ever level of 2.1 million. The Field report recommends a move away from measuring poverty based on material income and towards a broader set of 'life chance' indicators. This would entail withholding funding from state-funded benefits such as child tax credits and redirecting the money towards 'early years' education. The report does not focus explicitly on abuse and neglect but does note emerging research which indicates that the neurological development of maltreated children is characterised by significantly reduced growth compared with non-maltreated children. The government's response to this report and others (such as the Allen report (2011) on early intervention) has been to set out a new strategy for consultation, focusing on 'addressing the causes of poverty' rather than the symptoms. In April 2011, the government published a policy document, *A New Approach to Child Poverty: Tackling the Causes of Disadvantage and Transforming Families' Lives* (Department for Work and Pensions/

Department for Education 2011). This report argued that child abuse and neglect are most certainly not confined to poverty and that support and treatment facilities should be universal.

Finally, another way of understanding the impact of poverty on child well-being is via the levels of inequality in a society. As Wilkinson and Pickett (2010) argue, a smaller gap between rich and poor leads to happier, healthier and more successful populations, including children. A range of health and social problems, including life expectancy, infant mortality, teenage births, mental illness and drug and alcohol addiction, are all worse in more unequal counties (the UK is the third most unequal country out of the 50 richest, established, market economies, according to the World Bank). While it is difficult to see what individual child protection professionals, or even larger organisations such as local authorities, can do to address this issue, it does highlight how, without concerted effort from successive governments, these types of health and social problems are likely to persist and will, therefore, continue to impact on the well-being of British children.

A plea for therapy

In 2012, our knowledge base about the abuse and neglect of children has developed into a vast array of scenarios. We are now aware of physical, sexual, emotional abuse and neglect of children in their own homes, in residential and hospital services and in sports clubs; of children being bullied at school; being abused by the clergy; living on the streets; being involved in prostitution and pornography; being trafficked and economically exploited; being damaged by war experiences; and being assaulted and killed by strangers.

We know that some children and young people are exposed to many forms of abuse and that abuse can create a vulnerability to further abuse. We also know that the experience of abuse can lead to the abuse of others. We are beginning to realise that quite large proportions of adults experiencing problems in living, such as mentally ill persons, and those who have serious drug and alcohol problems, have some history of being abused as children.

Given this, one of the most pressing problems is surely the need to develop responsive and readily available therapeutic services for abused children and for adults who have been abused or neglected in the past. It is important to bear in mind in this instance that what is therapeutic is also preventive, i.e. it may well have the effect of improving future parenting or of reducing the likelihood of future child abuse and neglect. Nevertheless, there is still little in the way of a comprehensive therapeutic service available for those who have been abused or for members of their families. We are not without examples of good therapeutic responses to child abuse, particularly with regard to sexual abuse, and although there is an increasing interest in understanding how best to help children (or adults) who have been abused, the problem is that the therapeutic response is patchy and not systematic.

In 2009, *The Lancet* published a review of interventions used in the prevention of child maltreatment and treatment of associated impairments (MacMillan et al. 2009). The results showed that cognitive-behavioural therapy (CBT) brought benefits for sexually abused children with post-traumatic stress symptoms and that child-focused therapy had some benefit for neglected children (although no interventions with neglected children were found to be significantly effective), whereas therapy involving mother and child was beneficial following situations of intimate partner violence. For physically abused children, the study found that parent-child interaction therapy was perhaps the most promising intervention. This finding has also been confirmed by other studies (such as Carr 2009), especially when the therapy also involved a non-abusive carer. For emotionally or psychologically abused children, no interventions were shown by this study to be particularly effective. In all areas, the study called for more research into 'what works', with a focus on clear outcome measures and studies that rely on methods other than self-reporting of benefits.

In a review of attachment-related interventions, Bakermans-Kranenburg et al. (2003) found that 'less is more'. They studied 88 different interventions involving 7,636 participants and found that early interventions aimed at enhancing infant attachment security and increasing caregiver sensitivity were more likely to be effective when they consisted of a small number of sessions. They also found that interventions consisting of fewer than 5 sessions were as effective as interventions with between 5 and 16 sessions and both were more effective than interventions with more than 16 sessions. They identified more success when intervention was aimed at improving caregiver sensitivity. If we accept the mounting research indicating a link between disorganised attachment in children and child abuse and neglect (see Chapter 6 for more detail), then any evidence indicating the effectiveness of interventions aimed at increasing caregiver sensitivity and thereby increasing the incidence of organised attachment in children must be taken seriously.

However, despite this improving knowledge base about what works for child abuse victims, further research is needed, especially with regards to neglected or emotionally abused children and, as often seems to be the case with mental health support, provision of these services is patchy across the country.

An integrated approach

The Children Act 2004, which came into force on 1 April 2005, placed a 'duty to cooperate' (via Section 10) on local authorities and other public bodies. This Act sought to improve and integrate services for children in local areas, with local authorities taking a lead role in bringing together other agencies and professionals to achieve the outcomes of the *Every Child Matters* agenda. Greater levels of cooperation were to be achieved by the appointment in local authorities of directors of children's services, who would be responsible not only for the local authority's children's services but also for any services provided by the National Health Service (NHS) to children under Section 31 of the Health Act 1999. 'Lead members' for children were also to be appointed. Local authorities were required to produce children's and young people's plans, setting out the strategy for meeting the needs of children and young people locally, and by the establishment of children's trusts, new organisations to bring together health, education and social services for young people. Not all trusts were necessarily to be the same – the *Every Child Matters* Green Paper recognised that no single model was likely to be applicable in every area. Therefore, some were arranged to take responsibility not only for child protection services but also for services such as speech and language therapy, while other trusts would focus specifically on vulnerable groups, such as disabled children.

The Act also replaced area child protection committees, by April 2006, with LSCBs. LSCBs include representatives from the local authority, police, the probation service, district councils where relevant, strategic health authorities and primary care trusts, the Learning and Skills Council (LSC), youth offending teams, the Children and Family Court Advisory Support Service (CAFCAS), and the governors of any prisons or secure units in the area which routinely detain children. *Working Together* 2006 further established the roles and functions of LSCBs, and stated they should have as wide a membership as required. In some areas this led to charitable and/or religious groups becoming members. LSCBs' primary function is to hold agencies to account for their statutory duty to safeguard children.

In 2008, the Audit Commission produced a report into the effectiveness of children's trusts and found them to be lacking in clear direction and making slow progress. Although the Labour government rejected the findings, in October 2010 the Conservative-Liberal Democrat coalition administration withdrew the statutory guidance on children's trusts and revoked the requirement for local authorities to produce comprehensive children and young people's plans. The new government also announced an intention to withdraw the requirement for schools and further education colleges to cooperate with children's trusts. Groups such as the Association of Directors of Children's Services (ADCS) objected to this, arguing that it would undermine the integrated approach. Some local councils have already announced an intention to maintain their children's trusts, although the future of children's and young people's plans is less clear. In essence, the government's intention was to allow authorities to formulate their own local arrangements for partnership working while leaving in place the general 'duty to cooperate' of the Children Act 2004. The Munro report on child protection recommended that the current arrangements for directors of children's services should remain in place, advising against any dilution of the direct accountability of their roles.

Despite these statutory changes, the government does appear the accept the benefits of an integrated approach. Via the proposed Health and Social Care Bill, local authorities will be required to establish health and well-being boards, which will then take the lead in the strategic coordination of commissioning across local health services, social care and other related agencies. In a report published in January 2011 – *Early Intervention: The Next Steps* – Graham Allen MP recommended that these health and well-being boards should also have a role in ensuring that local early intervention services are integrated in terms of approach and sharing best practice.

Therefore, as in many other areas, there has been great upheaval in terms of the arrangements for integrating local child protection and other services between local authorities, the NHS and other bodies and what the longer-term effects of these changes will be is not yet clear. What is clear is that there will be different approaches in different areas, in contrast to the centrally mandated requirements of the previous Labour government.

Concluding comments

Trying to develop neat analyses of where child protection/safeguarding children policy currently stands is a difficult task. The picture is very untidy. Child abuse concerns have changed dramatically in the first decade of the twenty-first century although some aspects of child protection work never seem far from major controversy. Currently, for instance, there are major debates about what it is realistic to expect child protection professionals to achieve as well as important major changes due from the Munro report.

However, what is clear is that the major shift that took place in the 1980s and 1990s – towards an approach that looks more holistically at child abuse and neglect within the family – is unlikely to be reversed.

There are many ways of accounting for the direction that events have taken in Britain since 2000. As identified in Chapter 2, there has been tension for a considerable time between two schools of thought about how best to ensure the protection of children within families. There are those who have been in favour of more positive pro-family measures as an indirect means of meeting the needs of children at risk, and there have been those who have argued for more direct child protective measures (Fox-Harding 1991). The former are now in the ascendancy for a variety of possible reasons. Arguably, the more direct approach to dealing with child protection concerns simply has not worked. Arguably, also, the economic cost of the child protection system is too high (Allen 2011). Finally, particularly following the advent of the Conservative-Liberal Democrat coalition administration, the political emphasis has shifted to reducing public expenditure, reducing the role of the state, opening the public sector to a broader range of providers via the 'Big Society' agenda and focusing again on the 'need' for parents to be in work.

Key events in child protection 2000–11

2000
- Publication of the *Framework for the Assessment of Children in Need and Their Families*
- Criminal Justice and Courts Services Act
- Leaving Care Act
- Care Standards Act
- Publication of the Waterhouse inquiry report into the abuse of children in a residential home in North Wales
- Publication of *Working Together* guidelines to safeguard children involved in prostitution
- Murder of Sarah Payne

2001
- Review report into the death of Lauren Wright
- Review report into the death of Kennedy McFarlane
- Publication of Department of Health research, *The Children Act Now*
- Review of child protection in Scotland

2002
- Review report into the death of Ainlee Labonte
- Murders of Jessica Chapman and Holly Wells

2003
- Publication of the Victoria Climbié inquiry report (Lord Laming)
- Publication of the Green Paper *Every Child Matters*
- Publication of *What to Do if You're Worried that a Child is Being Abused*
- LSCBs established
- Every Child Matters agenda launched

2004
- Children Act
- Publication of the Bichard report
- Publication of the *Hidden Harm* report on the children of parents who misuse drugs

2007
- Death of Peter Connelly

2009
- Publication of *The Protection of Children in England: A Progress Report* (Lord Laming)

2010
- New *Working Together* guidelines

2011
- *The Munro Review of Child Protection*

Recommended reading

Brandon, M., Bailey, S. and Belderson, P. (2010) *Building On the Learning from Serious Case Reviews: A Two-year Analysis of Child Protection Database Notifications 2007–2009*. London: The Stationery Office.

Munro, E. (2010) *The Munro Review of Child Protection – Part One: A Systems Analysis*. London: The Stationery Office.

Munro, E. (2011) *The Munro Review of Child Protection – Interim Report: The Child's Journey*. London, The Stationery Office.

Munro, E. (2011) *The Munro Review of Child Protection: Final Report*. London: The Stationery Office.

Parton, N. (2005) *Safeguarding Childhood: Early Intervention and Surveillance in Late Modern Society*. London: Palgrave Macmillan.

Wilkinson, R. and Pickett, K. (2010) *The Spirit Level*. London: Penguin.

4

Defining child abuse

Introduction

Clearly any logical approach to a problem entails describing its nature and size, so that the response to it can be appropriate and sufficiently well resourced to ensure an effective solution. However, it should be clear from reading Chapters 2 and 3 that, in fact, the notions of child abuse and neglect are complex, subject to constant change and realignment. They are highly contested concepts, underpinned by and subject to a range of political and cultural factors particular to the society in which they occur. In much of the literature on this subject, the words 'abuse', 'neglect' and 'maltreatment' are used interchangeably, indicating that we are far from establishing a consensus on what they might mean (Mennen et al. 2010). For these reasons, child abuse and neglect are not phenomena that lend themselves to easy definition or measurement. Nevertheless, there is much to be learned from the various attempts that have been made to achieve this. Although the two phenomena are closely interrelated, for the purposes of analysis they will, as far as possible, be considered separately. This chapter will critically consider issues relating to the definitions of child abuse *and* neglect.

Before we look at different categories of child abuse, some general considerations should be taken into account.

The cultural context of child abuse definition

Child abuse and neglect are socially defined constructs. They are products of a particular culture and context and are not absolute unchanging phenomena. As we have seen in the historical chapters, what is considered to be abusive or neglectful in a particular society alters over time. Kempe argued that children have a right to be protected from parents who are unable to cope at a level deemed reasonable by the society in which they reside (Kempe and Kempe 1978). However, the question of what is 'reasonable' is not a fixed one. Place is another factor. Anthropological studies show clearly that what is viewed as abusive in one society today is not necessarily seen as such in another. Korbin (1981) cites examples of culturally approved practices in societies in the southern hemisphere that we would almost certainly define as abusive:

These include extremely hot baths, designed to inculcate culturally valued traits; punishments, such as severe beatings, to impress the child with the necessity of adherence to cultural rules; and harsh initiation rites that include genital operations, deprivation of food and sleep, and induced bleeding and vomiting.

(Korbin 1981: 4)

She points out that the reverse is also true:

Practices such as isolating infants and small children in rooms or beds of their own at night, making them wait for readily available food until a schedule dictates that they can satisfy their hunger, or allowing them to cry without immediately attending to their needs or desires would be at odds with the child-rearing philosophies of most of the cultures discussed.

(Korbin 1981: 4)

The lesson to be learned from anthropological studies is that the cultural context within which behaviour takes place and the meaning attributed to it by those sharing that culture are important factors to be taken into account when labelling certain acts as abusive or neglectful.

However, although such comparisons rightly sensitise us to the culturally relative nature of child abuse and neglect, this does not mean that there are no common standards at all. Korbin (1981) stresses that the sort of abuse described by Kempe et al. (1962) as the 'battered child syndrome' would not be sanctioned by any society. More recent research seems to confirm this point – Korbin et al. (2000) studied the views of African-American parents and compared them with European-American parents. They found that although there were differences in emphasis, there was a remarkable congruence regarding behaviours that most respondents agreed would be abusive or neglectful. Finkelhor and Korbin (1988) argue strongly that other culturally approved practices, such as ritual circumcision and female genital mutilation, should be universally seen as abusive and addressed as such.[1]

Nevertheless, there are many things happening to children worldwide which are more entrenched and harder to challenge. In the last two decades or so, as a result of the development of improved information and communications technology (ICT), we have become increasingly aware of these. It is clear that the experiences of children in parts of eastern Europe, South-East Asia, Africa and South America are massively different from others. UNICEF (2003) estimated that in the preceding decade 2 million children died as a direct result of armed conflict, 6 million were permanently disabled or seriously injured and there were an estimated 300,000 child soldiers in the world. UNICEF acknowledges that these types of figures can be unreliable and also estimated that there were 158 million children aged 5–14 working worldwide.

Equally staggering figures apply to societies beset with problems of AIDS, child trafficking, widespread child abandonment and children living on the streets and in poor standard institutions. Clearly, the answers to children's problems in these societies are, above all, political (Uzodike 2000).

Returning to child abuse in Britain, it should also be noted that culture has an impact on its definition within societies. However, just the same sort of care needs to be taken with a culturally relativist approach in these circumstances. Dingwall et al. (1983) were of the opinion that the standards applied by social workers observed in their study ran the risk of being too low. They were so used to dealing with poor families and poor parenting skills that they accepted them as the norm for that culture. Such views are borne out by some of the public inquiry cases and go some way to explaining the extraordinary degree of apparent tolerance shown by social workers in cases like that of Stephanie Fox.[2]

Webb et al. (2002) show how a whole range of factors, such as cultural stereotyping, misplaced cultural sensitivity, fear of being seen to be racist and inadequate training can result in professional workers failing to protect children in black and ethnic minority families from abuse. The cases of Tyra Henry (Lambeth 1987)[3] and Victoria Climbié (Laming 2003)[4] provide examples of this.

Differentiating between culturally normative and abusive/neglectful parenting is a critically difficult but essential task for all practitioners involved in safeguarding children.

The concerns of the definers

Legislators, by and large, favour non-specific definitions of abuse because they allow flexibility and room for manoeuvre. Therefore, most legal definitions of child abuse are phrased in very general terms, such as 'improper treatment' or 'significant harm'. However, researchers into child abuse are very much concerned with achieving precision and consistency. Clear identification of the object of research and common standards of measurement are important ingredients of such work. Definitional inconsistencies between studies may well account for major differences in estimates of prevalence (Finkelhor and Baron 1986).

Defining child abuse and neglect in practice

A further general issue relates to the process by which child abuse and neglect are actually defined in practice. Here we are considering what Gelles (1982) termed *operational* as opposed to *nominal* definitions (that is, those used in law and research). How do social workers and other professional groups in fact decide what does and does not constitute abuse or neglect from the large number of referrals they receive?

While it is now a somewhat dated study, the issues raised and examined by Giovannoni and Becerra (1979) remain highly pertinent today. They were of the opinion that there were no adequate definitions of abuse or neglect that could be operationalised by professionals: 'A major thesis of this book is that child abuse and neglect are matters of social definition and that the problems that inhere in the establishment of those definitions ultimately rest on value decisions' (Giovannoni and Becerra 1979: 5). To test this hypothesis, they devised 78 pairs of vignettes briefly describing potentially abusive situations.[5] The researchers assigned 60 vignettes at random to four groups of professionals (police, social workers, paediatricians and lawyers) and also to non-professional inhabitants of Los Angeles, who were asked to rate them on a 1 to 9 scale of seriousness. The main finding was that there was little agreement between the professional groupings about the seriousness of the various types of maltreatment. Overall, there was most agreement between the police and social workers, who together took a more serious view of nearly all incidents than did the paediatricians and lawyers (in that order). This lack of agreement was attributed to the requirements of occupational roles. Thus the reason for higher ratings on the part of police and social workers was seen to be their greater involvement in the early investigative stages of maltreatment. The police rated vignettes where a crime had been alleged as more serious than the other professionals. Social workers were ahead of the others with regard to emotional abuse and lawyers tended to rate everything lower than the rest because their concern was whether there was enough evidence to prove a case in a court of law.

With regard to non-professional people, Giovannoni and Becerra found that, as a whole, they were more likely to judge the scenarios as more serious than all the professionals and that those from poorer social groups 'generally saw mistreatment as more serious than did those of higher socioeconomic status' (Giovannoni and Beccera 1979: 189). This is in contrast to the widely held perception that professionals have higher standards in this respect than the general public. The main conclusion drawn from Giovannoni and Becerra's study was that there was much confusion among professionals over deciding whether cases were sufficiently abusive or neglectful to justify intervention.

Later studies have highlighted a related difficulty, namely that the heterogeneous nature of child maltreatment does not lend itself to very strict operational definitions, even when the study involves only child protection social workers. Mennen et al. (2010) studied the case records of 303 children identified as being maltreated by a child protection social work agency. The study also identified five areas of parental behaviour deemed by the agency to be neglectful: neglect of basic care, environmental neglect, medical neglect, educational neglect and supervisory neglect. Based on these measures, they found that 71 per cent of the case records contained evidence of neglect, compared with only 41 per cent of the children who were formally classified as being neglected. The conclusion of the study was that even based on the agency's own definition of neglect, they had not formally identified a large number of children who fitted this definition, despite a high level of involvement and recognition that other forms of maltreatment were present.

Nevertheless, considerable effort has been made to tighten official definitions over the last 20 years in the UK. There have also been constant attempts to get various professionals to work closely together to achieve greater consistency. However, on the basis of these sources of evidence, the only safe definition is that it is a judgement reached by a group of professionals on the examination of the circumstances of a child, normally (in the UK) at a child protection conference.

Formal definitions of child abuse

The 1989 Children Act

In the UK, child abuse and neglect are not clearly defined anywhere in the legislation. The nearest it comes to a definition is in Section 31(2) of the 1989 Children Act when setting out the grounds for care proceedings, which states:

A court may only make a care order or supervision order if it is satisfied –

(a) that the child concerned is suffering, or is likely to suffer, significant harm; and

(b) that the harm, or likelihood of harm, is attributable to –

    (i) the care given to the child, or likely to be given to him if the order were not made, not being what it would be reasonable to expect a parent to give to him; or

    (ii) the child's being beyond parental control.

Thus the key legal concept in relation to abuse and neglect is the notion of *significant harm*. Harm is defined in Section 31(9) (as amended by the Adoption and Children Act 2002) as 'ill-treatment or the impairment of health or development, including any impairment suffered from seeing or hearing the ill-treatment of another'; development is defined as 'physical, intellectual, emotional, social or behavioural development'; health is defined as 'physical or mental health', and ill-treatment is defined as including sexual abuse and forms of ill-treatment which are not physical. Section 31(10) addresses the issue of how to measure 'significant harm', as follows:

> Where the question of whether harm suffered by a child is significant turns on the child's health or development, his health or development shall be compared with that which could reasonably be expected of a similar child.

As Lyon points out, the sort of comparisons being required are: 'invidious, if not well nigh impossible, but do raise incredible spectres of class, cultural, racial, religious and ethnic considerations' (Lyon 1989: 205).

As operational definitions, therefore, the law offers little help, and much is left to the judgement of professionals and ultimately of the courts to decide on whether child mistreatment is sufficiently serious to warrant making care or supervision orders.

Working Together guidelines

However, formal definitions of child abuse and neglect are to be found in Department of Health guidelines and these will be used as a framework for the rest of this discussion. Four categories of maltreatment are identified in the 2010 *Working Together* guidelines: physical abuse, neglect, emotional abuse and sexual abuse. Consideration will be given to the four base categories before moving on to consider the others.

Every Child Matters

As we have seen in the earlier chapters, much of the focus from 1997 onwards has been on widening access to services for many more children than only abused children. The clearest example of this in policy terms was the *Every Child Matters* reforms, supported by the Children Act 2004, which remain government policy at the time of writing. As indicated elsewhere, the *Every Child Matters* reforms set out five outcomes for all children to achieve:

- be healthy
- stay safe
- enjoy and achieve
- make a positive contribution
- achieve economic well-being.

These reforms significantly widen the scope of which children local authorities and their partners should be concerned about and broaden the discussion beyond more 'traditional' concepts of harm and abuse.

Physical abuse

Physical abuse was the original concern of those who brought child abuse to public attention in the 1960s. In the 2010 guidelines, physical abuse is defined as involving:

> hitting, shaking, throwing, poisoning, burning or scalding, drowning, suffocating or otherwise causing physical harm to a child. Physical harm may also be caused when a parent . . . fabricates the symptoms of, or deliberately induces, illness in a child
>
> (Department of Health 2010: 38)

As a nominal definition, this categorisation is more specific than that provided in earlier guidelines. However, it is not particularly useful as an operational definition because there is little guidance as to when behaviour such as hitting or shaking becomes serious enough to warrant protective intervention, especially when considering that smacking children is not a criminal offence in the UK. Clearly, for physically abusive behaviour such as poisoning or drowning, single incidents will always be enough to warrant statutory intervention. Although the defence of 'reasonable chastisement' has been removed, Section 58 of the Children Act 2004 only states that the battery of a child resulting in actual or grievous bodily harm cannot be justified on these grounds. It is still permissible to hit a child as long as the consequences are so minor that they would not provide sufficient evidence to warrant an assault charge. This is open to different interpretations, but satisfies the demands of those who wish to retain the right to smack children.[6]

Therefore, the only guidance in this respect comes from the concept of significant harm in the 1989 Children Act which, as noted above, is still too vague to be of any great use. In practice, there are many factors taken into account in deciding whether officially to define a situation as abusive.

Seriousness

The seriousness of the injury plays a part. Minor bruising, for instance, is generally not seen as sufficiently serious to require a child protection plan, whereas a series of

unexplained bruises is more likely, under the same circumstances, t
sufficient cause for such action.

Intention

Intention has generally been considered to be a key variable in deciding whether
an action is abusive or not (although it is not one that is specified in the 2010
guidelines). Again there is variation with regard to this. Dingwall et al. (1983)
identified among some hospital doctors what they termed a strict liability approach
(Dingwall et al. 1983: 36). From this point of view, if a child suffers a serious injury,
even accidentally, the child's carer at the time should accept responsibility for
the outcome and can be judged to be abusive. For the majority of child protection
workers, however, intentionality is seen as an influential factor. However, more recent
developments in our understanding of the impact of unresolved loss and trauma
on behaviour pose a challenge to these ideas about intentionality, as do recent
developments in our understanding of empathy (Baron-Cohen 2011a). If a parent
has experienced an unresolved loss or trauma that leads them to display disconnected
and/or extremely insensitive caregiving, which their child then experiences as abusive,
one can question how useful the concept of intentionality is. Likewise, if a parent
has an intermittently or more permanently malfunctioning sense of empathy (because
of differences in their brain circuitry over which they have no control; Baron-Cohen
2011b), the concept of intentionality is again of questionable use. This is not to
say that abusive behaviours towards children can be excused or that there is no
difference between genuine accidents and more intentional abuse; however, this
does make the question of intentionality less clear-cut than perhaps it appeared
to be before.

Age of child

A factor often taken into consideration in defining physical abuse is the age of the
child. Generally, the younger the child suspected of being physically abused, the
greater the likelihood of official registration. This response is frequently justified by
the fact that young children (particularly those under school age) are physically more
vulnerable and less open to being monitored by health and welfare professionals.

Context and risk

An analysis of the circumstances surrounding the reporting of a physical injury is
also important in deciding whether or not to define it as abusive. Much reliance
here is placed on professional judgement. Factors to be taken into account about
physical injuries include their actual nature and the likelihood that they are inflicted
rather than accidental ones, the coherence of the account given by a parent or
carer about how the injury occurred, whether there has been any delay in reporting
the injury and whether or not there has been a previous history of abuse (Meadow
1997). A key issue for those working with cases of physical abuse is that of risk of
further abuse.

Poisoning, suffocation and fabricated or induced illness

The official definition of physical abuse in the *Working Together* guidelines includes poisoning, suffocation and fabricated or induced illness (FII; formally known as Munchausen's syndrome by proxy). The change in terminology is explained by a realisation among health care professionals in the main that the term 'Munchausen's syndrome' focuses on the person perpetrating the abuse rather than the victim of that abuse, and because the term was being increasingly used as if it represented a psychiatric diagnosis of the perpetrator rather than, more properly, a description of a particular pattern of abuse. These three forms of abuse probably should be seen as separate, but there has been a good deal of linking up between them. The deliberate administration of harmful substances was included in Kempe's early descriptions of child abuse (Kempe and Kempe 1978) and the government's revised 2008 guidance *Safeguarding Children in Whom Illness is Induced or Fabricated* (Department for Children, Schools and Families 2008b) highlights the need for immediate protective action if it is known that a child is being intentionally suffocated or poisoned.

There has been some recent controversy in the UK about whether FII actually exists, primarily because of a series of court cases in which a number of women, such as Sally Clark and Angela Cannings, were originally convicted of murdering their children; convictions which were later overturned by the Court of Appeal. Despite the cases of Clark and Canning being unrelated to FII, some media commentators drew the mistaken conclusion that their exonerations undermined the evidence of FII as a real phenomenon.

Taking the case of Sally Clark as an example, she was accused of murdering two of her children, the first in 1996 and the second in 1998. Both died in a similar manner and Meadow, a British paediatrician and author, testified that the chance of two children from the same family dying of sudden infant death syndrome (SIDS) was 1 in 73 million.[7] Clark was convicted in 1999 but this was overturned in 2003. In 2001, the Royal Statistical Society had released a public statement saying that Meadow had no statistical basis for his claims and, in the appeal trial in 2003, it became apparent that the prosecution had failed to disclose evidence that the second child may have died of natural causes.

The controversy surrounding these and other cases led to a review of how cases of suspected FII should be managed, both in the court arena and by local authorities. The 2010 judgment of HHJ Clifford Bellamy (made in regard to three children, known only as X, Y and Z) set out a number of case management points, including reminding local authorities of the seriousness of accusing a parent or carer of FII, that the views of health professionals involved with the child should be sought, in addition to any reports from independent experts, that independent experts should have regard to *Fabricated or Induced Illness by Carers (FII): A Practical Guide for Paediatricians* (Royal College of Paediatrics and Child Health 2009) and that any reports from independent experts should be examined thoroughly.

The *Working Together* guidelines on dealing with FII were introduced in 2002 and, as noted above, revised in 2008. This guidance sets out what is known about the incidence and prevalence of FII, concluding that in the UK the prevalence is 0.5 per 100,000 children aged under 16 and 2.8 per 100,000 for children aged under 1 year

(McClure et al. 1996). This would give an estimated incidence rate of 1 child per million per year.

These guidelines place the focus of intervention more on the abuse of the child than on the condition of the parent, although clearly there is a need to tackle both aspects once the child has been safeguarded.

Physical neglect

Neglect is defined in the Department of Health 2010 draft guidelines as:

> The persistent failure to meet a child's basic physical and/or psychological needs, likely to result in the serious impairment of the child's health or development. Neglect may occur during pregnancy as a result of maternal substance abuse. Once a child is born, neglect may involve a parent or carer failing to provide adequate food, clothing and shelter; protect a child from physical and emotional harm or danger; ensure adequate supervision or (failing to) ensure access to appropriate medical care or treatment. It may also include neglect of, or unresponsiveness to a child's basic emotional needs.
>
> (Department of Health 2010: 39)

The main development in this definition is the inclusion of neglect during pregnancy (see below). As an operational definition, this paragraph is problematic. Practitioners must determine what counts as 'persistent failure' and 'serious impairment'. They must also be able to define basic psychological and emotional needs.

In the USA, following on from the pioneering work of Polansky and his colleagues (1985) there have been some recent attempts to develop more specific models on which to base child neglect work. For instance, Burke and her colleagues define child abuse and neglect as:

> Deficits or omissions in the parental role performance related to inadequate use of the parental environment that results in a serious threat to or observable decline in the well-being of the child.
>
> (Burke et al. 1998: 394)

Such a definition clearly places a great deal of responsibility on the parents and this has always been an area of some dispute in dealing with neglect, perhaps more so in Britain than in the USA.

To what extent, for instance, should consideration be given to notions of cultural difference, material resources and intellectual capacity in assessing whether a parent is neglectful or not? Stevenson (1998) considers whether we can distinguish between low standards of care brought about by poverty and ignorance, and those that result from lack of parental care or concern. She concludes that we often cannot.

A more recent study considered the relationship between child experiences characterised as neglectful prior to age 4 and child outcomes at age 4, and found that certain problems (such as a poor level of home safety, cleanliness and a failure to provide adequate shelter) resulted in impaired language and other developmental difficulties. Other problems (a high turnover of caregivers and medical neglect) resulted in less developmental concerns (English et al. 2005). The conclusion to take from this is that children's experiences of serious neglect and its consequences should override, at least initially, concerns about parental culpability and the rights and wrongs of intervention.

Other researchers take a different view – Straus and Kantor (2005) give the following definition:

> Neglectful behavior is behavior by a caregiver that constitutes a failure to act in ways that are presumed by the culture of a society to be necessary to meet the developmental needs of a child and which are the responsibility of a caregiver to provide.
>
> (Straus and Kantor 2005: 20)

They recognise themselves the 'controversial' part of this definition as being 'behavior by a caregiver', which they explain is included to rule out other possible causes of neglect such as poverty, mental illness or malevolent motives. Straus and Kantor go on to argue that they have attempted to define neglectful behaviour without considering harm – actual or potential – to the child. They do so not only because, in their view, this makes the phenomenon easier to study but also because it is important in practice. They give the example of a carer who repeatedly leaves a child unsupervised but, via good fortune, the child remains unharmed. On the other hand, a child could be left alone on just one occasion and could die as a result. Clearly, the more often a developmentally young child is left unsupervised the greater the *chance* of harm and this is why they highlight the importance of *chronicity*; it is also why professionals are often concerned in practice with establishing the pattern of behaviours as the basis for a judgement regarding the significance or otherwise of the risk of harm.

All the same, the issue of standards of care and the concerns about parental culpability make tackling neglect a very problematic issue for health and social care workers. A further problem lies with the difficulty of proving neglect in care proceedings. As a consequence of these uncertainties, neglect cases have been less likely to be vigorously pursued than other forms of abuse.[8]

Clearly there is much work to be done in clarifying what is meant by neglect but, as has been noted, chronic neglect has been overlooked to a large degree because of the focus on more specific forms of abuse – yet neglected children are likely to suffer worse outcomes in the long term.

Failure to thrive

The 2010 *Working Together* guidelines do not refer specifically to the 'failure-to-thrive' syndrome which was included in the 1991 and 1999 guidelines. The 2010 guidelines do say that new-born babies require love, adequate nutrition, sleep, warmth and to be kept clean in order to thrive (p. 280). Despite the lack of direct reference, a failure to thrive in babies is a serious and potentially life-threatening form of neglect. Because it can be subjected to measurement, it is technically easier to define and can be thought of as easier to prove than general neglect (Iwaniec et al. 1985). Babies have an expected normal level of growth (weight and length), which is based upon their birth weight and size. Those that fall well below this expectation, with no apparent physical explanation, are considered to be at risk; neglect (both physical and emotional) is thought to be a likely cause of this.[9]

However, perhaps because the syndrome was described initially by paediatricians, it has attracted more attention in medical journals than in social work or child abuse journals. Various medical causes for failure to thrive have, of course, been identified (with cystic fibrosis and Russell-Silver syndrome being two of the most common); nevertheless, there are other, rarer medical causes, such as Classic Bartter syndrome (see Samayam et al. 2011), which are harder to detect and which could potentially cause difficulties for professionals wishing to be clear about the reasons for a child failing to thrive. Close monitoring of a child's physical growth when placed away from the parents may show that, with reasonable care and feeding, normal development will take place, thus proving that some form of neglect lies at the heart of the problem. However, this form of intervention is clearly not without cost, both financially but also – and more importantly – to the child, especially if there was no improvement in their development in substitute care.

More recently, the usefulness of the dichotomy between 'organic' failure to thrive (cases where an underlying medical condition is found) and 'non-organic' failure to thrive (cases in which no underlying medical diagnosis can be made) has been called into question. This is because the dichotomy often leads to children undergoing a battery of extensive medical tests, some involving prolonged hospitalisations. Jaffe (2011) argues that any investigation into a suspected case of failure to thrive must take a multi-factorial approach, considering the child's caregiving environment as much as their physical condition – the argument being that whether or not a child has an underlying medical condition, it is important that this does not preclude an investigation as to whether they are receiving good enough care at home.

Sexual abuse

Sexual abuse is defined in the 2010 guidelines as 'forcing or enticing a child or young person to take part in sexual activities' where 'sexual activities' are defined as:

> penetration . . . or non-penetrative acts such as masturbation, kissing, rubbing and touching outside of clothing . . . involving children in looking at, or in the production of, sexual images, watching sexual activities, encouraging children to behave in sexually inappropriate ways, or grooming a child in preparation for abuse.
>
> (Department of Health 2010: 38)

This definition specifies the fact that sexual abuse need not involve physical contact and it provides some specific examples of such non-contact abuse. The definition also includes grooming a child in preparation for abuse, which was not present in 1999 (although it was in 2006). The inclusion was made in response to the growing awareness of children being contacted by potential abusers via the internet. However, there are still many gaps to be filled. For instance, the definition makes no distinction between intra-familial and extra-familial abuse, and says nothing about the age of the perpetrator, other than to point out that sexual abuse may be perpetrated by children as well as adults. Glaser and Frosh's (1988) definition still seems to be more compre-hensive than that offered in official guidance:

> Any child below the age of consent may be deemed to have been sexually abused when a sexually mature person has, by design or by neglect of their usual societal or specific responsibilities in relation to the child, engaged or permitted the engagement of that child in any activity of a sexual nature which is intended to lead to the sexual gratification of the sexually mature person. This definition pertains whether or not it involves genital contact or physical contact, and whether or not there is discernible harmful outcome in the short-term.
>
> (Glaser and Frosh 1988: 5)

In 2009, the government issued further supplementary guidance regarding sexual abuse, *Safeguarding Children and Young People from Sexual Exploitation* (Department for Children, Schools and Families 2009c). This guidance defined sexual exploitation as being when children or young people receive 'something' (such as food, accom-modation, drugs, alcohol, cigarettes, affection, gifts, money) as a result of engaging in sexual activities. This would include sending sexually explicit images to a third party via ICT and could take place without the child realising they had been exploited. Furthermore, this guidance made explicit the judgement that sexual exploitation is a form of sexual abuse and the children involved should be treated not as criminals but as victims in need of safeguarding. In 2010, a report by Dr Linda Papadopoulos, on behalf of the Home Office and entitled *Sexualisation of Young People Review*, consid-ered how 'sexualised images and messages' may be affecting children's development and also examined the link between sexualisation and violence. The report concluded that children, especially girls, were under pressure to conform to unrealistic body images, that sex industry jobs (such as lap dancing) were being normalised and that sexism and sexual violence have increased. With regard to child abuse, the report argued that the increased sexualisation of girls has contributed to an increased market for child abuse images. In 2011, the newly elected Conservative-Liberal Democrat coalition government commissioned a further report into the commercialisation and sexualisation of children. The report (Bailey 2011) concluded that the UK is an increasingly sexualised culture and that 'public spaces' contain far too many sexual-ised images to be considered 'family friendly'. The report made various recommenda-tions, such as regulating the display of magazines with sexualised images on their covers, reducing the amount of street advertising containing sexualised imagery and making it easier for parents to control their children's internet access. The government broadly welcomed the report and its recommendations and committed to reviewing the progress of the recommendations in 18 months' time (in December 2012).

The issue of defining sexual abuse, sexual exploitation and sexual commercialisa-tion in practice is both complex and problematical. There is now a general awareness not only that child sexual abuse is far more common than was previously thought, but also that it affects very young children as well as older ones (Macfarlane and Waterman 1986). In what follows, it should be noted that the focus is on intra-familial abuse.

This is largely because this form of abuse lies more squarely in the domain of health and social care workers. However, the importance of responding to the needs of children and families where the former have experienced abuse outside the family should not be underestimated (Bolen 2001). For a useful discussion on the similarities and differences between intra- and extra-familial sexual abuse, see Fischer and Macdonald (1998).

Medical, social and behavioural factors in defining sexual abuse

There are few clear-cut medical signs of sexual abuse. Thus, most medical examinations of children suspected of having been abused yield little by way of evidence. It is now generally accepted that medical evidence without some form of corroboration from a social and behavioural assessment is not sufficient to prove child sexual abuse in court.

With regard to behavioural indicators, a variety of factors have been identified as associated with sexual abuse of children, for example withdrawn presentation, para-suicide and suicide, running away from home and anorexia nervosa (see Porter 1984). However, these correlations do not prove connections and can, therefore, only sensitise professionals to the possibility of sexual abuse. They have limited value in terms of the standard of evidence required in courts. The best indicator, particularly in younger children, is that of precocious sexual behaviour (see Brilleslijper-Kater et al. 2004). However, even sexual behaviour in children is not a clear indicator of sexual abuse. The development and exhibition of sexual behaviour is, after all, a normal part of healthy development. Children aged between 0 and 4 will normally kiss or hug other children, as well as show an interest in and talk about body parts, including genitalia, and they may engage in masturbatory behaviour. As in many cases, the best way for professionals to ensure they do not mistake normal childhood behaviour for a sign of something more worrying is to educate themselves as fully as possible about child development.

The child's testimony

As a consequence of the fact that there are few reliable external indicators of child sexual abuse, considerable emphasis has been placed on the child's account of events. While there is now much more openness among professionals to listening and responding to these accounts, there are still many problems in substantiating that abuse has occurred, particularly if it is alleged to have taken place within the family. As was seen in Chapter 2, following the Cleveland and the Orkney inquiries, there was concern that social workers and clinical psychologists were too willing to believe children and were possibly guilty of leading them too much. In America, the case of Frederico Macias raised similar concerns. Macias was convicted of murder in 1984 and was given the death penalty. The prosecution relied heavily on the testimony of a 13-year-old witness. Four years later, the same witness reported:

> Because different people asked me so many questions about what I saw I became confused. I thought I might have seen something that would be helpful to the

police. I didn't realize that it would become so important. I thought they wanted me to be certain, so I said I was certain even though I wasn't . . . the more questions I was asked, the more confused I became.

(Ceci and Bruck 1995: 304)

Fortunately, this statement was made two weeks before Macias' scheduled execution and he was later exonerated in 1993.

The concerns highlighted by the Cleveland and Orkney inquiries led to the introduction, in 1992, of the *Memorandum of Good Practice* for interviewing children which was to be used in all child abuse cases where a serious crime had been alleged (Home Office/Department of Health 1992). This document was revised in 2001 and then replaced by *Achieving Best Evidence in Criminal Proceedings* (Ministry of Justice 2011), for use when interviewing all children under the age of 17, regardless of the offence involved. The Achieving Best Evidence (ABE) protocol is a semi-structured interview and aims at eliciting as much free recall as possible by the interviewee. For example, the interviewer asks 'What shall we talk about?' rather than employing more direct questions. Many studies have indicated the benefits of this approach in providing the required information (e.g. Korkman et al. 2006). In spite of the supposed widespread usage of the ABE protocol, research has found that, in practice, closed questions, suggestive summaries, inappropriate prompts and the repetition of questions remain prevalent (see Westcott and Kynan 2006; Westcott et al. 2006). As we saw in the example of the Macias case from the USA, the use of repetitive questions has been shown to result in changes to the interviewee's responses and a decline in accuracy and consistency (Krähenbühl and Blades 2006). Children giving evidence in court also continue to be placed under tremendous pressure (Westcott and Page 2002).

Emotional abuse

Emotional abuse for the purposes of registration is defined in the 2010 guidelines as:

the persistent emotional maltreatment of a child such as to cause severe and persistent adverse effects on the child's emotional development. It may involve conveying to children that they are worthless or unloved, inadequate, or valued only insofar as they meet the needs of another person. It may include not giving the child opportunities to express their views, deliberately silencing them or 'making fun' of what they say or how they communicate. It may feature age or developmentally inappropriate expectations being imposed on children. These may include interactions that are beyond the child's developmental capability, as well as overprotection and limitation of exploration and learning, or preventing the child participating in normal social interaction. It may involve seeing or hearing the ill-treatment of another. It may involve serious bullying (including cyberbullying), causing children frequently to feel frightened or in danger, or the exploitation or corruption of children. Some level of emotional abuse is involved in all types of ill-treatment of a child, though it may occur alone.

(Department of Health 2010: 38)

This definition has been updated since 2006, making reference now to bullying and cyberbullying as well as including aspects which seem to relate specifically to disabled children ('"making fun" . . . of how they communicate'). Defining emotional abuse for practical intervention purposes is extremely difficult. Social workers seem to be particularly aware of, and concerned about, the emotional ill-treatment of children, but find it very hard to pinpoint their concerns. This is because they are tackling areas of major uncertainty and sensitivity, which are both controversial and difficult to prove. Styles of parenting are brought into question by the issue of emotional abuse. For instance, are authoritarian or extremely permissive parenting styles abusive? Is constant criticism of a child an abuse? Can it be proved that such parenting styles have ill-effects? Where is the line between acceptable and unacceptable psychological parenting to be drawn? Is it abusive actively to prejudice a child against people of different races and sexes? Some would argue that it is, but would be hard pressed to prove that such upbringings are actively harmful to individuals, even though it is likely that society as a whole will be the poorer for such forms of socialisation. It is difficult to prove links between causes and effects in this area; Garbarino and Vondra (1987) describe 'stress-resistant' children who, despite apparently rejecting parents, survive to be reasonably well-adjusted adults.

In the USA, Wald (1982) has argued that there should be intervention only where a child is suffering serious emotional damage, evidenced by severe anxiety, depression or withdrawal, or aggressive behaviour or hostility towards others, and the parents are unwilling to provide treatment for the child. Whether this would include parents who decline to allow their children to be prescribed medication such as Ritalin adds another difficult element to the debate, given the well-known concerns, from respected quarters, about the over-medication of children (see Sparks and Duncan 2004). Burnett (1993) has tried to develop a specific set of definitions of emotional abuse. Using vignettes with the public and professionals in a moderate-sized city in north-east USA, he found general agreement on nine forms of what he termed psychological abuse:

- confining a child in a small place
- severe public humiliation
- the 'Cinderella' syndrome
- severe verbal abuse
- encouraging or coercing a child into delinquency
- threatening a child
- refusal of psychiatric treatment
- not allowing social and emotional growth
- not providing a loving, nurturing atmosphere.

(Burnett 1993: 446)

In Britain, greater emphasis has been placed on emotional abuse following the refocusing shift in child protection work that took place in the second half of the 1990s, and this is reflected in the official reporting statistics (see Introduction). Glaser (2002), however, notes that there are continuing uncertainties over definition. She points to the need for careful psychological assessment of children whose parents are thought to be emotionally abusive using the following areas of focus on their behaviour:

- emotional unavailability, unresponsiveness and neglect
- negative attributions and misattributions to the child
- developmentally inappropriate or inconsistent interactions with the child
- failure to recognise or acknowledge the child's individuality and psychological boundary
- failing to promote the child's social adaptation.

(Glaser 2002: 703–4)

Such a framework seems to be a useful aid in raising practitioner awareness and structuring assessment and intervention, but it would still be hard to prove emotional abuse in care proceedings on this basis. Indeed, in 2006, Justice McFarlane found that cases of emotional abuse will rarely, if ever, warrant an application for an emergency protection order, and even rarer still would be an application for such without giving notice to the child's carers. In 2008, the Ministry of Justice published research into the profiles of children and families involved in care proceedings under Section 31 of the 1989 Children Act (Masson et al. 2008). In considering the concerns of children's services, it found that maternal emotional abuse was present in 59 per cent of cases and paternal emotional abuse in 50.8 per cent of cases. This data tells us that, contrary to the *Working Together* guidance, many applications for care orders were made without considering the emotionally abusive aspects of the child's care (*Working Together* states that some level of emotional abuse is involved in all types of child maltreatment), but what it cannot tell us is on how many occasions care proceedings were issued solely on the basis of emotional abuse. We suspect that the answer would be very few.

Factors common to all types of abuse

It has to be stressed that there may be overlaps and connections between the different forms of abuse. Thus, a child may be physically and sexually abused, physically abused and neglected and so on. As the 2010 guidelines stress, emotional abuse, while theoretically able to occur by itself, is also almost certain to accompany or to be a consequence of the other forms of abuse. Until the late 1980s, the emotional impact of physical abuse and neglect received little attention. This has been less true in the case of sexual abuse. Currently, the emotional or psychological effects of all forms of abuse are being seen as a unifying factor in identifying and responding to them. Focus on the emotional aspects of abuse is seen as a way of moving forward more positively to improving the quality of life of all children who experience any form of mistreatment.

Other forms of abuse

There are a wide range of other forms of child mistreatment about which concern has been expressed.

Abuse during pregnancy and foetal abuse

Abuse during pregnancy also features in the 2010 guidelines. It is a wider concept than what has been termed 'foetal abuse'. The issue of foetal abuse has been a concern for some time in the USA and in some states it is considered a clear grounds for taking protective action. It is a term used in relation to behaviours on the part of pregnant mothers, such as excessive use of tobacco, alcohol and prohibited drugs that are considered harmful to the unborn child. There is a good deal of speculation about the impact of the use of these substances during pregnancy and their short-term physical and longer-term physical, behavioural and social consequences (Mackenzie et al. 1982). However, more recently, research has confirmed the association between alcohol, cocaine, cannabis and tobacco during pregnancy and a number of serious complications for mother and foetus, including spontaneous abortion, low birth weight and impaired foetal growth (von Mandach 2005). What is less clear is the impact of 'party drugs' such as ecstasy and LSD. More generally, children whose parents have used alcohol or drugs during pregnancy are more likely to be referred for neglect during childhood (Street et al. 2003). The 2010 *Working Together* guidelines refer to maternal substance abuse during pregnancy as a form of neglect, and pre-birth child protection plans can be put in place if required.

In terms of abuse during pregnancy (as distinct from foetal abuse), the 2010 guidelines highlight the increased risk of domestic violence, stating that an estimated one-third of such abuse begins or escalates during pregnancy. Guidelines for health professionals were issued in 2005 regarding this issue entitled *Responding to Domestic Violence: a Handbook for Health Professionals* (Department of Health 2005).

Ritual and organised abuse

Following on from the research conducted by La Fontaine (1994), ritual abuse is not included in the 2010 guidelines, as it was previously not included in the 1999 guidelines. However, organised or multiple abuse is defined as 'abuse involving one or more abusers and a number of children. The abusers concerned may be acting in concert to abuse children, sometimes acting in isolation, or may be using an institutional framework or position of authority to recruit children for abuse' (Department of Health 2010: 194). The complexity of this form of abuse is reflected in the emphasis that the guidelines place on careful inter-agency planning and coordination, particularly between police and social services agencies, prior to intervention.

Female genital mutilation

Female genital mutilation (FGM) has been a criminal act in the UK since 1985 but the more recent Female Genital Mutilation Act 2003 added a new offence, prohibiting any UK nationals or permanent UK residents from carrying out FGM abroad or aiding, abetting or otherwise allowing the carrying out of FGM abroad, including in countries where the practice is legal. The 2010 *Working Together* guidelines note the abusive nature of FGM and clearly indicate that local authorities should use their child protection powers to intervene if they have reason to believe a child is likely to suffer or has suffered FGM. However, they also note that many parents do not intend FGM to be an act of abuse, genuinely believing that it is in the girl's best interests.

The World Health Organisation (WHO) defines FGM as procedures that intentionally modify or injure female genital organs (for non-medical reasons). The impact of FGM can include serious bleeding, difficulties urinating and potential childbirth complications in the future. In 2008, the WHO expressed concern about the increasing trend for trained medical professionals performing FGM. In 2010, it was widely reported in the media that the practice of FGM was growing in the UK, with girls being especially at risk during the longer summer school holiday, when their absence from the UK or their recovery from the procedure would be less noticeable. One story in the *Observer* newspaper (2010) stated that 63,000 girls and women in the UK have already undergone FGM.

Forced marriages and honour-based violence

The 2010 guidelines refer to 'honour crimes', '*izzat*' or 'honour-based violence' and state that these terms refer to a range of different violent crimes. Primarily, they are linked by the violence being used to 'punish' individuals (usually, but not always, women) for perceived transgressions against 'correct codes' of behaviour.

Forced marriage is when one or both parties have not consented to the marriage and is linked to honour-based violence because a failure to comply can result in a violent response. Although there is no specific criminal offence in England and Wales of 'forcing someone to get married against their will', those involved could be guilty of a range of offences such as assault, kidnap, theft (of passports), threats to kill and so on. The guidance also notes that sexual intercourse without consent, whether before or after a marriage ceremony, is rape. The Home Office and the Foreign and Commonwealth Office jointly run the UK Forced Marriage Unit and reported that in 2010 there were 1,735 instances when advice was given on possible forced marriages in the UK. Of these, 50 cases involved disabled people and 36 involved lesbian, gay, bisexual or transsexual people. It was not noted how many cases involved children.

Peer abuse

'Peer abuse', a term used to convey the significance of bullying as a form of abuse, has been popularised in academic discussions of child abuse (see Bennett 2006) as well as in government guidance (the term first appeared in *Working Together in* 1999). In addition, bullying of children in day schools is included, which has traditionally been seen as a school behaviour problem falling within the province of education authorities. Peer abuse need not only take place face to face. Bullying via the internet or other related communication methods is also a serious concern. The most recent research on cyberbullying indicates that one in five young people (aged 12 to 18) report experiencing bullying of this type (O'Brien and Moules 2011).

Increasingly, linkages are being made between behaviours outside the family and those within. Thus, physical bullying, sexual bullying, racist bullying and rape in schools are viewed as possible symptoms of intra-familial abuse as well as abuses or crimes in their own right. In 2009, the Office for Standards in Education (Ofsted) published a report, *The Exclusion from School of Children Aged Four to Seven*, which highlighted the underlying issues that can link sexually inappropriate behaviour at school and wider family difficulties.

The concept of peer victimisation has also become more prevalent, developing from research into the bully-victim relationship. This research has shown how the victims of peer abuse are more likely to exhibit poor school engagement and to experience emotional and mental health difficulties (Seeley et al. 2009).

Children affected by gang activity

The issue of children and young people affected by gang activity has also attracted more attention recently. In 2010, the government published non-statutory guidance, *Safeguarding Children and Young People Who May Have Been Affected by Gang Activity* (Department for Children, Schools and Families/Home Office 2010). This guidance recognises that young people in or around gangs can be both perpetrators and victims of harm. Indeed, the guidance explicitly states that 'children who harm others are both victims and perpetrators' (p. 6). This point is supported by research undertaken on behalf of Victim Support (Owen and Sweeting 2007), which highlighted three pathways from victimisation to offending behaviour, namely retaliatory violence, displaced retaliation or the victim befriending offenders (partly in order to seek protection from future victimisation). The same research highlighted two pathways from offending behaviour to victimisation, namely being subject to retaliatory violence and a lack of protection from adults in authority.

In August 2011, primarily in response to the English riots of that year and under the guidance of Home Secretary Theresa May and Work and Pensions Secretary Iain Duncan Smith, a review of gang culture was launched. It must be noted that the focus of this review does appear to be on the criminalisation of children involved in gangs, rather than on a view of these children as victims in need of protection.

Children involved in prostitution

There have been considerable developments in official thinking about children involved in prostitution. Previous guidance, *Safeguarding Children Involved in Prostitution* (Department of Health et al. 2000), was superseded by the 2006 *Working Together* guidelines, now superseded by the 2010 guidelines. The latest guidelines include information on the Sexual Offences Act 2003, which introduced a range of specific new offences such as paying for the sexual services of a child, causing or inciting child prostitution, arranging or otherwise facilitating child prostitution and controlling a child prostitute.

Reference is also made to the offence of trafficking children for the purposes of prostitution, introduced by the Nationality, Immigration and Asylum Act 2003. Any suspected victims of child trafficking should be referred via the national referral mechanism (NRM) to either the UK Border Agency (if the matter involves immigration processes) or to the UK Human Trafficking Centre, part of the UK's Serious Organised Crime Agency.

Child abuse and Information and communications technology

The 2010 guidelines note that a range of abuse is now taking place via, or involving, the use of ICT. The internet in particular is seen as being a significant tool, not only for the distribution of indecent images of children but also as a means of contacting and grooming children for future abuse. The guidance states that those found in possession of indecent images (or pseudo-images) of children should be investigated by the police as to whether they may also have been involved in direct child abuse. Beyond the internet, the guidance also refers to the use of SMS text messaging, email and instant messaging services as other potential tools for similar ends.

The guidelines also note the rise of bullying or peer abuse via ICT and another area of concern identified is that of violent extremism. The guidelines point to how young people, especially teenagers, can be vulnerable to the influence of radical groups and that increasingly such groups are using the internet to circulate their ideas and spread their influence. Radical groups are described as those that condone violence as a means to a political end.

Abuse of disabled children

The 2010 guidelines have a specific section on abuse of disabled children. There is clear evidence that disabled children are at an increased risk of abuse compared with their non-disabled peers and the presence of complex and multiple impairments increases the risk of abuse and neglect. This may be for a number of reasons, including the increased likelihood of disabled children being socially isolated, the child's potential dependency upon parents and carers for personal and intimate care, an impaired capacity to avoid and report abuse and an increased vulnerability to peer abuse. Clearly, the same procedures should be followed in terms of child protection for disabled children as for non-disabled children but extra effort is likely to be needed on the part of the professional to ensure the disabled child's wishes and feelings are understood and that the child is given the means and tools to communicate as fully as possible.

In 2009, the government issued specific guidance, *Safeguarding Disabled Children* (Department for Children, Schools and Families 2009d), offering advice on issues such as supporting families to provide the best possible care for disabled children, possible indicators of abuse and neglect for disabled children and therapeutic services for disabled children who have been abused.

Self-harm and suicide

While the 2010 guidelines do not contain a specific section on self-harm or suicide, it is noted that children who self-harm may have suffered sexual abuse, peer abuse, have experienced domestic violence or been involved in a forced marriage. Similarly, suicide or attempted suicide can also be a consequence of these types of abuse. It is also noted that where parents have severe mental health difficulties which include delusional beliefs about their child, this may lead to the parent making a 'suicide plan' that involves the child; clearly, this is recognised as a significant risk. Whenever a child death occurs and suicide is suspected *and* abuse or neglect is a known or suspected factor, local safeguarding children boards (LSCBs) are required to conduct a serious case review (SCR).

Children who go missing or live away from home, children with families of unknown whereabouts and unaccompanied asylum-seeking children

There has been a considerable amount of research carried out in relation to measuring the numbers of children and young people who run away from home or care (Biehal et al. 1995; Thompson 1995). The findings of these studies have been used in framing the Leaving Care Act 2000. Clearly, a key concern is the potential for children who run away from home to be abused and exploited, to become involved in prostitution, drug misuse and to end up in custodial settings. The 2010 guidelines also refer to the broader concept of abuse of children living away from home.

In addition to this, the guidance refers to children who go missing not from home, but from education. Specific guidance was issued in 2004, *Identifying and Maintaining Contact with Children Missing, or at Risk of Going Missing, from Education* (Department for Education and Skills 2004c). As we saw in the preceding chapter in the discussion of the death of Khyra Ishaq, the law regarding children educated at home remains unchanged, in that no registration is required and there is no oversight by Ofsted of the quality of the education being provided.

The 2010 guidance also highlights the risk of families moving in order to avoid involvement with agencies such as the police and children's social care. The guidance also notes the potential use of legal interventions where there is reason to believe that a child might be removed from the UK in order to avoid safeguarding interventions.

Finally, the 2010 guidance refers to unaccompanied asylum-seeking children. In most cases, such children would be referred to the relevant local authority by the UK Border Agency soon after their arrival in the UK. It is likely that these children would be accommodated by the local authority and the guidance makes clear that they should have their needs assessed and addressed as with any other child in need. Similarly, the guidance makes clear that any safeguarding concerns that arise in relation to an unaccompanied asylum-seeking child should also be fully addressed. In planning for such children, the advice is to consider that the child may not be long-term resident in the UK and therefore future planning would need to take into account that the child may be returned to their country of origin.

Concluding comments

As can be seen, what is defined as child abuse has grown from the battered child of 1962 to a vast range of practices and behaviours. The field is a very complex one: increasingly health and welfare professionals are being required to take on new issues and concerns, even though their primary focus may well continue to be on physical, sexual, emotional abuse and neglect within the family. The emphasis now is truly on providing safeguards for a wide range of threats to child development, and increasingly the expectation is that professionals will work together proactively to prevent harm to children both within and outside the family. Not only is the breadth of concerns now facing child protection professionals breathtaking, but so is the speed with which new issues arise – currently there are concerns being raised in relation to gang activity and 'troubled families' more generally, but undoubtedly other concerns will also crop up in future, and just as unexpectedly.

Despite this wide focus, Harris (1995) has argued that what we choose to focus on in terms of concerns about children are culturally specific. While this undoubtedly remains true, consideration of the international scene should provide some perspective on domestic concerns without reducing any commitment to tackling them. Awareness of these matters and of the complexities involved in defining child abuse in our own society which have been thus far reviewed should sensitise professionals to the ever-changing nature of this challenging area of work.

Recommended reading

Cawson, P., Wattam, C., Brooker, S. and Kelly, G. (2000) *Child Maltreatment in the United Kingdom: A Study of the Prevalence of Child Abuse and Neglect.* London: NSPCC.

Department of Health (2010) *Working Together to Safeguard Children: A Guide to Inter-agency Working to Safeguard and Promote the Welfare of Children.* London: The Stationery Office.

Ferguson, H. (2004) *Protecting Children in Time: Child Abuse, Child Protection and the Consequences of Modernity.* London: Palgrave Macmillan.

Lyon, C. (2003) *Child Abuse,* 3rd edn. Bristol: Jordan Publishing.

Stevenson, O. (2007) *Neglected Children and Their Families.* Oxford: Blackwell.

5

Perpetrators of child abuse

Introduction

A vast quantity of research has been conducted into the characteristics of perpetrators of child abuse and neglect and into the characteristics of the children most likely to be the victims of such maltreatment. This research has largely been undertaken to predict and prevent future abuse and neglect.

First, if it is possible to identify those adults who are most likely to abuse or neglect children, then early and decisive intervention is likely to afford those children greater protection.

Second, it is clear that there is a close association between who is most likely to be the victim of abuse or neglect and the question of perpetration. Children in close proximity to likely perpetrators are obviously those who are most at risk. However, not all children in these situations seem to be equally at risk. Some children seem to have more resilience than others and some seem to be singled out for mistreatment.

Third, the causation of child abuse and neglect is very closely linked to the question of perpetration and the interrelationship between these three aspects of child abuse cannot be sufficiently emphasised. However, for the purposes of analysis, these issues will be looked at separately. In this chapter the first and second questions will be considered. Theories of causation will be the subject of Chapter 6.

Researchers have considered a wide range of variables that seem likely to be associated with abusive and neglectful behaviour towards children. Inevitably, given the amount of research carried out, this summary will be a selective one. The factors selected for closer inspection in respect of those who abuse are as follows:

- gender
- age
- poverty and race
- adults who have themselves been abused
- family structure
- psychological capacities
- the impact of alcohol and drugs

- mental health difficulties
- domestic violence.

Much of the research focuses on abusers within family settings although extra-familial abuse is also significant and will also be addressed. However, it should be noted that, with the exception of child sexual abuse, children are most likely to be abused or neglected by their parents and/or carers (Lamont 2011).

Causal connections

Before considering the characteristics of perpetrators and victims of child abuse and neglect, special comment needs to be made regarding the absence of causal connections. Often, research finds an association or a correlation between a certain characteristic or variable – such as 'parents with mental health difficulties' or 'a child aged less than 12 months' – and child abuse or neglect. While helpful, this is very different from being able to claim that the presence of these types of characteristics or variables is causally *predictive* of child abuse or neglect.

For those unfamiliar with statistical language, there are precise differences between the terms 'association' or 'correlation', and 'causation'. An association or correlation between two or more things indicates any statistically dependent relationship between them. Two (or more) things are associated (or correlated) if some of the variability in one can be accounted for by the other(s). For example, there is an association between personal wealth and voting for right-wing political parties and a similar association between personal poverty and voting for left-wing political parties (Huber and Stanig 2009). However, while this association is demonstrably accurate, it does not allow one to draw conclusions about the voting records or future voting intentions of individuals. All it allows you to say is that if you picked one wealthy person at random (ignoring all other variables), he or she would be more *likely* to vote for a right-wing party than a left-wing party, but in many cases you would be wrong. The same holds true for less wealthy individuals.

The relationship between the types of variable in this example is not causal. The saying 'correlation does not imply causation' is well known and absolutely accurate. Indeed, to say that correlation does imply causation is a logical fallacy. Further examples of this mistaken belief are the numerous studies which found that women taking a certain type of hormone replacement therapy (HRT) had a lower risk of heart disease. This led to the proposition that HRT might in some way protect women against heart disease. However, a randomised trial showed that HRT actually raised the risk of heart disease. A deeper analysis of the original data showed that women who took HRT were more likely to be from higher socio-economic groups and as a result they tended to have better diets and engage in more exercise. Both the use of HRT and a reduced incidence of heart disease were caused by being a member of a higher socio-economic group.

Munro (2008) has explored these issues in relation to the field of child protection. Many people intuitively think that the more risk factors are identified for a particular family or child, the stronger the prediction of future harm – Munro points out that this is incorrect. In addition to knowing about the factors identified in relation to perpetrators or victims of abuse, we also need to be able to compare this to the incidence of the relevant factors in the general population (the 'base rate'). Take poverty as an example (as Munro does). In 2001, in the UK, around 21 per cent of children lived in poverty. To understand how strong a predictive factor poverty is for child abuse, we need to compare this general level of poverty with the incidence of poverty in abusive families. If found at the same level in abusive families as in the general population, poverty would have no predictive value in terms of abuse. If found to be more common in abusive families, poverty would be a predictive factor and the more common it was in abusive families, compared with the general population, the stronger the predictive value would become. If found to be less prevalent in abusive families than in the general population, poverty would be contra-indicative of abuse. Munro identifies a variety of factors that do seem to be relatively strong predictors for perpetration of abuse or neglect, many of which are discussed below, such as a record of previous violence, personality disorder, a history of mental health problems and being male. Munro also identifies a variety of risk factors for victims, including being young and being born prematurely – again, these are discussed in more detail below. As Munro argues, the best predictor of abuse would be a factor that occurs in all abusive families and very rarely in the general population. Munro concludes that given the ambiguous nature of child abuse and neglect (as discussed in Chapter 4), one commonly identifiable factor of causation is unlikely. In the next chapter (in detail) and in this chapter (more briefly), we discuss a combination of psychological and attachment-related factors that appear to be the closest we can currently come to identifying the causal and strongly indicative factors that Munro identifies would be so helpful.

In summary, research into the characteristics and variables related to perpetrators and victims of abuse has so far identified associations or correlations rather than causal connections. Munro's argument about the importance of appreciating the base rate of any given factor is also of significance. The greater the differential between the incidence of a particular factor in abusive families and in the general population, the more predictive it is of abuse (either as an indicator or a contra-indicator). Unless we understand the base rate of that factor, we cannot say whether or not it is a stronger or weaker predictor of abuse or neglect. We must consider the association and correlation between the variety of factors discussed below and not causal links.

The gender of those who abuse and neglect

Overall, children are more likely to be maltreated by females than males (but they provide most of the caregiving). Statistics from the US Department of Health and Human Services from 2000 to 2009 (the most recent available) all show that most perpetrators of child maltreatment are female. In 2009, 53.8 per cent of recorded cases of child abuse or neglect were believed to have been perpetrated by females (and 44.4 per cent by a male; in the remaining 1.8 per cent of cases, the gender of the perpetrator was unknown). In 2008, the figures were 56.2 per cent female, 42.6 per cent male; in 2007, 56.5 per cent female, 42.4 per cent male; in 2006, 57.9 per cent female, 42.1 per cent male; and in 2005, 57.8 per cent female and 42.2 per cent male (US Department of Health and Human Services 2007a, 2008, 2009, 2010a, 2010b).

Physical abuse

Nevertheless, in situations of physical abuse, fathers or social fathers are generally seen as the more likely perpetrators when compared with mothers. Men are almost universally considered to be more violent than women, which probably accounts for this. In a study of an accident and emergency hospital department over a two-year period, Steen and Hunskaar (2004) found that out of 1,680 assault victims, the vast majority (1,588 or 94.5 per cent) reported that they had been the victims of male perpetrated violence. In practice, social workers and other professionals tend to carry out much of their work in such cases almost exclusively with women (O'Hagan and Dillenberger 1995; Scourfield 2001).[1]

However, clearly women as well as men physically abuse children. In 2005, a survey of over 15 million Australians aged 15 and over found that 55.6 per cent of respondents reported having been physically abused by their father/step-father before the age of 15, compared with 25.9 per cent who reported having been physically abused by their mother/step-mother. A British study on behalf of the National Society for the Prevention of Cruelty to Children (NSPCC) found that mothers were more likely to physically abuse their children than fathers (49 per cent of recorded incidents by mothers compared with 40 per cent by fathers – May-Chahal and Cawson 2005). The evidence does suggest that fathers or social fathers are more likely to be responsible for serious injuries or fatalities (US Department of Health and Human Services 2007a). For example, Kajese et al. (2011) studied 170 child homicides in Kansas, USA, between 1994 and 1997. The most commonly identified perpetrator was the child's biological father (in 26.6 per cent of cases), with slightly fewer killed by their biological mother (24.9 per cent) and fewer again by the child's mother's male partner (19.8 per cent). These figures are more 'balanced' than those of an earlier study by Brewster et al. (1998), who studied 32 cases of infanticide on United States Air Force bases between 1989 and 1995, and found that 84 per cent of the perpetrators were men looking after children on their own at the time of the fatal abuse episodes.

Sexual abuse

Fathers or social fathers are also seen as more likely to be responsible for nearly all acts of intra-familial sexual abuse of children (Bornstein et al. 2007). Assumptions about the nature of female sexuality are the likely reason for this, with women generally thought far less likely to abuse children sexually. It is notable that, despite this view, women are still held to be partly responsible for what happens – hence the term 'collusive mothers'.[2]

The evidence to support this general view is quite clear-cut – overwhelmingly, sexual abuse is perpetrated by males (Australian Bureau of Statistics 2005; McCloskey and Raphael 2005). Of 411 sexually abused children referred to the Great Ormond Street Hospital for Sick Children between 1980 and 1986, only 8 children (2 per cent) had been abused by females (Bentovim et al. 1988).

Intra-familial sexual abuse implicates not only fathers – there have been studies of abuse by grandfathers (Margolin 1992), uncles (Margolin 1994) and male siblings

(Adler and Schutz 1995). Some writers have considered there to be important distinctions between male intra- and extra-familial abusers. Becker and Quinsey, for instance, point out that 'extra-familial child molesters are more likely to recidivate than strictly intra-familial child molesters and men who choose boy victims are more likely to recidivate than men who abuse girl victims' (Becker and Quinsey 1993: 170). More recently, Hanson and Morton-Bourgon (2005) found that when studying persistent sexual offenders, deviant sexual preferences (for children) combined with anti-social attitudes were the major predictors of sexual recidivism.

Others, particularly from a feminist perspective, see little distinction between intra- and extra-familial abuse. Bolen (2001) notes that although intra-familial abuse accounts for between 11 and 40 per cent of all sexual abuse of children, and between 7 and 8 per cent of all sexual abuse is committed by parental figures, nevertheless this model of abuse dominates our thinking. From her perspective there is little in the way of qualitative difference between intra- and extra-familial abuse.

There are a small number of studies of intra-familial female sex abusers. Krug (1989) studied eight cases in detail and came to the conclusion that female sexual abuse of children mirrored that of male sexual abuse:

> The sexual abuse typically involved the mother satisfying her own emotional and physical needs for intimacy, security and perhaps power by actively seeking out the son, either on a nightly basis, or when she and her living [live-in] partner were in conflict.
>
> (Krug 1989: 112)

In 2011, Testa et al. noted that as most victims of child sexual abuse are girls and most perpetrators are male, the likelihood of the abuse being transmitted inter-generationally is low when compared with other types of abuse. However, the same paper also notes that when a female child is sexually abused, it is more likely her mother was also sexually abuse in childhood.

There is a need for some degree of perspective when considering the likely gender of child sex abuse perpetrators. While it is wrong to assume that women do not sexually abuse children, one should not fall into the trap of seeing such abuse as perpetrated equally by men and women.

We know almost nothing about women who sexually abuse outside the family, but turning finally to male extra-familial abusers we are moving into the terrain of paedophiles. Pritchard (2004: 57) identifies three types of extra-familial child abuser: 'career paedophiles, whose lives are dedicated to the covert sexual pursuit of children', casual offenders with disorganised personalities, and violent offenders. Sullivan et al. (2011) found that, when compared with intra-familial abusers, extra-familial abusers were likely to be significantly more preoccupied with sex and to emotionally over-identify with children.

The research distinguishes between internet sex offenders (ISOs), who view child pornography, and general sex offenders (GSOs). Tomak et al. (2009) argue that the former are a different group of offenders from the latter – that is, ISOs are not 'just' GSOs making use of a new technology. ISOs are less deviant, less physically aggressive and less impulsive compared to GSOs. However, they are still overwhelmingly male. In the USA, there were 3,672 arrests for possession of child pornography in 2006 compared with 1,713 in 2000. Almost everyone arrested was male (Wolak et al. 2011).

Categorising sexual abusers is clearly important in terms of managing them once convicted, but one of the key problems is that these typologies are based only on known offenders and for that reason they surely do not represent the whole picture.

Emotional abuse

If there is little research into the gender of perpetrators of neglect (see below), there is even less where emotional abuse is concerned. Searching the British Library's collection of over 20,000 individual journals for the terms 'emotional abuse' and 'perpetrator' returns just seven articles, none of which is relevant to the question of gender. In a study of emotional abuse of pupils by teachers in Zimbabwean primary schools, Shumba (2002) found that the majority of teachers and teaching assistants who shouted, scolded, humiliated or negatively labelled pupils were female. However, how this might relate, if at all, to emotional abuse of children by their parents is not at all clear.

Neglect

It is generally thought that mothers are mainly responsible for mistreating children in cases of neglect (Daniel and Taylor 2006). This is likely to be because of common assumptions about parenting roles, with child care largely seen as the responsibility of women and, therefore, when things go wrong, the fault is thought to lie with them. When faced with suspected or proven child neglect, professional practice is almost solely focused on mothers (Daniel and Taylor 2006). However, there is little direct separate research into the issues of gender and neglect. In 2008, Dufour et al. under-took an in-depth analysis of parents involved with neglect and found that children of single mothers do seem particularly vulnerable.

However, the limited nature of our knowledge as to the gender of the perpetrators of neglect should lead us to be cautious about making assumptions as to the respon-sibility for it, especially in situations where more than one carer is involved. Nevertheless, it can be concluded that for a variety of reasons, associated largely with male gender-biased assumptions, women are thought to be more implicated in the neglect of children than is in fact the case.

The age of those who abuse

Traditionally, physical abuse and neglect of children has been associated with young and immature parents (Greenland 1987). By contrast, Gil's sample of 1,380 cases of reported abuse in the USA in the late 1960s led him to state that the age distribution of parents did 'not support the observation of many earlier studies of physically abused children and their families, according to which the parents tend to be extremely young' (Gil 1970: 110).

A more recent study carried out in Northern Ireland investigated children subject to a child protection plan for a long period of time (over 23 months), with more than one child protection plan (i.e. sequentially registered, then de-registered, then registered again), or who suffered further significant harm while already subject to a child protection plan. This study (Devaney 2009) found that 21 per cent of the children's mothers had been aged 20 or under at the time of the child's birth and 9 per cent of fathers had also been aged 20 or under. This would indicate that a significant proportion of children subject to child protection plans in these circumstances were born to relatively young parents. However, the same study also considered the age of parents at the time of registration and found that the mean age of mothers was 31 and the mean age of fathers was 36. The study does not provide a breakdown of these figures and a mean average can provide a distorted result, depending on the distribution of ages in the sample (for example, a small number of much older parents would increase the mean disproportionately). Sidebotham and Heron (2006) found that neglected children tended to have younger parents than other children. However, the Devaney (2009) study did not support this. Instead, Devaney found that children made subject to child protection plans for sexual abuse and emotional abuse had the youngest mothers and fathers respectively at the time of the child's birth. At point of registration, children made subject to child protection plans for physical abuse and sexual abuse had the youngest mothers and fathers respectively. Devaney also found that teenage parents who had made use of family support were far less likely to experience these types of difficulties than other young parents. Thus the evidence about low parental age and abuse and neglect is not consistent enough to provide clear connections. It may be convenient to associate child abuse with young parenthood. However, the evidence is not nearly strong enough to have much predictive value, even in association with other factors considered indicative of risk.

Abuse by adolescents and children

Abuse of children by other children and adolescents has been the focus of much attention by researchers. This includes the abuse of children by siblings ('sibling abuse'). By some measures, sibling abuse is more prevalent than the abuse of children by adults (and indeed, more prevalent than the abuse of children and spousal abuse combined – Wiehe 1991). Just as worryingly, Hotaling et al. (1990) found that in abusive families of more than one child, 100 per cent of children in their study had committed at least one act of serious abuse against their sibling. More recently, Irfan and Cowburn (2004) found that among the British Pakistani community, 35 per cent of physically abusive acts were committed by siblings, as compared with 33 per cent by mothers and 19 per cent by fathers. Several studies demonstrate that brothers are more likely to abuse their sisters although sisters do also abuse their brothers (Graham-Bermann et al. 1994). Parents may also view aggression by their sons as more significant than similar acts of aggression by their daughters (Schwartz et al. 1997).

Research into the sexual abuse of children by other children paints a similar picture, in that over a third of child sexual abuse is thought to be committed by someone aged under 18 (i.e. another child – Stop It Now 2007). In the USA, Fehrenbach et al. (1986) found in their study of adolescent sex offenders that 95 per cent were male, 19 per cent had been sexually abused themselves, the bulk of their victims were known to them and one-third were relatives. Johnson (1989) carried out a study of 13 female child perpetrators, aged between 4 and 12. Her main findings were that, first, these girls had all been severely sexually abused over long periods of time and, second, most of their victims were members of their own families. Considering the differences between young people and children who sexually abuse younger children and those who abuse their peers, Gunby and Woodhams (2010) found that peer abusers were more likely to have witnessed family violence and had family members more likely to be associated with criminal activity. Young people and children who sexually abused younger children had greater deficits in self-esteem and social isolation and were also more likely to know the victim, to lack age-appropriate friends and to be the victims of peer abuse.

Peer abuse, or bullying, of children by other children outside the family is also a widespread phenomenon. Information about its extent is mixed and much depends on definition, reporting practices and recording. However, a survey of 4,000 children in the UK, aged between 5 and 16, indicated that 60 per cent of children reported having been bullied, with 38 per cent reporting that they had been bullied severely at least twice (Elliot 2002). Earlier research found that around 30 per cent of bullied pupils aged 10–14 did not report this to anyone (Smith and Shu 2000). Finally, Oliver and Candappa (2003) found that 51 per cent of Year 5 pupils in the UK (aged 9–10) reported being bullied. In an NSPCC study, 43 per cent of respondents said they had been physically bullied, discriminated against or made to feel like an outsider by other young people (Cawson et al. 2000).

Overall, we know more about young sex abusers than we do about young people who are physically aggressive, even though the latter probably far outnumber the former.

Poverty, ethnicity and child abuse

Neglect

Partly because of a traditional focus on individual and psychological factors in the understanding of child abuse, there has been less direct attention paid to the association between broader social factors, such as poverty and class, and child abuse. However, as we saw in Chapter 3, connections between social exclusion and child abuse are evident. In a very extensive longitudinal study of 3,835 children in the USA, Slack et al. (2011) found that indicators of poverty were linked to an increase in the likelihood of neglect, even when the indicator of poverty might be interpreted as a family asking for support (such as receiving financial support from family members). Slack et al. also found that the association between poverty and neglect was not significantly affected by parental stress, parental involvement with the child's activities (e.g. playing sports or games with the child), or the use of physical chastisement. This could indicate that interventions based on modifying these types of parenting concerns will not prove as successful as a more targeted, anti-poverty intervention. Slack notes that poor economic indicators should be used as a warning sign that the family is likely to be struggling in other areas as well.

Abuse

It is not just neglect that is associated with poverty. In the USA in 2010, the fourth National Incidence Study of Child Abuse and Neglect (NIS-4) (Sedlak et al. 2010) found that children living in low socio-economic households (those with household income below $15,000 per year, parents with low educational attainment or members of the household reliant on food stamps, subsidised school meals and so on) were more than three times as likely to be psychologically, physically or sexually abused as other children and more than seven times as likely to be neglected. In Britain, Cawson et al. (2000), in a large-scale survey, found that children from lower socio-economic backgrounds were more likely to report being physically or emotionally abused (and neglected) than other children.

Nevertheless, it has been argued that physical abuse and neglect of children is a cross-class phenomenon and that the high proportions of lower-class families being suspected of such abuse result from the fact that they are more open to state surveillance. This is because of their need for state resources, application for which is at the cost of reduced privacy and independence. From this point of view, the official figures merely demonstrate that the children of the poor who are being abused are more likely to be *spotted* than those in the higher social classes.

NIS-4 also found that, for the first time in the history of National Incidence Studies (previous studies having been produced in 1981, 1988 and 1996), there were race differences in the incidence of maltreatment, with higher rates reported for black children. These differences were found across a variety of measures, including overall maltreatment, overall abuse and overall neglect and physical abuse. The report notes the need for further analyses of whether these race differences remain once the effect of family circumstances is taken into account.

In the UK, data from serious case reviews (SCRs) indicates that while black or black British children made up 3 per cent of the under-16 population (Office for National Statistics 2001a), they accounted for 13 per cent of SCRs in 2003–5 and 8 per cent in 2005–7. Comparable figures for children of mixed ethnicity were 3 per cent (general population), 6 per cent (percentage of SCRs 2003–5) and 13 per cent (percentage of SCRs 2005–7); for Asian or Asian British children, the figures were 6 per cent, 6 per cent and 5 per cent and for children from other ethnic groups the figures were 1 per cent, 1 per cent and 2 per cent respectively. In England, in the year ending 31 March 2010, there were 39,100 children subject to a child protection plan, of which 5.6 per cent were black or black British, 8.2 per cent were of mixed ethnicity, 5.5 per cent were Asian or Asian British and 1.4 per cent were from other ethnic groups.

Several factors could account for this over-representation. Black and ethnic minority families are likely to be more open to state surveillance as a result of figuring highly among indices of deprivation.[3] Lack of cultural knowledge and awareness and the operation of both institutional and direct racism may increase the chances of suspicions of abuse in black families being confirmed. On the other hand, issues of cultural sensitivity and stereotyping have resulted in less vigorous pursuit of child protection concerns particularly in respect of Asian families (Webb et al. 2002).

Whatever the genuine situation with regard to physical abuse, most incidence studies of child sexual abuse point to its existence among all strata of society. Finkelhor et al. (1986) argue that class, ethnic and regional factors do not seem to affect the incidence of sexual abuse of children in the USA. In a national survey held in 1985, the only exceptions to this were boys of English or Scandinavian heritage, who were at higher risk than those from other ethnic groupings (Finkelhor et al. 1990). The NSPCC incidence study in the UK also found that sexual abuse was spread across social classes (Cawson et al. 2000).

However, most reported child sexual abuse is located disproportionately among poorer families. In the USA, the 2010 NIS-4 found that child sexual abuse rates were 0.7 children per 1,000 for children not in low socio-economic status families but 2.4 children per 1,000 for children in low socio-economic status families, a rate nearly 3.5 times as high (Sedlak et al. 2010). However, in comparison with earlier National Incidence Studies, this was a relatively low difference, with the 1996 study finding a rate 18 times as high for children from low socio-economic status families (Sedlak and Broadhurst 1996). The 2010 survey authors comment that in part this decline in the rate of difference is consistent with declines overall in sexual and physical abuse and they conclude that these declines are real, as they are supported by other sources of data (such as US Department of Health and Human Services 2007b). The bulk of families coming to the notice of the NSPCC in the UK as a result of child sexual abuse were also from the poorer classes (Creighton and Noyes 1989: 18–19).

The argument that high rates of physical abuse and neglect are found among poorer families simply because they are more exposed to state surveillance, could, it seems, be more justifiably applied in the case of child sexual abuse. Finkelhor is unequivocal about the implications of the disparity of findings between research studies and officially reported statistics, arguing that professionals need to be cautious about using inaccurate, class-biased stereotypes in their work and, in addition, that detecting and reporting abuse in higher social classes needs to be improved (Finkelhor 2008).

Parents who have been abused themselves

The issue of the inter-generational transmission of abuse is a thorny one indeed (Kaufman and Zigler 1989). Because of what we know about the impact of abuse on self-esteem, it seems reasonable to believe that parents who have been abused are likely to struggle to provide good enough parenting for their children. However, attention needs to be paid to the discontinuities as well as the continuities, and knowledge of the circumstances in which abused parents do *not* abuse their own children is of as much importance to child protection professionals as that of the circumstances in which they do. Yet there has been very little research addressing this issue.

Physical abuse and neglect

Oliver (1985), using official records, uncovered 147 families out of a population of 200,000 in north Wiltshire where abuse of children had happened in successive generations. However, the potential usefulness of this study, as with many others, is diminished by the fact that we are not told how many of the parents who were abused themselves in the first generation did *not* go on to abuse their own children. In other words, studying parents who have already abused their children tells us nothing about the proportion of parents who have been abused but do not go on to be abusive themselves.

A study by Hunter and Kilstrom (1979) neatly illustrates this. They interviewed 282 parents of new-born children admitted to a regional intensive care nursery for premature and ill infants. Of these parents, 49 (17 per cent) had themselves been abused. At follow-up a year later, 9 of these had abused their children. Only one child from the rest of the sample had been abused. Thus the inter-generational rate in this prospective study was 18 per cent. However, if the 10 children who were abused had become the subject of a *retrospective* study, it would have been found that 90 per cent of their parents had been abused and this could give an exaggerated impression of the extent of inter-generational abuse.

It is worth noting an issue raised earlier: that all these studies focus almost entirely on transmission of violence and abuse through mothers whereas, to the best of our knowledge, men are responsible for at least half of all physical abuse. There is very little research into the antecedents of male adults who physically abuse.

Sexual abuse

The picture is only slightly better in this respect with regard to sexual abuse. Despite the fact that males are responsible for nearly all such abuse and that girls are by far the most likely victims, there is still considerable focus on women as the key link between sexual abuse over two generations. Faller (1989) found that nearly half the mothers of a sample of 154 sexually abused children either had experienced or knew of sexual abuse in their own families of origin. This study is particularly useful in that it also checked the experiences of the male offenders in these cases; nearly 40 per cent of them had also experienced or knew of sexual abuse in their families as children.

Studies of male perpetrators of sexual abuse who have been imprisoned show relatively high proportions of these men having been sexually abused themselves as children. Simons et al. (2008) found that 73 per cent of their sample of convicted child sex abusers had themselves experienced sexual abuse in childhood. Yet in an earlier study, only 5 out of 274 perpetrators reported having been sexually abused themselves (Bentovim and Boston 1988). The differences may be explained by the fact that these studies were looking at two different types of sexual abuser: persistent offenders who are a danger to many children outside their families, and offenders who have targeted children within their own family. However, one should not assume that intra- and extra-familial sexual abuse are totally unconnected phenomena.[4]

It is also worth noting that although sexual and physical abuse have been considered separately, several of the studies point to sexual abusers having themselves experienced both forms of abuse in childhood, although Simons et al. (2008) found that adult sex abusers (rapists) were more likely to have experienced physical abuse in childhood than child sex abusers, and they were also more likely to have experienced emotional abuse and parental violence.

Emotional abuse

As with other areas, there is a paucity of research on the inter-generational transmission of emotional abuse. Various documents make an assumption that emotional abuse is transmitted in this way (such as Prevent Child Abuse America 2005) but there is limited empirical research either way. Given that emotional abuse is generally held to play a part in both physical and sexual abuse (a child abused in these ways is also being emotionally abused), then the discussion above would also apply, in some form, to the inter-generational transmission of emotional abuse.

The topic of inter-generational transmission of abuse of all types is clearly a problematic one. It has been argued that focusing on this issue is pessimistic so far as those who have been abused are concerned. That continuities exist is not in dispute but, as Straus pointed out in the late 1970s, there are more pertinent questions to be asked:

> The time has come for the intergenerational myth to be put aside and for researchers to cease arguing 'Do abused children become abusive parents?' and ask, instead, 'Under what conditions is the transmission of abuse likely to occur?'
> (Straus 1979: 191)

Family structure, child abuse and neglect

There is considerable debate about how child abuse is related to different family structures. Official statistics show that lone parenthood has increased dramatically since the 1960s, as has divorce (although recent figures also show that the rate of divorce in England and Wales is now dropping – Office for National Statistics 2009).[5] Two facets of family structure have been particularly considered by child abuse researchers: lone parenthood and step-parenting (particularly with regard to sexual abuse).

Lone-parent families

In the USA, the NIS-4 (Sedlak et al. 2010) states that 'Children living with two married biological parents had the lowest rate of overall . . . maltreatment, at 6.8 per 1,000 children' (pp. 5–19). The report goes on to say that 'Children living with one parent who had an unmarried partner . . . had the highest incidence of . . . [overall] maltreatment (57.2 per 1,000) [and] their rate is more than 8 times greater than for children living with two married biological parents'. The incidence of overall maltreatment for children living with just one parent (and no partner) was found to be 28.4 per 1,000. However, the overall figures mask some differences between the incidence of abuse and neglect.

The rate of abuse for children living with two married biological parents was found to be 2.9 children per 1,000, compared to 33.6 per 1,000 for children living with one parent and that parent's unmarried partner. The rate for children living with just one parent was 10.2 per 1,000. For neglect, the figures are reported in a slightly different way but do show that the rate for children living with two married biological parents was 4.2 per 1,000 and 19.6 per 1,000 for children living with just one parent.

However, in England and Wales, an analysis of SCRs (Brandon et al. 2008a) found that of the 161 published between April 2003 and March 2005, 73 per cent of the children were living with two biological parents at the time of the significant incidence of harm, compared with 13 per cent who were living with one biological parent and their partner and 20 per cent who were living with just their mother.

These results do not generally fit with earlier findings from research. For example, Sack et al. (1985) carried out a study of 802 adults in Oregon, USA, and found the prevalence of abuse to be twice as high in single-parent households as in those with two parents. Creighton and Noyes (1989) found somewhat surprisingly that one-fifth of children registered for sexual abuse came from lone-female headed homes.

Therefore, on the one hand, children in lone-parent families can appear as significantly more at risk of abuse and neglect than their counterparts in two-parent families, but there is some evidence, especially from recent official reports, that this is not necessarily so. Bald statistics also cannot tell us anything about the dynamics or processes that might help to account for variations in abuse rates between these two family types. Clearly economic stress is likely to be an important factor. The higher incidence of neglect cases among lone-parent families shown up in the NIS-4 (Sedlak et al. 2010) could support this, although rates of neglect for children living with two married biological parents were also found to be higher than rates of abuse for the same children.

With regard to sexual abuse, Finkelhor et al. (1986) argue that children in lone-female headed households could be exposed to a greater number of male adult figures than those in two-parent households and that this could place them at statistically greater risk of being sexually abused. This rather contributes to a somewhat negative picture of lone parenting. The advantages of such families should also be taken into account, such as the potential for less interpersonal conflict between parents, a factor that has been associated with emotional abuse. There is need for much more research into the impact of lone parenting (benefits and costs) on childrearing in general.

Step-parents and social fathers

The term 'social father' is a relatively new one and is used to describe a person (male) who has responsibility for caring for a child to whom they are not biologically related. Therefore, the category of social father is in some senses wider than just step-fathers (that is, fathers who have married the child's mother), and refers to any male figure with caring responsibility for a child to whom they are not genetically related.

The research evidence on the effect of a social father or a step-parent on a family is mixed. Starting with step-parents, the term 'Cinderella effect' has been used to describe the significantly increased incidence of children being abused by step-parents than by genetic parents (Daly and Wilson 2005a). A wealth of data has found links between step-parents and child abuse. It has also been found that in families in which the parent has both step-children and genetically related children, it is the step-children who are more likely to be abused (Crawford and Krebs 2008). Other studies have also shown that not only are step-children more likely to be abused, they are also more likely to experience neglect, especially in the form of lack of parental supervision. For example, based on information from Australia, step-children aged under 5 are more likely to experience unintentional injuries than genetic children. Comparing data from lone-parent families to two-parent families suggests that the absence of a biological parent does not increase the risk but adding a step-parent to a family does (Tooley et al. 2006).

Reconstituted families are thus well over-represented in these abuse statistics, but there has been little follow-up research as to why this is the case or into the process of abuse in such families. In any event, one hugely significant caveat needs to be borne in mind – there is a danger of assuming that all step-parents present a risk to children, and clearly this is not true. The majority of step-parents do not abuse or neglect their step-children.

However, there is other research, focused specifically on social fathers, which indicates that this group of male carers is likely to exhibit at least as good care as biological fathers and, in many cases, higher quality care. Social fathers who married the child's mother (in other words, step-fathers) appeared to engage more with the children in the family, take on more responsibility for their care and were more trusted by mothers than non-married social fathers (Berger et al. 2008). However, on closer analysis, much of this difference could be attributed to background individual or family characteristics although, significantly, not all of it.

There is clearly a need for more broad-based research into the impact of family structure on children in reconstituted families and, as with lone-parent families, there is need for attention to be paid to positive features and adaptations as well as to negative consequences.

Other significant factors associated with those who abuse or neglect children

This section looks at four other significant factors associated with child abuse and neglect: learning difficulties and the 'toxic trio' of mental health difficulties, substance misuse and domestic violence. Finally, research into the psychological make-up of child sexual abusers will be considered.

Abuse and neglect: parents with learning difficulties

In their studies of SCRs between 2001 and 2007, cited above with regard to parental mental health difficulties, Brandon et al. did not find any significant incidence of parental learning difficulties. However, parents with learning disabilities have, nevertheless, typically been viewed as posing an increased risk to children (Social Services Inspectorate 1999). In some studies, this view has been justified by the data. For example, Booth and Booth (1998) studied 30 adults who had been cared for by a parent with a learning difficulty and found that over half reported childhood physical or sexual abuse, although primarily the abuse was perpetrated not by their parent but by a partner of their parent. In other words, it appeared that parents with learning difficulties were more vulnerable to being targeted by perpetrators, rather then being perpetrators themselves. In general terms, while it is safe to assume – as with all groups of parents – that some parents with learning difficulties will abuse or neglect their children, few studies have actually assessed whether the risk for children is significantly greater than for any other group of parents. What is clear is that parents with learning difficulties are over-represented in terms of having children subject to child protection plans. Creighton and Noyes (1989) found that 10 per cent of mothers and 5 per cent of fathers of children listed on child protection registers (now replaced by child protection plans) had attended special schools, which points to a significant correlation between learning disability and officially reported child abuse.

There are, however, several factors that could account for this association, the most obvious being that the heightened concern that exists with regard to people with learning difficulties bringing up their own children results in their child care practices being exposed to greater scrutiny than those of parents without learning difficulties. Care should be taken not to see all people with learning difficulties as a homogeneous group with similar characteristics. They do share some common problems, but these stem mainly from their potential for being undervalued and exploited by others. Indeed, the government has issued advice on this issue, entitled *Good Practice Guidance on Working with Parents with a Learning Disability* (Department of Health/Department for Education and Skills 2007), which notes that parents with learning difficulties often face other difficulties as well, including mental or physical health difficulties, domestic violence and substance abuse.

Research that demonstrates the circumstances in which parents with learning difficulties abuse their children is more useful than research that simply demonstrates correlation rates between low intelligence and child abuse. Booth and Booth (1993) argue that disentangling fears about parents with learning difficulties from the reality of their parenting behaviours is highly problematic – they note that parents with learning difficulties should be seen 'not as a different kind of parent but as a more vulnerable one' (Booth and Booth 1993: 477). Certainly this is borne out by the experiences of such parents in court care proceedings in the USA and elsewhere where the rates of child removal are around 50 per cent (McConnell and Llewellyn 2000).

The 'toxic trio': mental health difficulties, substance misuse and domestic violence

In their most recent two studies of over 350 SCRs, held between 2005 and 2009, Brandon et al. (2009, 2010) identified what has been referred to as a 'toxic trio' of risk factors for child abuse, namely domestic violence, mental health difficulties and substance misuse. They also included a fourth factor: poverty or poor living conditions. The authors found that in nearly 75 per cent of cases from the 2009 study one or more of these factors was present. Therefore, it appeared to them that these factors, especially in combination, increase the risk to children. Before we consider the wider evidence base for this 'toxic trio', it is worth noting, as discussed above in the section on the lack of causal connections for child abuse and neglect, that Brandon et al. are not claiming that to detect and prevent child abuse we only need identify families where these factors are present. In their own words:

> The environment in which the child lives is crucial to his or her health, safety and well being. Living with adversity compromises the life opportunities of the child and of the child's parents. As in other studies of serious child abuse and child deaths, we found evidence of many parents and carers struggling with mental ill health, domestic violence, substance misuse and poverty, often in combination. Nearly three quarters of the children lived in an environment where one or more of these factors were present. We emphasised in our 2003–2005 study . . . that the presence of these characteristics, even when they co-exist, do [sic] not predict serious abuse or death of a child. They do, however, increase the risks of harm to

the child and often present a hazardous and frightening home life for the child and a toxic caregiving environment.

(Brandon et al. 2009: 45)

Mental health difficulties

In considering all of the SCRs held in England and Wales between 2005 and 2007, Brandon et al. (2009) found that of all the characteristics of parents involved, mental health difficulties was the second most frequently cited, only behind domestic violence. In a detailed study of 40 of these cases, the same authors found that nearly 75 per cent of the children lived with domestic violence and/or parental mental health difficulties, and/or parental substance misuse. These findings were very similar to those for SCRs held between 2003 and 2005, in which mental health difficulties (including personality disorders) were identified in over 50 per cent of the cases selected for more in-depth study (Brandon et al. 2008a). Looking further back to SCRs held between 2001 and 2003, a similar pattern was again identified, in that significant numbers of the children concerned were again found to be living with parents experiencing mental health difficulties. So (relatively) common is the occurrence of parental mental health difficulties in cases of serious child abuse and/or child deaths that it is perhaps hard to remember that the 'obviousness' of this link was not always recognised. Early child abuse pioneers such as Steele and Pollock (1974) were of the view that parents who abused their children had psychological incapacities to nurture and care for their babies and children because of their own emotionally poor upbringing (and not because of specific mental health difficulties). Kempe and Kempe (1978) argued that only a small number of abusive parents were thought to be experiencing mental illness, usually at the more serious end of the spectrum – they used the term 'psychotic' to describe these parents.

However, this was primarily the case because of a fairly strict definition of what constituted mental health difficulties. Studies that have taken a broader definition of mental illness have demonstrated a closer association with physical child abuse. For example, Oliver (1985) found that 50 out of 147 mothers (34 per cent) had been treated psychiatrically for depression, as had seven of the fathers (5 per cent). In a more recent study, Stith et al. (2009) conducted a meta-analysis of 155 studies into parental characteristics identified with child abuse and found that addressing the mental health needs of parents who abuse or neglect their children was likely to be important. However, as with other areas (such as step-parents), certain caveats must be borne in mind. As pointed out in the Social Care Institute for Excellence (SCIE) report *Think Child, Think Parent, Think Family: A Guide to Parental Mental Health and Child Welfare*, 'adult mental health problems are [not] the only serious risk for children's safety. The research evidence suggests that other factors (such as parental drug and alcohol misuse, domestic violence and/or learning disability) are often present in serious abuse or neglect situations [as well]' (Diggins 2009: 26).

It may be the case that there are some forms of psychological state, such as depression, the effects of which are underestimated as contributory factors to the abuse and neglect of children. Sheppard (2003) has demonstrated in a series of studies that between 36 and 46 per cent of mothers receiving child welfare services are clinically depressed (using the Beck Depression Inventory). Indeed, parental depression, as a specific mental health difficulty, has been studied quite widely and it has been shown that it is associated with emotional and behavioural difficulties for children (National Research Council and Institute of Medicine 2009). The literature on the negative effects of parental depression for children is relatively consistent (see Jaser et al. 2005; Burns et al. 2009). The female carers of children, such as Christine Mason (Lambeth, Lewisham and Southwark 1989), Beatrice Henry (Lambeth 1987) and Rosemary Koseda (Hillingdon 1986), have all been described as showing symptoms of depression.[6]

However, one of the key questions – and certainly the key question here – is how much does child abuse and neglect account for (or mediate) the negative effect of parental depression? Two main parenting styles have been found to be associated with parental depression: harsh parenting and disengaged parenting. Harsh parenting occurs when a parent is more negative towards their child, more likely to be irritated by them and/or to be verbally or physically aggressive towards the child (Lyons-Ruth et al. 2002). Disengaged parenting occurs when a parent is more likely to withdraw from their child, less likely to respond to emotional needs and less likely to engage in positive interactions with the child (Goodman and Brumley 1990). Although the research base for clear links with abusive or neglectful behaviour is less clear, harsh parenting behaviours associated with parental depression may, in certain circumstances, escalate to the threshold of physically abusive behaviour (Silverstein et al. 2009). Perhaps surprisingly, the link between parental depression and neglect is less clear than the link between parental depression and abuse (Knutson and Schartz 1997). A recent study, which sought to examine in more detail the mediation between parental depression and poor outcomes for children, actually found little evidence to support the view that physically abusive parental behaviour was a mediating variable, finding instead that neglectful parenting partially mediated the link (Mustillo et al. 2011).

In Britain, with the broadening of focus onto children in need in the last two decades, there has been an significant shift in thinking about the importance of adult mental health in the safeguarding of children. In 2003, SCIE released a protocol for partnership working for local agencies working with adults with mental health difficulties (and other issues), and agencies with specific child protection functions, noting that effective coordination between these two different types of agency was a key way of promoting the well-being of children by ensuring appropriate support was available for parents (Kearney et al. 2003). There is of course a danger that focusing on the role of depression in child abuse could serve to place even more emphasis on women as key carers. Nevertheless, both in relation to serious and fatal abuse of children and more general concerns about good-enough parenting, there is clearly a need to make much more use of the growing awareness and knowledge base about the links between mental health and child abuse and neglect (Stanley et al. 2003).

Substance misuse – alcohol

Alcohol has been closely linked with child abuse from the early days of the NSPCC at the time when the temperance movement had a high profile and it has long been cited as a contributory factor to physical child abuse (Browne and Saqi 1988). In a study of all SCRs between 2005 and 2007, Brandon et al. (2009) found that alcohol misuse was a feature in 19 cases, less than domestic violence (49), mental health problems (32) and drug misuse (28) but more than the parent being a teenager (18), the parent being formally in care (5) or the parent currently being in care (4).

However, contrary to this and to common perceptions, research findings linking alcohol misuse with child abuse or neglect are inconsistent. There is a much stronger relationship between adult alcohol abuse and a childhood history of abuse – i.e. adults abused as children have a higher likelihood of misuing alcohol (Widom and Hiller-Sturmhofel 2001). A history of abuse in childhood has also been found to be a signif-icant risk factor for adolescent binge drinking (defined as five or more drinks in a row, at least two to three times a month – Shin et al. 2009).

Alcohol misuse does have a higher association with child neglect. Studies in the USA point to as many as half of all families known to the public welfare system being affected by alcohol or drug misuse (see Curtis and McCullough 1993). However, as we have seen, there are major difficulties involved in defining neglect, and the term 'alcohol problems' is also open to widely varied interpretation.

As we develop broader concerns about the care and development of children beyond abuse, the issue of alcohol misuse and its effect on children also grows in importance. Research shows that a million children could be living with parents with problematic drinking habits in Britain and that such children have higher levels of behavioural problems, school problems, emotional disturbances, lower self-esteem, anxiety and depression, and disrupted routines. They are likely to experience more disrupted routines, less supervision, more financial problems and witness more domestic violence (Kroll and Taylor 2003). Pregnant women who misuse alcohol can cause problems for the foetus; foetal alcohol syndrome (FAS) is the leading known environmental cause of learning disability in the western world (National Institute of Alcohol Abuse and Alcoholism 1993).

While there are no causal links between alcohol abuse and all these problems, the fact that they are so prominently correlated means that awareness of alcohol misuse in families is acting more and more as a warning signal about children being at risk of neglect.

Substance misuse – drugs

As noted above, in SCRs, parental drug misuse is a common feature. That this is so is not a new phenomenon; in 1995, Dore et al. pointed to very high rates of drug misuse among substantiated child mistreatment cases in the USA. As with alcohol, it is not clear from these figures whether drug misuse is associated more with physical abuse or with neglect. It is probably the latter. However, research also suggests that drug misuse (and alcohol misuse) features in the majority of cases of emotional abuse as well (Bijur et al. 1992).

As with alcohol, there are concerns about the impact of drug misuse on the foetus. However, research into this topic is inconclusive in that it is not easy to separate the impact of drugs from other frequently associated factors such as poor nutrition and lack of proper antenatal care (Keen and Alison 2001). Again, most of the concerns centre around the issue of neglect. There is little research directly linking problem drug use with physical or sexual abuse. The key concerns are supervision, the impact of drug-seeking lifestyles and the longer-term psychological impact on the child

(Kroll 2004). In broad terms, the research suggests that children of substance-misusing parents are likely to suffer deficits in their development which has clear implications for preventive and supportive programmes.

Domestic violence

Domestic violence typically involves patterns of physical, sexual or emotional abuse and can be understood as the misuse and exercise of power and control by one partner over another. As noted previously, the definition of harm derived from the 1989 Children Act now includes 'impairment suffered from seeing or hearing the ill-treatment of another' (as amended by the 2002 Adoption and Children Act). Children living with domestic violence are over-represented among those referred to children's services and domestic violence is a factor in up to two-thirds of cases discussed at child protection conferences (Humphreys 2006). Domestic violence can also affect unborn children: Gazmararian et al. (2000) estimated that 324,000 pregnant women are battered by their male partners each year, leading to, in some instances, subsequent birth problems and depression in mothers.

In Britain, research has indicated that between 30 and 66 per cent of children living with domestic violence experience direct abuse (Humphreys 2006). Children and adolescents exposed to domestic violence can present with a range of difficulties; childhood trauma symptoms have been linked to such exposure, as has the presence of externalising behaviour problems, especially in boys (Evans et al. 2008).

However, as with much of the other research referred to in this chapter, there is a pressing need for studies that go beyond correlations and explore in greater depth the dynamics of the family processes where child abuse and partner abuse coexist, so that child protection intervention in these circumstances can be better informed (Coohey and Braun 1997).[7]

Sexual abuse

There has been little linkage between particular psychological characteristics and child sexual abuse, and much more emphasis on interactive rather than individualistic factors than in the case of physical abuse and neglect. There has been no research linking mental illness with sexual abuse. Traditionally, incest has been linked to families of low intelligence, but there is little research evidence to show this to be the case.

In 2008, Whitaker et al. undertook a meta-analysis of 89 studies, published between 1990 and 2003, examining risk factors for the perpetration of child sex abuse. They compared the characteristics of sex offenders against children, sex offenders against adults, non-sex offenders and non-offenders. They found that while sex offenders against children were different from non-sex offenders and non-offenders, with regard to categories such as family factors, externalising behaviours, sexual problems and attitudes and beliefs, they were not significantly different from sex offenders against adults. As noted by the study's authors, this strongly suggests that the presence of general risk factors can lead to a variety of extremely negative behavioural outcomes, including sex offences against children, but does not support the view that there are qualitative differences between offenders against children and offenders against adults, despite perhaps fairly strongly held and common views to the contrary.

Who is abused?

All children are potentially vulnerable to abuse by those adults who look after them through childhood because they are dependent on them for all aspects of physical and emotional protection and care. Most children are not mistreated by their parents because protective behaviour is considered natural and instinctive (Bowlby 1971). Finkelhor and Korbin (1988), writing from an international perspective but with an eye to poorer countries, point out that children are most vulnerable to abuse and neglect if they are:

- less healthy than others
- disabled (although in a few societies, disabled children are protected by being accorded a special status)
- female
- born in unusual, stigmatised or difficult conditions
- unwanted
- born with 'dis-valued' traits and behaviours
- considered to be 'illegitimate' in some way
- born in situations of rapid economic change.

While such children are less obviously at risk in richer societies, they are still more vulnerable to abuse and neglect than those who do not share these characteristics. Many of the factors listed above have been considered in the first section of this chapter. The factors that remain to briefly be discussed are: age, gender, factors inherent to the child and disability.

Age

Using Department for Education statistics for 2010, the age breakdown of children subject to child protection plans is set out in Table 5.1. The unborn category of children includes those about to be born to parents who have already seriously abused siblings and, increasingly, those due to be born to parents involved in substance misuse or domestic violence. Concerns about children under 1 are largely in relation to physical abuse and neglect. Children in this age group are more likely to be made subject to child protection plans for these reasons than those in older age groups, reflecting the concerns created by their particular vulnerability. Around 80 per cent of children that die from abuse in the USA are under the age of 4 (US Department of Health and Human Services 2010a). However, the most recent National Incidence Study in the USA (Sedlak et al. 2010) found that the youngest children (aged 0–2) experienced the most severe type of maltreatment ('harm standard') at a much lower

Table 5.1 The age of children subject to child protection plans during the year ending 31 March 2010 (figures do not add due to rounding)

Age	No.	%
Unborn	660	1.7
Under 1	4,400	11.3
1–4	12,300	31.5
5–9	10,900	27.9
10–15	10,000	25.6
16+	780	2
Total	**39,100**	**100**

rate than children aged 6 or older (8.5 per 1,000 compared with 17.6 per 1,000 or higher).

The age group most likely to be made subject to child protection plans in the UK for sexual abuse are those between 10 and 15. However, one must be careful in using these figures not to assume that certain forms of abuse are confined to certain age ranges. For example, Boyer and Fine (1992) found that 24 per cent of female child sexual abuse survivors were first abused at age 5 or younger. Finkelhor (1993) also notes that children under 6 constitute at least 10 per cent of child sexual abuse victims in the USA. The case of Stephen Menheniott (Department of Health and Social Security 1978) provides a salutary reminder that physical abuse of young people can persist into adulthood.[8]

Gender

The gender breakdown for children subject to child protection plans on 31 March 2010 is set out in Table 5.2. Boys are slightly more likely than girls to be registered for child abuse. They are more exposed to physical abuse, neglect and emotional abuse than girls, as far as official intervention is concerned. There seem to be no obvious reasons that this is so. It could be speculated that, in the case of physical abuse, physical punishment of boys is more generally sanctioned as a means of control in our society than of girls and that this cultural norm leads to more excessive violence in their case. It has generally been thought to be the case that the sexual abuse of boys is less likely to be officially reported than that of girls.

It was noted in Chapter 4 that in many of the poorer societies throughout the world (southern India, for example) girls are more subjected to abuse because they are less valued for their economic utility. Clearly these economic factors do not apply in our society.

Factors inherent to the child

Difficult though it may be to contemplate, there are certain factors that make some children more likely to be the victim of child abuse than others. In other words, aside from

Table 5.2 The gender of children subject to child protection plans during the year ending 31 March 2010 (figures do not add due to rounding)

Gender	No.	%
Boys	19,800	50.6
Girls	18,600	47.6
Unborn	660	1.7
Total	**39,100**	**100**

the factors related to parents and to the environment, many of which we have discussed above, there are certain inherent characteristics that make some children more at risk. Infants and children who persistently cry are more at risk of physical abuse (being shaken). Disabled children are more likely to be abused or neglected but we will consider this group separately below. Children with more difficult temperaments, children with aggressive behaviour, attention deficits and other behaviour problems are also more likely to be abused. On the other hand, children with robust and high self-esteem, higher intelligence, creativity, humour and independence have a level of resilience against any abuse and this also makes abuse less likely to occur (Masten et al. 1990; Benard 1995).

Behaviourists and family therapists are interested in the dynamics of child abuse and why certain children are 'selected' for such abuse and not others. Children who are not wanted or who are considered to be the wrong sex by their parents are seen to be at greater risk (Roberts et al. 1980). The dynamics of the situation are seen by Belsky and Vondra (1989) to be important factors here:

> The undermining effect of a difficult child on parental functioning will be lessened when the parent has an abundance of personal psychological resources. Conversely, an easy-to-rear child can compensate for limited personal resources on the part of the parent in maintaining parental effectiveness.
>
> (Belsky and Vondra 1989: 188)

Turning to extra-familial sexual abuse, including that which takes place in institutions, the following comments from Finkelhor seem pertinent:

> First, a child is more vulnerable to abuse if the child's activities and contacts are inadequately supervised and monitored. Secondly, a child who is emotionally neglected or physically or psychologically abused is also more vulnerable to the ploys of child molesters who offer attention and affection, or even intimidation, to involve children in sexual contacts.
>
> (Finkelhor 1993: 69)

Disabled children

One of the key problems with research into disability and child abuse lies with the problem of consistent definition of the two concepts. Nevertheless, sufficient evidence has been generated over the last decade or so to conclude that disabled children are disproportionately at risk of child abuse and neglect of all kinds. In the USA, where it is estimated that 8 per cent of children have disabilities, official reports of abuse show considerable differences between the extent of abuse of disabled and non-disabled children. Kendall-Tackett et al. (2005) show that across the USA in the late 1980s the rate per 1,000 for all kinds of abuse of disabled children was 35.5 compared with 21.3 for the non-disabled population. Sullivan and Knutson (2000a) studied 40,000 children in an American city and found that disabled children were 3.4 times more likely to be abused or neglected than non-disabled children; 31 per cent of disabled children in their sample had been abused or neglected.

In Britain, there are few large-scale studies of this kind to give a clear picture of abuse and neglect of disabled children (Miller 2002). It is estimated that 3 per cent of children have disabilities (Department of Health 2000c) but make up around 10 per cent of the looked-after population. Among the reasons for this are a combination of complexity of need and a lack of local support services, along with abuse or neglect. Children who are disabled and living away from home are seen to be particularly at risk. Gordon et al. (2000) found that disabled children are more likely to be in residential care than are non-disabled children and Utting (1997) found some time ago that children in residential care are extremely vulnerable to abuse of all kinds.

There is clearly much that needs to be done in terms of researching the extent of such abuse and the reporting of it. Equally important is the need for a whole range of better supportive facilities for families with children with disabilities, particularly in relation to those at the lower end of the socio-economic scale. This does seem to have been recognised now by two successive governments (Labour, 1997–2010; Conservative-Liberal Democrat coalition, 2010–present), both of which have provided extra funds for better local support for disabled children.

Concluding comments

The research studies considered in this chapter have all sought to answer questions about the perpetrators of abuse and who is abused. As we have seen, there are weaknesses and biases in most of the research studies that pose questions about their usefulness for practice. The main weaknesses of these studies have been repeatedly stressed. They are, first, that they have focused too much on general correlations and not enough on particular details. We know, for example, that children living in reconstituted families are overall more at risk than those living with both natural parents. Yet we know little about the degree of risk, what factors exacerbate the risk or in what conditions reconstituted families do a good job of rearing children. These sorts of criticism apply to almost all of the factors that have been associated in the research studies with child abuse and neglect. The reasons for this weakness lie in the mislaid emphasis on predicting and targeting the problem, the constant need to note the difference between correlation and causation and the need to consider the hows and whys of child abuse. Second, many of the studies demonstrate gender blindness and slip into the easy assumption that the mother is the key figure in the child abuse process. Again, such a view does not do justice to the hows and whys of child abuse.

This does not completely invalidate the work that has been done, but stresses that it needs to be used in a careful and critical manner. If used in this way, such research can sensitise professionals to risk potential, but so far it provides a basic starting-point only.

One overriding factor that pervades much of the research and many of the findings is the impact of poverty, stress and deprivation. Except in the case of sexual abuse, which is commonly agreed to be more broadly spread across classes, almost all studies of abuse and neglect point to one or more of these factors being significant. It has been argued that known cases are likely to be found disproportionately in poorer families because of the nature of state surveillance. While this may be so to some extent, the evidence from incidence and prevalence studies on abuse and neglect (apart from sexual abuse) suggests that maltreatment of children is closely linked to socio-economic background and the strains and deprivations that are associated with this for many people.

Recommended reading

Howe, D. (2005) *Child Abuse and Neglect: Attachment, Development and Intervention.* Basingstoke: Palgrave Macmillan.

Humphreys, C. and Stanley, N. (2006) *Domestic Violence and Child Protection: Directions for Good Practice.* London: Jessica Kingsley Publications

Pritchard, C. (2004) *The Child Abusers: Research and Controversy.* Maidenhead: Open University Press.

6

The causation of child abuse

Introduction

Health and welfare professionals involved in the field of child abuse have arguably paid less attention to why such abuse happens than they have to the type of person who abuses and the type of child who is most vulnerable to abuse. This is probably because the latter two questions seem to have a more direct impact on prediction and prevention (if we can identify those most likely to be at risk, then we can do something about it). Also, the question of why child abuse happens is not considered so directly significant to the day-to-day practicalities of child protection work. Such an inquiry has traditionally been seen to be more the province of theorists than of practitioners. This state of affairs is understandable given the increased volume of child protection work and the pressures on practitioners not to make mistakes. However, endeavouring to understand why the abuse of children takes place serves three main functions: it gives a greater sense of control to the worker over events that may otherwise seem inexplicable; it gives a sense of direction for intervention and treatment; and it informs those responsible for policy-making in this field. For these reasons, understanding why abuse has happened has a very important contribution to make to child protection work.

There is another reason, however, why studying the causes of child abuse – and as will become evident in the next chapter, the consequences of child abuse – is problematic, and this centres, as we have seen, upon the well-documented problem concerning the precise nature of causality generally (for example, Pearl 2009). The ever-present problem of causation is, to some extent, tackled in contemporary research by newer methodologies such as meta-analysis, structural equation modelling and path analysis, allowing the more precise isolation of mediating variables which was only possible in the past by rigorous experimental design (but which is often impracticable or unethical in the field of child maltreatment).

An example of this kind of approach is evident in a large sample study (n = 4,351) by Dixon et al. (2005). The researchers explored the 'mediational properties of parenting styles and their relation to risk factors in the intergenerational cycle of child maltreatment' (p. 58). They found that:

> Mediational analysis found that intergenerational continuity of child maltreatment was explained to a larger extent (62% of the total effect) by the presence of poor parenting styles together with the three significant risk factors (parenting under 21 years, history of mental illness or depression, residing with a violent adult). The three risk factors ... were less explanatory (53% of the total effect) ... Hence, prevention may be enhanced in [such] families by the promotion of 'positive parenting' in addition to providing additional support to young parents, tackling mental illness/depression and domestic violence problems.
>
> (Dixon et al. 2005: 58)

A broad range of theoretical perspectives has been brought to bear on the aetiology of child abuse. They derive from diverse sources, survey the problem at different levels and, as a consequence, do not necessarily complement each other. Indeed there is a good deal of conflict and disagreement between adherents of different approaches. On the other hand, there are those whose theoretical focus has been on the development of integrative approaches to understanding why child abuse happens (Garbarino 1977; Jack 2000; Belsky and Jaffee 2006), and there is some evidence of the adoption of this type of thinking in the *Framework for the Assessment of Children in Need and Their Families* which was introduced in April 2001 in England (Department of Health 2000a). Although we have seen that *The Munro Review of Child Protection* in the UK (Munro 2011a) promoted a rethink about the timing of an assessment of need during the early stages of an inquiry, arguing that, initially, the assessment of risk in the context of family strengths and gaps is paramount, it nevertheless recognises the importance of a more comprehensive understanding of the family's circumstances and the child's developmental needs later on.

One potential drawback of the integrative approach is that, although it provides a richer explanatory account of the problem of child abuse, it is inevitably more complex and practitioners can find this harder to apply than single-cause accounts. Overall, however, particularly given the contested nature of a good deal of child protection work (see Chapters 3 and 4), the fact that multi-dimensional theories of child abuse causation may lead to questioning of certainty and the need for greater caution in practice may be no bad thing.

There are three main groups of broad theoretical perspective:

1   Psychological theories: those that focus on the instinctive and psychological qualities of individuals who abuse.
2   Social psychological theories: those that focus on the dynamics of the interaction between abuser, child and immediate environment.
3   Sociological perspectives: those that emphasise social and political conditions as the most important reason for the existence of child abuse.

This categorisation will be used as the structure for this chapter. In addition, consideration will be given to attempts to combine these perspectives to provide a more holistic picture.

Psychological theories

In this section consideration will be given to the contributions of the disciplines of biology, attachment theory, psychodynamic theory, learning theory and cognitive approaches.

Biology and child abuse

Biological explanations were not applied directly to the understanding of child abuse until the late 1980s although it did underpin some key theories such as that of attachment and psychodynamics. It now finds its latest application in approaches which link evolutionary psychology, neuroscience, biochemistry and genetics to our understanding of child abuse and neglect.

In the 1970s and 1980s the discipline of sociobiology emerged which aimed to reinstate the role of nature in the explanation of social behaviour.[1] Sociobiologists applied Darwinian theories, such as that of natural selection and the survival of the fittest, to a range of human behaviours, of which child abuse was one. Reite (1987) put forward the view that there are many factors common to human child care and neglect and that of animals: 'Human and non-human primates share a substantial common evolutionary history, and many of the behavioral systems we are talking about, including perhaps much of that underlying social attachment, are likely biologically determined to a significant degree' (Reite 1987: 354). He points out that animals abuse their young in circumstances where there are aberrations or disturbances in early mother-infant attachment, and where environmental stresses such as overcrowding or lack of social support prevail. In similar vein, other writers have drawn comparisons between certain types of child abuse and what is termed 'the culling process' among animals, whereby the weakest in the litter are neglected in times of food shortage (Barash 1981).

Sociobiologists have in a very general way applied these principles to the question of step-parenting, substitute parenting and child abuse. Some non-genetic parents in the animal world have been noted to be very cruel to infants. Hrdy (1977, 2009) found that in one species of monkey, males seeking to mate with females already with litters, but with no male protectors, killed the young. The explanation for this behaviour, according to sociobiological theory, is simply that, as these monkeys have no investment in the genes of these infants, the sooner they are out of the way the more quickly they (the male adults) can produce offspring of their own. On the other hand, sociobiologists point to examples of altruism where infant birds and animals are nurtured and protected by non-relatives. Such behaviour is attributed to a species survival instinct and, it is argued, takes place only where there are benefits for the giver (Barash 1981: 132–69). In a more recent study, Maestripieri et al. (1997) found evidence of inter-generational transmission of physical abuse of infant macaque monkeys in a longitudinal study covering 30 years.

The views of Krugman (1998) show how far thinking moved on in the 1990s in relation to genetics and child abuse. He described an experiment carried out in the USA comparing the nurturing behaviours of two mice, one of which had been deprived of a single gene:

> One mother mouse is in a cage with her newborn pups nursing avidly in a nest she made in the corner of the cage. The other mother is sitting (she even looks depressed) in the corner of her cage. There is no nest and all of her pups are dead at 24 hours of age.
>
> (Krugman 1998: 477)

Krugman asserted that these sorts of studies should be further explored:

> Some of us who've spent most of our time worrying about global issues find it pretty difficult to focus on single genes, but I would suggest that if we're going to get anywhere in this field, we need to start bringing neuroscientists, geneticists and others together with us, to just sit down and talk.
>
> (Krugman 1998: 478)

Talk of a 'child abuse gene' seems somewhat far-fetched, but research into the impact of sensory deprivation on the growth and development of the brains of young children does provide food for thought. 'Feral' children, i.e. children who have been abandoned or severely neglected, and either partially or wholly reared by animals, have been shown to have suffered irreparable brain damage, affecting their capacities to communicate and relate emotionally to humans later on. While these are very rare and extreme cases, they have led to greater concern about the impact of serious neglect and institutionalisation on the capacity of children psychologically and emotionally to overcome early deprivation (Glaser 2000; Schore 2000, 2001; Perry 2002). With the use of technology, including functional magnetic resonance imaging (fMRI), electro-encephalography (EEG) and positron emission tomography (PET) scans, we can now see these processes in operation. For example, EEG maps comparing maltreated and non-maltreated children shown photos of angry, happy and neutral faces demonstrate that maltreated children process the images in a different part of the brain – behind the eyes – compared with non-maltreated children (McCrory et al. 2010). This means that they tend to think 'What have *I* done to make him so cross?' when looking at the 'angry face'. The non-maltreated child thinks 'What's made *him* angry?' because they make sense of the image using brain circuits in the centre of the brain, allowing the image to be processed in a more balanced and measured way.

Similarly, genetic research is beginning to indicate that certain genes, especially (i) the DRD4 7-repeat polymorphism – a dopamine neurotransmitter responsible for how we deal with reward and pleasure – (ii) the MAO-A, so-called 'aggression' gene and (iii) the 5HTT 'depression' gene, all play a part in explaining some of the variation in the causes and consequences of abuse and neglect. But there is clearly a long way to go before any single genetic rationale to explain child maltreatment will be forthcoming, if ever; and current indications are that 'gene × environment' interactions and the notion of 'differential susceptibility' (Belsky et al. 2007) – that the interaction of genes and environment operate differently within different people under different circumstances – are likely to offer the most convincing explanations

Initially, much of the theorising of sociobiologists appeared to be reductionist, even overstated, but today neurological, biochemical and genetic research is beginning to be accepted by researchers across all disciplines. Although this brand of child abuse research has its critics it does remind us of the part that genetic capacity and instinct can play in certain behaviours and it is a variable not to be overlooked. Unthinking and indiscriminate use of such theory could, however, fuel prejudice and lead to over-reliance on instinct as a tool for understanding the way in which people behave. We will return to neurobiological, biochemical and genetic research in the next chapter when we look at the consequences of abuse.

Attachment theory and child abuse

The main theoretical tenets of attachment theory are derived from the work of one person, John Bowlby. In the period immediately after the Second World War, he carried out studies into the nature and effects of 'maternal' deprivation on young children (Bowlby 1951). Although attachment researchers would now use terms such as 'parental' or 'caregiver' instead of 'maternal', Bowlby initially hypothesised that any significant separation of a child from the mother in the first five years of life could have deleterious effects on its emotional development and could lead to a variety of psychological and social difficulties in later life, such as the development of an affectionless personality. Originally, the reasoning for this process was derived from psychodynamic theory; that is, that the child developed a psychologically healthy sense of self through consistently rewarding emotional contact with the mother. As his work developed, Bowlby drew more and more from the biological sciences and ethology, thus placing more emphasis on the physical aspects of carer-to-child bonding and child-to-carer attachment. In the final analysis he argued that a child securely attached to the mother gains the dual benefit of physical protection and psychological security.

While retaining many of Bowlby's initial insights, contemporary attachment theory is today supported by burgeoning neurological, biochemical and genetic research. It is described by Shemmings and Shemmings (2011) as:

> [a] behavioural system . . . responsible for regulating the infant's propensity to monitor physically and psychologically the accessibility of the attachment figure. Bowlby concluded that from a very early stage the attachment system acts initially to protect the child from harm, threat and, in particular, fear and danger, but later provides a 'secure base' from which the child can explore the environment . . . Attachment behaviours intended to increase proximity – such as crying, gazing and calling – are unconsciously selected if the child cannot reach their attachment figure, depending not just on the *physical* distance from the attachment figure but also their perceived *emotional availability*: the fact that a parent is nearby physically does not assuage attachment needs unless s/he is emotionally present. Perceived emotional closeness also determines how much hugging, clinging and smiling is required to ensure the caregiver stays near. When attachment is de-activated, it is replaced by exploration, feeding etc.
>
> (Shemmings and Shemmings 2011: 18)

Bowlby's early theorising was criticised by Rutter (1978) for not taking into account that the child could become attached to other significant figures as well as the mother: Hrdy's concept of the 'allo-parent' (Hrdy 2009). According to Rutter's argument the consistency and positive nature of the relationship were more important. Thus the roles of the father and other relatives in the emotional development of the child needed to be given more consideration. This is now seen as a 'given' in modern attachment theory.

Feminists initially criticised attachment theory on the grounds that it had limiting and restrictive implications for women, because of its prescription that mothers should be in close proximity to their children for the whole of their infancy. Most attachment theorists now agree that children at around the age of 3 can cope with separation because they can, by use of language and reasoning, understand and accept explanations of what is happening.

Until the late 1980s, attachment theory was not directly applied to the problem of child abuse, although it has had a major influence on general child care policy and practice. Crittenden and Ainsworth (1989) argued that repeated consistent and rewarding interactions between a caregiver and child lead to high self-esteem and the capacity to trust. Conversely, non-responsive, rejecting and inconsistent responses lead to anxiety, insecurity, a lack of self-worth and a restricted ability to relate to others. This problematic interaction is considered to lessen the child's chances of making satisfying peer relationships later on in life because a sense of self and trust of others, which are essential to this process, do not exist. The pattern may then be repeated with the child's own children, thus providing some explanation of how abuse is transmitted from one generation to the next (Bakermans-Kranenburg and Van IJzendoorn 1997; Morton and Browne 1998). This process is not considered inevitable because the effects of poor early attachment experiences are thought to be remediable by attachment to a surrogate figure or by successful counselling.

However, because over 40 per cent of the world's population is likely to show an insecure-avoidant or insecure-ambivalent attachment in close relationships, contemporary attachment research instead now stresses the role of *unresolved loss and trauma* (see Madigan et al. 2006), *very insensitive and disconnected caregiving* (see Lyons-Ruth and Jacobvitz 2008; Out et al. 2009) and *low mentalisation capacity* (the inability to appreciate that others have different thoughts, feelings hopes and intentions from one's own (see Fonagy and Target 2005; Allen et al. 2008) because they are more likely to lead to disorganised attachment behaviour, which is both an indicator and a consequence of child abuse and neglect (Crittenden 2008; Slade 2008; Shemmings and Shemmings 2011). Disorganised attachment occurs frequently in intra-familial abuse situations because the child cannot rely on the caregiver for support due to the fact that they are, at one and the same time, the source of danger. When a child's safe haven is simultaneously the source of fear and foreboding they experience what Mary Main called 'fear without solution' (Main and Solomon 1990). As we will see in the next chapter the consequences of prolonged attachment disorganisation can be profound in the short, medium and long term.

What are the strengths and gaps in this theoretical approach? The strengths lie in its convincing and detailed explanation of the process whereby abuse and neglect potential can be derived from particular dynamics within adult-child relationships (Howe 2005; Cassidy and Shaver 2008; Crittenden 2008; Shemmings and Shemmings 2011). Initially the gaps were, firstly, its inability to account more fully for the fact that the majority of parents who have been abused themselves do *not* go on to abuse their own children and, second, the fact that insufficient account is taken of the total dynamics of the family. Nowadays, these gaps have largely been filled and certainly the focus is no longer exclusively on the mother-child – or even caregiver-child – pairing. The challenge for attachment theory in the coming years will be to explain the interactions between genes and the immediate caregiving environment, as well as the connection between social factors such as poverty and unemployment, and attachment and the combined effect upon child abuse and neglect.

Psychodynamic theory, physical child abuse and neglect

Freud's work forms the kernel of psychodynamic thought, but it has been subjected to considerable variation by his followers. There are several good overviews of Freudian theory.[2] The key arguments of this perspective are that human beings mentally adapt their instinctive drives to the demands and requirements of their social circumstances. In the process of so doing, they develop personality traits that persist throughout life and influence their relationships with others. Freud's belief was that the dominant human instinctual drive was libidinal, or sexual. He also theorised that very young children had such sexual drives and he devised an elaborate explanation of how these were moulded into pro-social behaviours and internalised to shape an individual's character.

Summarised very briefly, Freud postulated that in the first five years of life infants go through three psychosexual stages: the oral, the anal and the genital. These stages of development are linked to sources of physical pleasure – the oral stage to feeding, the anal stage to elimination and the genital stage to sexual stimulation. For Freud, socialisation meant the suppression of these pleasures in order to function as a responsible person in society. Parents carry out this socialising task. As a result, childhood sexuality goes through a latency stage only to reassert itself in adolescence, by which time individuals are considered to be more able to manage their libido for themselves. As a result of this process, the psyche of each individual is made up of the id (libidinal drive), the superego (the conscience or voice of the parent, which represses the id) and the ego (the integrating element which balances the id and superego and forms the visible or social aspect of the personality). The personality is also made up of different levels of consciousness as a result of this socialising process – the conscious (that part of the mind used in everyday life), the preconscious (that part of the mind from which past material could be summoned with prompting) and the unconscious (that part of the mind to which libidinal drives and urges have been exiled; these are normally unavailable to consciousness).

How does this relate to child abuse? With regard to physical abuse, Freudian or psychodynamic theory has arguably been the most dominant explanatory model since its rediscovery in the early 1960s (see, for example, Letourneau 1981; Halston and Richards 1982). It saw a decline during the 1990s but has since seen a resurgence as a result of a series of texts which now broadly speaking can be subsumed under the soubriquet 'relationship-based social work' (see McCluskey 2005; Ruch et al. 2010).

In terms of Freudian psychodynamics, from the very early stages the children of abusing parents are not responded to in a way that helps them to progress through all the necessary psychosexual stages. They are frustrated by lack of adequate response almost from the first contact and, therefore, are unlikely to develop the sort of integrated personality that enables them to relate responsively to others:

> Stimulation of the aggressive drive with its accompanying anger toward the frustrating caretaker, coupled with the parallel development of strict superego rudiments, inevitably leads to a strong sense of guilt. This guilt, largely unconscious, predominantly in relation to the mother, persists throughout the patient's life and leads to turning much of the aggression inward towards the self. When the parent misidentifies the infant as the embodiment of his own bad self, the full aggression of his punitive superego can be directed outward toward the child.
>
> (Steele and Pollock 1974: 122)

Thus, put simply, child abuse is seen to be the result of excessive superego demands. The carer's psychological make-up is the key. Psychological treatment, focusing on improving his or her ability to relate to other people, is seen to be the solution to the problem. Such treatment is to be achieved by insight development (through a psychotherapist) and by the effects of a rewarding relationship with a practitioner over a period of time.

The strengths of this approach, as with attachment theory, are that it can help professionals to understand the intra-personal and inter-personal dynamics of child abuse and point to intervention aims and strategies (Searing 2003). It is still hard for many in the child protection field to comprehend and tolerate violence to children; the psychodynamic approach provides a tool for this purpose. The weaknesses lie in the very heavy focus placed on the individual without sufficient consideration of the circumstances in which they are operating and in the lack of attention to social and environmental factors.[3]

Psychodynamic theory and child sexual abuse

With regard to the sexual abuse of children, psychodynamic thought has rather a mixed history. According to Jeffrey Masson (1984), before Freud developed the psychosexual personality theories outlined above he hypothesised that 'hysteria' in women may have been caused by them having been sexually abused as children. This hypothesis, according to Masson, was based on disclosures to him by women whom he was treating. He relayed his ideas to fellow doctors in Vienna but they rejected his hypothesis, mainly because, as 'hysteria' was such a commonly diagnosed illness, the implication was that incestuous abuse was of epidemic proportions. Freud's response was to go away and look at his material again. Soon after, he laid the foundations of the theory of psychosexual development. Reference has already been made to the oral, anal and genital stages. With regard to the last, Freud hypothesised that, as part of their normal development, boys and girls at the genital stage 'desired' their parents of the opposite sex. This desire was repressed and the repression led to modelling along the lines of the same-sex parent. When this process was disturbed, this led to developmental problems and the possibility of neurosis. Thus Freud argued that when he dealt with adults with such neuroses and tried to help them unlock these childhood repressions, it was not surprising that a lot of sexual material should arise. However, contrary to his original view, he saw these accounts as fantasies or wish-fulfilments rather than as recollections of fact.

Such theorising was highly influential in psychoanalytic circles and was one factor in predisposing psychotherapists and psychiatrists for many years to disbelieve accounts of sexual abuse. However, throughout the mid-1980s, influenced by the writings of Rush (1980), Herman (1981) and Masson (1984), there was a major shift in psychodynamic thinking with the development of a 'believing' school among psychoanalysts, the most famous example being Alice Miller (1985). Indeed, psycho-analysts and others went to great lengths to elicit accounts of child sexual abuse based on beliefs that many of their patients and clients had repressed events. Particularly in the USA (Loftus and Ketcham 1994) this so-called 'repressed memory syndrome' was challenged in the 1990s by critics (and lawyers) who argued that therapists had 'persuaded' their clients that they had been abused when they had not ('false memory syndrome').[4]

Psychoanalysts as a whole, however, have still not theorised in great depth about why child sexual abuse happens. Most would consider such abuse to have a very damaging effect on personality development, particularly if it took place in the first five years of a child's life, because of its distorting effect on the process of psychosexual development, but little has been written from this point of view about the causation of sexual abuse. Finkelhor et al. (1986), reviewing research on child sexual abusers, found two main views among psychoanalytic writing on this subject: first, that they have arrested psychosexual development and choose to relate at a child's emotional level; second, that they have general low self-esteem and, therefore, gain a sense of dominance and control by victimising children. However, neither explanation properly explains why such people resort to sexual abuse in response to these emotional difficulties.

Learning theory and child abuse

Learning theory, while embracing many different approaches, is based on the view that behaviour is shaped, or learned, by the interaction of an individual with the environment. The internal processes described by psychoanalysts are completely rejected. Classical learning theorists (Pavlov 1927; Skinner 1953) see behaviour as a response conditioned by external stimuli or reinforcers and dismiss the notion of any internal functioning at all. From this point of view, what is not observable does not exist. However, since this early theorising, learning theorists such as Bandura (1965) and Michenbaum (1977) have incorporated social modelling and the notion of internal cognitive reasoning processes into their analyses of how behaviour operates, and these more complex theories are generally accepted by most learning theorists now. An example of how social learning theory has been applied to modern-day child protection practice – specifically in the London borough of Hackney's Reclaim Social Work (RSW) innovation – can be found in McCafferty (2011). The RSW approach also incorporates elements of a 'strengths-based' orientation (see Gaughan and Kalyniak 2011) which is to say that as the past cannot be changed it is often more productive to concentrate on how the future could be different. This orientation partly derives from the late Steve de Shazer's pioneering work on 'solution-focused therapy' (de Shazer 2005); there are also similarities with some of the tenets of 'motivational interviewing' (Miller and Rolnick 2002) as well as Andrew Turnell's 'signs of safety' (Turnell 2009). Some of these ideas were first articulated for use in practice in Parton and O'Byrne's (2000) notion of 'constructive social work' for social workers. Along with RSW, many of these ideas are referred to in the Munro report in the UK (Munro 2011a) and we return to them in Chapter 8 when we consider the evidence-base for interventions.

From this general perspective, child abuse is a problem resulting neither from personality traits nor from lack of attachment. Rather, it is largely the result of having learned dysfunctional child care practices or, alternatively, of not having learned functional child care practices. The question of punishment looms large here. Adults who have themselves experienced punitive treatment may well rely on such methods to discipline their own children. Most learning theorists see punishment as effective in the short term, but less so in the long term. It also has unwanted side-effects for both the punisher and the punished. The dysfunctional effects of punishment have been put forward as important reasons for banning all forms of corporal punishment (Leach 1999). Positive reinforcement of pro-social behaviours and negative re-inforcement (such as ignoring) of anti-social behaviours are seen as more effective and enduring influences on behaviour.

Dubanoski et al. (1978) described a set of behavioural explanations of why children are physically abused:

- parents may lack effective child management techniques
- parents may deliberately use punitive childrearing practices
- the abuse may result from explosive acts triggered by the child
- there may be a high level of stress
- parents may have seriously negative attitudes towards the child.

Each of these problems might lead to the need for a variety of responses, including teaching new techniques, teaching self-control and focusing on attitude change.

Learning theorists have been applying their ideas to child abuse cases in the USA and the UK since the mid-1970s. Early British studies (e.g. Reavley and Gilbert 1979; Smith and Rachman 1984), for example, proved mostly unsuccessful. They found that simply teaching new child management techniques was in many cases inadequate, and stressed the need for attitudinal change on the part of parents as well, particularly where problems had been well established over a long period of time and motivation for change was low.[5] Pure behaviourist interventions are rare now, having largely been replaced by cognitive and cognitive-behavioural therapies (see below). Today social learning theory underpins many aspects of the 'Incredible Years', one of the most popular parenting programmes available (Webster-Stratton and Reid 2005).

The strengths of the learning theory perspective lie to some extent in its clarity and specificity. The learning theorist intervening in a case of child abuse would, for instance, focus on the actuality of the abuse, the situational factors, the anteced-ents and the consequences of the event, the attributions placed on the child by the parents, and their attitudes towards punishment and control. The personality of the parents and their developmental history would not be a major concern. There is also more potential for change than with the psychodynamic perspective, in that early experiences are not considered to be as deterministic.

Learning theory suffers from the same weaknesses as those of other psycholog-ical theories so far reviewed, namely that it often focuses on the individual abuser to the exclusion of the impact of wider networks. It may be that the strength of learning theory with regard to child abuse is also its weakness: it runs the risk of oversimpli-fying the problem in its search for clarity. In addition, it has so far paid little direct attention to child sexual abuse.

Cognitive approaches to child abuse

There has been an increase in interest, particularly in the USA (Newberger and White 1989), in the application of cognitive theory principles to the understanding and treat-ment of child abuse. The essential feature of this approach is that the way people perceive, order, construct and think about the world is an important key to their behaviour. It was noted earlier that parental attitudes were perceived to be important, as well as their actual behaviour. Cognitive theorists point to the value of finding out how parents who have abused children perceive their children's behaviour. Larrance and Twentyman (1983) argue that attribution theory could help to explain why parents who have not been abused as children do abuse as adults. Their argument is that they may have developed a 'frame' or view on a child and/or on themselves that leads on to child abuse.

Newberger and White (1989) put forward a useful model of levels of parental awareness. At the first level, the child is seen by the parents purely as an extension of themselves. At the second level, the parents ascribe conventional roles to the child. At the third level, the child is seen by the parents as an individual with its own changing needs. They argue that abuse is more likely to take place when parents are at the first level. Although most parents progress to the highest level with time and experience and without outside help or intervention, this is not true in all cases. According to this view, intervention must be focused on helping parents to perceive their children differently, and such activity can help to prevent recurrence of abuse.

Deblinger and her colleagues (1999) successfully used cognitive-behavioural interventions in the treatment of 100 sexually abused children diagnosed as suffering from post-traumatic stress disorder (PTSD) in New Jersey, and this success was maintained over a two-year follow-up period. The therapy involved gradually encouraging children mentally to confront their abuse and to develop everyday coping strategies. Non-abusing parents were also helped by similar means with a view to increasing supportive behaviour to their children. It was found that where both parents and children were involved in the therapy, there were most improvements in terms of the child's psychological health.

Until relatively recently there was little evidence of the use of cognitive approaches with abused children in the UK (Verduyn and Calam 1999) but cognitive-behavioural therapy (CBT) is now increasingly used with traumatised children (see Trickey and Black 2009). Scott (1989) developed such work in relation to families with more general child care problems with some success, though mainly with parents who had less complex and less well-established problems. Cognitive-behavioural approaches have been used with adult sex offenders.

American studies suggest that, particularly in relation to treatment, there are encouraging possibilities for cognitive-behavioural interventions. While cognitive theory shares with other psychological theories the danger of not paying sufficient attention to the social context, nevertheless its approach to child abuse problems is clear and understandable and supports individuals in taking responsibility for their own futures.

Social psychological theories

In this section attention will be paid to theories that consider behaviour as follows:

- to be a product of interaction between individuals
- to be determined by family dynamics
- to be influenced by social networks and supports.

These approaches may be termed 'middle range' in that they fall between a focus on the individual and a focus on broader social factors. Essentially the relationships between individuals and their immediate environments are seen as key determinants from these perspectives. The three areas of interaction have been separated from each other for analytic purposes, but many theorists of these persuasions see close linkages between them.

Individual interactionist perspectives and child abuse

The key defining factor of the individual interactionist approach is that behaviour is seen to be determined less by intra-personal factors such as prior experiences, or by learning, and more by interactions between people (Deacon and Gocke 1999). From this perspective, greater attention is placed on the dynamics of current relationships than on parental background or characteristics. Thus, interactionists take the child's contribution to situations of abuse much more into account, and also that of the spouse or partner (Kadushin and Martin 1981).

A climate of abuse can result from parents lacking skills to cope with difficult behaviour and from certain children continually exposing that inadequacy. From this perspective, the combination of factors is as important as the weight of them, if not more so. Thus, a difficult crying baby with two parents with low tolerance of stress and high aggression levels is particularly at risk, whereas a more easily comforted and responsive child with parents who have the same characteristics may not be. The child can, from this perspective, reward the parents and enhance their skills or further de-skill them and lower their self-esteem. Similarly, the parents' responses will affect the responses of the child in a circular process.

Wolfe (1985) argues that parents do not have to have been abused themselves as children for them to abuse their own children, because he sees violence as a product of interactional events rather than a result of factors such as parental upbringing. He argues that it is possible for a frame of violence to develop within families. Similarly, Dibble and Straus (1980) point out that violence to children can and does take place in families where parental attitudes are disapproving of such violence. This, they argue, is because such violence is often situational, not a product of attitudes. Their study involved only families with two parents and they found that violent behaviour on the part of one parent was likely to influence the other parent to be violent even if he or she was personally opposed to using violence against children. These studies lend support to the view that violence breeds violence.

This perspective on violence in the family offers another dimension with regard to the dynamics of why and how physical abuse of children occurs and persists. However, as is true of all the perspectives so far considered, a major weakness is that individuals are seen in isolation from wider social influences and stresses.

Family dysfunction theory, physical child abuse and neglect

Family dysfunction theory broadens the focus a little more in that its concern is with the impact of family dynamics on the behaviour of its members. This theory and family therapy, the treatment method derived from it, originated within the field of psychiatry and the aetiology of mental illness.

Family therapy is a theoretically eclectic discipline. Initially, it drew mainly from psychodynamic theory and concentrated on the impact of family life on the psychological development of the individual (Dallos and Draper 2005). Many practitioners adopt a systems perspective based on the work of Minuchin (1974), which theorises that there are two main subsystems within the family, that of the parents and that of children, and emphasises the need for boundaries (with some degree of permeability) to be maintained between the two in order to ensure a healthy climate for all family members. Therapy is focused on examining the nature of current boundaries and on improving communication between family members.

Another family therapy approach is termed 'strategic'. Family therapists of this school see the family as a powerful system that resists attempts to change it from the outside (Dale et al. 1983). Carefully worked-out tactics and strategies are needed to break down this resistance to create the best conditions for change.

Dysfunctional family theory has been used in the UK to help explain the dynamics of physical abuse of children within the family and the interplay between professionals and parents where serious abuse has taken place. Asen et al. (1989) refer to the notion of 'stand-in abuse' where the child is subjected to violence by one parent as a means of 'getting at' the other parent. The notion of a child as scapegoat, the bad one in the family and the reason for all the family's ills, is another example of a family dysfunction explanation of child mistreatment. Reder et al. (1993) used material from public inquiry reports to examine both intra-familial dynamics and the way in which parents relate to professionals involved in working with them. They focused particularly on the way in which parents tend to oscillate between revealing what is going on (what are termed 'covert warnings') and concealing it.

Family therapy techniques have also been used in the assessment of families. Dale et al. (1986) reported successfully using strategic family therapy to determine whether it was safe for children who had been abused to return to the care of their families.

There is a general lack of focus on causes of behaviour among family therapists. Their concern is with the here-and-now dynamics of family life and how to break or change patterns of behaviour. From this point of view, the notion of 'cause' in the linear cause-and-effect sense is seen to be less relevant than the process.

Family therapy and child sexual abuse

Family therapy thinking has played a major role in the explanation of the causes of child sexual abuse. This is largely due to the pioneering work of Arnon Bentovim (see Bentovim et al. 1988) at the Great Ormond Street Hospital referred to in Chapter 8. This approach, which incorporates both psychodynamic and systems theories, is broadly based on the hypothesis that child sexual abuse serves the function of keeping together families that would otherwise collapse. The classic scenario is that of the abuse of a teenage daughter by her father, who is considered to be seeking emotional and sexual gratification because communication and sexual relations with his wife have broken down. It is believed in many cases that the wife/mother knows (whether consciously or subconsciously is not made clear) what is happening and passively colludes in the continuance of this situation. This collusion is thought to serve the function of freeing her from responsibility without sacrificing the unity of the family. The solution to the problem is seen to be one of opening up the secret to all family members, disentangling the knotted relationships and freeing individuals to decide on their futures. The means for achieving this is by family meetings and the use of family therapy techniques.

The strengths of the family dysfunction approach are that it heightens awareness of the powerful nexus of relationships that the family can be sheltering and demonstrates how it can sustain unacceptable forms of abuse. However, it suffers from the problem of many systems-based theories, in that although it describes well how dysfunctional families operate, it is much more limited in explaining the reason that they function in the way that they do. The Great Ormond Street team explained sexual abuse by reference to the emotional need of the perpetrator and the structural dependence on adults of the child victim. Feminist critiques of family dysfunction theory stress the lack of attention paid to gender power relations. Family therapy thinking has also been criticised for focusing too much on the family as a closed system cut off from wider systems and social influences. There is evidence of the development of more flexible family dysfunction approaches that take into account both of these concerns (Barratt et al. 1990; Masson and O'Byrne 1990; Jenkins and Asen 1992).

A final criticism is that the explanatory value of the family dysfunction approach is limited to the types of abuse situation outlined above. It does not help to explain the wide range of forms of sexual abuse that can take place in families, such as abuse of infants and abuse by siblings, uncles and grandparents (Corby 1998) and, of course, it contributes little to our understanding of abuse outside the family (but it does not set out to).

Social ecological approaches

General systems theory was adapted by social work theorists in the USA and the UK in the early 1970s to broaden this profession's traditional emphasis on personal problems and to move away from concentration on personal pathology (Pincus and Minahan 1973; Hingley-Jones and Mandin 2007). The influence of systems theory and ecological approaches (see Jack 2000) in understanding and interpreting social problems has been particularly influential in the USA with the development of general concerns about the environment. Germain and Gitterman (1980) provided a good example of the thinking behind this model:

> The ecological perspective provides an adaptive, evolutionary view of human beings in constant interchange with all elements of their environment. Human beings change their physical and social environments and are changed by them through a process of continuous reciprocal adaptation . . . Like all living systems, human beings must maintain a goodness-of-fit with the environment. The Darwinian concept of 'fit' applies both to organisms and their environments: to the fitness of the environment and the fitness of the organism, each with the other and through which both prosper.
>
> (Germain and Gitterman 1980: 5–6)

From this perspective, human behaviour is influenced, or determined, more by the context in which a person lives than by intra-personal or inter-personal factors. In the particular case of child abuse, it is hypothesised that where environmental conditions are unfavourable to families, the incidence of abuse is likely to be higher. In the USA, Garbarino (1977, 1982) has been particularly active in exploring these connections. He found in both rural and urban areas that officially reported abuse was higher in those neighbourhoods where indicators of social stress, population mobility and poverty were highest. A major factor was seen to be isolation from possible support systems, be they the extended family or community-based systems such as neighbourhood centres and day-care facilities: 'A strong pro-social neighbourhood climate can have a beneficial impact – by increasing participation – on persons whose individual predilection is to be isolated' (Garbarino and Crouter 1978: 606).

Garbarino (1977) linked this theoretical approach to others in that he did not preclude individual history as an additional causative factor and he acknowledged the impact of culture. Nevertheless, given these factors, stress, created from living in environments that are not conducive to psychological health and development, is seen to be a major contributory factor to child mistreatment and points to solutions other than a focus on the individual, most notably community-based initiatives to break down isolation and create a sense of belonging and shared problems.

There are difficulties with 'proving' the validity of social ecological theories in relation to child abuse causation, not least because of the fact that poorer communities are more likely to come under the close surveillance of public authorities and, therefore, produce higher official rates of abuse. There is also a need for closer attention to be paid to which particular deficits in what circumstances contribute to child maltreatment and the process by which this happens (Seagull 1987; Coohey 1996). In Britain, Department of Health initiatives in the second half of the 1990s (see Chapter 2) led to greater attention being paid to social stress as a causative factor in certain types of child abuse and to the use of broader-based assessments of families referred for child protection concerns (Department of Health 1995). In the early 1990s there were developments to support families at risk by use of community-based projects such as the Sure Start and Children's Fund programmes, but critics of these schemes alleged that they did not reach the families for whom they were intended. Social ecological thinking underpins these developments (Jack 2000). In the USA, where they have a longer established community-based programme (Healthy Start/Healthy Families), concerns have been raised that too much reliance is being placed on broad-based initiatives of this kind (Chaffin 2004).

Despite this type of reminder about not putting all your eggs in one basket, the main strength of the social ecological approach lies in the way in which it broadens the scope of thinking about why the abuse of children occurs. It shifts the focus from individual pathology to the influence of the immediate environment and the need to tackle the problem at that level. At the other end of the spectrum, however, it is argued that exponents of this approach pay little attention to political factors that contribute to the deterioration of neighbourhoods and the disorganisation and break-up of social networks. Attention to these points might well lead to quite different solutions to the problem.

Sociological perspectives

Sociological perspectives on child abuse did not have a major influence on child protection thinking and work in the UK before the 1990s, except in the case of sexual abuse and the question of gender. The reason for this is probably twofold. First, such perspectives do not provide clear indicators for practice in that they look broadly at the conditions that create the climate for child abuse rather than at how this works out in individual cases. Second, many sociological perspectives provide a challenge to those who are intervening into families to protect children, in that they question the ethics and politics of mainstream assumptions (Howe 1991). Thus, they have an unsettling quality in that they locate the 'cause' of the problem outside the sphere of influence of the professional worker and they consequently pose uncomfortable questions about the validity of that professional intervention. The main sociological perspectives to be considered in this section are those that have been articulated by researchers and others involved in the child abuse field:

- the social cultural perspective, which points to linkages between child abuse and general social approval of the use of violence to maintain control and order
- the social structural perspective, which relates child abuse to the maintenance of general inequality in northern industrialised societies
- perspectives that link child abuse to gender and generational inequality – that is, feminist and children's rights perspectives.

The social cultural perspective and child abuse

The work of Straus and Gelles (1986) in the USA has already been referred to several times in relation to their national surveys into the incidence of physical child abuse. In these studies, they and their colleagues reported high levels of intra-familial violence of all kinds. They came to the conclusion that such violence was the norm and that individuals were more likely to be subjected to violent acts within families than outside them. In an attempt to explain these high rates, they argued that violence is a socially sanctioned general form of maintaining order and that it is approved of as a form of child control by most people in US society. It can be argued from this perspective that a society that approves of the corporal punishment of children in schools and endorses the old adage 'spare the rod and spoil the child' sets the scene for a variety of unwanted forms of violence, of which physical child abuse is one. Child abuse, therefore, is seen as being on the same spectrum as socially approved forms of violence rather than as a separate pathological phenomenon.

Adherents of these views point to the dysfunctions of physical punishment for individuals in later life (which can include lowered self-esteem and poor social relationship skills), their families (as a result of the inter-generational transmission of punitive parenting) and for society as a whole which is increasingly looking in the job market for individuals with flexible problem-solving skills, a style of behaviour not generally created by the use of physical punishment as a key form of discipline (Straus 1994).

From this perspective, it is clear that there is a need for change at a broad societal level to the way in which we treat and control children. There is a need to encourage non-violent means of ensuring pro-social behaviour. There have been moves in this direction in Britain, but an outright ban on the use of physical punishment has been seen as a step too far because the vast majority of parents use such punishment as a form of discipline (Nobes and Smith 1997). Support for physical punishment is perhaps even more entrenched in the USA where research has found that 94 per cent of parents 'spank' their children by the time they are 3 or 4 years old (Straus and Stewart 1999). However, as has been seen, other European countries have been much more proactive in this respect. In Sweden, where the ban on the use of physical punishment of children by parents has been in operation the longest, there have been reductions over time in youth involvement in crime and decreases in substance misuse, rape and suicide (Durrant 1999).[6]

Nevertheless, there are others who take the view that what they call 'non-abusive' corporal punishment does not inevitably or necessarily lead to aggression, and indeed this viewpoint informs the 'chastisement practices' within some cultural groups. One of the central tenets of this view is that Sweden's anti-spanking laws have never really been evaluated fully – indeed Lyons et al. (1993) argue that physical abuse actually increased after the ban in Sweden, the reason being that, drawing upon the work of Baumrind (1973) and Patterson (1982), parents can become excessively violent if they feel 'mild spanking' is not available. There were also fears that emotional abuse – in the form of excessive criticism, persistent mocking and derogation – could increase when 'non-abusive' corporal punishment is forbidden.

Returning to the question of how society sanctions or condones certain behaviours, whether implicitly or explicitly, the same sort of analysis can be applied to sexual abuse: that because sexual exploitation of women and, to a lesser extent, of children, is societally tolerated in, for instance, art, cinema, advertising (and today there are concerns about the over-sexualisation of very young children), pornography and prostitution, a climate is set whereby sexual abuse results. Again, from this perspective, it is seen as part of a continuum rather than as an act of a totally different quality or dimension.

The clear strengths of the social cultural perspective are that it broadens the focus in comparison with psychological and social psychological theories and helps in the understanding of how societal influences can contribute to the incidence and form of child mistreatment despite the fact that society officially sets out to reduce and prevent such occurrences. The implications for social policy are that there is a need to tackle matters on a broader front and that intervention into individual cases alone is not sufficient for dealing with the problem. The major weakness of this perspective lies in the fact that it does not help to explain why some people within our flawed culture abuse and others do not.

The social structural perspective and child abuse

Gil's research and writing, already referred to, form the cornerstone of this perspective. Gil's (1970) early work convinced him that child abuse was class related and that 'psychological' explanations of abuse by themselves were too narrow and grossly

underestimated the contribution of stress, caused by poverty and material deprivation, to the causation of child abuse.

He developed his ideas further to lay some of the blame for child abuse on the
policies of the state (Gil 1975, 1978). He put forward a broad definition of abuse
which included all children whose developmental needs could not be met, whatever
the reason.

This definition clearly places responsibility for child abuse on the state over and
above the person who actually abuses, on the grounds that it sanctions inequality and
low standards of housing, health, education and leisure for the children of the poor.
From this point of view, the state, far from being the benign rescuer of children when
parents ill-treat them, is actually the villain of the piece because it abuses children
directly by its failure to provide adequate facilities for them to lead a fulfilling life, and
also creates stresses for parents that increase the likelihood of their committing acts of
abuse or neglect. Nigel Parton (1985, 2007) has lent considerable support to this
perspective in Britain:

> Child abuse is strongly related to class, inequality and poverty both in terms of
> prevalence and severity . . . Locating the problem in terms of social structural
> factors has important implications for the way we define the problem, the way we
> explain it and the best way of doing something about it. For solving the problem
> requires a realignment in social policy which recognises the necessity of attacking
> the social, economic and cultural conditions associated with the abuse.
>
> (Parton 1985: 175–6)

The strength of the social structural approach is that it does justice to the accepted
fact that physical child abuse has a close association with deprivation. As we have
seen, this is particularly so with regard to neglect (Wolock and Horowitz 1984). Its
weakness lies in the fact that not all poor people abuse their children and, therefore, it
is not a sufficient explanation. Also, until relatively recently, this perspective had not
taken into account structural factors other than class and poverty. In particular it has
been silent on the question of gender and generational inequalities (Parton 1990).
Finally, it does not address the aetiology of child sexual abuse, which is generally
considered not to be linked to class and poverty; nor is emotional abuse. There are
signs that post-structuralist and post-modernist understandings may complement the
social structural approach (see, for example, White 1997; Fook 2002); they certainly
include gender and cultural dimensions.

The social structural approach has not had a great deal of support in child abuse
circles. Pelton (1978) pointed to the fact that structural inequality explanations pose
a threat to those who espouse clinical and medical approaches to child abuse. Other
writers have seen Gil's views as 'idealistic' (Greenland 1987) or beyond the scope of
the helping professions and, therefore, not applicable to day-to-day practice.

Child protection policy in the UK during the 1990s began formally to take
into account structural inequality and social exclusion through the third side of
the 'assessment triangle', family and environment factors, which incorporates
family history and functioning, wider family, housing, employment, income, family's
social integration and community resources into the family assessment. Thus, in

addition to the components of the other two sides of the triangle – the child's developmental needs and parenting capacity – professionals involved in child protection and welfare are required to take account of the 'world outside the family'. The New Labour focus on the early years of childhood, with its greater emphasis on more broad-based safeguarding measures and on provision of preventive facilities, could be seen as an indicator of a shift towards tackling the sort of structural problems that created the conditions for child abuse and neglect (Parton 2005). Clearly, however, there are tensions between the demands of a liberal democratic society and the sort of social engineering likely to be required to have lasting impact on social inequality.

Feminist perspectives and child abuse

One of the key developments during the past 10 years is that there is no longer consensus over the existence of one 'feminism' or indeed 'family' (Featherstone 2007). Most commentators agree that there are different distinct emphases within an overall feminist discourse and some of the earlier forms of feminism have been criticised for being geared towards white, middle-class perspectives. But most of the perspectives so far outlined are considered by radical feminists, for example, to be gender-blind. From their point of view, all of the psychological perspectives assume that women are the key carers of children and that, if things go wrong, then the spotlight falls on their behaviour. The interactionist perspectives broaden the focus, but assume an equal power base between men and women.

The radical feminist perspective on child abuse began to emerge in the 1980s. The stimulus for this came from the 'discovery' of child sexual abuse, an act committed predominantly by males, and feminist explanations have been highly relevant to it. From this starting point, the feminist perspective has now been applied to all forms of abuse. This perspective on child sexual abuse has been articulated by many writers in the USA and the UK (for example, Dominelli 1986; Nelson 1987; Macleod and Saraga 1988; Driver and Droisen 1989; Cox et al. 2001; Smart et al. 2001; Ferguson 2004; Featherstone 2007).

There is little equivocation about the reason for the existence of child sexual abuse and the form that it takes:

> Generally boys and men learn to experience their sexuality as an overwhelming and uncontrollable force; they learn to focus their sexual feelings on submissive objects, and they learn the assertion of their sexual desires, the expectation of having them serviced.
>
> (Macleod and Saraga 1988: 41)

> Abuse in the form of violence against women is a normal feature of patriarchal relations. It is a major vehicle that men use in controlling women. As such it is the norm not an aberration. The widespread incidence of child sexual abuse reveals the extent to which men are prepared to wield sexual violence as a major weapon in asserting their authority over women.
>
> (Dominelli 1986: 12)

The attention of these writers is not on individual males. Individual pathology is discounted as a cause of child abuse (as is family pathology). Rather, abuse is seen as an extreme example of institutionalised male power over females. The implications for policy of this perspective are similar in kind, if not focus, to those of the other sociological perspectives. Sexual abuse needs tackling at a societal level as well as at the individual level. Men abuse children because of the general power imbalance between the sexes and the different forms of socialisation that they experience as a result, not because of psychiatric illness or emotional deficits.

With regard to physical abuse and neglect, feminist perspectives are less clear-cut (Featherstone 1997). The argument that such abuse is created by the conditions of patriarchy does not rest as easily in this case as with that of sexual abuse. However, women spend far more time with children than do men and cope with the stresses of child care, often with little support. The argument has been taken further by some feminists in that they see the notion of motherhood, a product of patriarchy which reinforces the idea that children's welfare and needs are best met by mothers, as exacerbating the already existing stresses placed on women looking after children (Ong 1985). Under such conditions, it is surprising that the numbers of women who abuse and neglect children do not vastly exceed those of men, and, from this point of view, men are disproportionately violent to children. The implication is that women's violence to children is much more likely to be stress related than that of men. Another area opened up by the feminist perspective is that of domestic violence (Dobash and Dobash 1992) – or as it tends now to be referred to, 'intimate partner violence' – and its linkage with child abuse (Mullender and Morley 1994).

The strength of feminist perspectives on child abuse as a whole is that it opened up a dimension that had been missing from previous explanations about why child abuse occurs. We saw earlier that (in the case of physical abuse and neglect) men have been, until fairly recently, overlooked in terms of intervention. Feminist perspectives points to the error in this, in that understanding and challenging the nature of male-female power relations at an institutional and individual level is of major importance in the theory and practice of child protection work (Scourfield 2003). The challenge should be both to the impositions placed on women within the family and to the way in which males are socialised (Hearn 1990).

The weakness of *the* feminist perspective is in assuming that there is one perspective. 'Post-feminist' perspectives have questioned the determinism of radical feminism and argued the need for more flexibility in understanding female identity and of the roles that this might play in child abuse (Featherstone and Trinder 1997). This goes a long way to counter the argument that feminist perspectives can be used in a reductionist and exclusive way, attributing everything to patriarchy, thus overriding other explanatory accounts.

The children's rights perspective and child abuse

Freeman (1983) identified two main schools of thought on children's rights: the protectionist and the liberationist. Protectionist thinking about children has been applied to the question of child care through legislation since the late nineteenth century and still underlies much of current policy and practice in the field of child abuse. Essentially the argument from this viewpoint is that children have the right to protection from their parents by outside bodies in circumstances where their health and welfare are at risk. In the absence of these conditions, parents have the responsibility of determining their children's rights up to prescribed ages.

The liberationist perspective is a product of the late 1960s and derives mainly from the field of education. Holt (1974) provided a good example of the extreme end of this type of thinking. His argument is that childhood is an oppressed status and that the current state of affairs in which parents grant concessions to children who have little redress against their actions and decisions is unjust and reinforces their oppression. He proposed a series of rights that children should have, such as the right to choose where to live, the right to vote and the right to have the same financial status as adults. In short, his view is that children should have exactly the same rights as adults. Age is seen as irrelevant and self-determination as paramount.

In the late 1980s and 1990s there was a shift in official thinking about children's rights away from a traditional protectionist perspective towards viewing children in a more independent light. This was largely due to events in Cleveland. The view that children are either the responsibility of the family or, where abuse occurs, that of the state, was thrown into question by what happened there. The Cleveland report (Butler-Sloss 1988) was highly critical of the way in which children were treated during investigations. It pointed out that there is a danger that in looking to the welfare of children believed to be the victims of sexual abuse the children themselves may be overlooked: 'the child is a person not an object of concern' (Butler-Sloss 1988: 245). The 1989 Children Act took children's rights of this kind into consideration.[7] However, neither the Cleveland report nor the 1989 Children Act could possibly be seen as liberationist in the way in which Holt (1974) proposed. In fact they reflect a half-way house position between the protectionist and liberationist viewpoints. Children's views are to be taken into account, but there is no suggestion that they should prevail.

In respect of physical abuse, the development of anti-corporal punishment legislation and policy reflects the influence of liberationist views. The thinking is clear: if children had the same rights in society as adults and, therefore, similar individual status (one that was not prescribed by family relations), they would be less likely to be the object of physical abuse and neglect. For instance, we do not consider it proper to smack adults for misbehaving. Were children to have individual rights without reference to their parents, we would not consider such treatment to be acceptable in their case either.

The main strength of the children's rights perspective is that it compels us to consider matters from the child's point of view as an individual rather than purely as a family member and points to changes in the status of children at a societal level as a solution to the widespread problem of child abuse. While the relevance of this perspective has no bounds, it should be stressed that the notion of children's rights has a particular role to play in the protection of children living away from home. Various reports (Utting 1991, 1997; Warner 1992) on the care of children being looked after in local authority care and elsewhere demonstrate the consequences of children not being able to assert rights of complaint against those in power over them.

Although there were considerable general developments in the 1990s to establish and assert children's rights – for instance, the UN Convention on the Rights of the

Child, adopted by the United Nations in 1989 and ratified by the UK government in 1991, and the setting up of a formal representations procedure in the 1989 Children Act – there has not been any obvious evidence of overall improvement in respect of children in care (see Lyon 1997). However, there has existed a UK children's commissioner for the past 10 years and the post of minister of state for children in the UK was established in 2003.

The weakness of the children's rights perspective lies in the fact that most children living at home cannot be easily seen in isolation from their parents because of their dependence on them. Children's rights protagonists tend to ignore this fact and also the fact that many parents do not have the means to achieve the high standards that the children's rights perspective properly demands.

Attempts at integration and ecological perspectives

Social workers and other professional workers in the field of child protection need to be open to a wide range of explanations of child abuse in order to intervene effectively into families where children are thought to be at risk, even though this approach may be more complex than that of following a single theory. Attempts to integrate the different approaches to child abuse have been made. Using an ecological framework, Belsky (1980) and Belsky and Jaffee (2006) pointed to a four-level approach, similar to that of Bronfenbrenner (1979):

1   Ontogenic development is concerned with what the individual parents bring to the situation, their developmental background and experiences.
2   The microsystem is concerned with the interaction of individuals within the family.
3   The exosystem is concerned with the immediate social environment within which the family functions.
4   The macrosystem takes into account broader structural factors, such as cultural attitudes to violence.

The way in which these different systems interact is the key to the likelihood of abuse occurring or not. Wiehe (1989) and Coohey and Braun (1997) have developed integrative models in relation to physical abuse. Finkelhor et al. (1986) provided a similar type of model for child sexual abuse. The way forward is clearly in the direction of further attempts at integrating ongoing research into the aetiology of child abuse. While practitioners may be more concerned with what is directly relevant to practice, it should be borne in mind that a broad range of integrated knowledge provides a strong base from which to operate.

Integrated thinking about the causation of child abuse does of course have implications for far more people than child protection workers. However much we develop understandings of abuse and neglect at the micro level, the implications of the broader sociological theories of child abuse causation cannot be avoided by society as a whole. A more concerted effort needs to be made to give consideration to child abuse prevention in all areas of planning and policing of society.

Most researchers into the field of child abuse point to the dangers of adopting single-cause explanations of the phenomenon. While some explanations may seem to be particularly useful for the understanding of certain forms of abuse (for example, attachment theory appears to have particular relevance in the case of physical abuse or emotional rejection of young babies) they are unlikely to be sufficient in themselves.

Concluding comments

There has been (and still is) a polarisation between different perspectives on why child abuse occurs, with single explanations dominating within different 'camps'. In the field of physical abuse, for example, the cases of Victoria Climbié and Peter Connelly highlight the clash between different perspectives, especially those of the needs of the child and the rights of carers. Social workers and other child protection professionals, in both cases, were heavily criticised for overlooking what, with hindsight, were key indicators of abuse. Similarly, the social workers in the Jasmine Beckford case (Brent 1985) focused on improving the social circumstances of the parents of the child by helping them find more suitable accommodation, by providing Jasmine's mother with supportive help at home and by obtaining nursery school provision for Jasmine. The focus was on external factors improving quality of life, thereby reducing stress and enhancing parent-child relationships. The report criticised the social workers on a variety of grounds, including not taking into account the psychological background of the parents. Again, with the value of hindsight, this criticism was justified and greater attention to inter-personal and intra-personal factors may have led to greater caution in decision-making.

The scandals in Cleveland, Rochdale and the Orkney Islands criticised paediatricians and social workers for over-reacting to a series of allegations and indicators of alleged sexual and 'satanic' abuse. It is cases such as these that, in their wake, alter significantly the thresholds within which child protection agencies make decisions about how to respond to allegations: cases such as Jasmine Beckford, Victoria Climbié and Peter Connelly lowered the threshold, whereas the Cleveland, Rochdale and Orkney scandals raised it. Either way, it remains true that legislation drawn up in the aftermath of such high profile tragedies inevitably produces restrictive and defensive practice. The Munro report in the UK (Munro 2011a) was not requested as a result of such tragedies and, hence, the hope is that it will produce more lasting changes in policy and practice.

Recommended reading

Cassidy, J. and Shaver, P. R. (2008) *Handbook of Attachment: Theory, Research and Clinical Applications*, 2nd edn. New York: Guilford.

McCrory, E., De Brito, S. A. and Viding, E. (2010) Research review: the neurobiology and genetics of maltreatment and adversity, *Journal of Child Psychology and Psychiatry*, no. doi:10.1111/j.1469–7610.2010.02271.x, accessed February 2010.

Trickey, D. and Black, D. (2009) Child trauma, in M. Gelder et al. (eds) *New Oxford Textbook of Psychiatry*, 2nd end. Oxford: Oxford University Press.

Turnell, A. (2009) *Of Houses, Wizards and Fairies: Involving Children in Child Protection Casework*. Perth: Resolutions Consultancy.

7

The consequences of child abuse

Introduction

In the past there has been less attention paid to the consequences or effects on a child of being abused than to ways of preventing such abuse happening in the first place. This could not be so easily argued now. Particularly since the greater emphasis paid to child sexual abuse in the 1980s, there has been an explosion of interest in, and studies about, the consequences both of this form of abuse and of all others as well. This concern with the effects of sexual abuse is largely attributable to the pressure of the feminist movement, but it may also reflect increasing societal concerns about risk to individuals identified by, among others, Ulrich Beck (1992, 2008). Beck argued that such concerns are characteristic of modern, more affluent societies which possess increasingly more effective technological means of controlling broad aspects of life and which thereby create a strong desire to reduce risk to a minimum. This argument has been applied to child abuse concerns generally (for example, Parton 2007). However, it seems particularly persuasive in explaining the growth of attention paid to the consequences of abuse, because in relation to the physical punishment of children, it is not only those who are abused who may pay a cost, but their relatives and society as well.

Moving on to the concerns of child protection policy-makers and practitioners, there are several good reasons for careful study of the consequences of child abuse. First, there are the support and treatment needs of children, young people and adults who have been abused. Awareness of the short- and long-term impacts of various forms of abuse and neglect are central to the development of appropriate resources and services for meeting such needs.

Second, there is a preventive aspect to focusing on the consequences of abuse, and the question of the inter-generational transmission of abuse was discussed earlier. Greater focus on the effects of abuse and the consequent development of better treatment measures can help reduce the likelihood of abuse being repeated in the next generation (even though many children who are abused do not go on to become abusers).

Third, informed knowledge about the consequences of different forms and intensities of abuse and neglect can help shape intervention practices, although it is important to bear in mind that some forms of intervention may add to the harm already created by the abuse that the child has suffered rather than alleviate it (for example, being taken into care and certain 'invasive' forms of therapy).

As we saw in the previous chapter, the nature of causality is complex and it is difficult to isolate precisely what is actually 'causing' which outcome. The same is true when we explore the effects or 'consequences' of child abuse and neglect. For example, some emotionally abusive experiences can result in mental illness for one person, but leave another relatively unscarred. Similarly, many people are mentally ill who were not abused, as with the more heritable conditions such as schizophrenia and bipolar depression. But there are some forms of abuse that lead more directly to certain outcomes: 'non-organic failure to thrive' often results in restricted growth, for example; shaking a baby can damage the spinal cord and neck or *in extremis* lead to brain damage. But with emotional abuse, and even sexual abuse, it is more difficult to say accurately whether a particular outcome in adulthood was the direct result of the events in childhood. The child's resilience, for example, can be a key factor in determining whether she or he will be able to 'bounce back' from adversity (for an excellent website devoted to resilience in children visit www.boingboing.org.uk).

As with the 'causes' of maltreatment, in this chapter we consider the mediating connections and pathways that we can more confidently expect to exist between abusive acts towards a child and the outcomes later on in adolescence and adulthood, in order to understand more completely the way abuse affects individuals in different ways.

Whatever the consequences of child maltreatment they can be profound and may endure long after the abuse or neglect occurs; they may include minor physical injuries, low self-esteem and an inability to focus attention, or brain damage, extremely violent behaviour and, in extreme situations, suicide.

Up until the past 5–10 years most quantitative studies of the consequences of child abuse were correlational in design. That is to say, they looked for statistical connections between the types of abuse and outcomes. Few involved control groups of children who were *not* abused (and how does one ever know that a child has not been abused?). The use of control groups has not significantly increased in the recent past but two other developments have been noted. Firstly, the use of meta-analytic statistical methods and systematic reviews allows researchers to combine studies. Secondly, there has been an increase in neurological, biochemical and genetic research into the causes and consequences of abuse, and such techniques permit the isolation of mediating processes more than any other. For example, a typical contemporary research study into consequences of early abuse can be found in Kim and Cicchetti (2010). Their very precise focus was the longitudinal pathways linking child maltreatment, emotion regulation, peer relations and psychopathology with 215 maltreated and 206 non-maltreated children (aged 6–12 years) from low-income families (again, a very precise sample). The study involved exploring boundaried research questions aimed not at a broad inquiry such as 'is mental illness an effect of child abuse?' but with a much tighter focus of the mediating effect of 'emotion regulation' and 'peer support'. The findings indicated 'emphasize the important role of emotion regulation as a risk or a protective mechanism in the link between earlier child maltreatment and later psychopathology through its influences on peer relations' (p. 706).

Another example is Yampolsky et al.'s (2010) study of these indicators compared with high risk-pregnancy status in survivors of childhood sexual abuse. The researchers took a random sample of 1,835 mid-pregnant Jewish women recruited in Israel over an 18-month period in 2005–7. They explain the design as follows:

> Participants were divided into three sub-groups consisting of the different combinations between pregnancy at risk (yes/no), childhood sexual abuse (yes/no), other than childhood sexual abuse trauma (yes/no), and no trauma (yes/no). They completed a self-administered questionnaire consisting of five scales: a demographic variables scale, the Post-traumatic Stress Disorder Symptom Scale, Center for Epidemiologic Studies Depression Scale, Traumatic Events Questionnaire, and Childhood Sexual Experiences Scale.
>
> (Yampolsky et al. 2010: 2025)

They found that:

> Pregnant survivors of childhood sexual abuse suffered higher distress levels which heightened poor health, hence increasing the probability of high risk pregnancy compared to women who had had other than sexual abuse trauma or reported no trauma. Post traumatic stress symptoms and avoidance (a sub-category) were found to explain chronic illnesses, whereas depression was found to explain gynecological problems in pregnant sexually-abused survivors.
>
> (p. 2025)

Confidence is a key theme in this edition; this is why it is prominent in the subtitle. For practitioners and policy-makers to feel more confident in their practice they need to be able to rely upon sound, robustly designed research. To date, and as we shall see in some of what follows, research has often produced ambiguous and conflicting results, due to poor design, imprecise sample focus and the research questions being too wide-ranging. The two examples above, we argue, correct this tendency.

Although we have tended to concentrate on quantitative research, qualitative research that is similarly focused also produces findings which are capable of being used directly by practitioners and policy-makers alike. Bernard's 1999 study of child sexual abuse and black children with a disability is a good example. Very precise research questions enabled her to explore 'how the interlocking dimensions of race, gender and disability compound the problems that they are faced with in the after-math of sexual abuse' and 'concludes with some reflections on the implications for making risk assessment for black disabled children' (p. 325). Similarly, in separate areas of child protection, Sue White's critical study of the micro-worlds of practitioners' responses to the UK's Integrated Children's System (see, for example, White et al. 2010; Wastell et al. 2011) and Brid Featherstone and Jonathan Scourfield's work on men as parents and carers (Featherstone et al. 2010), as well as Scourfield's on self-harm among young people (Scourfield et al. 2011) are excellent examples of qualitative research.

We first summarise correlationally based studies, incorporating where relevant the meta-analyses and systematic reviews, and then consider more recent 'bio-psychosocial' studies. A number of caveats exist with most of the studies. First, samples have tended to drawn from lower socio-economic backgrounds, prisoners, mental health patients or other clinical populations. Other than attachment-based research (e.g. Out et al. 2009) it is rare to find examples of research conducted in so-called low-risk populations. Secondly, data collection is often achieved through the use of official records or by the self-reporting of current or past child maltreatment and this may result in a misrepresentation of the true prevalence levels of child abuse and neglect. Thirdly, there are problems about agreed definitions of what constitutes abuse. Lack of definitional clarity makes comparability between different studies difficult; it is not always possible to be sure that you are comparing like with like. Some studies are careful to differentiate between types of abuse and degrees of severity, while others are not. Fourthly, the difficulty of deciding on the length of time to be allowed for follow-up of cases is a problem. Research that is carried out soon after the abuse has occurred will obviously miss out on evaluating longer-term effects.

On the other hand, the greater the gap between the abuse event and the later behaviour, the less chance there is of causally linking the two because of the existence of more intervening variables.

The consequences of physical abuse and neglect

Research into the consequences of physical abuse and neglect has been patchy, particularly in the UK. There has been a generally held view that the consequences of physical abuse are self-evident, with provision of protection and security in serious cases being the key requirements, and studies of the consequences of neglect have been few and far between. Between 1990 and 2000, however, more interest began to be shown in the effects of physical child abuse, and particularly in the effects of neglect, as policy has shifted from a focus on abuse events to broader consideration of ongoing neglectful (and abusive) climates within families.

Separating out the effects of physical abuse and neglect in order to pinpoint which causes what, however, is highly problematic in that the two are often closely linked. It would be rare for a child experiencing regular physical ill-treatment not to be experiencing neglect (especially emotional harm). On the other hand, parents can be seriously neglectful without actually physically abusing children. This must be borne in mind throughout the following commentaries.

Beginning with physical abuse, it tends to be associated with:

> . . . various types of injuries, particularly when exposure to such abuse occurs in the first three years of life (Vinchon et al. 2005). Shaking an infant may result in bruising, bleeding, and swelling in the brain. The physical consequences of 'shaken baby syndrome' can range from vomiting or irritability to more severe effects, such as concussions, respiratory distress, seizures, and death (Conway 1998). Two-thirds of subdural haemorrhages in children under two are caused by physical abuse (Vinchon et al. 2005). It is estimated that 10 per cent of admissions to paediatric burns and plastic surgery units are related to child maltreatment (Chester et al. 2006).
>
> (Lazenblatt 2010: 5)

Other possible consequences of physical abuse include partial loss of vision or blindness, learning disabilities and paralysis (Conway et al. 1998). Neglected infants may experience 'non-organic failure to thrive', resulting in the child's weight, height and motor development being significantly below that expected for the child's age, as well as learning and psychological problems.

Short- and medium-term effects on emotional development

The emotional impact of physical abuse
Physically maltreated children will often become passive and withdrawn (internalising behaviours) or, alternatively, overactive and aggressive (externalising behaviours). Both physically and sexually abused children sometimes exhibit both extremes (Kaplan et al. 1999). Emotional and psychosocial problems identified among

individuals who were maltreated as children include: low self-esteem; depression and anxiety; post-traumatic stress disorder (PTSD); attachment disorganisation or disorders; eating disorders; and self-harming behaviour, including suicide attempts (Silva et al. 2000; Widom 2000).

Calam and Franchi (1987) provide a useful – and timeless – overview of psychological characteristics displayed in the short term by children who are physically abused. Many of these characteristics can be seen as survival tactics adopted by the powerless in the face of harsh treatment. Such abused children can develop a form of 'pseudo-maturity' that manifests itself in behaviour aimed at keeping their parents happy. Generally they have a lack of appetite for, or confidence in, play. Such children become self-critical and lack self-esteem. 'Frozen watchfulness' is another response, usually to more extreme forms of abuse and deprivation; that is, the child seems to be wary of human contact and to lack emotional reaction. Hyperactivity and inability to settle for any substantial length of time have also been seen as typical of the behaviour of physically abused children.

These initial responses may or may not persist. Calam and Franchi studied a small number of abused/neglected children attending a National Society for the Prevention of Cruelty to Children (NSPCC) day centre with their mothers and came to the conclusion that 'severity of injury was not the major determinant of the degree of disturbances that they showed; the family environment that they were continuing to experience was likely to play a more significant part' (Calam and Franchi 1987: 191). From this viewpoint, early negative psychological development is caused not so much by the actual physical abuse as by the way in which parents relate emotionally to their children, and it is maintained by the way in which they continue to interact with them regardless of whether they use physical violence again or not.

In the USA, Steele (1986), arguing along similar lines, stressed that the main feature of being an abused child is inconsistent care, which in general terms leads to a sense of insecurity. This evidences itself in low self-esteem, problems in developing a sense of self-identity, a diminution in the ability to cope with life and its stresses, a lack of ability to take pleasure in things and to make lasting attachments, depression, delinquency and masochism. For Steele, as for Calam and Franchi, physical abuse per se is not the issue. It is the *emotional quality* of parenting that is the key:

> Physical abuse does not necessarily cause trouble. Most people have had physical injuries, fractures or bumps during childhood due to purely accidental causes and they have not been harmed by it because they have been comforted and cared for by good caregivers at the time of the incident. Damage comes when the injuries are inflicted by those to whom one looks for love and protection and there is no relief from the trauma.
>
> (Steele 1986: 283–4)

Steele goes on to argue that the emotionally incapacitating effects of this type of early mistreatment can be alleviated only by positive interpersonal experiences. In both these accounts, therefore, physical abuse is seen more as a symptom of emotional abuse, and the important consequences, provided a child's physical safety is ensured, are linked to the child's emotional and attachment needs.

The emotional impact of neglect

The impact of neglect alone on children (i.e. unaccompanied by any specific incident of physical or sexual abuse) has been relatively under-researched (Hildyard and Wolfe 2002). However, the Minnesota Longitudinal Study of Parents and Children (Egeland et al. 1983; Erickson et al. 1989; Sroufe et al. 2009) – which included emotional abuse – began in 1975 and has been of considerable influence in the development of child protection policy in the UK. It was drawn upon in the 1995 *Messages from Research* series to support the need for re-focusing services on the broader issue of children in need (Department of Health 1995). The Minnesota Study is still running and in 2009 the researchers summarised the findings in *The Developing Child* (Sroufe et al. 2009).

This longitudinal study followed the development of 267 children born to first-time mothers identified as being at risk for parenting problems over a period of six years. The study focused on 84 of these children, all of whom had been reported as being abused, and used 85 non-abused children, selected from the original sample of at-risk mothers, as a control group. The researchers categorised their experimental group children under four main abuse headings:

1   Children who were physically abused.
2   Children whose parents were hostile and verbally abusive.
3   Children who were neglected.
4   Children whose parents were psychologically unavailable (that is, they were emotionally abusive).

Children from all the 'abused' groups were generally rated as having less confidence and lower self-esteem than those in the control group. However, the main aim of the study was to see whether there were differences between the experiences of children who were abused and neglected. The study found that there were differences, though not as great as between the abused and non-abused groups as a whole. At age 4, the neglected and emotionally abused children were the cause of most concern. With regard to those who were emotionally abused, the researchers write:

> The sharp decline in the intellectual functioning of these children, in their attachment disturbances and subsequent lack of social/emotional competence in a variety of situations is cause for great concern. The consequences of this form of maltreatment are particularly disturbing when considered in light of the fact that it is probably the least likely pattern of maltreatment to be detected.
>
> (Erickson et al. 1989: 667)

However, at age 6 these children, whose parents were described as psychologically unavailable, fared as well as the other groups of abused children. The group giving most cause for concern at this stage was the neglected children, who were very low achievers in school. Such children were found to show disorganised attachment with their parents, negative self-representations, to be isolated and withdrawn in social situations and to have poor problem-solving skills. The study pointed to the persistent and ongoing nature of neglect as the cause of the severity of the outcome compared with that of other forms of abuse. Other studies have also pointed to the fact that neglected children seem to be lower in self-esteem than children who have been physically abused (e.g. Toth et al. 1997).

Summary

What comes across clearly from research into the early effects of child abuse and neglect is that it is the emotional impact of children's experiences that debilitates and disadvantages them. This provides a focus for treatment for all abused children. It tells us that with regard to children who are being physically ill-treated, it is not sufficient just to ensure their physical safety (important though this is). With regard to neglected children, it tells us clearly that, even though there are no incidents of inflicted abuse, they may have major emotional deficits that need attending to, arguably of greater severity than for other abused children.

Before moving on to the next section, which considers social and intellectual functioning, it should be noted that the consequences of abuse and neglect considered above lay the foundation for what is to follow. Children who are psychologically disturbed or emotionally deprived at an early age lack the internal cognitive map and hence behavioural skills needed to develop socially and intellectually. As will be seen, the deficits in these areas result in frustrations and avoidance behaviours which elicit further negative responses from those with whom they interact, and so on.

Medium-term effects on social and intellectual functioning

Relationships with peers

As children get older, peer relationships take on an increasingly important role (Tajima et al. 2011). Children who have been mistreated seem to fare badly in peer relationships according to research findings (Camras and Rappaport 1993; Bolger et al. 1998). These studies find that physically abused and neglected children are either more aggressive or more withdrawn than their non-maltreated peers and that they are likely to experience more conflict and hostility in their relationships with them. Higher levels of aggression are found among physically ill-treated children; neglected children tend to be more withdrawn (Erickson and Egeland 1996). Bolger et al. (1998), in a study of 107 maltreated children, found that the earlier the onset of maltreatment and the longer it persists, the less likely such children are to be popular with their peers. They also note that maltreated children find it harder to maintain friendships in adolescence as these become more intimate and complex.

The reason for poor social functioning on the part of abused children might not be the result of the psychologically incapacitating effects of being poorly cared for or ill-treated. An alternative explanation is that their parents are themselves socially isolated and do not provide, or value, peer contacts for their children. There could be factors other than these that mark out ill-treated children for fractured peer relationships. They may have been disruptive in school, poorly dressed by the standards of the rest of the neighbourhood and avoided by their peers for these reasons.

Clearly both psychological and social factors need to be taken into account. However, the research leaves us in little doubt that abused and deprived children do not generally enjoy good peer relationships and this, therefore, can add to the difficulties they may already be experiencing in their intra-familial relationships.

School performance

Differences exist among the findings on the consequences of maltreatment on cognitive development, verbal abilities and problem-solving skills. Some studies find evidence of lowered intellectual and cognitive functioning in abused children compared with children who have not been abused (Veltman and Browne 2001; Porter et al. 2005), whereas others found no differences (Allen and Oliver 1982). This may be connected with confounding variables such as the timing, nature and severity of the abuse. For example:

> Children maltreated in multiple developmental periods had more externalizing and internalizing problems and lower IQ scores than children maltreated in only one developmental period. Chronically maltreated children had significantly more family risk factors than children maltreated in one developmental period and these accounted for maltreatment chronicity effects on externalizing and internalizing problems, but not IQ. The timing of maltreatment did not have a unique effect on cognitive or behavioral outcomes, although it did moderate the effect of maltreatment chronicity on prosocial behavior.
>
> (Jaffee and Maikovich-Fong 2011)

Far less equivocal is the finding that child abuse results in lower academic achievement as well as impaired school performance generally – for example, through lower grades. This finding has emerged consistently over the years, including from the Minnesota Study (Sroufe et al. 2009). Poor educational achievements have also been found among children in care in the UK, many of whom are likely to have experienced some form of abuse or neglect (see Jackson 1996).

Two important messages come across from research into the short- and medium-term effects of physical abuse and neglect so far reviewed. The first is that early depriving experiences can set up a cycle of events that can reinforce the ill-effects of those early events (Howe 2011). The second, linked to the first, is that incidents of abuse, while traumatic and occasionally causing lasting physical damage, even death, are not as such the major determinants of negative consequences. The ongoing climate within the family seems to be of prime importance in determining whether or not such consequences persist.

'Runaways'

Both in the USA and in Britain, an association between physical abuse and neglect has been found with children who run away from home and are then homeless. Kaufman and Widom (1999), in a study of 587 reported runaways, found that just under half had been physically abused. In the UK, there has been a series of studies carried out by the Children's Society into the backgrounds and experiences of children and young people who have run away from home (Rees 1993; Rees and Smeaton

2001). Rees (1993), in a study of 80 children staying in a safe house, found that physical violence was the most commonly cited reason for running away from home, occurring in just under a half of all those interviewed. In a sample of 416 adolescents drawn from a longitudinal study conducted in Pennsylvania, Kim et al. (2009: 19) found that 'physical and psychological abuse predicts a child's running away from home and that running away predicts later delinquency and victimisation as well as partially mediating the effect of earlier abuse'. In a study in the USA, Sullivan and Knutson (2000b) found very high levels of children with disabilities among their sample of runaways, with maltreatment being seen as the main cause in the majority of these cases. Today, 'Railway Children' (www.railwaychildren.org.uk) acts as an awareness-raising organisation in 24 countries.

Resilient children

Not every child who is maltreated experiences the negative consequences presented so far. 'Protective factors' such as optimism, high self-esteem, high intelligence or a sense of hopefulness can insulate or 'buffer' some children (Heller et al. 1999). The Minnesota data also found that relationships with supportive adults and friends also helped (Sroufe et al. 2009). Mrazek and Mrazek (1987) list 12 factors that can account for resilient survival behaviours. Most of these are associated with the child's personality and intelligence, but some are linked to situational circumstances, such as access to good educational and health facilities. However, a number of commentators are now questioning whether this 'trait-based' operational construction of 'resilience' is the most appropriate one (Liebenberg and Ungar 2009). They prefer instead to conceptualise resilience as the ability to recognise, seek, acquire and then negotiate successfully the right kind of help and support when it is needed; they see it as a dynamic process, not a static personal attribute, even though it contains a genetic component.

   Kinard (1998), however, poses the following important questions about resilience in children, particularly in relation to defining the concept. Are there objective measures of resilience? Who decides whether a child is resilient? How long does a child have to be resilient to be termed as such? She also notes that resilience does not necessarily signify emotional health in that a child could simply be internalising problems, factors that need to be borne in mind when supporting families where children are acting as carers (Dearden and Becker 2001; Cree 2003). Clearly, therefore, much care is needed on the part of professionals in using the notion of resilience. On the positive side it may inform supportive help given to children coping with adverse circumstances, but there are dangers that children could be too easily identified as resilient and not be helped in an effective way.

Severe psychological difficulties and impairments to young children as a result of physical abuse

Studies have linked physical abuse with hyperactivity in children (Whitmore et al. 1993). Originating in the USA, the diagnosis of PTSD is increasingly being used elsewhere (Perrin et al. 1999). This diagnosis has been applied to adults and children experiencing disturbingly high levels of stress following either being the victim of or witnessing extreme violence or threat of it, or some form of catastrophe (Seng et al.

2011). Symptoms of PTSD in children include sleep disturbance, loss of concentration, constant re-experiencing of the trauma-inducing events and separation anxiety. Perrin et al. (1999: 277) define PTSD as an 'abnormal reaction to an abnormal event'. Clearly there are many variations in relation to PTSD – often connected with the under-identification of mediating factors, making diagnosis problematic. However, there is sufficient evidence to link PTSD to children exposed to physical and sexual violence within and outside the family.

Longer-term pathological effects of physical abuse and neglect

As was stressed in the introduction to this chapter, the longer the gap between the abusive incident and the behaviour associated with it, the greater the uncertainty about the linkage. This is demonstrated in the case of child sexual abuse and prostitution, for example, and should be borne in mind throughout this discussion, in which two long-term effects linked to physical abuse and neglect are considered: mental illness, and general life experiences and outlook. Drug-taking, delinquency and violent crime are not explored in any detail because the trajectories and pathways are too loosely coupled to be reliably considered as direct effects of child abuse; although, clearly, many children who are abused follow criminal pathways and abuse drugs – the problem is that so do lots of children who have not been abused. These particular outcomes are notoriously hard to pin down, and that is why they have been excluded from the discussion.

Mental illness

The link between parental mental illness and physical child abuse and neglect was considered in the previous chapter. Here the concern is whether mental illness is a consequence of being abused or neglected as a child. Because of the impact of mediator variables, we often encounter wide variation in results – and this is why there are few studies today which consider such research questions as 'Does child abuse lead to . . . ?' Here are two examples which illustrate this problem.

An early study into the prevalence of the experience of child abuse among a sample of mentally ill participants was undertaken by Carmen et al. (1984). They analysed the case records of 188 in-patients in a US psychiatric hospital to see if there was evidence of abuse (as children and wives) in their backgrounds. They found that 80 (43 per cent) of these patients had histories of some form of abuse; 64 of these (80 per cent) had been physically abused and half sexually abused; 72 (90 per cent) had been victimised by family members; 52 (65 per cent) were female. The researchers argue that these figures are probably an underestimation of the real incidence of abuse in this population because they included only those cases where there was unequivocal evidence that abuse had occurred. But some years later Read (1998), reporting on an examination of the records of 100 consecutive admissions to an acute psychiatric in-patient unit in New Zealand, found a considerably lower rate of abuse than Carmen et al. – namely 22 per cent. However, patients who had been physically or sexually abused, or both, were more likely to be suicidal, to have longer stays in hospital and to show the most severe disturbances in symptoms and behaviour. Read (1998: 366) concluded that these findings raised 'the possibility that child abuse may have a causative role in the most severe psychiatric conditions, including those currently thought to be primarily biological in origin'.

Greater sensitisation to the fact that such relatively high numbers of people who are treated as psychiatric patients are likely to have been ill-treated as children can only be of benefit to them and their treatment. However, it should be noted that there are many other possible factors apart from childhood abuse that could account for the psychiatric illnesses found in these studies and, as we have demonstrated, by no means all physically and sexually abused children develop psychiatric illnesses. There are also problems relating to the definitions and diagnoses of psychiatric illness.

A more promising approach to the study of pathways between child abuse and subsequent mental ill-health looked at the 'impact of child abuse on neuro-endocrine functioning and the structure of the brain, in particular on the amygdala, hippo-campus, left hemisphere, and corpus callosum' (Coates 2010: 391), and then considered the effects on mental disorders. All were implicated to a greater or lesser degree in moderating the effect on adult mental health. The author went on to look specifically at what the implications were for practitioners and in essence stressed the need for stability, consistency and predictability in close relationships.

General life experiences and outlook

Most of the studies looking at how abuse impacts on victims when they reach adulthood are retrospective ones. As was saw in the previous chapter, such studies tend to exaggerate the extent of the influence of abuse on later life. Also there is a problem with retrospective studies that the memory of the research respondents becomes less accurate over time (Widom et al. 2004). Colman and Widom (2004) in a study of 1,196 substantiated physical abuse and neglect cases (followed up after 20 years) found that they were more likely to have experienced problems in close relationships with other adults than those in a control group. This was indicated by higher rates of cohabitation, walking out and divorce.

A British study by Gibbons et al. (1995b) followed up 144 children 10 years after they had been placed on child abuse registers for physical abuse reasons. They used a control group of a similar number of children from similar backgrounds and came to the conclusion that there was little sign that the severity of abuse had any direct effects on the child's development 9 or 10 years later.

A 20-year follow-up study of 44 children identified as 'non-organic failure to thrive' showed that some children had by adulthood developed more positive attachment styles where others had not (Iwaniec and Sneddon 2001). Key variables were seen to be the type of professional support that these individuals had received and their experience of rewarding close relationships.

As can be seen, therefore, important though these prospective studies are, the findings are not sufficiently consistent to provide the basis for safe judgements about the long-term effects of physical child abuse and neglect.

The consequences of extra-familial physical abuse – bullying

While children are exposed to a wide range of physical abuse outside the family, little focused research into its consequences has been carried out. The main exception is in relation to bullying. It is estimated that 16 children per year commit suicide in the UK as a consequence of school bullying and links have been made between bullying and PTSD (Marr and Field 2001). Clearly not all children by any means will develop this disorder following school bullying and the emphasis of central government policy in England is on prevention. Nevertheless, the consequences of school bullying are likely to be severe in the short term for a small number of children and it is important to ensure a prompt and appropriate response where it occurs.[1]

Summary

Many of the studies reviewed here suffer from the problems of causally linking abuse and outcome, from weak and vague definitions of abuse and from a lack of attention to social factors as influences on behaviour, such as the differential impact of abuse on women.[2] Having noted these problems, however, the following general picture of the consequences of physical abuse and neglect emerges from the research that exists. Many physically abused children suffer considerable emotional and psychological problems in their early childhood, leading them to have problems in trusting other people and to suffer from a sense of personal worthlessness. Socially and intellectually they do not perform well because of this. Many physically abused children tend to be both aggressive and withdrawn; neglected children as a whole seem to be less aggressive, but are more likely to exhibit withdrawn behaviour. A relatively small number of children suffer permanently from the physical effects of injury and severe neglect. Some children seem to survive well and cope despite all the odds. Much depends on the quality of their relationships with members of their family and others during childhood and also on the individual personality and intelligence of the child in question. In the longer term, there is evidence of linkages between being physically abused and mental illness, drug abuse, delinquency and violent criminality and general adjustment to life. The connection between child abuse and these behaviours in adult lives is harder to prove, but nevertheless, particularly in the field of mental illness, the consistency of the findings is highly persuasive and has important implications for psychiatric practices.

The consequences of child sexual abuse

Research into the impact of sexual abuse on victims has been, and continues to be, more in evidence than that into physical abuse and neglect. This stems to a large extent from the way in which sexual abuse was emphasised in the 1980s, often as a result of women recounting their childhood experiences and the effects these continued to have in their adult lives. Such accounts have led to greater sensitivity to the consequences of such abuse, particularly with regard to its long-term effects. Generally, although there are the same methodological problems as in studies of the consequences of physical abuse, particularly in relation to definitions and the use of control groups, research into the effects of child sexual abuse seems to be more systematic and detailed. Nevertheless, there are still major difficulties in sifting out the direct impact of the abuse from that which may be attributed to other variables, such as pre-existing problems, responses to the abuse by significant adults (including professionals) and later depriving experiences.

From the mid-1980s studies tended to differentiate between short-term and long-term effects (Browne and Finkelhor 1986; Beitchman et al. 1991, 1992). Also, clear distinctions are made between the impact of intra-familial and extra-familial sexual abuse of children in only a few of the research studies.

Short-term effects

These include a higher level of severe consequences for children of all ages who have been sexually abused, in particular: fearfulness, depression and withdrawal, hostility and aggression, low self-esteem, guilt and shame, physical symptoms, cognitive disability, developmental delay, impaired school performance and showing inappropriate sexual behaviour.

Two conclusions can be drawn. The first is that, while an appreciable number of sexually abused children do experience behavioural and emotional problems in the two years following abuse, compared with children who have not been abused, the linkage between these behaviours and sexual abuse is weak and other factors could account for them. As Beitchman et al. (1991) stressed:

> We do not know whether many of the symptoms reported in the literature are specific to sexual abuse or whether they are attributable to other factors such as the child's pre-morbid level of functioning or a disturbed home environment. The contribution of these preexisting constitutional and familial factors to observed psychopathology needs to be more carefully examined.
>
> (Beitchman et al. 1991: 552)

The only relatively clear direct outcome is that of inappropriately sexualised behaviour, which occurs in between 25 and 33 per cent of all sexually abused children (see also Brilleslijper-Kater et al. 2004).

The second conclusion is that sexual abuse per se has different effects on children. Browne and Finkelhor note that: 'In the immediate aftermath of sexual abuse one-fifth to two-fifths of abused children seen by clinicians manifest some noticeable disturbance' (1986: 164). It should be stressed that this apparently strange conclusion may result from the fact that a broad definition of sexual abuse is used in most of the studies, including, for instance, various degrees of seriousness and both intra-familial and extra-familial abuse. It should be noted that the timing of the research is also important. Calam et al. (1998) found that, overall, their sample of children was experiencing more problems two years after the abuse incident than they were at four weeks afterwards. It has to be stressed that research into this area is still relatively new and experimental; it is important, therefore, to interpret the findings carefully and not to draw hasty conclusions from them.

Long-term effects

Many of the behaviours and emotions discussed in relation to short-term effects of sexual abuse are also to be found in studies of long-term effects. As stressed at the start of this chapter, the linkages, seen to be problematic in the case of short-term effects, are even more problematic with regard to long-term effects because of the greater length of time between the abuse and the observed behaviour and because of the possible effect of a much wider range of intervening variables. Nevertheless, there are a number of consequences that have emerged. For example, Swanston et al. (2003), in a nine-year follow-up of 103 sexually abused children in Sydney, Australia, found that they suffered significantly more from *fear and anxiety* than individuals in their non-abused control group.

The same authors also found high rates of *depression and low self-esteem* in their study. Again in Australia, Martin et al. (2004) carried out a study of 2,485 14-year-olds. They found that 5.4 per cent of girls and 2 per cent of boys in their sample had been sexually abused and that those who had been sexually abused were far more likely than their non-abused peers to entertain *suicidal thoughts*. Boys who had been sexually abused were more likely than girls to attempt suicide (55 per cent to 29 per cent).

Low self-esteem is another longer-term consequence of sexual abuse in childhood. Swanston et al. (2003) confirm a significant link between self-esteem and sexual abuse in their study. For the same reasons as outlined earlier, it is very difficult to untangle the links between childhood sexual abuse and longer-term psychiatric problems; the same applies to connections with sexual abuse and eating disorders, abusing other children as adults and running away from home. Less problematic, however, is the almost self-evident finding that there are physical consequences of sexual abuse. For example, Jaudes and Morris (1990) collected data from a sample of 138 sexually abused children referred to hospital between 1979 and 1987 and found that one-third of them had a sexually transmitted disease; nowadays 'chlamydia and pelvic inflammatory disease [are] the most common infections' (Kelly and Koh 2006: 434). Their average age was just over 6 years. Although, despite their name, it is possible for sexually transmitted diseases to be passed on in non-sexual ways, the chances of this are very small (Neursten et al. 1984). Interestingly, and perhaps somewhat controversially, for 'the most part, physical symptoms were of no value in differentiating between those who had been sexually abused and those who had not' (Kelly and Koh 2006: 112).

The findings of research into the general long-term effects confirm that women who have been sexually abused are more likely than women who have not to have problems in later life with regard to fear, anxiety, self-esteem, depression, satisfactory sexual relations, substance misuse and general mental health, and to be vulnerable to further abuse. However, such consequences are not inevitable. In the section that follows, the focus is on those factors that can be influential in leading to the worst outcomes.

A number of other variables have been associated in the literature with influence on the harmful effects of child sexual abuse: age at onset of abuse; gender of child; degree of seriousness of the abuse; duration of abuse; relationship of the abuser to the abused; abuse accompanied by violence; and the way in which the abused child was helped and responded to at and after the time of disclosure. However, today the only *relatively* consistent finding among these variables is that concerning the gender of the victim.

For example, according to the *Fourth National Incidence Study of Child Abuse and Neglect* (NIS-4) (Sedlak et al. 2010, n = 16,875), girls are now sexually abused five times more often than boys (but to illustrate the point about variation, in the third study – only a decade earlier – it was three times more prevalent). The NIS-4 survey still confirms David Finkelhor's earlier finding that both boys and girls are most vulnerable if sexual abuse occurs between the ages of 7 and 13 (Finkelhor 1994).

Beitchman et al. (1991, 1992) referred to several other studies that confirmed the influence of family response on both short- and long-term harm. Their view was that victims of child sexual abuse are more likely than non-victims to come from disturbed families and, therefore, that they are particularly likely to be responded to by their families in a negative way. Clearly this argument is more relevant to intra-familial abuse. Also of importance in this area is the response of professionals to allegations of sexual abuse. Elwell and Ephloss (1987) found that bad handling of intervention by the police and other professionals was associated with increased short-term trauma. Gomes-Schwartz et al. (1990) found that children removed from their families showed the most short-term problems but, as Browne and Finkelhor (1986) comment, these might have been the most problematic cases in the first place.

There seems, therefore, to be reasonable evidence to suggest that sexual abuse is likely to be most harmful in the following instances:

- where the abusive act involves penetration
- where the abuse has persisted for some time
- where the abuser is a father-figure
- where the abuse is accompanied by violence, force and/or the threat of it
- where the response of the family is negative.

While the age and sex of the abused child have some impact on the outcome, the research does not provide clear indications of the direction of these variables' effects. There is not sufficient information on the impact of professional intervention to evaluate conclusively its effect for good or ill.

For some health and welfare practitioners, the degree of detail of all this research may seem unnecessary, in that child sexual abuse of the type in which they frequently become involved – largely intra-familial and often of a very serious nature – clearly has harmful effects on the child. It can seem to be somewhat hair-splitting to separate which element of abuse in a generally abusive situation causes the most harm. Similarly, research that suggests that children who are removed from families do less well than those who remain can be frustrating when it is apparent that removal is the only feasible course of action. Nevertheless, there are some important and relevant findings, in particular that sexual abuse of children is not necessarily incapacitating for them in later life. There is a tendency among professionals to make this assumption, which can in itself have negative effects. In particular, awareness of the impact of the variables just discussed is an important starting-point for assessing the consequences for the child and how to organise a response. Such knowledge provides a framework for intervention, not a blueprint. Children whom one would expect to suffer less harmful effects on the basis of known research findings may in fact experience considerable trauma. As has been repeatedly stressed, there are weaknesses in the research, and findings need to be carefully interpreted. Nevertheless, despite its limitations, this is the best formal available knowledge and it should, therefore, have relevance for policy and practice in this field.

The consequences of disorganised attachment

There is a bi-directional relationship between disorganised attachment and child maltreatment: most maltreated children show attachment disorganisation and between 80–90 per cent of abused children are likely to show disorganised attachment (Cicchetti and Curtis 2006; Lyons-Ruth and Jacobvitz 2008). Research on the consequences of disorganised attachment can, therefore, be used as a relatively reliable proxy measure of the consequences of child maltreatment. The added benefit of doing this is that research into disorganised attachment is more dependent on observable behaviours whereas the definition of 'child abuse and neglect' has always led to methodological problems which have proved difficult to overcome. Similarly, disorganised attachment 'occurs in the present' whereas child maltreatment will have taken place often many years ago and in a variety of forms.

There is a general consensus in attachment research that mere 'insecurity' of attachment is unlikely *on its own* to lead to mental health disorders. These studies are in little doubt that it is 'the absence of a coherent strategy (i.e. *disorganisation*) rather than insecurity *per se* that is linked to maladaptation' (Deklyen and Greenberg 2008: 649). Furthermore, 'the only clear connections between infant attachment and adult psychopathology are between disorganised attachment and dissociative symptoms in adolescence and early adulthood' (Dozier et al. 2008: 736). Again, it is thought that a 'sensitized neurobiology' (p. 736) is the most likely cause, and specifically 'attachment-related trauma to later dissociative symptoms' (p. 720).

Five consistent factors emerge which mediate the pathway between more global caregiver 'risk factors' and disorganised attachment: i) unresolved loss and trauma (see Madigan et al. 2006) – especially when accompanied by ii) dissociation as it can lead to iii) disconnected and extremely insensitive parenting (see Out et al. 2009) – and iv) a low capacity for mentalisation – i.e. the inability to appreciate that others have different thoughts, feelings, hopes and intentions from one's own (see Fonagy and Target 2005; Allen et al. 2008). As we shall see in the next section, from genetic research it now emerges that v) caregivers' high levels of *impulsivity* explain why some cannot inhibit fast enough their tendency towards low mentalising capacity.

These five factors offer great promise in explaining much of the variation in the aetiology of child abuse and neglect Not surprisingly, therefore, we see these same factors re-emerging as explanatory mechanisms when exploring the conse-quences and effects of child maltreatment, specifically in terms of subsequent mental illness, as this is the 'downstream effect' that is most researched in the child protection literature.

Disorganised attachment and subsequent mental disorder

Because both forms of depression – unipolar and bipolar – have a significant genetic component, the connection to disorganised attachment tends only to be consistently strong when there is accompanying unresolved loss and trauma (Deklyen and

Greenberg 2008) and/or persistent and prolonged maltreatment. Similarly there are no clear links between disorganised attachment and schizophrenia.

A clearer picture emerges when examining dissociative disorders, borderline personality disorders (BPDs) and anti-social personality disorders. Not surprisingly *dissociative disorders* are strongly connected to disorganised attachment (see Carlson 1998; Liotti 2004; Sroufe et al. 2005) because dissociation is often a feature of it. Interestingly, childhood abuse and emotional neglect are very high among adults who develop dissociative disorders (which do not have a high heritability factor). In some studies the correlation is actually 100 per cent. Furthermore, with disorganised attachment no 'associations emerged between disorganised attachment and any variables assessing endogenous vulnerability, such as prenatal difficulties, difficulties during childbirth, or maternal drug or alcohol use . . .' (Dozier et al. 2008: 729).

Because BPD includes neurotic and psychotic behaviour, high correlations are found consistently between the condition and disorganised attachment in early childhood. The same is true of anti-social personality disorder, the adult equivalent of 'conduct disorder' in adolescence (Deklyen and Greenberg 2008).

Van IJzendoorn and Bakermans-Kranenburg (2003) state that 'Disorganised attachment has been shown to be indexed with clear-cut behavioural markers . . . and have serious developmental consequences . . . Extreme indications of disorganisation may be regarded as psychiatric disturbance with more or less severe symptoms and consequences' (Van IJzendoorn and Bakermans-Kranenburg 2003: 317). Because of strong and consistent linkages between disorganised attachment and child maltreatment, it may prove more fruitful to continue to explore the consequences and effects of the latter by continuing to study the former.

We now move on to discuss recent studies which look at how brain biochemistry and genetics are helping us understand more clearly the consequences of child maltreatment, again in many of the studies by considering disorganised attachment as the key intervening variable.

Neuro-biochemical and genetic research into the effects of maltreatment

The design of neuro-biochemical and genetic research

Magnetic resonance imaging (MRI) scanners measure the structure and function of the brain by showing two- and three-dimensional 'slices'. Electroencephalography (EEG) 'nets' cover the head and use small 'suckers' to measure electrical activity.

Functional magnetic resonance imaging (fMRI) scans measure the amount and location of blood in different areas of the brain to reveal precisely the areas that are active when an individual undertakes a task (such as looking at photos expressing different emotions). For example, McCrory et al. (2010) asked adolescents exposed to family violence, and controls, to look at pictures of male and female faces showing sad, calm or angry expressions. Worryingly, they found that children exposed to family violence show a similar pattern of brain activity to soldiers exposed to combat, specifically in the amygdala and anterior insula regions.

The HPA axis connects the hypothalamus, the pituitary gland and the adrenal glands, which regulate, among other things, cortisol levels produced when the body experiences fear and danger (the axis also helps to regulate temperature, digestion and the immune system, and plays a large part in the system controlling our reaction to stress, trauma and injury). Measuring cortisol levels is achieved by taking saliva samples. Too much or too little cortisol can cause problems. The under- or over-production of cortisol has been called 'toxic stress' (National Scientific Council on the Developing Child 2005) as the effects can be severe and lead to psychopatho-logical conditions and psychiatric vulnerability in adulthood, as well as altering brain circuitry.

Genetic research usually needs large samples to overcome the problem of tracking single pathways from a specific genotype to something as complex as 'maltreatment', partly because the statistical power needed is large (Lyons-Ruth and Jacobvitz 2008). As a consequence:

> Until recently, the preferred way to explore the effect of genetics was to compare monozygotic (identical) with dizygotic (non-identical) twins. Fortunately, complementary methods are now available to study the possibility of DA [disor-ganised attachment] being partly heritable. They involve analysing the structure of genes at the molecular level. This is achieved by taking 'buccal swabs' – a saliva sample taken from inside the cheek.
>
> (Shemmings and Shemmings 2011: 93)

Most studies direct their attention at two neurotransmitters: oxytocin and dopamine. Oxytocin plays a significant role in the care of new-born infants, and low oxytocin levels are strongly related to emotional abuse (Heim et al. 2009). Dopamine regulates reward and attentional strategies and increases when we are under stress. At that point, the more logical and measured parts of the brain that delay gratification – especially the prefrontal cortex – disconnect and our sub-cortical, more impulsive areas take over, resulting in increased impulsivity. The HPA axis controls the entire system when we are stressed. When a child has been maltreated the HPA axis is often on 'red alert': 'even though there may *actually* be no real threat, the body stays on permanent "look-out" and remains in an almost permanent state of hypervigilance and anxiety. It is this state that can eventually impair or impede the structure, function and neural circuitry of the brain' (Shemmings and Shemmings 2011: 90). This is what Luyten refers to as a 'bio-behavioural switch' (Luyten et al. 2009). Chronic maltreatment in childhood leads to the switchover kicking in a lot earlier.

Bio-psychosocial research is beginning to reveal more precisely the mechanisms that produce the ambiguous and sometimes contradictory findings typical of this whole field; it helps in our understanding of why someone who is sexually abused, for example, might go on to abuse others, or develop mental illness, etc. whereas others do not. Until now, researchers have assumed that the differences would be the result of 'age of onset' or the 'duration of the abuse' but, as we have seen, two studies will reveal different results, even though the designs are similar. This research is expanding our understanding of the mediating processes between independent (e.g. 'early child abuse') and dependent (e.g. 'mental ill-health in adulthood') variables.

Specific findings: neurological and biochemical

McCrory et al. (2010) offer the best summary of these findings to date. In their detailed review they found, firstly, some evidence that abused or neglected children have smaller cranial and cerebral volume. Secondly, however, although there appears not to be any reduction in hippocampal volume – a sub-cortical area responsible for, among other things, long-term memory – in maltreated children, it *has* been noted in adults maltreated as children and who *also* exhibited PTSD or experienced chronic stress. Notice the need, again, to separate out stress as a confounding or mediating variable to understand the complexity of this finding – this is why it was built into the design. Thirdly, maltreated children were noted to have a smaller corpus callosa – a key area of the brain responsible for arousal, emotion and higher cognitive abilities.

Genetic explanations

We now consider the growing field of genetic research and its connection to child maltreatment. To do this, we draw upon the larger volume of work on disorganised attachment. Because it is a known indicator of maltreatment (see Shemmings and Shemmings 2011), what applies to disorganised attachment is likely to apply in large measure in cases of child abuse and neglect.

The dopamine D4 receptor (DRD4) gene crops up regularly as having a mediating effect in children with disorganised attachment (Lakatos et al. 2000, 2002), as well as in adults who were abused as children. It also appeared at first to be related to attention-deficit hyperactivity disorder (ADHD) (Lasky-Su et al. 2008), but there are now doubts as a result of methodological problems similar to those that have bedevilled the field of research in the aetiology of child maltreatment (Turic et al. 2010). Dopamine is a neurotransmitter involved in the regulation of reward.

Two subsequent papers (Bakermans-Kranenburg and Van IJzendoorn 2004; Spangler and Zimmermann 2007) contended that Lakatos et al. did not take account sufficiently of 'gene × environment' interactions. For example, 'children might inherit the tendency to be overweight, but if there is very little food around for them to eat, and they end up poorly nourished, they will be underweight for their age' (Shemmings and Shemmings 2011: 95).

Genes operate in complex, interactive ways. For example, certain 'polymorphisms' (small gene variants) provide resilience to maltreatment in one person while, in another, they will lead to vulnerability. To confuse matters further, the same genes can be connected to different outcomes. For example, the serotonin transporter 5-HTT gene has been linked to PTSD, depression *and* anti-social behaviour (Feder et al. 2009).

Applied to child protection, the fundamental idea behind 'gene-environment interaction' (GxE) is that some children are more susceptible to abusive parenting than others. It is referred to as 'differential susceptibility' (see, for example, Belsky 2005). At one level this appears to be a restatement of the concept of resilience – the difference is that the resilience factors, in genetics research, are not the same as those identified in psychosocial research (for example, the child's intelligence, having a sense of humour). In the field of genetics research this is known as 'differential susceptibility', as elaborated by Jay Belsky (Belsky 2005). Genetic explanations stress how and why different environmental features can produce different reactions and responses in different children.

Finally, in addition to the concept of GxE, some genes also interact with other genes. For example:

> there are now thought to be nine genes which help us 'pick up the baby' soon after its birth (and not do much else): if all goes well 'your ticket is punched when you hold your baby' . . . or, at least it is for most parents; for others, it can be a time of unbearable emotional pain, full of regular reminders of insensitive parenting provided during their own childhood.
>
> (Shemmings and Shemmings 2011: 95)

With these points borne in mind, two other key genes so far identified (see McCrory et al. 2010) in maltreatment are monoamine oxidase-A (MAO-A), the so-called warrior gene as it is connected to aggression (Beach et al. 2010) and serotonin transporter (5-HTT), often referred to as the 'depression gene'. Combined with the dopamine neurotransmitter DRD4 7-repeat, which helps us deal with reward and impulse, we may have the ingredients of a genetic admixture in part responsible for stress reactivity and impulsivity (Maestripieri 2010) that, as we saw above, may be a key component in low mentalisation. The effect is that, in combination with caregiving, social support and other environmental features, G (× G) × E interactions can confer vulnerability or resilience (McCrory et al. 2010).

Dante Cicchetti and his colleagues completed two studies into the GxE interactions. The first considered the combined effect on child maltreatment of the serotonin transporter (5-HTT) and monoamine oxidase-A (MAO-A) genes specifically in relation to depression. The researchers note:

> Adolescents (mean age = 16.7 years) from low socioeconomic backgrounds with a history of child maltreatment (n = 207) or no such history (n = 132) were interviewed and provided buccal cells for genetic analysis. Gene × Environment interactions were observed. Heightened depressive symptoms were found only among extensively maltreated youth with low MAO-A activity. Among comparably maltreated youth with high MAO-A activity, self-coping strategies related to lower symptoms. Sexual abuse and the 5-HTT short/short genotype predicted higher depression, anxiety, and somatic symptoms. This gene × environment interaction was further moderated by MAO-A activity level. The results highlight the protective functions of genetic polymorphisms and coping strategies in high risk youth and offer direction for understanding resilience and its promotion from a multiple levels of analysis perspective.
>
> (Cicchetti et al. 2007: 1161)

In their second study, a slightly different variant of the serotonin transporter – this time the 5-HTTLPR – was shown to mediate the effect of child maltreatment on suicidal thoughts among school-aged children. The sample was 850 children from low-income families, divided into 478 maltreated and 372 non-maltreated. It was found that 'higher suicidal ideation was found among maltreated than non-maltreated children . . . but the protective effect of the 5-HTTLPR . . . genotype on suicidal ideation was limited to maltreated children experiencing fewer subtypes' (Cicchetti et al. 2010: 536).

Concluding comments

We return briefly to a point made at the beginning of this chapter: that there are consequences to society of child maltreatment, because abuse and neglect extend far beyond the child and the family. Advanced econometric modelling techniques now permit the forward projection of current problems into future scenarios, enabling governments to predict, albeit within wide reliability tolerance levels, the financial consequences of societal problems and challenges. Trying to 'put a figure' on something as complex as the effects and consequences of child maltreatment might sound like a futile task but anecdotal evidence already exists that policy-makers are often more persuaded by 'money talks'-type arguments than they are by empirical research. This seems to have been the case with the recent report by Graham Allen MP's into the need for 'early intervention' across the UK in respect of child welfare and protection services (Allen 2011).

In conclusion, the *financial* consequences of child maltreatment are staggering: as estimated by Prevent Child Abuse America, a reputable body which uses reliable statistical data, the total annual cost of child abuse and neglect in the USA is estimated be in the region of $103,754,000,492 (Ching-Tung and Holton 2007): over $103 billion.

While not restricted to child abuse and maltreatment, the 'cross-party' report in the UK, *Early Intervention* by Graham Allen, included the following sobering figures relating to the costs of inaction:

- The productivity loss to the state as a result of youth unemployment is estimated at £10 million every day.
- The average cost of an individual spending a lifetime on benefits is £430,000, not including the loss of tax revenue.
- The cost of youth crime in 2009 alone has been estimated by the National Audit Office at £8.5–11 billion.
- The costs associated with mental health problems in the UK are estimated at £105.2 billion.
- The total cost of drug misuse in the UK is estimated at £77.7 billion.
- The current total cost of children in care is estimated at £2.9 billion. About half of this is spent on children who have been abused – dealing with a problem after it has become acute and costly rather than preventing it from happening.

(Allen 2011: 34)

As the Allen report concludes, in the executive summary (p. ix):

every taxpayer pays the cost of low educational achievement, poor work aspirations, drink and drug misuse, teenage pregnancy, criminality and unfulfilled

lifetimes on benefits. But it is not just about money – important as this is, especially now – it is about social disruption, fractured lives, broken families and sheer
human waste.

It may be, therefore, that this more recent focus on the economic and financial consequences of child maltreatment and 'unnecessarily' impaired development of children
and young people offers more hope for change.

Recommended reading

Allen, G. (2011) *Early Intervention: The Next Steps*. London: HM Government.

Beck, U. (2008) *World at Risk*. Cambridge: Polity Press.

Featherstone, B., Hooper, C-A., Scourfield, J. and Taylor, J. (eds) (2010) *Gender and Child Welfare in Society*. Oxford: Wiley-Blackwell.

Lazenbatt, A. (2010) *The Impact of Abuse and Neglect on the Health and Mental Health of Children and Young People*. London: NSPCC.

Liebenberg, L. and Ungar, M. (eds) (2009) *Researching Resilience*. Toronto, ON: University of Toronto Press.

Out, D., Bakermans-Kranenburg, M. J. and Van IJzendoorn, M. H. (2009) The role of disconnected and extremely insensitive parenting in the development of disorganized attachment: the validation of a new measure, *Attachment and Human Development*, 11: 419–43.

White, S., Wastell, D. G., Broadhurst, K. and Hall, C. (2010) When policy o'erleaps itself: the
tragic tale of the Integrated Children's System, *Critical Social Policy*, 30(3): 405–29.

8

The evidence base for child protection practice

Introduction

The aim of this chapter is to analyse what research tells us about the way in which health and welfare professionals respond to child abuse and neglect concerns and the effectiveness of this response.

Prior to the early 1990s, the amount of research into British child protection practice was very limited. There were few studies of the work of mainstream statutory agencies (Dingwall et al. 1983; Corby 1987). Child protection public inquiry reports gave glimpses of practice approaches, but as such inquiries were held when things appeared to have gone wrong, they formed a rather skewed sample. There were more, but still relatively few, accounts and evaluations of intervention into physical and sexual abuse cases by those working in voluntary agencies and hospital settings (Baher et al. 1976; Lynch and Roberts 1982; Dale et al. 1986; Bentovim et al. 1988) and a few accounts of action research projects (Smith and Rachman 1984; Browne and Saqi 1988). Overall, there were very few studies of the effectiveness of child protection interventions, only a small amount of research into the consumer end with regard to parents (Brown 1986; Corby 1987) and no formal research data on the views of children.

The picture changed considerably from the mid-1990s. There was a fuller body of research, largely sponsored by central government following events at Cleveland (see Chapter 4). There were two main tranches of this research: that summarised in *Child Protection: Messages from Research* (Department of Health 1995) and that summarised in *The Children Act Now* (Department of Health 2001), in all incorporating 44 research studies. The following key areas of child protection practice were among those focused on in the first tranche: responding to referrals (Gibbons et al. 1995a), carrying out investigations (Cleaver and Freeman 1995; Farmer and Owen 1995), involving parents in the initial stages of intervention and at child protection conferences (Thoburn et al. 1995), inter-professional collaboration (Birchall with Hallett 1995) and responding to sexual abuse allegations (Sharland et al. 1996). In the second group of studies, there has been focus on responding to referrals of children in need in England and Wales (Aldgate and Tunstill 1995; Tunstill and Aldgate 2000), child protection interventions within a context of family support (Brandon et al. 1999; Thoburn et al. 2000), and the views of parents involved in child protection care proceedings (Freeman and Hunt 1998). These studies have largely been concerned to explore the way in which practice is conducted. They have emphasised the extent of poverty and ill-health in most of the families referred for services and interventions. They have sought out the views of parents and of children about being on the receiving end of state intervention.

By and large, they have not examined outcomes of interventions but have tried to distil what is seen to be best practice. They have been particularly influential in the shaping and development of safeguarding children policy in the UK in recent times and in drawing closer links between child protection and child welfare thinking and activity.

There have also been other studies reported during this period, most of them smaller, more independent studies, into child protection investigations (Wellbourne 2002), child protection assessments (Holland 2000), parental participation at conferences and reviews and meetings (Corby et al. 1996; Horwath and Calder 1998; Marsh and Crowe 1998; Bell 1999; Shemmings 1999, 2000; Spratt and Callan 2004), and ongoing management and treatment of sexual abuse cases (Roberts and Taylor 1993; Corby 1998; Farmer and Pollock 2003). More recently, there has been research into the impact of Quality Protects targets on child welfare practice (Devaney 2004), into re-focusing on child protection within a framework of children in need (Spratt 2001), and into the implementation of the new assessment procedures (Corby et al. 2002; Cleaver and Walker 2004). Thus, the research scene in the UK is very active, although it has to be stressed again that the focus of much of this research is on understanding how the processes work rather than on their effectiveness in terms of successful outcomes. So, while we now have a clearer picture of how the British child protection system operates, we still lack a strong body of information about which preventive measures, which intervention strategies and which treatment initiatives work and which do not.

In the USA, child protection research is on a much larger scale in terms of resources. The National Center on Child Abuse and Neglect was set up in the 1970s specifically to promote research initiatives into child protection issues. The emphasis of much North American research is more on evaluating the outcome of intervention than in Britain, but, even so, there remains much concern about the lack of knowledge about effectiveness (Melton and Flood 1994; Leventhal 2003).

Studies and accounts of practice will be considered in the following way. First, those relating to prevention and prediction will be examined. Second, the focus will be on studies and accounts relating to assessment and decision-making at the early intervention stage and later in the process, when important long-term plans are being considered. Third, consideration will be given to provision of ongoing support and treatment, and, finally, general effectiveness studies will be examined.

We decided to sub-divide this chapter into the 'evidence base' pre- and post-2006, the date of the earlier edition.

BEFORE 2006

Prevention

Patterns

Prevention of child abuse appeared more on the agenda in both Britain (Tunstill and Aldgate 2000) and the USA (Leventhal 2001) after the mid-1990s. As was seen in Chapter 2, the way in which British child care policy developed during this period was to shift the emphasis from abuse incidents onto the more ongoing welfare needs of families. Study after study showed that the families being responded to under the child care system had multiple problems and difficulties. The *Children Act Now* report (Department of Health 2001), in an overview of the families involved in its 24 research projects, pointed to the following facts:

- high numbers of lone-parent families (between one-third and one-half in eight of the studies)
- high levels of partner changes in families
- high levels of poverty (98 per cent in one study)
- high numbers living in poor standard rented accommodation
- high levels of mobility
- high levels of social isolation
- high levels of disorganisation in neighbourhoods
- high levels of chronic health problems (physical and mental) and inability to carry out parental functions as a result
- high levels of acute illness
- high levels of problem substance misuse
- high levels of domestic violence and relationship problems with partners.

The wider picture

Not all families experienced all these problems all the time, but, particularly in the case of families whose children were the subject of care proceedings as a result of abuse or neglect, such problems were seen as 'multiple, long-standing and entrenched' (Department of Health 2001: 30). However, as we have pointed out on a number of occasions, not everyone in the above circumstances abused their children; and, to complicate matters, a number of carers were (and are) harmful to children who do not show any of the above 'risk factors'. Nevertheless, data such as these were rightly used to stress the need for a broad range of policies, services and practices that would support, meet the needs of and engage with parents in the process of preventing child abuse and at the same time address other behaviours damaging to the well-being of children – failure to engage with education, involvement in crime and teenage pregnancy. From this point of view, the whole thrust of central government policy outlined in the Green Paper *Every Child Matters* (Department of Health 2003b) was preventive. The key instruments in this process were the 250 Sure Start programmes for children under 5, and the Children's Fund initiative which aimed to bring agencies together to develop initiatives to encourage social inclusion of 5- to 12-year-olds in their communities. Initial evaluation of the Children's Fund projects was rather mixed, suggesting a degree of uncertainty about achieving broad preventive goals (Department for Education and Skills 2004b). Other developments taking place at that time included the setting up of multi-purpose children's centres, and improved nursery, day-care and after-school provision. The aim of all these initiatives was to prevent social exclusion in a broad sense.

By and large, child protection concerns were not seen as best tackled by broader anti-poverty programmes. Thus, they might have what could be seen as a narrower conception of prevention in mind. For instance, Gough (1993) considered what sorts of preventive programmes were being implemented to raise awareness of child abuse and the means of tackling it. He found that, in this sense, there were three types of preventive strategy: those aimed at the whole population, such as community education programmes; those aimed at certain communities, usually those afflicted by poverty and deprivation; and those aimed at certain groups of families in which children were considered to be at risk.

The first level of prevention

With regard to the first type of preventive strategy, Gough (1993) found little evidence of abuse awareness campaigns in Britain. The main exceptions to this were educational programmes in schools aimed at equipping children to protect themselves against sexual abuse. Gillham (1991: 48–63) provided a useful overview of such programmes and research related to them. He questioned their effectiveness, which has generally not been rigorously tested. Most programmes of this kind tended to focus on extra-familial abuse, and one study demonstrated that they have only limited impact (Kelly et al. 1991). In the USA, Finkelhor et al. (1995) found from a study of 2,000 children that 'victimisation prevention instruction', as they termed it, did increase knowledge among children and the likelihood of disclosure.

Much changed in this respect, however, from the mid-1990s. Voluntary agencies in the UK played an increasingly important role in highlighting and raising awareness of child abuse with a view to prompting preventive measures. The National Society for the Prevention of Cruelty to Children (NSPCC) led campaigns about child deaths and the psychological abuse of children. Agencies such as Barnardo's and the Children's Society played a significant role in highlighting challenges in relation to children's involvement in sex work. Childline, which was set up in the late 1980s to provide direct confidential help and support to children, has campaigned to keep all forms of abuse, but particularly sexual abuse of children, in the public eye. An example of the work of child protection lobby groups is the 'Children are Unbeatable! Alliance' which is opposed to all forms of corporal punishment of children. However, while these examples of preventive lobbying and campaigning are clearly very visible, we have little research knowledge about the impact they have had on policy, practice or public perception.

The second level of prevention

The second strategy identified by Gough (1996) involves lay and professional people operating in community centres to provide general help and support with parenting for any family in a particular geographical area. Such provision is open to whole communities; however, some facilities take (or assist) only families referred with child care problems. The former tend to be more family oriented, i.e. designed to provide social support to families (Pithouse and Holland 1999). The latter are more child-focused and work more specifically on parental capacities. There has been little evaluation of the effectiveness of such centres, although a study by Ghate et al. (2000) demonstrates that very few men participate in their activities for a variety of gender-based reasons. The broader-based family support approach is well used in European countries such as Belgium, the Netherlands and Germany. Thyen et al.'s study (1995) of the Child Protection Center in Liibeck, Germany, which worked on a supportive and voluntaristic basis with families where child maltreatment was a concern, demonstrates how an indirect approach can work well. While broad-based supportive approaches are an attractive option, there remain doubts as to whether all families where there are child protection concerns will agree to attend such centres through reasons of low motivation and sense of stigma.

The third level of prevention

The third preventive strategy involves selecting certain types of parents who are considered to be potentially abusive to their children in order to provide extra support from community health and welfare services. This type of approach has not been a mainstream one in Britain, although it has been used in evaluative action research (Browne and Saqi 1988). In the USA, however, it formed the basis of what were termed 'Healthy Start' programmes which have been adopted in most states. These programmes consist of trained family workers or community nurses carrying out regular visits over several years to families whose children are identified at birth as at risk of abuse. The results of these initiatives have been mixed (Chaffin 2004). Olds et al. (1997) carried out a 15-year follow-up of a nurse home visitation programme and found a correlation between this intervention and reduced anti-social behaviour on the part of the children involved in it. Duggan et al. (2004), however, in an evaluation of a similar type of programme in Hawaii (though employing trained family aides rather than health professionals), found that home visiting had little impact on the reduction of abusive behaviour in the short term. They attributed this largely to the fact that the focus of support offered was not sufficiently directed towards abuse prevention.

Assessment and decision-making

There are two key assessment points in child protection work: the first is at the point of referral when there is a need for short-term decision-making; the second is when there is a need to decide on the action required to ensure the longer-term future protection and well-being of the child.

As with many other aspects of child protection work in Britain, there have been considerable changes in thinking about assessment work as a result of the 'refocusing' shift – away from a more reactive approach based on 'child protection' to a more preventive and collaborative 'family support' approach – which began in the mid-1990s. Prior to this, the effect of public inquiries into circumstances where professional intervention was seen to have failed to provide adequate child protection was to emphasise the need for speedy and decisive intervention wherever a child was thought to be at risk of being abused. Following the publication of the Cleveland report (Butler-Sloss 1988), which recommended more strategic forms of intervention in relation to sexual abuse concerns, and research findings that pointed to children who were persistently in need being overlooked because of over-concern with abuse (Gibbons et al. 1995a), health and welfare professionals were required to carry out more broad-based assessments which took into consideration both needs and risks. This culminated in the introduction of the *Framework for the Assessment of Children in Need and Their Families*, which was implemented in April 2001, and two new assessment processes: *initial*, to be carried out at the point of referral; and *core*, in more complex cases, including those raising child protection concerns (Department of Health 2000a). It is within this context that the implications of the research findings to be discussed are considered.

Short-term decision-making in child protection cases

The lack of detailed research into short-term assessment and decision-making in child protection cases made it hard to know how it was actually carried out. The process by which child abuse or neglect concerns become child protection cases is complex and shrouded in some mystery. The procedures to be followed are described in the 1999 *Working Together* guidelines (Department of Health 1999), the most recent of which was produced in 2012. All child protection concerns should be reported to social services department personnel who decide whether a case is of sufficient seriousness to warrant a child protection investigation. If it is not, but welfare needs are identified, then an initial assessment follows, to be completed within seven days of the referral. If there is a serious child protection concern and an offence is believed to have been committed against a child, then the police should be informed and this may result in a joint interview of the child. In addition, an inter-disciplinary child protection conference would be held within 15 days after the referral to determine whether a child protection plan is needed and to appoint a key worker to lead a core group of professionals to work with the family concerned. In these circumstances a core assessment is required to be completed within 35 days of the initial referral. Should a child need immediate protection, this would be achieved by the use of a protection order under Section 47 of the 1989 Children Act. Alternatively, where a criminal charge is being brought against an alleged abuser living in the child's household, it is a condition of bail that she or he reside elsewhere until the matter has been resolved in court.

Gibbons et al.'s (1995a) research demonstrated how this system operates in terms of numbers. In their study of 1,888 child concern referrals, they found that about a quarter were filtered out at the point of referral, and a further 50 per cent following closer investigation of the circumstances. Only a quarter of all child protection referrals resulted in conferences being held. Finally, 17 per cent of the total number originally referred remained as cases being worked with by health and welfare professionals (15 per cent needing a child protection plan).

What this study could not tell us is which cases were filtered out of the system and why. Attention to decision-making at the early stages of intervention was limited. Dingwall et al. (1983) and Buckley (2003) carried out ethnographic studies of child protection practice which gave some insight into how 'referrals' become 'cases'. Dingwall demonstrated how societal expectations and normative values influenced decision-making and argued that social workers operated by three general criteria: those of natural love (belief that parental care for children is instinctual and therefore normal), cultural relativity (belief that standards of care need to be seen in a context of cultural norms) and the rule of optimism (belief in the potential for parental care to improve with support). These factors led social workers and others to filter child care cases out of the system where the concerns were not clear-cut, rather than draw them in. Buckley (2003) studied 72 child abuse referrals made to a social work health board in Ireland over a six-month period in the mid-1990s, at the end of which there were 14 open cases receiving attention from social workers and related professionals. She showed how social workers were as keen to eliminate potential cases from the system as they were to accept them, a state of affairs resulting from their need to realistically manage the amount of work coming to them. A range of devices are used to achieve this, some socially supported, such as those found by Dingwall et al., and others not, such as inter-agency buck-passing and avoidance of violent men. Earlier studies pointed out that social workers carrying out initial assessment do take into account factors such as the seriousness of the abuse, the cooperativeness of the parents and histories of previous abuse, but often do not make this explicit (Corby and Mills 1986).

Initial assessment at conferences and other inter-professional meetings

Initial child protection conferences and meetings are important for early decision-making in child protection work and several studies exist that have examined these processes. Most of the findings from these studies support the notion that there are many factors militating against reaching knowledge-informed decisions. Hallett and Stevenson (1980) made much of inter-professional defensiveness and dysfunctional group processes as impediments to good early assessment and decision-making. Dingwall et al. (1983) came to the conclusion that most assessments made at case conferences were, for a variety of structural reasons, including inter-professional conflict, likely to result in an underestimation of the degree of risk to a child. Dale et al. (1986) considered that there were grave dangers of professionals becoming polarised over case conference decisions and exacerbating already existing difficulties. Corby (1987), while finding little inter-professional disagreement over cases of serious abuse, reported a good deal of confusion in more marginal cases about why some children were registered and others were not. Decisions did not seem to be reached on the basis of a rational assessment of the degrees of risk (see also Campbell 1991). Farmer and Owen (1995), in their study of child protection conferences, showed how one of their key functions is that of meeting the needs of professionals to demonstrate their accountability.[1]

It is notable that little use is made of risk assessment models in screening child protection referrals in Britain. Greater use has been made of such tools in the USA. However, Murphy-Beaman (1994) has pointed to the dangers of using risk assessment schedules as part of initial assessments:

> Accurate predictions of violence are considerably more difficult to make for individuals who have not yet clearly behaviorally demonstrated harmful acts, but only show an apparent proneness for such acts. This would be the case with many parents who are suspected of being at risk for child abuse.
>
> (Murphy-Beaman 1994: 194)

In relation to screening children for broader social needs, all new referrals are assessed using the assessment framework document which looks at the child's needs, the family's strengths and the environment in which the family is living. Initial research suggested that some parents appreciated the explicitness of this assessment approach and the speed of response (as we saw, such assessments are required to be completed within seven days) (Corby et al. 2002; Cleaver and Walker 2004).

Sexual abuse

The research and practice so far discussed have been concerned mainly with physical abuse and neglect. Short-term assessment in the field of child sexual abuse followed a different line. The focus of such assessments was much more on children than on adults. This came about because there are few observable signs of child sexual abuse and, therefore, the main means of assessing whether or not a child has been sexually abused or not is likely to be via the child's testimony.

While indicators of sexual abuse were devised (see Finkelhor 1979; Porter 1984), they tended to be used as supportive evidence to a child's testimony. Similarly, physical evidence of sexual abuse, following events at Cleveland, tended to be used as supportive rather than main evidence. However, securing a child's evidence proved to be a highly controversial matter. More in-depth early assessments focused on children were actively discouraged. Thus, for example, the use of methods involving anatomically correct dolls diminished considerably, despite reports of positive applications in research carried out in the USA (Everson and Boat 1994). Later, reliance was placed on a child being interviewed by police and social workers following guidelines designed to ensure that a child's statement, if used, reaches the standard of evidence required in a criminal trial (Home Office/Department of Health 1992). While these procedures have gone some way to checking the 'excesses' of disclosure interviews, it should be noted that children do not often reveal to order the full truth about being sexually abused. Shapiro Gonzalez et al. (1993: 288) point out that: 'Clinicians treating child abuse victims must understand that disclosure is a continuous process and be aware that some aspects of the abuse may not be revealed until months into therapy'. Wellbourne (2002), in a study of 36 taped interviews, found that, although 50 per cent of the children did disclose abuse, all had done so previously. In other words, the interviews did not elicit any new disclosures at all. There is also some evidence to suggest that the inflexibility of the procedures is particularly problematic for pre-school children and children with communication difficulties, and that child sexual abuse criminal prosecutions have declined since their introduction.

The context of initial child protection assessments

Much of the foregoing material has been critical of the way in which early assessments of child protection referrals are carried out. However, it should be noted that these often take place in highly stressful and hostile circumstances (Farmer and Owen 1995), and that, therefore, opportunities for calm and careful analyses of situations are relatively rare (Corby 1996). In situations of extreme hostility, assessments can often only be carried out with the backing of the courts.[2] This was the thinking behind the introduction of child assessment orders under Section 43 of the 1989 Children

Act, which empowers social workers to carry out assessments in situations where parents are denying them access to a child, although the orders have been rarely used (see Dickens 1993).

Another approach to facilitating early assessments in conflict situations was to remove suspected abusers from the household. Under Schedule 2.5 of the 1989 Children Act, local authorities were empowered to pay the expenses of an alleged abuser living away from home pending the outcome of an investigation. Under the 1996 Family Law Reform Act, courts could, on making an interim care order, enforce the removal of a parent from the family home, provided the remaining parent was in agreement.

A final contextual factor to be borne in mind is that of the conditions in which frontdoor health and welfare professionals operate. Munro (2002) noted that staff shortages, poor working environments and information systems, lack of adequate supervision and stress all contribute to the difficulty of developing more analytical approaches to making decisions about child abuse and neglect risks at the early stage of referral.

Summary

Research into and accounts of short-term assessment and decision-making in child protection work have pointed to a different approach being adopted depending on whether the subject of inquiry was a case of physical or of sexual abuse. In the former, assessment tended to focus on the parents and in the latter on the children. In the case of physical abuse and neglect, there was little evidence of use of research findings in carrying out assessments, and some reasons were put forward to account for this. Initial assessment practices in child sexual abuse changed considerably following the events of the late 1980s and early 1990s. There was a shift towards the gathering of practical evidence and away from more child-centred approaches.

Longer-term assessment and intervention

The bulk of cases that come into the child protection system involve moderate abuse and low standards of child care (Thorpe 1994; Thoburn et al. 2000). In most of these cases decisions are reached to monitor families, provide support services and review progress at a later date. Recognition of the fact that concerns about this type of abuse or neglect dominate child protection work has led to much greater encouragement of a more family-supportive approach. The guidelines for core assessments produced by the Department of Health (2000a) reflected this shift. They contained three areas of emphasis: the needs of the child, the capabilities of the parents, and the material and social environment in which the family is situated. The focus was far less on the identification of abuse and risk, and much more on meeting the needs of the child and the family. This was in sharp contrast to the child protection assessment guidelines, known as the 'Orange Book', published over a decade earlier (Department of Health and Social Security 1988), which reflected the then prevalent concern with risk of serious abuse. The Orange Book was based on risk assessment principles and was designed as an aid to making key decisions about the direction of social work intervention with families. However, its use was never made a requirement by the

Department of Health and there was little research into the way in which it was implemented (although, as we will see later in this chapter, recent research has been carried out in connection with the Integrated Children's System – the computerised records system which complements it). A study by Holland (2000) of 16 assessments carried out using these guidelines found that decisions were based more on the degree of cooperation shown by the parents in the process of assessment than on an objective analysis of the data derived from the assessment process.

While the focus was less directly on abusive incidents, there was much emphasis on the ongoing quality of care provided for children within the family. Use of various schedules to assess factors such as depression and self-esteem was also encouraged by the Department of Health. Small-scale research (Corby et al. 2002) pointed out that, used flexibly by experienced workers, core assessments can be well received by some parents and effective in achieving the general aim of determining the quality of care being received by a child and the type of help/support needed by parents to achieve 'good enough' parenting standards.

Cases of serious child abuse are the main focus of the rest of this section, i.e. children previously subjected to serious abuse, or who are thought to be at risk because of previous serious abuse of their siblings or because their carers/parents have been convicted or suspected of previous serious abuse. While, as we have seen, they form only a small percentage of all those referred, nevertheless the consequences of inadequate assessment in relation to them can be disastrous. Difficult decisions have to be reached about whether it is best for children in these situations to remain with or, since in such cases emergency removal is likely to have occurred, return to their parents and, if so, under what circumstances, with what services and safeguards.

Physical abuse

In the field of physical abuse and neglect, this has perhaps been the most pressing issue of all. In most of the cases publicly inquired into, the main concerns have not been the effectiveness of initial assessments and interventions. Several of the children in public inquiry cases died while *legally* in the care or supervision of the authorities (or at least the subject of an assessment), but *actually* living at home with their parents – for example, Maria Colwell (Department of Health and Social Security 1974), Jasmine Beckford (Brent 1985), Tyra Henry (Lambeth 1987), Victoria Climbié (Laming 2003), Peter Connelly (Haringey 2008) and Khyra Ishaq (Birmingham 2010). The focus of concern was whether these children should have been allowed to stay with their parents or whether they should have been returned to their parents' care, and whether the supervision or assessment they received was of an acceptable standard.

Generally the practice of the statutory agencies has been heavily criticised for being too parent-centred in its thinking in this area and for not being sufficiently thorough in its assessments. It is with cases such as these that risk assessment schedules are thought by many to be most effective. Such schedules were first brought to professionals' attention in the late 1980s.

As is true of initial assessments, checklists and risk schedules have not been much used in the UK for this type of assessment either, despite the great outcry about child deaths for nearly two decades following the publication of the Maria Colwell inquiry report (Department of Health and Social Security 1974). To some degree there has been distrust, particularly by social workers, of using knowledge derived from public inquiry reports in any systematic way (Corby et al. 1998). Yet recently there has been an increase in interest in risk assessment in some circles, prompted partly by concerns about the shift towards a family-support approach (Bridge 1998b).

Much of the research about rehabilitation of seriously abused children is derived from medical settings and was pessimistic about the effectiveness and advisability of this course of action (Jones 1987). A study by Dale et al. (1986) came to more positive conclusions about the potential for successful rehabilitation. They used techniques derived from strategic family therapy to assess 26 sets of parents whose children had been removed from home following abuse, and to decide whether rehabilitation was a safe prospect. Their main concern was to secure acknowledgement from the parents of the seriousness of the abuse done to their children and acceptance of their responsibility for it. On this basis they successfully rehabilitated half the children in the sample with no injury recurrences (although the time period is unspecified). The remaining 50 per cent stayed in care on a long-term basis.

Another study with implications for successful rehabilitative work was reported on by Farmer (1992). Case records of a sample of 150 abused and neglected children placed home-on-trial were studied to see what factors were associated with success or failure; 45 per cent of placements were considered to be beneficial to the children and 19 per cent detrimental. Abuse or neglect reoccurred in just over 25 per cent of all cases. Successful rehabilitation was seen to be linked to purposeful social work involvement, planning and regular visiting. It was also linked to the number of placements that the child had experienced while in care. Those who had been placed with only one foster-parent did better than those with more than one placement (but it could be that these were the least problematical cases in the first place). However, what this study demonstrates is that social workers in mainstream services can achieve successful rehabilitations without attempting to bring about major changes in parental attitude. They need to select the cases with the best prospects, have regular direct contact with families and work purposefully and in a planned way to achieve rehabilitative goals.

Sexual abuse assessments in statutory agencies

With regard to longer-term assessments in serious sexual abuse cases, Corby (1998) found little evidence of systematised assessment taking place. Often there was little opportunity for carrying out formal assessments because abuse continued to be denied, sometimes throughout long periods of involvement. As with short-term assessments, the difficulties of trying to analyse situations characterised by conflict and deception should not be underestimated. Similar findings were reached by Sharland et al. (1996).

Waterhouse and Carnie (1992) found that the main factors taken into account in deciding on a child's protection needs in cases of sexual abuse were the response of the non-abuser to the abused child, the age of the children and their degree of assertiveness and ability to protect themselves in future. It should be noted that all these studies focused on the work of local authority social workers. Another finding that all these studies reached was that little or no work is done by statutory-based workers in relation to adult abusers. The main concern with regard to them is the threat that they might pose to children, and the main solution adopted is to find means of ensuring that they are separated from the children concerned.

The Great Ormond Street approach

The picture is somewhat different in hospital and voluntary agency-based services. Bentovim et al. (1988) devised a form of assessment, based on family therapy principles, which involved all members of the family. They argue that intra-familial abuse is a product of faulty family functioning and is sustained by secrecy, and therefore that it is a prerequisite to successful treatment that family members communicate openly with each other about what has happened in the past and what they wish for the future. This entails abusers admitting to all their family members what they have done and the opening up of emotional blockages. Openness and explicitness are seen as essential counters to the secrecy that has helped to maintain the abusive situation, and they must be achieved regardless of the pain and anxiety created in the process (Furniss 1991). Often by the stage at which this assessment is carried out the family has broken up, usually as a result of a prison sentence being imposed on the abuser. This form of assessment requires family attendance at monthly meetings over a period of 12–15 months and is supplemented by children and parents attending separate groups or in some cases receiving individual therapy. Bentovim et al. (1988) conducted a follow-up (no time period specified) of families who were assessed between 1981 and 1984 (55 per cent of the families completed the full course of assessment). They found that 83 of 120 children (69 per cent) had not been re-abused, whereas 19 (16 per cent) had, and it was not clear whether re-abuse had taken place in the remaining cases. Most of the family structures had changed by the time of follow-up. After their prison sentence 15 per cent of abusing parents had returned home.

Clearly Bentovim et al.'s (1988) work has similarities with that of Dale et al. (1986) in the case of physical abuse. Both studies focused on the need for full acknowledgement of the abuse. Both see faulty family dynamics as at the root of abuse and both merge assessment to a large extent with therapy. Both also require considerable time, resources and expertise. Both control the inflow of work, in terms of type and quantity of cases worked with.

In more recent times, as has been noted before, there has been very little written about assessment of sexual abuse cases which coincides with a general reduction in activity in this field, a situation reflected in the USA as well. There, attempts have been made to explain the decline. While some attribute it to a backlash following controversies over false memory syndrome and ritual abuse of children, others have surmised that there is a genuine reduction in such abuse taking place because of the way in which it has become a much more open issue over the past 20 years or so (Finkelhor and Jones 2004). The focus in this area of work is much more on therapy, which will be discussed below.

Summary

In overview, the picture of longer-term assessment and decision-making in the child protection field was as follows. With regard to physical abuse and neglect, statutory agencies did not follow a particular theoretical approach, and generally, unlike the situation in the USA, the use of risk assessment schedules was not popular. State social workers in the UK operate under a philosophy that oscillates between a preference for rehabilitation where possible, in the belief that ultimately a child is better off in its own family, and a preference for non-rehabilitaton as the safest course of action in terms of the protection of the child. Assessments and decisions are frequently based on the actions of parents after the abuse and, particularly, on their cooperativeness and desire shown to retain the care of their child. Some research shows a reasonable degree of success with rehabilitation (Dale et al. 1986; Farmer 1992). Other research, particularly that carried out by the medically oriented professions, points to clean-break approaches being more beneficial for children.

With regard to sexual abuse, the lack of formal theory-based assessment in statutory social work is also evident. Before Cleveland, there is evidence that social workers and psychologists were applying approaches, methods and knowledge derived particularly from the USA. To a large degree this type of work has been seen as too intrusive and too narrowly focused on the child, and is now relatively rare. In longer-term assessments, social workers seem to be less likely to favour rehabilitation with the continuing presence of an abuser in the household than is the case in physical abuse and neglect. Bentovim et al.'s (1988) approach in a specialist setting has been more optimistic in relation to rehabilitation and demonstrated some success.

Providing support and treatment

It is important to understand clearly what we mean by the use of terms such as 'support' and 'treatment' in child protection work. There is an assumption that they are separate forms of activity. However, providing support can have therapeutic effects and, similarly, receiving more specific therapeutic help and relating to a therapist can have a supportive effect. In general terms, the notion of providing therapeutic aid is less culturally encouraged in the UK than in the USA. Thus if we look particularly for therapeutic inputs (and outcomes) in the UK we find that they are fewer and further between than is the case in the USA. In this section, we will consider the provision of support first and treatment next. Finally, consideration will be given to the effectiveness of the help provided by therapists and others, taking into account objective data and the views of parents and children on the receiving end of intervention.

Supporting families

The key challenge currently facing child protection workers in the UK is how to shift the focus onto providing more general support while at the same time maintaining awareness of the needs of children to be protected. As we have seen, government-sponsored research in the 1990s was critical of social work practice because of its concentration on abuse incidents to the neglect of other work (Department of Health 1995, 2001). Thus, families with considerable needs for support because of factors such as ill-health, domestic violence, financial problems and low standards of hygiene, were, according to the research findings, unlikely to receive ongoing help or support unless there was evidence of an incident of physical or sexual abuse. This same research painted a picture of interventions that were systems-led and which, to a large degree, alienated parents because they resulted in conflict and disputes over care standards but offered little in the way of supportive help.

Research by Brandon et al. (1999) found that in the majority of cases being referred, provision of supportive help without resort to the more formal aspects of the child protection system met needs without increasing risks to children. Indeed there was a positive response to the provision of practical and supportive help. Statham and Holtermann (2004) found a similar appreciation of supportive services in a study in North Wales – a problem, however, was the lack of consistent ongoing support for a group of parents on the edge of family breakdown. These findings were echoed in a study by Tunstill and Aldgate (2000) which found that the most requested form of help by parents was social work support, including direct casework and advocacy. They were more likely, however, to receive a specific service to bolster a particular need such as referral for day-care or to a family centre.

Stevenson (1998) argued for more ongoing support to be provided for neglecting families, stressing the fact that entrenched problems realistically need more consistent intervention over time if they are to be solved. Similar views were put forward by Searing (2003), who argued the merits of casework with its focus on interpersonal dynamics and bringing about change through emotional experience rather than through case management.

Treatment for children

Generally research suggests that there is a lack of treatment provided for children who have been abused. This is particularly true in the case of children who have been physically abused and neglected, where direct forms of treatment or therapy have been found to be lacking, often because the focus is on working with parents to ensure that they are more responsive to their children's needs (Greenwalt et al. 1998).

It is also true, though to a lesser extent, in the case of child sexual abuse. An Australian study (Humphreys 1995) found that 56 per cent of children received counselling despite a policy of providing such a facility for all sexually abused children. Tingus et al. (1996) reported slightly larger numbers receiving counselling in California, but found that white children were more likely to be counselled than black children, as also were children who were removed from their families. The picture in the UK with regard to therapeutic inputs has not been very encouraging in the 1990s. Sharland et al. (1996), Corby (1998) and Calam et al. (1998) all reported very low levels of child-focused treatment. By contrast Lindon and Nourse (1994) recounted the work of an excellent group-work project for sexually abused girls. But such projects are relatively rare and that therapeutic provision is patchy across the country. Corby (1998), in his study of 40 child sexual abuse cases dealt with by statutory agencies in the north-west of England, commented as follows:

> As far as the children were concerned, only a few offers of therapeutic help either in the form of group or individual work were made, and by no means all of these were taken up. Selection for, and allocation of, therapeutic help was a very hit-and-miss affair, depending on the availability of resources, knowledge of them by social workers and openness to them by both children and parents.
>
> (Corby 1998: 135)

Nevertheless, there are more examples of therapeutic work with children who have been sexually abused than with those who have been physically abused and neglected. The main forms of intervention include psychotherapy and cognitive-behavioural therapy (CBT) carried out with individuals or groups. Ross and O'Carroll's review (2004) notes that although few of the studies into treatment are methodologically sound, there is general evidence that all forms of treatment have some positive effects. Cognitive-behavioural approaches are cited as the most effective, by demonstrating that helping children come to terms at a cognitive level with their abusive experiences is more beneficial than harmful. Ramchandani and Jones (2003) concurred with these findings, but note that the relative success of these approaches is not so great as to warrant priority over other forms of intervention and that it is important to take into account the whole context of the situation before deciding on courses of treatment. They also note that interventions that provide therapeutic support for non-abusing parents as well as children seem, by and large, to be more effective than those that focus on children alone. Also, there seems to be little difference in outcome between group and individual therapy (Nolan et al. 2002). Policy-makers and managers could be tempted by findings such as these to provide only group therapy because of its cost-effectiveness, but accounts of therapeutic interventions point to the importance of acceding to the preferences of the children themselves (Richardson and Bacon 2001). It should be noted that most of the studies referred to in Ross and O'Carroll's review are North American, a study by Trowell et al. (2002) comparing the outcomes of individual and group psychotherapeutic treatment being an exception.

Treating adults who have been abused

There is limited reporting of therapeutic work with adults who have been physically abused or neglected as children. Such adults are more likely to receive help and support as parents if their own children are at risk of abuse or in need.

There is greater emphasis on the need for therapeutic responses to adults who have been sexually abused. Hooper and Koprowska (2004) have shown the importance for professionals working with non-abusing parents of sexually abused children to be sensitive to the possibility that they may have been sexually abused as well. They need to bear in mind that these parents may not have come to terms with their experiences, that they may as a result be feeling additional psychological and emotional stress in relation to their children's abuse, and thereby be less able to respond adequately to their needs.

However, there is little evidence of therapeutic provision for adults sexually abused as children in the UK and very little research carried out into this topic. Kessler and her colleagues (2003) completed a systematic review of 13 studies of group treatment for women who had been sexually abused (nearly all North American). They found that most of the studies showed that group treatment based on a range of theoretical approaches (feminist, problem-solving, transactional and group process) could be effective in terms of reducing depression and anxiety, and raising self-esteem. Women most likely to benefit from such treatment were those who had experienced less traumatic and intrusive forms of abuse. Most of the studies found that gains persisted, although follow-up periods for many were relatively brief (6–12 months). Some studies compared individual and group treatment and found little difference in terms of outcome. Questions about cost-effectiveness raised above in relation to treatment for children are relevant here as well. Stalker and Fry (1999) compared the experiences of 32 women receiving short-term individual therapy and

33 receiving short-term group therapy. Both forms of therapy were equally effective in terms of reducing adverse symptoms associated with sexual abuse. The conclusions reached by the researchers were as follows:

> Given the apparent efficacy and cost-effectiveness of group interventions, the findings of this study suggest that most women seeking help for the effects of sexual abuse should be encouraged to participate in a psychoeducational group with other women survivors and that for many this will be a sufficient short-term intervention. Some of our participants, however, noted that the short-term nature of the treatment provided through this study left them feeling frustrated and abandoned, especially if further treatment was not immediately available.
>
> (Stalker and Fry 1999: 172)

It is important not to dictate the type of treatment that is best for sexual abuse survivors. It is obvious from these comments that there is a danger that treatment can objectify its subjects by telling them what is best for them in terms of both form and length of intervention. Providing choice in these matters clearly has an important empowering function which should be one of the key goals of therapeutic intervention.

Therapy for maltreating parents

Providing some form of intervention for parents who are physically aggressive towards their children has been developed over the past decade or so in Britain. The main forms of intervention include teaching parenting skills and anger management. There is little by way of evaluation of these interventions. However, Sanders et al. (2003) review developments internationally and report findings from North American studies that suggest that parent training leads to improvements in parenting competence. They go on to argue that a combination of approaches linking cognitive therapy and skills development pitched at a broader preventive level rather than targeted on specifically referred parents is the most likely to achieve success. With regard to sexual abuse, abusers (mainly male) are largely excluded from intra-family child protection interventions in Britain. Apart from the type of work carried out by Bentovim et al. (1988), which has been described above, therapy takes place mainly with offenders following conviction. There have been considerable developments in this field in the 1990s, led largely by the probation service and the police. The emphasis is mainly on management of offenders, but treatment is seen as part of this process. There were also a growing number of non-statutory approaches (Morrison et al. 1994). In the USA (Giaretto 1981), the Netherlands (Frenken 1994) and Belgium (Marneffe 1996), there are opportunities to provide therapeutic intervention services for certain abusers instead of criminal prosecutions. Frenken (1994) stresses that in the Netherlands such interventions are possible only for first-time offenders who did not use violence in their sexual acts and who would otherwise have been given short prison sentences. This seems to be a sensible attempt to differentiate between types of abusers, but adoption has not been evident in the UK because of the current social concerns about paedophiles.

By the millennium much attention was paid to the treatment needs of young sexual abusers in the UK (Erooga and Masson 1999). Two considerations drove: the first was that such offenders are also children and many may have been subjected to abuse themselves, and the second was that intervention at this stage may prevent them from becoming recidivist paedophiles and placing other children at risk.

The effectiveness of providing support and treatment

How effective are the various treatments and interventions outlined above? This can be judged by measurement of outcomes, and, to some extent, by the views of those at the receiving end, i.e. parents and children. The main findings are as follows. Supportive intervention was, by and large, well received by families, but most studies show that the services available are not sufficient to meet their needs (Aldgate and Tunstill 1995; Statham and Holtermann 2004). Studies seeking the views of parents about the support they receive from social workers and other professionals indicated that reliability, consistency, genuineness and respect for them as individuals were the qualities they valued (Thoburn et al. 1995; Corby and Millar 1997; Statham and Holtermann 2004). How effective this supportive work is in preventing child maltreatment is extremely hard to measure (Ghate 2001).

Treatment for children, where it is available, seems to be effective whether conducted in groups or individually. Cognitive approaches carried out with children and non-abusing parents have appeared to be particularly beneficial (Deblinger et al. 1999). Children seem to cope with openness and candour about the abuse they have experienced, particularly in relation to sexual abuse (Roberts and Taylor 1993; Berliner and Conte 1995). It is also clear that the views of children about how they wish to be helped are of key importance in achieving effective treatment. In general terms, the same messages hold true for adults on the receiving end of treatment programmes. Treatment of abusive parents in relation to physical abuse has not been well researched in terms of testing its effectiveness or of eliciting the views of those at the receiving end. There is evidence to suggest that family centre provision has been well received, provided it is pitched to the level of more general support (Pithouse and Holland 1999). What remains the case is the lack of involvement of men in the various programmes. With regard to sexual abuse, there is clearly more emphasis on males, but much of the work is focused on extra-familial abusers. Most of the interventions have been cognitive-behavioural with a view to reducing the risks of re-offending. As has been seen, the rates of re-offending remain high, which is not an argument against this type of provision – it is clearly important. However, it is also important to ensure that such treatment has a degree of flexibility and incorporates intra-familial abuse concerns as well. Bentovim et al.'s work (1988) has been an exception in this respect. In the current climate of fear about dangerous sexual offenders, such approaches remain relatively rare.

Clearly, there is work that needs to be done in this area. Research shows that therapy, by and large, has beneficial effects. Some would go so far as to say that any therapy is better than none, though this is not universally accepted. Jones (1987), in a review of British and US studies, focused on those families that do not respond to treatment and that he terms 'untreatable'. These include those who have carried out serious forms of abuse, such as non-accidental poisoning, burns, neglect resulting in psychosocial short stature syndrome and cases attributed to fabricated or induced illness (FII) (formally known as Munchausen's syndrome by proxy). Other factors *associated* with – but not necessarily 'leading to' in every case – untreatability have been parents who were severely maltreated themselves as children, parents with personality disorders or suffering from psychotic illness, and parents who deny abuse, lack empathy and drop out of treatment programmes. Important though this cautionary note is, as it stands it is of little use in the world of practice, where there is an expectation that parents will be at least considered for a second chance. The future challenge for treatment is to provide a comprehensive range of approaches that meets the needs of all children, adults, non-abusing and abusing parents and in a sensitive and flexible way. Adoption of a more treatment-focused orientation does not mean that there should be any less vigilance about children's needs for protection.

Overall effectiveness of child protection work

What did research tell us about the overall effectiveness of child protection work? At the serious end of the spectrum, research revealed that some children are best protected by separation from their parents and some studies show that carefully planned interventions can help maintain some children with support within their own families.

With less resistant and intransigent families success rates, as measured by re-abuse over two years, were around the 70 per cent mark in the UK in the early 1990s (Farmer and Owen 1995; Thoburn et al. 1995). Cohn and Daro (1987) in the USA found that 42 per cent of parents in federally funded programmes had reduced potential for neglect. They suggested that supportive interventions combined with individual work were more effective than working solely with individual families. Brandon et al. (1999) found that goals of intervention with families where there were child protection concerns could be just as well achieved by voluntary measures as by compulsory ones.

Several studies evaluated the effectiveness of sexual abuse interventions in terms of the likelihood of re-abuse and in terms of the perceptions of children and parents about professional intervention. In Britain, in relation to statutory interventions, Sharland et al. (1996) reported a 30 per cent rate of re-abuse (i.e. a 70 per cent success rate). Corby (1998) estimated that 35 per cent of children in his sample remained at risk of abuse when the cases were closed by the child protection professionals. As has already been noted, Bentovim et al. (1988) reported a 20 per cent re-abuse rate in families treated at Great Ormond Street Hospital. It seems, therefore, that the specialist agencies have higher success rates. This may well be because such agencies can select their clientele whereas statutory agencies cannot.

For many families at the receiving end of child sexual abuse investigations, these are not the only problems they face. In the USA, Gomes-Schwartz et al. (1990) found that most of the families in their study faced multiple difficulties and needed a wide range of long-term support and help, a finding echoed by Sharland et al. (1996) and Corby (1998) in Britain. Gomes-Schwartz et al. (1990) also argued that treatment programmes must recognise parents' needs for support and that collaboration between treatment and child protection services is essential for successful outcomes. Sharland et al. (1996) found that only 24 per cent of the parents in their study had positive feelings about the way in which intervention had been handled.

In relation to work with adult sex offenders, Furby et al. (1989) provided an overview of the effectiveness of such treatment programmes in the UK and USA and came to the rather pessimistic conclusion that there was no evidence that they reduce the reoccurrence of sex offending. Hall (1995) found evidence of some success with psychological interventions. It seems that intra-familial child abusers are the most likely to respond to treatment. And Erooga and Masson (1999) found more optimistic evidence in terms of outcomes with young sexual abusers. However, success is less likely in the worst cases, characterised by long histories of young people being abused themselves in childhood, high levels of anti-social behaviour and aggression, and low levels of social competence.

AFTER 2006

A shift towards 'systems' and 'interventions'

During the past few years, and certainly since the third edition of this book, the focus has arguably changed to a greater concentration on the efficacy of 'systems' and 'interventions' (but here using more quantitative approaches, as we see below) rather than on processes, such as prevention and assessment. Approaches have also become more explicitly outcome-focused.

Systems

One of the key targets of the Munro report is the

> skew in priorities that has developed between the demands of the management and inspection processes and professionals' ability to exercise their professional judgment and act in the best interests of the child. This has led to an over-standardised system that cannot respond adequately to the varied range of children's needs.
>
> (Munro 2010: 5–6)

As one social worker in the report put it 'timescales can end up replacing professional judgment' (p. 12). Furthermore,

> The ones who lose out most are the very children the system is intended to protect. The reforms have driven compliance with regulation and rules over time, with social workers increasingly operating within an over-standardised framework that makes it difficult for them to prioritise time with children, to get to know them, and understand their feelings, wishes, and worries.
>
> (Munro 2010: 7)

This thread runs through other reports written around the same time. Not surprisingly, in a recent review of safeguarding and child protection, Barlow and Scott (2011: 24) also report that:

> a recent overview of the evidence about effective interventions for complex families where there were concerns about (or evidence of) a child suffering significant

harm, showed the importance of providing 'a dependable professional relationship' for parents and children, in particular with those families who conceal or minimise their difficulties.

Munro also found that professionals were often reluctant to form negative assessments about a family which Robert Dingwall and his colleagues referred to in 1983 as the 'rule of optimism'. 'Thinking the best' of families is an admirable quality but uncritically applied it can be sentimental; moving too far in the opposite direction, however, can leave the professional acerbic – even aggressive and threatening. Other writers and researchers (e.g. Forrester et al. 2008a; Ferguson 2011; Shemmings and Shemmings 2011) have begun to articulate alternative child protection practices, aimed at avoiding the extremes of naive sanguinity and harsh confrontation when working with families, by returning to their relationship base (see also Ruch et al. 2010).

Children and young people are clear that they welcome workers who show empathy, who are reliable and respectful, but who can take action and be decisive (Munro 2011a: 41). This attention to what social workers actually do and how they do it is welcome because, as Harry Ferguson notes, there is 'a curious absence from a great deal of social work and child protection literature, policy and discussions about practice of any considered attention to the core dynamics, experience and methods of doing the work' (Ferguson 2011).

The Munro report also found that, over the years and as a direct result of the excessive proceduralisation of child protection practice, professionals and their employers have, no doubt inadvertently, lost sight of the person that should be at the centre of what they do, namely the child or young person. This is why she entitled her second report *The Child's Journey*. Such a re-focusing resulted in 2012 in all Office for Standards in Education (Ofsted) inspections having as their focus the 'child's journey' when looking at files and interviewing professionals and families. As Munro put it, 'The current performance management system provides detailed information about aspects of case management, such as time taken to complete an initial assessment but it does not provide a clear picture of a child's journey from the identification of need to actually receiving help' (2010: 19).

In addition, much publicity has been devoted to the unnecessary complexity of some of the software systems designed to support the assessment procedures in operation across the UK, notably the *Common Assessment Framework* and the *Framework for the Assessment of Children in Need and Their Families* (Department of Health 2000a). As Munro put it in her report 'computers have a lot to offer, but their use so far has been problematic' (2011a: 157). Other research, using a combination of quantitative and anthropological methods, has also been extremely critical (Bell et al. 2007; Shaw et al. 2009; White et al. 2009).

To change the prevailing system, the Munro report argues that the 'climate of fear, blame and mistrust that seems to be endemic within the child protection system' (Munro 2011a: 12) needs to be removed. We include below in full the principles and innovations her review considers essential in order to achieve this:

- the family is the best place for bringing up children and young people, but the child protection system faces difficult judgments in balancing the right of a child to be with their birth family with their right for protection from abuse and neglect;

- the child protection system is a multi-professional, multi-agency operation requiring all who work with children, young people and families to consider the effectiveness of their work;

- the child protection system should be child-centred, recognising children and young people as individuals with rights, including their right to participation in major decisions about them, in line with their evolving capacities;

- the child protection system understands its dual mandate to support families and help them provide adequate care and to intervene authoritatively when children and young people need protection;

- the general public and all who work with children, young people, families and carers have a responsibility for protecting children and young people;

- helping families involves working *with* them and therefore the quality of the relationship between the family and professionals directly impacts on the effectiveness of help given;

- children's needs and circumstances are varied and so the child protection system requires sufficient flexibility, with space for professional judgment to meet that variety of need;

- the complexity of the world means that uncertainty and risk are features of child protection work and that risk management cannot eliminate harm, only reduce its occurrence;

- a learning and adaptive system is characterised by regular questioning of how the system (locally and nationally) is functioning and whether children are receiving effective help;

- good professional practice is driven by knowledge of the latest theory and research.

(Munro 2011b: 19–20)

The Munro report points to an innovation – Steve Goodman and Isabelle Trowler's attempt to *Reclaim Social Work* in Hackney, London (Goodman and Trowler 2011) which has already begun to develop ways of overcoming the problems she identified in her review. Additionally, Julian le Grand's notion of organising social work in a similar way to that in which family doctors (general practitioners – GPs) operate across the UK is currently being piloted in five areas. The intention of *Consistent Care Matters: Exploring the Potential of Social Work Practices* (Le Grand 2007) is that social workers should become as independent as possible from the local authority and professionally – not managerially – led.

Interventions: the 'What works?' agenda

Increasingly, policy-makers have become interested in the notion of 'What works?' because such a question appears, at first sight, to offer budget-holders a more rational basis for the allocation of resources. This becomes even more important as finances for child protection services have to compete with other demands; during times of austerity, performance audits and inspection regimes beg questions such as 'Does what we do actually work?' which have percolated to the top of management agendas. But in their wake appear a series of equally important questions such as 'For whom does it work and under what circumstances?', 'When does it work . . . *and* why . . . *and* how?' And eventually, politicians, managers and professionals are forced to address a much more complex, ethical question: 'Even if it does work, does it offer value for money?' In other words, notions of whether one family should receive service X, costing Z pounds, when another 20 families could have received service Y, costing a lot less, have to be considered.

Consequently, a plethora of studies, using systematic reviews and meta-analyses (see, for example, MacMillan et al. 2009; Montgomery et al. 2009; Barlow and Schrader McMillan 2010; MacMillan 2010) and, albeit to a far lesser degree in the UK, experimental designs has now emerged. Other reviews and reports summarise the findings about specific interventions or participant groups and then translate them into practice (see, for example, Littell et al. 2005; Utting et al. 2007; Hicks and Stein 2010).

The most comprehensive UK review of interventions in child protection was conducted by Caroline Davies and Harriet Ward in 2011 and the findings are summarised in the second stage of the Munro report (2011b: 46–7). We provide the full summary as it contains a series of key messages:

In deciding how to help children and families change, research also provides valuable evidence. A recent overview of the research listed the following as examples of programmes that have been proven to be effective in addressing the needs of maltreated children and their families in evaluative studies:

Programmes for parents

- *Parents Under Pressure* (PUP) and *Relational Psychotherapy* are effective interventions for substance misusing parents;
- the *Post Shelter Advocacy Programme* is an effective intervention for women who have been exposed to domestic violence;
- the *Enhanced Triple P – Positive Parenting Programme* is effective in addressing adults' own experiences of poor parenting and the psychological consequences of abuse; and
- *Cognitive Behavioural Therapy* (CBT) can be effective in reducing emotionally abusive parenting, particularly when individual sessions are combined with group based sessions.

Programmes for parents and children

- *Infant-Parent Psychotherapy* is effective in improving maternal and child representations where there is a known history of abuse in the family;
- *Interaction Guidance* may be an effective intervention in improving parent/ child relationships in infants with faltering growth, but further evaluation would be valuable;

- *Parent-Child Interaction Therapy* is a cognitive behavioural model that has been shown to be effective in reducing physical abuse; and
- Abuse-focused cognitive behavioural therapy can be more effective in reducing physical abuse and parent-child conflict than traditional family therapy.

Programmes for children:

- *'Therapeutic Pre-school'* is an effective intervention for children aged 1–24 months who have been maltreated or are at risk of maltreatment. It has a significant and lasting impact on parenting and child behaviour;
- *Peer-led Social Skills training* is an effective intervention for 3–5 year olds with a history of maltreatment who are socially withdrawn; and
- *Multi-treatment Foster Care for Pre-schoolers* is an effective intervention for maltreated infants who require permanent placements. Trials in the USA have produced promising results.

So far we have considered individually based, tertiary interventions; others are aimed at the community or even wider (universal and secondary interventions). As the Munro report comments: 'preventative services can do more to reduce abuse and neglect than reactive services' (Munro 2011b: 7). In conclusion we consider the findings relating to such initiatives.

In 2010 Frank Field MP undertook an independent review on poverty and life chances. He reported in December 2010, outlining the actions 'required by government and other institutions to reduce poverty and enhance life chances for the most disadvantaged' (Munro 2011b: 17). The Field report was conducted in tandem with another review, headed by Graham Allen MP, into early intervention. The Allen report was published in January 2011. It identified 19 programmes that were considered to be more effective than others in helping children and young people to fulfil their potential and help break inter-generational cycles of disadvantage. One in particular, the Family Nurse Partnership (FNP), a preventive programme for vulnerable young first-time mothers based on over 30 years of research in the USA, was considered by the review team to offer significant benefits, alongside sizable cost savings. In October 2010 the government announced the doubling of places by 2015.

A third study, a review by Dame Clare Tickell entitled *The Early Years: Foundations for Life, Health and Learning*, reported in March 2011. It concluded that the entire process of supporting early learning needed to become less bureaucratic and more focused on young children's learning and development. If the aims and objectives in her review are achieved this could have a preventive and lasting effect on safeguarding policy and practice.

Concluding comments

In many respects, the findings in the 'post-2006' section of this chapter are a sad reflection of developments in child welfare and social care services generally in the UK: poorly coordinated, overly bureaucratic, procedurally led impersonal provision that seems to have lost sight of its purpose – the care, protection and welfare *of the child*. And professionals and practitioners themselves report high levels of stress and burn-out alongside reduced job satisfaction. This is precisely why the implementation of the Munro, Allen and Tickell reviews is being observed and noted with anticipation.

Recommended reading

Barlow, J. and Schrader McMillan, A. (2010) *Safeguarding Children from Emotional Maltreatment: What Works?* Available at: www.education.gov.uk/research.

Barlow, J. and Scott, J. (2011) *Safeguarding in the 21st Century: Where to Now?* Totnes: Research in Practice.

Ferguson, H. (2011) *Child Protection Practice*. Basingstoke: Palgrave Macmillan.

Goodman, S. and Trowler, I. (2011) *Reclaiming Social Work*. London: Jessica Kingsley.

MacMillan, H.L. (2010) *Interventions to Prevent Child Maltreatment*. PreVAiL: Preventing Violence Across the Lifespan Research Network, available at: www.uwo.ca/fims/prevail/docs.

Ruch, G., Turney, D. and Ward, A. (2010) *Relationship-Based Social Work: Getting to the Heart of Practice*. London: Jessica Kingsley.

Tickell, C. (2011) *The Early Years: Foundations for Life, Health and Learning*, available at: http://www.education.gov.uk/tickellreview.

9

Global and cultural perspectives on child abuse and neglect

Introduction

In this chapter, attention will be focused on some of the key issues currently being debated by researchers and practitioners in the field of child protection in areas of the globe beyond Britain and the USA. Consideration will be given to child abuse and neglect from a worldwide perspective.

Examining the world picture helps to put some of our domestic concerns in a broader context of understanding. The aim is not to comfort ourselves that, compared with children's circumstances in other parts of the world, our children's problems are relatively slight. Rather, a worldwide perspective can be used to examine some of our assumptions about children and their rights and needs, and even to question the complexity of the systems that we have devised for dealing with child protection concerns (Freeman 2000). In addition, we are not immune from the world's problems – children of asylum seekers and our responses to them are immediate pressing problems within our own society, as was highlighted by the Victoria Climbié case (Laming 2003).

It is worth reflecting that in many parts of the world, intra-familial child abuse and neglect remain low on the lists of priorities – for example, street children and children in substandard institutions dominate concerns in parts of South America. In many of the world's poorer countries child prostitution, child labour, infanticide and the impact of AIDS and war on children are also major concerns. In such countries, rife with poverty and deprivation, as was true of Britain in the late nineteenth century, abuse or neglect of children by their parents has relatively low priority. It should be noted that these concerns are not confined to these countries; concerns about institutional abuse, runaway and homeless children and child prostitution remained important issues in Britain and other rich countries at the end of the 1990s as well. However, the scale of these problems was quite different compared to that which faces poorer countries.

While richer countries can and should play a role in helping poorer countries tackle problems of child mistreatment, it is important to avoid assuming that our ways of dealing with problems are the solutions that other less advanced countries should follow. It is important to start where people are at, if one is to gain a full understanding of child care needs in poorer countries. Clearly for many such countries, the priority in relation to meeting the needs of their disadvantaged children is poverty reduction rather than the development of child protection systems. Analyses of the institutionalisation of children in eastern European countries such as Romania point to poverty as the reason for so many children living in orphanages. Many children are placed in such institutions simply because families cannot afford to care for them (Stephenson 1997). These findings can surely inform how we view difficulties in other countries as well. While much good work is being done by foreign agencies to improve standards and develop more preventive measures, ultimately poverty is the key determinant of so many events.

We could, of course, turn this thinking back on ourselves. While the proportions of children in state care in Britain are much lower than in some other poorer countries, nevertheless all the indices about accommodated children and children subject to child protection plans point to their coming largely from very poor and disadvantaged families (Bebbington and Miles 1989). Thus, the problems of two different countries, such as the UK and Romania, though different in form and degree, can actually share many similarities. In such circumstances, great care needs to be taken in assuming that our responses to child abuse are more sophisticated and therefore superior to those of poorer countries. On the other hand, we have, through our experiences in tackling child abuse and neglect, developed knowledge and skills that can be used to support and provide critical analyses on developments coming out of poorer countries. Clearly, however, it is a delicate business and there are no quick-fit transferable solutions across countries and cultures.

Child abuse and neglect: a worldwide perspective

Trafficking of children

In terms of issues that impact directly on British child protection services, another key area of worldwide concern is that related to child trafficking (UNICEF 2003). The UN *Protocol to Prevent, Suppress and Punish Trafficking Persons, Especially Women and Children, Supplementing the UN Convention Against Transnational Organisational Crime* (commonly known as the 'Palermo Protocol') defines person trafficking as 'The recruitment, transportation, transfer, harbouring or receipt of persons, by means of threat or use of force or other forms of coercion . . . for the purpose of exploitation. Exploitation shall include, at a minimum, the exploitation of the prostitution of others . . . forced labour or service, slavery . . . or the removal of organs'. This is a global problem involving very large numbers of children (and adults) and taking place within and between countries across the world. It involves children being taken away from their families by threat or deception for the purposes of exploitation. It is often assumed that the sole purpose of trafficking is sexual – i.e. children being coerced into prostitution and pornography – but it can also be for the provision of cheap labour, domestic service and adoption. Numbers of trafficked children known to have entered Britain between 1998 and 2003 are relatively small – 250 in all. In 2011, the Serious Organised Crime Agency in the UK issued a report, *Making Every Child Matter . . . Everywhere*. It stated that between January and September 2011, 202 children were identified as trafficked into or within the UK. Sixty-seven of these children were from Africa, 63 from Asia and 50 from eastern Europe; the rest were from other parts of the world or their origin was unknown. Most of the children from Africa (48) and eastern Europe (32) were female, whereas most from Asia (43) were male. Most were aged between 14 and 16 although the report acknowledges that it is more difficult to identify younger children as having been trafficked and therefore they are possibly under-represented in the figures. Most of the trafficked children were found to be victims of multiple types of exploitation; however, all the sexually exploited children were female and most victims engaged in cannabis cultivation were male. Because of the clandestine nature of trafficking, it is generally assumed that the overall figure – of 202 children trafficked in this period – is a considerable underestimate.

Where children arrive in the country and are identified as being unaccompanied (by an adult), they immediately become the responsibility of the relevant local authority and should be accommodated under Section 20 of the 1989 Children Act. However, there are several cases where they have since disappeared, presumably to do the work for which they were brought into the country by those exploiting them. Social services departments have been slow to adequately meet the needs of trafficked children. It should be clear by now that they need protection, not simply accommodation. In July 2011, Home Secretary Theresa May noted that the 2012 Olympic and Paralympic Games in London could provide a potential target for criminal gangs looking to take advantage of the higher numbers of people entering and leaving the UK and to use this as a cover for an increase in people trafficking (*The Daily Telegraph* 2011).

Asylum seekers

A linked issue relates to children who are asylum seekers, but who are not being trafficked. Such children and their families are disadvantaged by our asylum laws which provide closely monitored and restricted access to reduced state benefits, pending the often drawn-out business of securing asylum (Cemlyn and Briskman 2003). More recently, under Section 9 of the 2004 Asylum Act, children of 'failed' asylum seekers have been denied access to Section 17 resources under the 1989 Children Act (those relating to children in need). This means that if their parents do not return to their country of origin within the specified time limits, these children may well have to be accommodated by local authorities. In other words, children will be separated from their parents solely on the grounds of destitution. Cunningham and Tomlinson (2005) argue that this legislation is putting the politics of immigration before child welfare and will result in children being put at greater risk.

Thus, it can be seen that what is happening to children worldwide in terms of abuse and neglect is a challenge for child protection professionals in Britain. Clearly, we have a vested, as well as moral, interest in using knowledge and experience to support poorer countries in developing policies and practices that meet the needs of disadvantaged children within their own boundaries. We also need to develop much more sensitive and supportive policies for dealing with the way in which the consequences for children of poverty and social upheaval worldwide impact here.

International figures for child abuse and neglect

Measuring and comparing prevalence rates for child abuse and neglect between different countries and areas of the globe is an incredibly difficult task. Different legal jurisdictions have different conceptions and thresholds of what constitutes child abuse or neglect and these legal differences are often at least partly rooted in very different cultural or historical conceptions of what the role of parents should be, different ideas about parenting and caregiving and the status of children in society more generally. Compounding these difficulties is the fact that different countries use different ways of gathering and interpreting data on child abuse and neglect; even where official records do exist, these remain open to question and interpretation. It also needs to be borne in mind that as awareness and education regarding child abuse and neglect increases, there is typically an increase in the *reporting* of such problems (Creighton 2004). As Creighton notes, most academic studies of prevalence (and incidence) rates have been conducted in western countries, again making international comparisons outside western nations more difficult (see Table 9.1 for a comparison of the data from western countries).

Even within the four countries that make up the UK, it is not straightforward to compare statistics. This is because the four countries collect different information – for example, England, Scotland and Northern Ireland all collect data on the duration of child protection plans but Wales does not (Munro et al. 2011a).

Figures for non-western countries are typically, but not always, harder to obtain. A meta-analysis by Stoltenborgh et al. (2011) of 217 publications reporting on the prevalence of child sexual abuse from a wide range of countries, with a combined sample size of over 9 million participants (9,911,748 to be exact), found that the overall estimate of child sexual abuse prevalence was 180 per 1,000 girls (self-reporting) and 76 per 1,000 boys (also self-reporting). Lower rates for both girls and boys were found in Asia (113 per 1,000 and 41 per 1,000 respectively) and the highest rate for girls was found in Australia (215 per 1,000) and for boys in Africa (193 per 1,000). Although this meta-analysis confirms the global nature of

Table 9.1 A comparison of officially recorded rates of child abuse and neglect in different countries

Country	Sample	Source	Data
Australia	Official records	Munro et al. (2011b)	Sexual abuse – 10.2% of officially recorded cases Physical abuse – 21.6% Neglect – 28.5% Emotional abuse – 39.7%
Canada	Official records	Munro et al. (2011b)	Sexual abuse – 3.1% of officially recorded cases Physical abuse – 20.1% Neglect – 33.9% Emotional abuse – 42.9%
England	Official records	Munro et al. (2011b)	Sexual abuse – 6% of officially recorded cases Physical abuse – 13% Neglect – 46% Emotional abuse – 27%
Norway	Official records	Munro et al. (2011b)	Sexual abuse – 0.8% of officially recorded cases Physical abuse – 3.2% Neglect – 88% Emotional abuse – 8%
USA	Official records	Munro et al. (2011b)	Sexual abuse – 7.9% of officially recorded cases Physical abuse – 14% Neglect – 63.6% Emotional abuse – 6.3%

child sexual abuse as a phenomenon, it also points to the significant influence of methodology on estimates of prevalence.

Our knowledge of other forms of abuse and neglect are far less developed than for child sexual abuse.

Child abuse and neglect in two specific countries

In this section we consider several questions related to child abuse and neglect in China and Russia. Clearly, there has been a large degree of arbitrary choice in including these particular countries and this decision has been taken purely at the authors' discretion. The intention is simply to give the reader a flavour of how two different but globally significant countries have addressed the issue of child protection.

China

We have selected China because of its growing economic and social importance and because of distinctive polices in operation there, such as the 'one child' policy, as well as demographic considerations such as the having the world's largest population. Based on the results of the 2010 national government census, China has around 1.3 billion inhabitants, of which 16.6 per cent, or 222 million, are aged 0–14 years (the census groups people in age bands of 0–14, 15–59, 60 and over and 65 and over; therefore, figures for the number of children aged 0–17 are not available). Much of the research regarding child abuse in China focuses on the issue of child sexual abuse with far less attention being given to physical or emotional abuse. Neglect of children appears to be related at least in part to the effects of China's 'one child' policy. When discussing child abuse and neglect in China, one must bear in mind, despite impressive economic growth figures over the past 30 years, that marked poverty remains a daily reality for a significant minority of families and children (around 10 per cent of the population were living in poverty in 2004 – Ravallion and Chen 2007).

A study of nearly 500 university students in China found that around half reported having been hit, kicked or slapped in childhood. Around one-third reported being hit with an object such as a stick (Hester et al. 2009).

Other sources of research also confirm the widespread nature of child abuse in China, although, as with studies of child abuse and neglect in Britain, there are quite marked differences in estimated prevalence levels. For example, Chen et al. (2004) surveyed 3,261 students in Hubei, Henan, Hebai and Beijing and found that the prevalence of unwanted sexual experiences before the age of 16 was 16.7 per cent for females and 10.5 per cent for males. One per cent of all respondents reported child rape, 8.9 per cent of females reported other forms of contact sexual abuse, while 5 per cent of males reported the same. As with other countries, the results of having been sexually abused were found to be significantly negative. Both males and females in China reported more depression, suicidal thoughts and increased use of alcohol following child sexual abuse. Females were also more likely to engage in anorexic or bulimic behaviour while males were more likely to engage in violence (a fairly clear example of a split between internalising and externalising responses to traumatic experiences). Another study by Chen et al. (2007) examined Chinese parents' knowledge and attitudes towards child sexual abuse and found that while 95 per cent of respondents agreed that schools should seek to educate children about the prevention of child sexual abuse, around half (46.8 per cent) expressed a concern that such programmes would lead to children knowing 'too much' about sex.

In terms of physical abuse, as noted above, studies of this phenomenon are less prevalent than studies of child sexual abuse. Indeed, no studies of physical child abuse on mainland China could be found by the authors. Tang (1998) has studied physical child abuse in Hong Kong (prior to 1997, Britain had sovereignty over Hong Kong but in July of that year Hong Kong became a 'Special Administrative Area' of China). Tang interviewed 1,019 families in Hong Kong and found a rate of physical child abuse of 526 per 1,000 children for minor violence and 461 per 1,000 for serious violence (with a significant degree of overlap between the two groups). Tang also found that children aged 3–6 or children with no siblings were the most vulnerable to this type of abuse. Tang concludes that Hong Kong families showed slightly lower rates of minor violence than families in the USA but slightly higher rates of severe violence towards children. Tang does not hypothesise as to why this might be the case but does caution that relying on official statistics of child abuse in Hong Kong would have indicated a much lower level of physical child abuse.

The effects of China's long-standing 'one child' policy on the care of children are undoubtedly complex. Introduced in 1978 by Deng Xiaoping's administration, this policy restricts married, urban couples to having only one child, while exempting rural couples, ethnic minorities and parents without any siblings themselves. Foreigners living in China are also exempt from the policy. In combination with a long-standing historical and cultural preference in many parts of the country for sons over daughters (in common with some other parts of the world), this has led to a high male:female sex ratio in rural *and* urban areas (thus demonstrating it is not simply the 'one-child' policy that gives rise to such figures). Many studies have found that girls are more likely to be abandoned by their families and many of these children live in state-run orphanages, from which many of them are subsequently adopted internationally or nationally. In the 1990s, Human Rights Watch found evidence that the care that children received in these institutions was characterised by cruelty, neglect and abuse (Human Rights Watch 1996). Various bodies, including the US State Department, the British Parliament and Amnesty International, have also found that China's policies on family planning contribute to an increase in infanticide.

The law in China regarding child abuse and neglect is clear, despite the difficulties discussed above. Since 2007, the Law on the Protection of Minors has banned family violence against children. However, there is no national system in place for actively detecting child abuse or neglect and much of the work of protecting children is conducted by non-governmental institutions, although many of these work at the policy rather than the practical level. Where practical efforts are made, families can refuse entry to non-governmental officials visiting them following concerns regarding potential violence in the family home (*China View* 2007). Official statistics in China do indicate that increasing knowledge and understanding of child abuse and neglect has led to an increase in reporting. Between 2005 and 2009 there was an increase in reported incidents of child abuse of 35 per cent (*The China Post* 2010). However, even with this increase, in 2009 only 13,400 cases of child abuse were officially recorded out of the total child population of more than 200 million; this indicates an officially recognised prevalence of only 0.006 per cent, much too low a figure to be considered accurate.

In summary, China has recently passed laws banning family violence against children and official statistics do indicate that reported cases of child abuse are increasing. However, self-report studies seem to indicate that far more children in China than is officially recognised are being abused, physically and sexually. Reasonable estimates of children emotionally abused in China are not available and neither are figures for neglect. As we have seen, cultural preferences for boys and China's 'one-child' policy may have exacerbated particularly the neglect of girls as well as encouraged families to abandon girl babies, some of whom are then abused in state-run orphanages (or at least, they were in the 1990s – more up-to-date informa-tion is not available). As argued by Dunne et al. (2008), research which simply finds that Chinese children are maltreated is of limited value; we know that children in all societies in which studies have been undertaken are maltreated and therefore there is no real doubt that children in all societies are maltreated. The crucial question for researchers is whether there are different patterns in different societies, different prevalence rates for different types of abuse or neglect and, ultimately, what are the causes of these and how can they be addressed. Research in China is at a very early stage as far as these questions go.

Russia

We have selected Russia because of its dual role as both a European and an Asian country. It is also a developed and rich country with the tenth largest economy in the world. However, compared with other 'European' countries, Russia's national system of child protection is relatively undeveloped. According to the US Library of Congress, children in Russia are increasingly becoming involved in criminal activity, and drug and alcohol misuse among the child population is increasing. Russia also has a distinct problem with child trafficking and, according to Russian police statistics, between 30,000 and 60,000 women, most of whom are under the age of 18, are taken out of Russia each year and some may become sexually exploited (Roudik 2011).

Substance misuse by children will now be considered in more detail. According to the *British Medical Journal* (2005), young people in Russia are using cigarettes, alcohol or drugs in increasing numbers. The Russian health service estimates that 2.7 per cent (4 million) of Russia's 144 million teenagers are drug users and of those 1 million are 'hardened addicts'. Rates of drug use among teenagers in Russia are esti-mated to be 2.5 times as high as among Russian adults and 40 per cent of Russian schoolchildren are thought to regularly consume alcohol. Various studies have consid-ered why the rates of substance and alcohol misuse are so high in the Russian child population and Koposov et al. (2005) found that dysfunctional family dynamics and parenting factors are significantly related to alcohol abuse, even after controlling for psychopathology in the child.

The Russian Constitution of 1993 provides protection for children and their rights and there are also well developed child protection policies, including the Civic Code, the Federal Law on State Support of Youth and Children's Organisations and the Federal Law on Social Assistance. This differentiates Russia from countries such as China, which have only more recently introduced such laws. What this demonstrates clearly, if such demonstration were required, is that laws themselves, even good laws, are only a necessary condition of protecting children but they are far from sufficient.

Concluding comments

In this short chapter, we have sought to demonstrate the difficulty in believing that countries with less developed systems of child protection need only to copy the example of countries such as the UK or USA in order to improve the welfare of their child populations. As we saw perhaps most clearly with China, local policies, such as 'one child' can have profound effects on children's welfare that are not translatable into any western experience. We have also seen, as with Russia, that some countries face difficulties and challenges with issues such as substance misuse that would most likely overwhelm any western system of child protection as currently arranged. For both of these reasons, and others, the 'simple' imposition of western systems of child protection in non-western countries would be deeply problematic.

We have also sought to show that global difficulties can have significant local effects. The issue of the global trafficking of children from their country of origin to a country in which they are exploited in various ways is a clear example of this. The oft-found situation in which trafficked children are not seen primarily as children in need of protection, but children with the potential either to be engaged in criminal behaviour or to have links with criminals, poses a challenge to child protection professionals in the West. A comparison can be drawn between this and the state's response, in the UK, to children involved in gang activity; in both cases, the issue is seen as primarily one of the criminalisation of children rather than viewing children involved with gangs or those subjected to trafficking as primarily being in need of protection.

Recommended reading

Serious Organised Crime Agency (2011) *Making Every Child Matter . . . Everywhere*. London: Child Exploitation and Online Protection Centre.

Tiurukanova, E. and the Institute for Urban Economics (2006) *Human Trafficking in the Russian Federation: Inventory and Analysis of the Current Situation and Responses*. Moscow: UNICEF/ILO/CIDA.

West, A. (2005) *Hubs and Centres for Developing Children's Participation and Child Protection in China*. Beijing: Save the Children.

10

Reflections for future child protection work

Introduction

In this final chapter we offer an overview of how we see the challenges and possibilities within current child protection in the UK. We refer to comments made to us by numerous professionals over the past 15 months during training and dissemination events as well as at conferences at which we have spoken in connection with the Assessment of Disorganised Attachment and Maltreatment (ADAM) project, and to which we return at the end. These professional development activities have brought us into contact with well over 4,000 practitioners and supervisors. We have not inter-viewed them formally, nor have we asked them to complete questionnaires. Nevertheless we feel that their viewpoints are valid to report here as they reflect the opinions, expe-rience and practice wisdom of the people who undertake the job of helping to protect children, day in, day out. We recognise that our approach in what follows may seem somewhat unconventional but we urge the reader to keep an open mind.

At the time of writing, Professor Eileen Munro's review is poised to have a major effect on professional practice as well as on the management of the entire system of safeguarding and protection. Because professional *practice* has been neglected over the past 30 years in favour of systems, procedures, auditing and inspection, we unapologetically decided to focus on it, as we believe it is equally important. Andrew Turnell (2009: 4) writes:

> Since the 1970s, when the poorest organisational and casework practices began to be exposed through critical case reviews and death inquiries, proceduralisation has become the dominating paradigm for reforming child protection practice in all developed countries around the world . . . Unfortunately, proceduralisation has not created the transformation that was hoped for.

These problems are not confined to these shores, however. The following words from the US government's 1991 National Commission on Children are probably truer today than they were when they were penned: 'If the nation had deliberately designed a system that would frustrate the professionals who staff it, anger the public who finance it, and abandon the children who depend on it, it could not have not done a better job than the present child welfare system' (Turnell 2010 quoting Thompson 1995: 5). In what follows we contrast a 'pre-Munro world' – the way practice appears currently to operate in most areas of the UK – with a 'post-Munro world': a vision of child protection practice to which many professionals aspire. We aim no criticism at child protection professionals who, we believe, do an astonishing job under the most emotionally draining circumstances, and with caseloads that virtually everyone now accepts are far too high. Furthermore, they are constantly being inspected, evaluated and reorganised, and may face dismissal, de-registration and even public humiliation if they are thought to have made a mistake. This is the case across all professions involved in child protection but the most vilified and blamed are social workers. We are concerned that the system itself, most often devised after knee-jerk reactions to high profile cases, is the primary cause of the defensive practice we are about to describe. The Munro report, on the other hand, has been written more 'in the cold light of day' and we believe it offers a unique opportunity to steer our gigantic procedural supertanker onto a different course before it hits the rocks (many believe it already has).

'Pre-Munro' child protection practice: the current situation in the UK

The past 40 years of legislation and procedures in the UK arguably have produced practice with children and families based upon the sharing of concerns within written agreements aimed primarily at *protecting the practitioner* if things subsequently go wrong. So terrified are practitioners – as well as supervisors and managers – that the system is often geared to 'covering their backs' rather than helping families to keep their child safe. Managers often see the role of the worker as spelling out what a parent needs to do to protect the child and to minimise concerns; then it is the worker's job to monitor adherence and progress, often using the formal system of announced and unannounced visits, alongside child protection conferences and reviews. It is as if the worker is saying (for example): 'Your problems are concerned with substance misuse and mental ill-health and this results in poor parenting which, in turn, leads to your child being abused/neglected. What you have to do to get us out of your life is get off drugs, get help with your illness and improve your parenting. What we will do is get you on a parenting skills course, suggest a counsellor and insist that you attend and successfully complete a drugs rehabilitation programme. We will put this in writing and then monitor progress by visiting you.' Various veiled – and sometimes more transparent – threats are made about what will happen if the written 'agreement' is not implemented, most typically focusing on the removal of the child. This approach is basically saying, 'Get a grip, take responsibility, sort yourself out, because we are now keeping an eye on things and if they don't improve you could lose your child/ren.'

This form of professional practice can be implemented 'firmly but fairly'; on the other hand, practitioners can become acerbic, even threatening and punitive. The latter kind of practice is well documented in Donald Forrester's innovative research in which he asked actors to role-play a parent alleged to be experiencing drug problems and in which case there are child protection concerns. It exposed bureaucratic and sometimes insensitive practice, including confrontational, aggressive and disrespectful communication (Forrester et al. 2008a, 2008b). Ironically, the social work profession has spent the past 20 odd years stressing such laudable values as 'user empowerment', 'respect for persons', 'valuing the individual' etc., yet there is reason to believe that professional practice in reality may operate at some distance from these values: 'research has also demonstrated that working relationships, professional relationships and attitudes toward service recipients are very often negative, judgmental, confrontational and aggressive' (Turnell 2009: 18).

We now routinely ask practitioners on training events to 'write three words or very short phrases to describe how you think and feel about parents who abuse or neglect their children'. We have now asked 387 practitioners, during 15 different training and dissemination events, and the results are illuminating. (They were all experienced workers, most of whom were qualified.) Their words and phrases subdivide into three groups as follows (the relative proportions are shown in brackets):

Sympathetic (40 per cent), examples of which are:

- *Sad, frustrated, powerless, in need of help, unsupported, neglected, sympathy, stressed, personal problems, unloved, overwhelmed, desperate, curious about why, they need help and I want to help them*

Ambiguous (30 per cent), examples of which are:

- *Disturbed, frustration, pity, emotional deficit, damaged, uncontrolled, difficult to empathise with, angry, senseless, unrealistic, overwhelmed, shocked, disturbed, harsh/insensitive*

Judgemental (30 per cent), examples of which are:

- *Appalling, horrifying, dislike, disgusting, uneducated, need to be held accountable, irresponsible, cruel, evil, selfish, wicked, no capacity, no knowledge, inadequate, weak, 'What's wrong with you?', dangerous, put away and not let out, don't deserve children, should be locked up, thick*

Given that some of the *ambiguous* responses will contain negative and judgemental thoughts and feelings as well, it could be that nearly half of these, entirely representative, child protection practitioners harbour hostile, condemnatory and disapproving feelings about family members.

This, we argue, is likely to be a direct consequence of the present 'pre-Munro' system. It indicates a strong likelihood that there is inadequate supervision of the kind that is needed to address the highly emotional nature of child protection work. It is well known that professionals involved in child protection daily encounter some of the most distressing accusations and traumatic events. Recently in the UK, for example, a 1-month-old baby boy was allegedly raped by one or both parents; we heard about the case of a 9-year-old girl who was forced to watch her mother tortured and killed by a rebel soldier and then forced to watch her older sister raped, tortured and killed by the same man. He then cooked part of her arm and made the younger sister eat part of it.

Working within and among a sinister and cruel side of humanity has considerable emotional costs. Without effective supervision to address and help regulate such emotion, practice suffers, as does the practitioner, who may progressively become anaesthetised and inured to the families they work with. Decision-making is also compromised when 'hot cognitions' – thinking imbued with powerful emotion – are involved. Research with surgeons, for example, has shown that they forget basic medical procedures when faced with an aggressive actor/patient during the latter stages of their training; but what is more astonishing is that they are rarely aware that they have done so (Kneebone 2009). When asked how they rated their performance on these basic medical procedures – for example, administering a drip, monitoring blood pressure and oxygen, sterilising the site for the insertion of a needle – they often self-reported competent performance, but when they watched themselves on film they were astounded to learn that they often do not perform *any of these procedures* if the actor/patient increased their aggressive behaviour.

There is a flip-side to the defensive practice described above which veers towards the other end of the spectrum. In this version of child protection practice an excessive level of positive reinforcement and praise is shown to the parent or caregiver. An interchange might sound something like this:

Practitioner: How have things been for you?
Parent: Really good! I've decided to stop drinking after what you said.
Practitioner: Wow, I'm really pleased. I can tell too, as often when I've visited it seemed as though you *had* been drinking. Well done!

This visit may be written up in the record as indicative of 'positive change'. At one level, it could be dismissed as naive practice, perhaps undertaken by an inexperienced or newly qualified worker. But we have seen and heard experienced practitioners working in this way. They explain their approach as that of trying to encourage the parent and as a way of developing trust with them. Our view is that such an approach relies too heavily on what the parent tells the worker is happening (as the worker is usually not in a position to verify the parent's assertions). We are not suggesting that practitioners should end up interrogating parents, or looking in dustbins for evidence of empty spirit bottles. Our argument is that a different kind of interaction is needed when exploring parents' intentions about changing lifestyles and addictions. Using the principles of *motivational interviewing* (Miller and Rollnick 2002) the aim is to try and explore what it was like for the parent when they *did* drink – 'What problems did it solve?' 'How did it achieve that?' 'How did drinking help matters?' The practitioner then encourages the parent to try and speak at some length. She or he listens, attends fully and empathises and then, from time to time, sensitively challenges the parent, perhaps by adding – at the appropriate time – something along the lines of, 'Hearing you talk like this is helping me get a better idea of how drinking helps you. So, perhaps what I'm now going to say might surprise you: I guess I don't really understand how or why you would have given up, because it strikes me that the same problems are still there for you.' The practitioner will need to gently and sensitively challenge a parent who responds by saying something such as, 'Well, I've decided to do it for my children', or 'I've just realised how stupid it all is and how stupid I've been', or 'I've decided to turn my life around'. Such interchanges build trust. But real, lasting trust cannot be developed and sustained by over-praising unverified assertions, no more than it impresses a student if a teacher tells them they have done really well when they know they have not!

While a minority of parents and carers will deliberately seek to deceive practitioners – now usually referred to as 'disguised' or 'false' compliance – the majority struggle to cope and want to believe that they are changing in the intended direction. Many genuinely want to shake off addictions and become better parents, but a number of research studies now describe the neurological pathways that abusive and neglectful parents may have developed as a result of their own traumatised and chronically unhappy childhoods (see National Scientific Council on the Developing Child 2009; McCrory et al. 2010). These pathways can create a pernicious neurochemistry which leads to impulsivity, low distress tolerance and low consequence appraisal and makes it extremely difficult for a parent to change without help and support. However, another way of avoiding the problem of misguided over-praising is to adopt a different focus for the assessment entirely. We discuss this in more detail later.

It is worth remembering that the UK system of child protection has been emulated or implemented in many other countries across the world, the reason being that, for some families, it appears to have a negatively reinforcing effect: the Sword of Damocles motivates them to make marginal, even substantial, changes in order to keep 'social services' off their backs and out of their lives. But not all families are capable of change under threat: they simply cannot do the things required without help. Others are capable of making changes in the short term but cannot sustain the progress for very long; they only manage cosmetic, superficial improvement.

Another problem with the pre-Munro paradigm is that, not surprisingly, with the emphasis on 'caseload throughput' (i.e. closing cases as quickly as possible in order to open new ones), practitioners routinely *ask parents about their parenting* rather than *seeing them do it*; yet, as we saw earlier, the evidence indicates that simply asking parents about their parenting capacity is partial and often highly unreliable. In 2010, in a systematic review of working with 'reluctant or resistant' families, submitted to the UK's Centre for Excellence in Outcomes for Children and Families (C4EO), one of us (DS) wrote:

> One of the key implications of these findings is that professionals working with highly resistant families need to refocus their gaze towards the relationship between the parent and the child, rather than focusing too exclusively on the relationship between the parent and the professional (Juffer et al. 2008) . . . Being in a position to observe and witness the parent-child relationship directly enables an experienced worker to gauge the presence of disorganised attachment behaviours . . . which are linked . . . to both family risk factors and child maltreatment . . . This is a different approach to that of asking the parent to comment or reflect upon their parenting, which for someone feigning compliance offers a wonderfully simple opportunity to deceive the worker. Because it is unlikely that a parent will be uncooperative and aggressive with a social worker present, but loving, warm and responsive to their child, the professional's interest in the relationship they have with a resistant parent is the insight it can offer about what it must feel like to a child to be with someone so hostile and unpredictable.
>
> (Fauth et al. 2010: 11)

The team had earlier pointed out that:

> There is an urgent need to review practitioners' tendency to rely almost exclusively on interviewing parents about their parenting skills to assess capacity. Practitioners need information from a variety of sources using a variety of techniques, of which observation is an important one. Attention needs to be paid to observing parent-child dynamics in order to assess caregivers actually parenting, as distinct from describing how they parent. The use of standardised questionnaires and assessments may be useful here as well. Convincing evidence exists to show that simulating sensitive parenting is very difficult to sustain. But to accomplish such a shift in emphasis it is likely that specific observational techniques,

such as understanding and recognising disorganised attachment behaviour, will
need to be acquired by practitioners.

(Fauth et al. 2010: 8–9)

An additional problem with current practice is that there is a lack of focus on the
child. The practitioners we have spoken to regularly tell us that they sometimes have to
interpret the requirement to 'see the child' as literally that: 'I *saw* the child in the garden/
in the classroom . . . but I didn't actually speak to them.' Others who *do* talk to the child
tell us that it often amounts to little more than saying to the child 'How are you?',
'How's it going?', 'How are you doing?', 'How did your football match/contact visit/
maths test etc. go last week?' But such an approach rarely reveals much about the
child's world or their wishes and feelings; it is yet another procedurally based approach.
Again, we are not reporting these points in order to criticise practitioners: quite
the reverse, we are doing so in order that the context of their work is appreciated
more fully.

Talking to practitioners we also get the distinct impression that some families are
subjected to an indefinite amount of assessment, conducted by a range of professionals. On the other hand, the professionals themselves often tell us that, at the end
of such investigative processes, they may well end up feeling none the wiser about the
precise mechanisms leading to alleged abuse or neglect. Other than composing a
written agreement spelling out in detail what is wrong and what needs to change, they
remain at a loss to know how to help.

Finally, despite child protection practice being procedurally based and somewhat
adversarially driven, high court judges, magistrates and local authority lawyers will all
give examples of social workers and others losing cases because their evidence is not
well argued (see Dickens 1993), critically analysed or guided by research and theory
(this point also applies to recording and report-writing generally). We are not
suggesting that there were halcyon days when these problems were not present;
consequently we agree with Andrew Turnell when he contends that:

Anyone who was influenced by the open, almost-anything-goes field that was
social work in the 1970s, knows that while there was extraordinarily good child
protection work happening at that time, there was also correspondingly appalling
work happening at the other end of the practice continuum.

(Turnell 2009: 4)

'Post-Munro' child protection practice: a realistic vision for the future

The subtitle of this book is *An evidence base for confident practice*. We conclude, therefore, with some indications of what such practice needs to comprise. The problem is
that 'a significant difficulty is that little attention is given within the literature of social
work and the broader helping professions about how to build constructive helping
relationships when the professional also has a strong coercive role' (Turnell 2009: 18).
Referring to the same C4EO review into working with 'reluctant or resistant' families
as quoted above, one of us (DS) was part of the team that wrote:

... most parents who harm their children would prefer not to. As long as professionals remain alert to those individuals accomplished at responding with 'disguised compliance', this perspective is less likely to result in defensive social work. Such an 'eyes wide open', unsentimental approach recognises the profound harm and distress that befalls children who are maltreated, while simultaneously upholding the values of social work.

(Fauth et al. 2010: 8–9)

The Munro report as well as many serious case reviews (SCRs) comment unfavourably on the level of analysis in child protection reports and records. Visits, observations and conversations are described but they lack either a theoretical or an evidence base; even an argument threaded with sound 'practice wisdom' is often missing. Considerable amounts of information are gathered but it is often not assessed; it is not evaluated in the sense of different viewpoints being weighed and balanced against each other. Part of the problem seems to lie in a legacy over the years whereby social work in particular has developed a mistrust of 'expertise' and as a consequence has become ambivalent, disinterested and even hostile towards theory and research. From our involvement with practitioners, however, we detect a change here, possibly as a result of emerging neurological research in child development which shows clearly the effects of early maltreatment and delay on brain growth (see National Scientific Council on the Developing Child 2009).

Also missing is a 'child's-eye' view within assessments. The entire second report in the Munro review is entitled *The Child's Journey*; indeed the *Framework for the Assessment of Children in Need and Their Families* (Department of Health 2000a) was subtitled *The Child's World*. So when, in the Victoria Climbié report, Lord Laming used the phrase 'the child is "missing" from the files', he was among many to express his concerns about the invisibility of *children* in child protection practice (Laming 2003). We now offer two examples[1] which we believe offer a 'child's-eye view'. They include theoretical insights and draw heavily on research; notice how, in each, they do not read as 'academic assignments' as they are written in plain language and without references.

Example A

Specific indications of how Ricky experiences chronic lack of parental affection emerge when he is asked to complete a story involving mild conflict between two PlayPeople. In the story, one of them says 'You've lost my keys'; the other replies 'I haven't lost your keys'. The child is asked, 'Can you show and tell me what happens next?' Even quite *insecure* children will develop an *organised* way of finishing the story – there might be an argument, more shouting and the keys may never be found, but eventually there emerges an organised way to complete the task. Not so for Ricky; he is more than 'merely' insecure; his story ends very abruptly. The two PlayPeople immediately 'die' which Ricky confirms by saying, 'They can't get up.' This sudden and unexpected catastrophising after only mild disagreement is indicative of what experts refer to as 'disorganised attachment'.

Example B

During this visit Ms X gave Y his dinner. She made him a chocolate spread sandwich and gave him some crisps. She gave him a bottle of fizzy drink. Ms X did not encourage Y to sit at the table and consequently Y dropped part of his sandwich onto the floor, and he started to play with it and move it across the carpet.

Ms X became annoyed by this. She told him to stop it but he continued. Ms X then bent down near to him and said in an aggressive tone, 'Give me that to me.' When Y did not respond she repeated herself and pointed to the crust on the floor. Y did not respond and Ms X removed the crust herself and said to Y in an aggressive tone 'You're *disgusting*.'

I was surprised by this reaction. Ms X had given Y his sandwich while he was sat on the floor. The likelihood of a 2-year-old managing this without spilling some on the carpet is remote. Yet Ms X was unable to reflect on this and instead directed her anger and verbal abuse at Y.

'Disgusting' was used to describe Y on other occasions. The most worrying incident occurred when Ms X removed Y's nappy after I had informed her that it was leaking, as there were wet patches on his trousers. Ms X then dressed Y in the wet trousers, but did not put another nappy on him. While myself and Ms X were talking in the living room, Y went into the hallway, removed his trousers and 'pooed' onto the carpet. When Ms X discovered this she shouted 'Urgh – that is *disgusting*.'

This was an understandable response, but she then took hold of Y and held him against her with one arm (facing the poo). She said to him in an aggressive tone 'I am *not* happy. *What* do you say?' When he did not respond she repeated this in a louder tone of voice. Y remained still, with his eyes looking downwards. She then repeatedly said to him in an increasingly loud and aggressive tone, '*What* is it, tell me what it *is*?' When Y did not respond she removed her arm from around him and said, 'You're disgusting – *you're a disgusting child.*' Y then walked into the living room and repeated this, saying 'Disgusting child.' Ms X removed the faeces, but did not wipe his bottom.

The need for good communication skills are also highlighted in the Munro review. There is growing evidence that offering empathy increases mentalising capacity, thereby reducing some of the mis-synchronised interactions observed in maltreating parents (see, for example, Shemmings et al. 2012). The need, however, is for practitioners with counselling skills, but not skilled counsellors. Practitioners need to be able to discuss gaps in parenting in an open, honest and respectful way, but it is also important to be able to help a parent with the daily minute-to-minute interactions with their child. There is an impressive and developing body of research claiming that showing short, filmed vignettes of parent-child interaction, selected by the practitioner to highlight synchronised parenting and/or the child demonstrating their need and affection for the parent, re-sensitises caregivers with low capacity for mentalisation in ways which more didactic approaches are unable to achieve. Video-based interaction for positive parenting (VIPP – Juffer et al. 2008) is a manualised intervention run over four to six one-hour sessions but many of the principles can be used by busy child protection professionals, sometimes to help assessment accuracy. The following examples[2] show how this can be achieved.

> The following practice refers to a 60-minute contact session between a young father and his 3-month-old daughter

> Despite being advised by the regular contact supervisor that father's interaction with his baby was very positive, a few exploratory questions with him . . . *'Why do you think she did that?', 'Does she know how you feel about it?', 'So is she being sick on your shoulder on purpose?'* . . . identified that he had persecutory beliefs about his daughter and was placing negative attributions on age-appropriate behaviour: 'She's never been sick on her mum, and she knows I'm wearing a new shirt today!'
> Teams are beginning to advise contact supervisors to assess low mentalisation and emotional attunement. This guidance includes prompts like:
>
>> For infants, does the parent help interpret the child's presumed internal state using exaggerated expressions and tones? Does the parent show a willingness to understand their child? Is the parent able to speculate on their child's feeling states?
>
> By maintaining curiosity about what psychological traffic is passing between the parent and child, the worker needs to be prepared to ask specific, clarifying questions to the parent rather than maintaining a strictly passive, observational stance. We also try to assess low mentalisation and parental sensitivity by filming approximately 10–15 minutes of parent-child interaction, during a *guided parenting task,* and later inviting the parent to undertake a 'speaking for the child' exercise. This involves playing the footage back to the parent and stopping at frequent intervals to ask questions such as *'So, what's your child thinking/feeling here?', 'What do you think that cry means?', 'Is she upset about something in particular?', 'What's in her mind here?'*

A *guided parenting task* (see Juffer et al. 2008) comprises five stages, two of which involve short but mildly challenging components: the 'don't touch' task and the 'clear up' task. Even though they have to learn not to touch grandma's precious vase, or the electric plug, most children usually struggle when asked not to touch a particular toy. Equally, when they are having fun with a new toy they want to carry on doing so. The purpose of the guided parenting task is to observe parenting directly, rather than simply ask the parent to comment on their 'parenting capacity' because of the obvious problems of relying heavily on the truthfulness of their account. The practitioner also gently asks questions aimed at exploring the parent's mentalising capacity, in the way we saw above, such as, 'What do you think is in his mind when he's getting cross?', 'Why do you think he doesn't want to clear up?'

A guided parenting task
1   Child plays on their own with an unfamiliar toy (2 mins) – parent is asked to 'be with' their child but not to join in.
2   Parent joins in (5 mins) – parent has to tell the child they can't touch one of the toys yet.
3   Parent and child read a story, or make lunch, or sing a song – the aim is for them to do it together.
4   Parent and child play with paints, felt-tips, crayons etc. (5 mins).
5   Parent and child clear up.

We conclude this chapter by describing the ADAM project, which is attracting considerable interest in the UK and Europe because it puts into practice the ideas we have outlined in this section on a 'post-Munro world', but first we contextualise the project by discussing the problem of *prediction* and how ADAM seeks to sidestep it.

Problems with the current method of predicting child abuse and neglect: 'looking in the wrong place for the wrong things'

The promise of predicting abuse and neglect is an attractive one because of its preventive potential. It also has financial appeal because it raises the possibility of targeting limited resources at those areas where they are most needed and most likely to be effective. Predicting child abuse by observing caregiver responses to new-born babies and collecting other available data is still an important part of child protection policy and practice in the USA. There is a relatively long history of prediction studies, starting with Kempe and Kempe (1978) who claimed a 79 per cent successful prediction rate for their method of assessment. Montgomery (1982) criticised this study for its use of a very broad definition of child abuse. Judged by the rate of substantiated child abuse, Kempe's predictions were 16 per cent accurate rather than 79 per cent. In addition, even if the 79 per cent rate were accepted, this still means that 21 per cent were wrongly 'diagnosed'.

In Britain, where prediction of this kind is not part of mainstream policy, studies that have been conducted have not come up with encouraging results. Lealman et al. (1983), using maternity records to predict the likelihood of child abuse, forecast that 500 from a sample of 2,802 children were likely to be abused. In fact, 28 children were registered for abuse, 17 of whom were predicted. The remaining 483 were wrongly predicted (false negatives).

Browne and Saqi (1988) reported on a series of predictive studies carried out with health professionals in the Surrey area. Using a 12-item checklist at birth and after one month on a population of 14,238 families, they identified 949 of these as high risk. However, the results after two years were disappointing in terms of successful prediction – only 1 in 17 (6 per cent) had abused their children (using child protection conferences as an indicator).

A more recent study by Peters and Barlow (2003) conducted a systematic review of 220 published articles on the subject of predicted maltreatment around the time of birth. They found eight studies that met the criteria of using evaluated standard instruments (of which the Browne and Saqi study was one). However, none of these studies had a positive prediction value of over 50 per cent and only two approximated acceptable standards of accuracy.

In summary, therefore, the various studies considered here demonstrate that it is extremely difficult to predict future abuse. In this process, at least 20 per cent of any sample will be wrongly predicted of being likely to abuse or neglect their children, and if one uses a narrow definition of child abuse, such as that of child protection registration, then the rate of false prediction can rise to a much higher level. Therefore, it must be concluded that these studies fail in their aims of accurately targeting those families who might benefit from specialist help. In addition, the programmes to which parents are assigned following these predictions have not been proven to be consistently effective (Duggan et al. 2004).

It is not only the effectiveness of the predictive approach that is in question. There are also major questions about the ethics of this sort of activity. Is it, for instance, ethical to make an assessment of potential parental care without informing parents of what is happening? Is it ethical not to inform parents about concerns resulting from this assessment? The only justification for this lack of openness can be that secrecy is essential in order to ensure the well-being of the child. There is, however, no evidence that lack of candour is likely to improve the safety of the child. Working with parents on the basis of shared concerns may be a more effective strategy in achieving this goal. Peters and Barlow (2003) are also concerned about these questions:

> . . . it is not appropriate to screen parents for outcomes such as increased risk of child abuse for which they are not likely to consent to be screened. An alternative strategy would involve the provision of universal parenting support beginning during the ante-natal period, in which professionals already working with families identify parents in need of higher levels of intervention . . .
>
> (Peters and Barlow 2003: 437–8)

The problem with current prediction methods is that they are circumscribed by what Munro (2008) called the 'base rate problem'. We illustrate this by referring to what Marian Brandon calls the toxic trio of 'risk factors': mental ill-health, substance misuse and domestic violence. As experienced practitioners will quickly attest, one or more of these factors is usually present when maltreatment occurs; but retrospective associations and correlations are very different from prospective prediction.

Prevalence figures illustrate this clearly. They are derived from analyses of SCRs[3] in the UK (e.g. Brandon et al. 2008a, 2010) now totalling over 500. In around 27 per cent of families where serious child maltreatment has taken place one or more of the parents will have a mental health problem, but 25 per cent of the general population also has a mental health problem in any one given year (Office for National Statistics 2001a). The figures for substance misuse are 44 per cent in SCRs, but 34 per cent of the general population experiences significant addiction to drugs (9 per cent – Kershaw et al. 2008) and/or to alcohol (25 per cent alcohol misuse – Cheeta et al. 2008). The position is little different with domestic violence, with 34 per cent in SCRs but in the general population the figure is as high: 29 per cent of women and

18 per cent of men in the general population are victims or survivors of domestic violence (Coleman et al. 2007).

These data result in relative prevalence rates of 1.1:1 for the prevalence of mental ill-health between maltreating and general populations. For substance misuse the figure is 1.3:1 while for domestic violence it is only marginally higher at 1.4:1. Consequently, it is hardly surprising that the practice of trying to predict maltreatment from the so-called risk factors is rather hit and miss.

But there is another problem with existing 'risk factors': even if they contained more predictive validity, almost all of them are extremely difficult to change. How does a parent easily and quickly become drug or alcohol free? How do they overcome mental illness? We can help families with rehousing and even help alleviate chronic levels of poverty, but experienced practitioners know only too well that, while such social actions are essential in terms of social justice and equality, they may have little effect in the short, or even medium, term on child abuse and neglect.

So the problem may be expressed as follows: *some* parents who are mentally ill later go on to abuse their own children . . . *but others do not; some* drug users abuse their own children . . . *yet others do not.* In fact, the majority – around 75 per cent (see Crittenden 2008) – of parents who were abused themselves as children do not go on to abuse their own children. Another way of appreciating this is by considering that, although the majority of children who are sexually abused are girls, by far the greater proportion of sexual abusers are men, so clearly other mechanisms operate in the pathway from caregiver characteristics to child maltreatment.

The relative data on the prevalence of disorganised attachment (DA) in children, however, allows us to have much greater confidence because although between 10 and 15 per cent of the general population of children will display DA – and it is always of concern and may indicate that there is abuse from individuals other than parents or as a result of other traumatic events – around 80 per cent of a maltreated population will display DA. Therefore, the presence of DA strongly suggests that the child *has already been maltreated*, not that they are likely to be in the future; hence, it is an indicator of maltreatment, not a predictor of it. The indicative ratio for DA is 5.4:1 and, thus, is currently the best maltreatment marker available.

In terms of parents, to explore the ways in which caregiver 'risk factors' lead in some cases to maltreatment but not in others we need to assess the effect of the 'explanatory mechanisms' – which as we saw in Chapter 7 are *unresolved loss and trauma* (see Madigan et al. 2006), *disconnected and extremely insensitive caregiving* (Out et al. 2009) and *low capacity for mentalisation* (see Fonagy and Target 2005; Allen et al. 2008). A positive effect can be brought to bear upon these explanatory mechanisms by the use of interventions such as trauma-focused cognitive behaviour therapy (TF-CBT – Cohen et al. 2006), VIPP (Juffer et al. 2008) and mentalisation-based treatment (Allen et al. 2008), which are all proving to be effective ways of helping families. Furthermore, elements of these approaches can also be incorporated into assessments in a more agile and dynamic way (training is required to do this and is described fully in Shemmings and Shemmings 2011; much of it is provided at the Anna Freud Centre in London). We saw this in the earlier example of the father's perceptions when asked why he thought his baby daughter had been sick on his clean shirt. His response permits us to assess his capacity for mentalisation as well as the likelihood of his being able to change; if he becomes more flexible in his own thinking, if he can feel a degree of discomfort about his assumptions, if he can slowly move towards a more curious and less self-referential position about his baby's intentions, then the prognosis for change is more promising than if he continues to maintain an intransigent and incurious stance towards his baby.

The interplay between these explanatory mechanisms becomes clearer in the maltreatment pathway model shown in Figure 10.1 (see Shemmings and Shemmings 2011: ch. 2).

The approach we are describing implies a re-focusing of attention by child protection professionals. It requires an interest, awareness and genuine curiosity about the mental states of parents and children. The need for this change of gaze was expressed by Marian Brandon and her colleagues after analysing 350 SCRs from 2003 to 2007:

> One of the key bits of information that helps frame an ... understanding of parent-child interaction, children's psychosocial development and children's care and protection is the carer's state of mind. Caregiver states of mind can therefore be understood in terms of the parent's relationship history and current patterns of interaction with children, partners, peers, professionals.
>
> (Brandon et al. 2009: 63)

This shift in perspective stresses not what happened to people in the past, but the sense they make of it all *now*; the emphasis is not about people's current lifestyles in isolation but how they understand and make sense of close relationships. Above all, the key to understanding maltreatment crystallises when practitioners develop curiosity and skill in understanding whether parents can accurately make sense of their child's mental states.

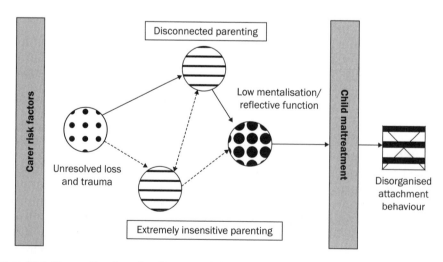

Figure 10.1 The maltreatment pathway model

Concluding comments: the ADAM project

The Assessment of Disorganised Attachment and Maltreatment (ADAM) project (see http://adamproject.tiddlyspot.com) started in May 2009 and is aimed at helping professionals feel more confident when assessing why it is that some parents abuse their children while others do not. By the end of a four-day course, spread over four months, participants are able to draw upon a number of assessment techniques adapted for use pragmatically by busy child protection practitioners. The organisations that have taken part are all interested in evidence-based skills to help families by incorporating them, seamlessly and in agile and creative ways, into assessment and intervention processes.

The ADAM project invites practitioners to work differently with parents, carers and children. They need to be more patient, more empathic, listen more carefully, show more genuine respect – in other words, maintain basic Rogerian conditions for an effective helping relationship. However, the relentless media hype, along with the ever-present fear of being pilloried, blamed or even losing one's job, has produced a perniciously bureaucratic and proceduralised system for child protection – not just in the UK, but in many other countries – which, while reasonably good at preventing child *deaths*, is far less effective at addressing abuse and neglect generally. It is chilling, as we saw earlier for example, to find consistently that around 15 per cent of parents will exhibit disconnected or extremely insensitive caregiving with their infants or toddlers. This leads to the emergence of disorganised attachment behaviour in children, which is one of the most reliable predictors of problems later in adulthood.

The main conduit for change in the carer is increased mentalising capacity, which has been shown to develop both more quickly and more permanently with an emotionally available practitioner. Over the past two years we have witnessed a number of practitioners, from each of the main child protection agencies, respond eagerly and enthusiastically to the new approach; that is why we dedicated this book to them. The urgent task for policy-makers, managers and supervisors is to create the right conditions for emotionally intelligent professionals to flourish; it's their turn now to step up to the plate and respond creatively to this challenge.

Recommended reading

Allen, J. G., Fonagy, P. and Bateman, A. W. (2008) *Mentalising in Clinical Practice*. Arlington, VA: APP.

Cohen, J. A., Mannarino, A. P. and Deblinger, E. (2006) *Treating Trauma and Traumatic Grief in Children and Adolescents*. New York: The Guilford Press.

Forrester, D., Kershaw, S., Moss, H. and Hughes, L. (2008) Communication skills in child protection: how do social workers talk to parents? *Child and Family Social Work*, 13(1): 41–51.

Juffer, F., Bakermans-Kranenburg, M. J. and Van IJzendoorn, M. H. (eds) (2008) *Promoting Positive Parenting: An Attachment-based Intervention*. New York: Lawrence Erlbaum/Taylor & Francis.

Miller, W. R. and Rollnick, S. (2002) *Motivational Interviewing: Preparing People to Change*, 2nd edn. New York: The Guilford Press.

Shemmings, D. and Shemmings. Y. (2011) *Understanding Disorganised Attachment: Theory and Practice for Working with Children and Adults*. London: Jessica Kingsley.

Notes

Introduction

1. It is important to distinguish between the terms 'prevalence' and 'incidence'. Prevalence studies measure how many people in a given sample have experienced a particular phenomenon at least once over a particular period of time. Incidence studies measure the number of occurrences of a particular phenomenon in a given sample of people over a particular period of time. Thus, if a sample of 100 people were asked if they had been sexually abused at least once before the age of 15, and 20 said that they had, the prevalence rate of abuse of such children would be 20 per cent. If these 100 people were asked how often they had been sexually abused before the age of 15, the answer would probably be higher. They might report abuse on 60 occasions. The incidence rate of abuse would then be 60 per 100 people over the first 15 years of their lives. La Fontaine (1990: ch. 2) gives a fuller, very useful account of these and other issues relating to prevalence and incidence studies.

2. The 'grave concern' category formed nearly 30 per cent of the whole in 1978 and just under 50 per cent of the whole in 1991. It was something of a miscellaneous category, originally incorporating cases where those convicted of offences against children had been living or were about to live in the same household as children, and cases where there had been strong suspicions of physical abuse, sexual abuse or neglect, but no definite evidence. This category was abandoned at the end of 1991. It is likely that the increase in neglect and emotional abuse cases between 1991 and 2004 is partly as a result of the elimination of this category.

Chapter 1 Childhood, child abuse and history

1. This day a quarter past two in the afternoone my Mary fell asleepe in the Lord, her soule past into that rest where the body of Jesus, and the soules of the saints are, shee was: 8 yeares and 45 dayes old when shee dyed, my soule had aboundant cause to blesse god for her, who was our first fruites, and those god would have offered to him, and this I freely resigned up to him[,] it was a pretious child, a bundle of myrrhe, a bundle of sweetnes, shee was a child of ten thousand, full of wisedome, woman-like gravity, knowledge, sweet expressions of god, apt in her learning, tender hearted and loving, an obedient child [to us.] it was free from [the rudenesse of] litle children, it was to us as a boxe of sweet ointment, which now its broken smells more deliciously than it did before, Lord I rejoyce I had such a present for thee, it was patient in the sicknesse, thankfull to admiracion; it lived desired and dyed lamented, thy memory is and wille bee sweete unto mee. [26 May 1650]

(Macfarlane 1970: 203)

2. It should be noted that Boswell (1990) has been criticised by some historians for being over-optimistic about the fate of abandoned children (see Tilly et al. 1992).
3. This statement, while demonstrating public concern about child sexual abuse, also shows that there was probably a hierarchy of concerns. No mention is made of female children and those of non-citizen status.
4. La Fontaine (1990: 210), drawing from anthropological work, lends some support to such a view with regard to sexual abuse.

Chapter 2 A history of child abuse and neglect 1870–2000

1. It would be wrong, however, to suggest that there was no relevant legislation at all. The 1868 Poor Law Act made wilful neglect by a parent of a child under 14 that threatened or resulted in serious injury an offence. The weakness of this law was that only Poor Law officials were empowered to bring cases of this kind to court and they very rarely did so. The 1861 Offences Against the Person Act could also be used to prosecute parents for assaults on their children, but no particular agency was mandated to report or seek out such abuse.
2. This may seem counter-intuitive but despite the Great Depression of the 1930s, from a long-enough perspective, as taken by Stevenson and Cook, by the late 1930s and early 1940s, the economy in the UK had grown substantially when compared with the 1910s. Unemployment dropped substantially from 1930 onwards and gross domestic product (GDP) was also higher in 1940 than it had been between 1900 and 1920 (see Hicks and Allen 1999).
3. The major legislative change of this period was the 1933 Children and Young Persons Act, which followed in the tradition of previous legislation by extending the range of prosecutable offences against children. It also blurred distinctions between neglected children and young offenders by such measures as the creation of approved schools for all who came into these two categories (before this they had attended separate institutions). By 1946, when the Curtis Committee reported, this type of thinking was well established: 'According to the evidence of the Home Office, it is often an accident whether a child is before the court for an offence or as a neglected child, and it is accordingly appropriate that the same methods of treatment be equally available' (Curtis 1946: 14, para. 38).
4. See Housden (1955: 209–10), which provides an extract of an NSPCC inspector's discovery of and response to a child sexual abuse case. The case is undated, but as the children involved were committed to industrial schools, it must have been before the implementation of the 1933 Children and Young Persons Act. The case involved a 12-year-old girl, her 11-year-old sister and her 9-year-old brother. Their mother was dead and they were living with their father and a 46-year-old male lodger. It was revealed that the two girls slept in the same bed as the lodger. The inspector's records described the children as being dirty and neglected. A medical examination was arranged by the inspector. 'This proved that the girl aged 12 had been interfered with.' The father and the lodger were prosecuted. The father, a first-time offender, received a light sentence and the lodger 18 months' hard labour. The children, as mentioned above, were committed to industrial schools. The tenor of the report is very factual. The response to this case comes across as insensitive by our standards but unequivocally child protective.
5. See Cleveland inquiry report (Butler-Sloss 1988: 64, para. 4.80). A 10-year-old girl and her two siblings were examined with their mother's consent by Dr Higgs in the hospital. Their father removed them. They were subsequently brought into police custody under place of safety orders and examined by a police surgeon, Dr Beeby. His diagnosis conflicted with that of Dr Higgs, who re-examined the children. The following day they were

re-examined by Dr Irvine, another police surgeon. The report adds that the children 'were later examined by three more doctors'.

6. La Fontaine (1998: 9–12) provided some useful information about the different terminologies used to describe this form of abuse. The term 'satanic' implies that children are being abused as part of devil-worship ceremonies. It is a term used usually by extreme fundamentalists who are committed to wiping out such forms of worship. The term 'satanist' is used by those who attribute the abuse to devil worship, but do not believe in the devil; their concerns are more objectively focused on child abuse issues. 'Ritual abuse' is a term used to describe any form of child abuse taking place within a ritual setting (including devil worship).

7. The accounts of the interviews with the child, MT, are a very good example of this (see Clyde 1992: paras 11.91–6). MT is described in the report as an 'articulate and able child who rarely showed visible signs of emotion. She appeared very grown up' (para. 11.91). In the following paragraphs she gives a clear and detailed account of taking part in a ritual where children were hurt 'in the wrong places'.

8. While the focus in this section has been on responses to two main forms of institutional abuse, those relating directly to the regime's measures of control, as in Pindown, usually involving psychologically cruel or physically abusive practices, and sexual abuse usually perpetrated by individual residential workers using the power opportunities provided by their positions in the homes, as in Leicestershire (Wardhaugh and Wilding 1993), there are two other forms of abuse that should also be considered. The first is that of neglect, in situations where children are not contained within the residential centre and become involved in unacceptable behaviours, such as offending, drug-taking and prostitution. Concerns of this kind were raised in the Islington inquiry (White and Hart 1995). More recently, there was an inquiry into the death of Aliyah Ismail (Harrow 1999), a 13-year-old girl in the care of Harrow Social Services Department. She died of a methadone overdose and was known by various child protection professionals to have been involved in prostitution. The other form of institutional abuse relates to bullying by peers within institutions. This has not aroused public concern but in a study by Sinclair and Gibbs (1998) was found to be the most pressing fear of children and young people.

9. Part 8 reviews were introduced in 1991 in the *Working Together* guidelines (Department of Health 1991b). Following the introduction of the 1999 *Working Together* guidelines (Department of Health 1999) such reviews are now termed 'serious case reviews'. They are required to be carried out by area child protection committees where child abuse has taken place resulting in death or serious injury likely to be of major public concern. The reports resulting from these reviews must be sent to the Department of Health (now the Department of Education and Skills) and the findings must be considered by the relevant agencies within the area where the abuse has taken place. A key aim of this review system is to ensure that lessons are learned and put into practice as soon as possible. One of the problems with it, however, has been that, except in a small number of cases where it has been deemed that there is exceptional public concern, the findings of these reviews have not been available to the general public or professionals involved in child protection work outside the particular areas concerned. This has now been remedied to some extent in that, under the current guidelines, a biennial report on all serious review cases is required. However, there is still a good deal of debate about the best means of inquiring into and learning from cases where child deaths by abuse have happened (Reder and Duncan 1998; Corby 2003a).

10. Jason Swift was a 14-year-old boy at the time of his death in 1985. He was living on the streets and had been doing sexual acts for money for some time. He was drugged and slowly suffocated to death while being sexually abused by four men, who were

later convicted of manslaughter. They were given sentences of between 2 and 19 years' imprisonment.

11. Another important piece of legislation passed at this time was the 1999 Protection of Children Act which requires child care agencies, when making appointments, to check Department of Health lists of individuals previously employed with children but considered to be a risk to them. This Act also requires agencies to refer individuals whom they have employed and dismissed because of risk-to-children concerns (Department of Health/ NHS Executive 2000).

Chapter 3 Protecting children and young people from harm: contemporary perspectives

1. Initially, these outcomes and this agenda seem difficult to object to – after all, who would not want children to 'stay safe' and 'be healthy', or could possibly argue that not all children matter? However, there are some who have found reasonable fault with the agenda – for example, Hoyle (2008) argues that the focus on 'be healthy' ignores the structural health inequalities in the UK. Other criticisms have included the charge that by asking Ofsted to inspect schools partly on the basis of the five outcomes of *Every Child Matters*, the focus of the inspections becomes less about educational outcomes and more about more general outcomes for children (*Guardian* 2009).

2. The Aiming High for Disabled Children agenda was aimed at transforming disabled children's services in England. It was discontinued in 2011 by the Conservative–Liberal Democrat coalition administration although additional money for short breaks for disabled children was allocated (£800 million over a four-year period, 2011–14). A new short breaks duty also came into force in April 2011 as an amendment to the Children and Young People Act 2008. This amendment requires all local authorities in England to provide services to people who care for disabled children. The government has also issued a Green Paper on special educational needs and has indicated a desire to improve transparency and access to information for carers of disabled children.

3. Although the national ContactPoint database (planned to be operational across England) was discontinued, individual local authorities are developing similar databases for children in their areas. For example, Westminster Council has developed Children's Hub to enable information-sharing between local services. There has been some speculation that local authorities may in future decide to exchange information between their local databases – in effect, creating reduced versions of ContactPoint in particular areas of the country. Given the debates about the likely efficacy and potential risks of a national database of children, it is perhaps somewhat concerning that these reduced versions of ContactPoint have been developed without nearly as much attention.

4. Sharp-eyed readers may have noted that no amendment to the timescales for initial and core assessments had taken place by December 2011 and neither had the two distinct assessments been replaced with one combined assessment. On 13 December 2011, Tim Loughton MP provided a written answer to a parliamentary question, stating that revisions to *Working Together to Safeguard Children* and the *Framework for the Assessment for Children in Need and Their Families* would be forthcoming by July 2012. Readers are advised to view *The Munro Review of Child Protection* website, www.education.gov.uk/munroreview, for further information.

5. For example, in 2011 the coalition government introduced the Welfare Reform Bill to Parliament with the intention of ensuring that being in paid employment is always financially beneficial when compared to an income based solely on benefits and tax credits.

6. All of these statistics can be found on the Department for Education website.

Chapter 4 Defining child abuse

1. The Female Circumcision Act was replaced in 2004 by the Female Genital Mutilation Act 2003. This was introduced to prevent children being taken abroad to have circumcision operations, thus blocking a loophole in the previous legislation. The Department of Education and Skills estimated that there were 7,000 girls under the age of 16 who were at risk of female genital mutilation (Department for Education and Skills 2004b).
2. Stephanie Fox was known by the health and welfare authorities to have suffered minor bruising on 30 occasions before she died as a result of a violent assault by her father. They had previously declined to remove Stephanie, probably because their expectations of the family were very low and it was felt that such bruising (largely perceived to be the result of careless supervision of the child rather than of physical mistreatment) was not remarkable given the background of the Fox family. The Lester Chapman case shows a similarly resigned acceptance of low standards of care, as does that of the case of Paul.
3. The social worker in this case made assumptions about Caribbean culture that placed heavy expectations on Tyra's grandmother to provide care and protection for her. West Indian grandmothers were stereotypically considered to be the linch-pins of the family. As far as Beatrice Henry was concerned, nothing could have been further from the truth. She had experienced the death of her husband and the severe mistreatment of her grandson. She was a lone parent dealing with the problems of her own three children, was inadequately housed and had multiple debts. As events proved, she was completely unable to protect Tyra.
4. At her second referral to hospital, Victoria presented with scald marks on her head and face which, according to her great-aunt, resulted from her pouring boiling water on herself to stop the itching being caused by scabies. This was a highly implausible account, and the fact that there had been several hours between the incident happening and Victoria being brought to hospital should have aroused much more suspicion than it actually did. Instead, there was a good deal of circumspection on all parts and eventually after a short stay in hospital Victoria was discharged home without any agreed follow-up arrangements (see Laming 2003: ch. 10, North Middlesex Hospital).
5. The following two vignettes, with consequences in parentheses, are taken from Giovannoni and Becerra's (1979: 116) study and give a flavour of the general approach used: 'The parents regularly left their child alone outside the house during the day until almost dark (neighbours have spotted the child wandering five blocks from home).' 'The parents banged the child against the wall while shaking him by the shoulders (the child suffered a concussion)' (Giovannoni and Becerra 1979: 113).
6. Currently (2011), the following European countries have banned all corporal punishment of children at home and in schools: Austria, Bulgaria, Croatia, Cyprus, Denmark, Finland, Germany, Greece, Hungary, Iceland, Latvia, Moldova, the Netherlands, Norway, Poland, Portugal, Spain, Sweden, Romania and Ukraine. The following countries have banned corporal punishment of children in schools but not entirely in the home: Albania, Belarus, Belgium, Bosnia and Herzegovina, Czech Republic, Estonia, Italy, Lithuania, Macedonia, Montenegro, Russia, Serbia, Slovakia, Slovenia, Switzerland, Turkey and the United Kingdom. France has not explicitly banned the corporal punishment of children in schools.
7. Such pronouncements were perhaps influenced by earlier work, such as the Doreen Aston report (Lambeth, Lewisham and Southwark 1989). Before Doreen's birth, her mother, Christine Mason, had had a child, Karl, who died aged 10 weeks. A post-mortem revealed that he had three fractured ribs and a subdural haemorrhage, but these injuries were not thought to have contributed to his death, which was finally recorded as a cot death (see Lambeth, Lewisham and Southwark 1989: 8, paras 11 and 12). The authors of the report felt that the cot death decision led social workers and others to overlook the fact that the

child had been abused and, therefore, that subsequent children might be particularly at risk. Although Sally Clark's conviction for harming her children was duly overturned, the cases of Doreen and of Sally Clark do evidence the difficulty that child protection practitioners have between not overlooking significant previous histories (as in the case of Doreen) but also having to leave room for the acceptance that on occasion (as in the case of Sally), terrible and tragic things do happen without the need for a perpetrator to have caused the harm.

8. Political factors may also play a part in this relative lack of attention to neglect. Wolock and Horowitz (1984) argued that neglect of children is far more common than physical abuse in the USA, but receives far less attention. This 'neglect of neglect', as they termed it, results from the fact that closer inspection of many children's lives would reveal the extent to which poverty contributes to neglect and this would create political embarrassment for governments.

9. The Jasmine Beckford report (Brent 1985: 69–74) provides useful detailed material on the failure-to-thrive syndrome. At birth, Jasmine weighed 2.58kg. By four months, she had reached an average weight for a child of her age and, therefore, would have been expected to maintain this average growth throughout her early childhood. After 10 months, Jasmine had slipped back and her weight was well below the average. It was below the third centile (that is, Jasmine was among the 3 per cent most poorly developed of all children). At age 15 months Jasmine weighed 8.33kg, even further down in the third centile. At 20 months, when she experienced her first serious injury, she was still well down in the third centile. At the age of 27 months, after she had been in foster care for seven months, Jasmine had grown considerably and weighed 11.48kg (on the 25th centile). At this point she was returned to her mother and step-father. She was not weighed again until her death 27 months later. She weighed 10.43kg.

Chapter 5 Perpetrators of child abuse

1. In the case of Wayne Brewer, who was killed by his step-father, Nigel Briffett, his mother was heavily implicated. In a report written for court when Wayne was made the subject of a care order, the social worker commented on her as follows: 'Her inability to restrain her husband, together with the rather negative handling of the child, characterised by her unwillingness to readily handle him, and to generally care for and stimulate him, indicate that she has not really been able to accept responsibility for him' (Somerset Area Review Committee 1977).

2. The views put forward on this subject in the Cleveland report are of interest. The term 'collusive mother' is not explicitly used. However, the implications are clear from the following extract:

> Again quoting Professor Sir Martin Roth, 'In many cases mothers play a role in the genesis of the sexual abuse of their daughters. They may be too physically ill or inadequate in personality to provide proper care and protection for their children. In other cases mothers elect the eldest or one of the oldest daughters to the role of "child mother". The girl in her early teens or even earlier is expected to take the responsibility for the caring of the younger children whose mothering role is allowed to slide into a sexual relationship with the father. This is tolerated with little or no protest. I refer to lack of protest of [sic] the part of the mother for a variety of reasons and the mother may in such cases deny what is happening. She conceals the truth from herself as well as others; the relationship continues and when the situation is brought to light it may be insisted by the mother that it had been unknown to her.'
>
> (Butler-Sloss 1988: 8, para. 29)

3. A survey conducted in 2000/1 found that Pakistani/Bangladeshi and black families were three to four times more dependent on social security benefits than other families in Britain. Only 36 per cent of Pakistani/Bangladeshi families were able to obtain income from earnings compared with 60 per cent for the rest of the population (Department for Work and Pensions 2002).

4. This is another difficult issue to untangle. Abel et al. (1987) report that 44 per cent of convicted sex offenders had committed sexual crimes within and outside the family.

5. In 2003, 41 per cent of all live births in England and Wales were outside marriage, and 24 per cent of children lived with lone parents. In 2003, there were 167,000 divorces involving approximately 150,000 children. Over 1 million children were living with a step-parent, approximately 10 per cent of the total child population (see www.statistics.gov.uk). More recently, in 2010, this had increased slightly to 52 per cent of all live births in England and Wales being outside of marriage or civil partnerships. In 2009, 23 per cent of families with dependent children were single-parent families and between 2006 and 2007 the divorce rate in the UK fell by 2.6 per cent (from the previous year) to 144,220, the lowest number since 1977. The number of divorces peaked at 180,018 in 1993.

6. Christine Mason, the mother of Doreen Aston, was known to have been depressed in October 1985, seven months before Doreen was born. In January 1985, her 10-week-old son, Karl, had died in suspicious circumstances (see Chapter 4, n. 7). Nine months later Christine was said to be continuing 'to give cause for concern as she was carrying the ashes of her dead child around with her' (Lambeth, Lewisham and Southwark 1989: 9, para. 15). There is no further reference to depression or grief reaction in the report. Beatrice Henry, Tyra Henry's grandmother, on whom great reliance was placed by Lambeth Social Services Department for her protection, had experienced the death of her husband and the maiming and loss of her grandson in 1982 (she had also previously suffered the death of her own son). The inquiry report points out that there was 'not a line in the contemporary records and not a line in the evidence given to us which recognises that by the time of Tyra's birth, Beatrice Henry was struggling with private grief along with the difficulties of her daily life' (Lambeth 1987: 112). The inquiry panel recommended that social workers receive training in this area and be directed to devote attention to such matters in future. The Koseda inquiry noted that the cohabitation of Heidi Koseda's mother, Rosemary, with Nicholas Price 'seems to have been the start of a marked deterioration in her mental state and way of life, which culminated in serious mental illness after the discovery of Heidi's body early in 1985' (Hillingdon 1986: para. 1.1).

7. There also needs to be more research into and understanding of situations when adults with relationship difficulties, including domestic abuse, do not abuse their children and where adults who seemingly or actually have very few relationship difficulties do nevertheless abuse their children. In the cases of Tyra Henry (Lambeth 1987) and Darryn Clarke (Department of Health and Social Security 1979) there do not seem to have been obvious signs of conflict. However, very little information seems to come to light about the relationships of parents or parent substitutes in public inquiry reports. Both Andrew Neil and Charles Courtney, who were convicted for the killing of these children, had histories of violence. The lack of conflict in their relationships with these children's mothers may have been the result of their being totally dominating and controlling figures.

8. Stephen Menheniott was 19 years old when he died as a result of multiple injuries inflicted on him over a long period of time by his father. Because of his age, this case could be seen to be the murder of a young adult, but this judgement would belie the true nature of Stephen's abuse. The events of his life and death all carry the hallmarks of a case of child abuse. His father, Thomas Menheniott, was brought up in public care institutions. Nearly all his eight children had had long spells in care. He had convictions for neglect and

ill-treatment of his children and had been acquitted after being charged with incest. Stephen was a rather pathetic, immature young man. He had spent the bulk of his life in residential care attending schools for maladjusted children and had developed few lasting relationships. He was returned to his father's 'care' at the age of 15. He was clearly exposed to prolonged physical abuse and intimidation.

Chapter 6 The causation of child abuse

1. Sociobiology emerged as an identifiable discipline in the 1970s (Wilson 1975). It is essentially a new form of social Darwinism, but is more subtly argued than its predecessor. Sociobiologists' main proposition is that social sciences have been too narrow in their interpretations of human behaviour, associating it almost exclusively with cultural and social influences. In this process, the fact that humans are, like any other form of living species, biologically driven, has been forgotten. From a sociobiological perspective, biological forces, particularly gene preservation, are paramount influences on behaviour (Dawkins 1976). Social scientists have responded by arguing that sociobiology has theoretical flaws and adverse political effects, such as the potential for encouraging racism, sexism and far-right views such as eugenics (Montagu 1980). One common misconception of the critics of this view is that sociobiologists are making arguments about the ways people 'should' behave, rather than studying the impact of genetics on how people apparently *seem* to behave. In many ways, this conflict is part of the continuing nature-nurture debate which has existed formally since the emergence of the social sciences in the eighteenth century. It rose again in the late 1990s with the publication of two influential books by Harris (1998) and Pinker (2002) which question the assumption that nurture is the key determinant of the way in which a child develops. Both place much more emphasis on the genetic base of behaviour. Harris in particular attacks the notion that children's personalities are shaped by the quality of parent-child interactions, placing much more emphasis on other external influences such as peer groups. However, the nature-nurture debate is essentially much less interesting than it once appeared; new branches of scientific research, such as epigenetics (the study of heritable changes brought about by factors or mechanisms other than DNA mutations), are increasingly showing that it is not either nature or nurture that effects particular traits but rather something more akin to nature-via-nurture.

2. For a mainstream analysis see Jahoda (1977). Kline (1981) provides details of empirical studies into Freudian theory. Feminist critiques of Freudian theory are to be found in Mitchell (1974: 61–108) and Sydie (1987: 125–67).

3. Steele and Pollock's (1974) views on the influence of socio-economic factors on the incidence of child abuse are that they are marginal:

   > Basically they are irrelevant to the actual act of child beating. Unquestionably, social and economic difficulties and disasters put added stress on people's lives and contribute to behavior which might otherwise remain dormant. But such factors must be considered as incidental enhancers rather than necessary and sufficient causes.
   >
   > (Steele and Pollock 1974: 108)

4. Webster's account (2005) of Freud's thinking about childhood sexual abuse and the recent debates about false memory syndrome are interesting. He rejects Masson's thesis, using evidence from Freud's writing to show that his early patients did not reveal being sexually abused without being prompted and that in fact he helped them to elicit memories that they had repressed. Webster argues that Freud did not later dismiss childhood sexual abuse altogether as a cause of psychological illness, but his psychosexual theory did create the conditions for psychoanalytical practice to pay it little attention for most of the twentieth

century. Webster clearly sees the revival of repressed memory syndrome in the 1980s in the USA to have led to excesses and to have created conditions for a backlash which, he argues, could be equally damaging. Much has been written about trying to achieve some balance in the debate, but this has been hard because of the impact of criminal prosecutions and compensation claims.

5. Behavioural interventions in the USA at this time were reported as being more successful (Denicola and Sandier 1980; Wolfe et al. 1981). Smith (1984) attributed this relative success to the fact that therapeutic change is more embedded in North American culture and intervention programmes are often enforced by court orders.

6. Beckett (2005) argues that Sweden's child-death-by-abuse rate has not changed over time and is not significantly lower than that of European countries that have not introduced a ban. However, as was noted in Chapter 5, because of the relatively small numbers involved, great care has to be taken in using child-death-by-homicide figures as indicators of the success or otherwise of child protection policies.

7. Smith (1991) outlines the parts of the 1989 Children Act that specifically enhance a children's rights perspective. Two examples are, first, Section 22, which emphasises the need to consult children of sufficient age and understanding with regard to all decisions that affect them (this section is very similar to Section 18 of the 1980 Child Care Act) and, second, Section 44(7), which gives a child of sufficient age and understanding the right to refuse a medical examination under an emergency protection order (a direct result of events in Cleveland, where it was felt that children were exposed to many assessments and examinations without having any recourse if they objected). In general, the 1989 Children Act was a move towards greater consideration of children as subjects rather than objects. However, the legislation still leaves a lot of room for adultist views to prevail.

Chapter 7 The consequences of child abuse

1. The longer-term impact of being bullied at school has not been demonstrated in research. More focus seems to have been placed on the progress of bullies in later life and in particular on their association with crime.

2. The study by Carmen et al. (1984) is an exception. These authors show considerable awareness of the potential impact of physical and sexual abuse on women:

> In our sample, the abused females directed their hatred and aggression against themselves in both overt and covert ways. These behaviours formed a continuum from quiet resignation and depression to repeated episodes of self-mutilation and suicide attempts . . . Markedly impaired self-esteem was prominent among these patients, as they conveyed a sense that they were undeserving of any empathic understanding or help by clinicians.

> (Carmen et al. 1984: 382)

These reactions were in contrast to the outwardly directed aggression that was most common among the mentally ill males in this study with a history of abuse. From this perspective, the form of the reaction to abuse is heavily influenced by social and socialisation factors.

Chapter 8 The evidence base for child protection practice

1. The potential for poor decision-making at case conferences and other inter-disciplinary meetings is clear from an analysis of a strategy meeting held about Victoria Climbié on

28 July 1999, four days after she had been admitted to North Middlesex Hospital with scalds on her head. The meeting was held at Harringey Social Services Department, not at the hospital. A key consequence of this was that none of the nursing or medical staff who had been involved with Victoria during her stay in hospital attended. The meeting was attended by a senior social work practitioner who acted as chairperson, a hospital social worker, a police officer from a child protection team and an emergency team social worker, none of whom had seen Victoria or her great-aunt. Hospital documents were not available at the meeting and any urgency that staff at the hospital had felt was not represented. Eighteen tasks were agreed upon and it was decided not to hold a full conference until these had been completed. In fact they were not properly allocated and the concerns just seemed to fizzle away (Laming 2003: 143–6).

2. There are many instances of aggression and hostility on the part of parents to health and social care workers to be found in public inquiry reports, most notably in the cases of Doreen Aston (Lambeth, Lewisham and Southwark 1989), Kimberley Carlile (Greenwich 1987), Sukina (Bridge 1991) and Ainlee Labonte (Newham Area Child Protection Committee 2002). In such circumstances, carrying out analytical assessments is virtually impossible. In all these cases, however, instead of bringing legal authority to bear on the families to enable proper assessments and monitoring to take place, the response was to back off and reduce involvement (with disastrous consequences).

Chapter 10 Reflections for future child protection work

1. The author of Example B is a practitioner who needs to remain anonymous to protect the identity of family members. Example A was written by DS.
2. They were provided by an experienced child protection practitioner colleague of ours, David Phillips, in Enfield Council, London.
3. In the UK, SCRs are independent investigations culminating in a formal report in cases where a child dies or where there is serious abuse and it is felt that there may have been 'systems failures'.

Bibliography

Abel, G., Becker, J., Mittelman, M. et al. (1987) Self-reported sex crimes of non-incarcerated paraphiliacs, *Journal of Interpersonal Violence*, 2: 3–25.

Adams, J., McLellan, J., Douglass, D., McCurry, C. and Storck, M. (1995) Sexually inappropriate behaviours in seriously mentally ill children and adolescents, *Child Abuse & Neglect*, 19: 555–68.

Adams-Tucker, C. (1981) A socioclinical overview of 28 sex-abused children, *Child Abuse & Neglect*, 5: 361–7.

Adler, N. and Schutz, J. (1995) Sibling incest offenders, *Child Abuse & Neglect*, 19: 811–19.

Aldgate, J. and Tunstill, J. (1995) *Making Sense of Section 17: Implementing Services for Children in Need Within the 1989 Children Act*. London: HMSO.

Allen, A. and Morton, A. (1961) *This is Your Child: The Story of the NSPCC*. London: Routledge & Kegan Paul.

Allen, G. (2011) *Early Intervention: The Next Steps*. London: HM Government.

Allen, J. G., Fonagy, P. and Bateman, A. W. (2008) *Mentalising in Clinical Practice*. Arlington, VA: APP.

Allen, R. E. and Oliver, J. M. (1982) The effects of child maltreatment on language development, *Child Abuse & Neglect*, 6(3): 299–305.

Angelides, S. (2004) Feminism, child sexual abuse, and the erasure of child sexuality, *GLQ: A Journal of Lesbian and Gay Studies*, 10(2): 141–77.

Angelou, M. (1983) *I Know Why the Caged Bird Sings*. London: Virago.

Archard, J. (2004) *Children: Rights and Childhood*, 2nd edn. Abingdon: Routledge.

Ariès, P. (1962) *Centuries of Childhood*. Harmondsworth: Penguin.

Armstrong, L. (1978) *Kiss Daddy Goodnight*. New York: Dell.

Asen, K., George, E., Piper, R. and Stevens, A. (1989) A systems approach to child abuse: management and treatment issues, *Child Abuse & Neglect*, 13: 45–57.

Association of the Directors of Social Services (1988) Press release, July.

Audit Commission (1994) *Seen But Not Heard: Coordinating Community Child Health and Social Services for Children in Need*. London: HMSO.

Audit Commission (2008) *Are We There Yet? Improving Governance and Resource Management in Children's Trusts*. London: HMSO.

Augoustinos, M. (1987) Developmental effects of child abuse, *Child Abuse & Neglect*, 11: 15–27.

Australian Bureau of Statistics (2005) *Personal Safety*, available at: http://www.abs.gov.au/ausstats/abs@.nsf/mf/4906.0.

Badman, G. (2009) *Report to the Secretary of State on the Review of Elective Home Education in England*. London: The Stationery Office.

Bagley, C. and Ramsay, R. (1986) Sexual abuse in childhood: psychosocial outcomes and implications for social work practice, *Journal of Social Work and Human Sexuality*, 4: 33–47.

Baher, E., Hyman, C., Jones, C., Kerr, A. and Mitchell, R. (1976) *At Risk: An Account of the Battered Child Research Department*. London: Routledge & Kegan Paul.

Bailey, R. (2011) *Letting Children be Children*. London: DfE.

Baker, A. and Duncan, S. (1985) Child sexual abuse: a study of prevalence in Great Britain, *Child Abuse & Neglect*, 9: 457–67.

Bakermans-Kranenburg, M. and Van IJzendoorn, M. H. (1997) Intergenerational transmission of attachment: a move to the contextual level, in L. Atkinson and K. Zucker (eds) *Attachment and Psychopathology*, pp. 135–70. New York: Guilford Press.

Bakermans-Kranenburg, M. and Van IJzendoorn, M. H. (2004) No association of the dopamine D4 receptor (DRD4) and -521 C/T promoter polymorphisms with infant attachment disorganization, *Attachment and Human Development*, 6: 211–18.

Bakermans-Kranenburg, M., Van IJzendoorn, M. and Juffer, F. (2003) Less is more: meta-analysis of sensitivity and attachment interventions in early childhood, *Pyschological Bulletin*, 129: 195–215.

Bandura, A. (1965) *Principles of Behaviour Modification*. New York: Holt, Rinehart & Winston.

Barash, D. (1981) *Sociobiology: The Whisperings Within*. London: Fontana.

Barker, J. and Hodes, D. (2004) *The Child in Mind: A Child Protection Handbook*. Abingdon: Routledge.

Barlow, J. and Schrader McMillan, A. (2010) *Safeguarding Children from Emotional Maltreatment: What Works?* Available at: www.education.gov.uk/research.

Barlow, J. and Scott, J. (2011) *Safeguarding in the 21st Century: Where to Now?* Totnes: Research in Practice.

Baron-Cohen, S. (2011a) *Zero Degrees of Empathy: A New Theory of Human Cruelty*. London: Allen Lane.

Baron-Cohen, S. (2011b) *Science of Evil On Empathy and the Origins of Cruelty*. New York: Basic Books.

Barratt, A., Trepper, T. and Fish, L. (1990) Feminist informed family therapy for the treatment of intra-familial child sexual abuse, *Journal of Family Psychology*, 4: 151–66.

Baumrind, D. (1973) The development of instrumental competence through socialization, in A. D. Pick (ed.) *Minnesota Symposia on Child Psychology*, vol. 7, pp. 3–46. Minneapolis, MN: University of Minnesota Press.

BBC (2008) Shannon Matthews timeline, available at: http://news.bbc.co.uk/1/hi/uk/7733586.stm.

Beach, S. R., Brody, G. H., Gunter, T. D., Packer, H., Wernett, P. and Philbert, R. A. (2010) Child maltreatment moderates the association of MAOA with symptoms of depression and antisocial personality disorder, *Journal of Family Psychology*, 1: 12–20.

Bebbington, A. and Miles, J. (1989) The background of children who enter local authority care, *British Journal of Social Work*, 19: 349–68.

Beck, U. (1992) *Risk Society: Towards a New Modernity*. London: Sage.

Beck, U. (2008) *World at Risk*. Cambridge: Polity Press.

Becker, J. and Quinsey, V. (1993) Assessing suspected child molesters, *Child Abuse & Neglect*, 17: 169–74.

Beckett, C. (2005) The Swedish myth: the corporal punishment ban and child death statistics, *British Journal of Social Work*, 35: 125–38.

Behlmer, G. (1982) *Child Abuse and Moral Reform in England 1870–1908*. Stanford, CA: Stanford University Press.

Beitchman, J., Zucker, K., Hood, J., Da Costa, G. and Akman, D. (1991) A review of the short-term effects of child sexual abuse, *Child Abuse & Neglect*, 15: 537–56.

Beitchman, J., Zucker, K., Hood, J. et al. (1992) A review of the long-term effects of child sexual abuse, *Child Abuse & Neglect*, 16: 101–18.

Bell, M. (1999) Working in partnership in child protection, *British Journal of Social Work*, 29: 437–55.

Bell, M., Shaw, I., Sinclair, I., Sloper, P. and Rafferty, J. (2007) *The Integrated Children's System: An Evaluation of the Practice, Process and Consequences of the ICS in Councils with Social Services Responsibilities*. York: SPRU.

Belsky, J. (1980) Child maltreatment: an ecological integration, *American Psychologist*, 35: 320–35.

Belsky, J. (2005) Differential susceptibility to rearing influence: an evolutionary hypothesis and some evidence, in B. J. Ellis and D. F. Bjorklund (eds) *Origins of the Social Mind: Evolutionary Psychology and Child Development*. New York: Guilford.

Belsky, J. and Jaffee, S. R. (2006) The multiple determinants of parenting, in D. Cicchetti and D. Cohen (eds) *Developmental Psychopathology: Risk, Disorder and Adaptation*, pp. 38–85. New York: Wiley.

Belsky, J. and Vondra, J. (1989) Lessons from child abuse: the determinants of parenting, in D. Cicchetti and V. Carlson (eds) *Child Maltreatment: Theory and Research on the Causes and Consequences of Child Abuse & Neglect*. Cambridge: Cambridge University Press.

Belsky, J., Bakermans-Kranenburg, M. and Van IJzendoorn, M. (2007) For better or worse: differential susceptibility to environment influences, *Current Directions in Psychological Science*, 16(6): 300–4.

Benard, B. (1995) Fostering resilience in children, available at: http://eric.ed.gov/PDFS/ED386327.pdf.

Bennett, E. (2006) *Peer Abuse Know More: Bullying From a Psychological Perspective*. Concord, MA: Infinity Publishing.

Bentovim, A. and Boston, P. (1988) Sexual abuse – basic issues: characteristics of children and families, in A. Bentovim, J. Elton and J. Hildebrand et al. (eds) *Child Sexual Abuse Within the Family: Assessment and Treatment*, pp. 1–15. London: Butterworth.

Bentovim, A., Elton, A., Hildebrand, J., Tranter, M. and Vizard, E. (eds) (1988) *Child Sexual Abuse Within the Family: Assessment and Treatment – The Work of the Great Ormond Street Team*. London: Wright.

Berger, L., Carlson, M., Bzostek, S. and Osborne, C. (2008) Parenting practices of resident fathers: the role of marital and biological ties, *Journal of Marriage and Family*, 70: 625–39.

Bergner, R., Delgado, L. and Graybill, D. (1994) Finkelhor's risk factor checklist: a cross-validation study, *Child Abuse & Neglect*, 18: 331–40.

Berliner, L. and Conte, R. (1995) The effects of disclosure and intervention on sexually abused children, *Child Abuse & Neglect*, 19: 371–84.

Bernard, C. (1999) Child sexual abuse and the black disabled child, *Disability & Society*, 14(3): 325–39.

Bichard, Sir M. (2004) *The Bichard Inquiry Report*, HC653. London: The Stationery Office.

Biehal, N., Clayden, J., Stein, M. and Wade, J. (1995) *Moving On: Young People and Leaving Care Schemes*. London: HMSO.

Bijur, P. E., Kurzon, M., Overpeck, M. D. and Scheidt, P. C. (1992) Parental alcohol use, problem drinking and child injuries, *Journal of the American Medical Association*, 23: 3166–71.

Birchall, E. with Hallett, C. (1995) *Working Together in Child Protection*. London: HMSO.

Birmingham (2010) *Serious Case Review Under Chapter VIII 'Working Together to Safeguard Children' In respect of the Death of a Child Case Number 14*. Birmingham: Birmingham Safeguarding Children Board.

Bolen, R. (2001) *Child Sexual Abuse: Its Scope and our Failure*. New York: Kluwer Academic Press.

Bolger, K., Patterson, C. and Kupersmidt, J. (1998) Peer relationships and self-esteem among children who have been maltreated, *Child Development*, 69: 1171–97.

Booth, T. and Booth, W. (1993) Parenting with learning difficulties: lessons for practitioners, *British Journal of Social Work*, 23: 459–90.

Booth, T. and Booth, W. (1998) *Growing Up with Parents Who Have Learning Difficulties*. London: Routledge.

Bornstein, B., Kaplan, D. and Perry, A. (2007) Child abuse in the eyes of the beholder: lay perceptions of child sexual and physical abuse, *Child Abuse & Neglect*, 31: 375–91.

Boswell, J. (1990) *The Kindness of Strangers: The Abandonment of Children in Western Europe from Late Antiquity to the Renaissance*. New York: Vintage.

Bourke, M. and Hernandez, A. (2009) The 'Butner Study' redux: a report of the incidence of hands-on child victimization by child pornography offenders, *Journal of Family Violence*, 24: 183–91.

Bowlby, J. (1951) *Maternal Care and Mental Health: A Report Prepared on Behalf of the World Health Organisation as a Contribution to the United Nations Programme for the Welfare of Homeless Children*. Geneva: World Health Organization.

Bowlby, J. (1971) *Attachment and Loss: Volume 1, Attachment*. Harmondsworth: Penguin.

Bowlby, J., Fry, S. and Ainsworth, M. (1965) *Child Care and the Growth of Love*. Harmondsworth: Penguin.

Boyer, D. and Fine, D. (1992) Sexual abuse as a factor in adolescent pregnancy and child maltreatment, *Family Planning Perspectives*, 24.

Brady, K. (1979) *Father's Days: A True Story of Incest*. New York: Dell.

Brandon, M., Thoburn, J., Lewis, A. and Way, A. (1999) *Safeguarding Children with the Children Act 1989*. London: The Stationery Office.

Brandon, M., Belderson, P., Warren, C., Howe, D., Gardner, R., Dodsworth, J. and Black, J. (2008a) *Analysing Child Deaths and Serious Injury Through Abuse and Neglect: What Can We Learn? A Biennial Analysis of Serious Case Reviews 2003–2005*. London: DCSF.

Brandon, M., Belderson, P., Warren, C., Gardner, R., Howe, D., Dodsworth, J. and Black, J. (2008b) The preoccupation with thresholds in cases of child death or serious injury through abuse and neglect, *Child Abuse Review*, 17(5): 313–30.

Brandon, M., Bailey, S., Belderson, P., Warren, C., Gardner, R. and Dodsworth, J. (2009) *Understanding Serious Case Reviews and their Impact: A Biennial Analysis of Serious Case Reviews 2005–2007*. London: DCSF.

Brandon, M., Bailey, S. and Belderson, P. (2010) *Building on the Learning from Serious Case Reviews: A Two-year Analysis of Child Protection Database Notifications 2007–2009*. London: The Stationery Office.

Brandon, M., Sidebotham, P., Ellis, C., Bailey, S. and Belderson, P. (2011a) *Child and Family Practitioners' Understanding of Child Development: Lessons Learnt from a Small Sample of Serious Case Reviews*. London: DfE.

Brandon, M., Sidebotham, P., Bailey, S. and Belderson, P. (2011b) *A Study of Recommendations Arising from Serious Case Reviews*. London: DfE.

Brent (London Borough of) (1985) *A Child in Trust: The Report of the Panel of Inquiry into the Circumstances Surrounding the Death of Jasmine Beckford*. London: London Borough of Brent.

Brewster, A., Nelson, J., Hymel, K. et al. (1998) Victim, perpetrator, family and incident characteristics of 32 infant maltreatment deaths in the United States Air Force, *Child Abuse & Neglect*, 22: 91–101.

Bridge (Child Care Consultancy Service) (1991) *Sukina: An Evaluation of the Circumstances Leading to her Death*. London: The Bridge.

Bridge (Child Care Consultancy Service) (1995) *Overview Report in Respect of Charmaine and Heather West*. Gloucester: Gloucestershire Area Child Protection Committee.

Bridge (Child Care Consultancy Service) (1997) *Report on the Professional Judgements and Accountability in Relation to Work with the Neave Family (on behalf of Cambridgeshire Area Child Protection Committee)*. London: The Bridge.

Bridge (Child Care Consultancy Service) (1998a) *Neglect and Developmental Delay: Part 8 Case Review. Overview Report re: Case 1/99 in Caerphilly (on behalf of Caerphilly Area Child Protection Committee)*. London: The Bridge.

Bridge (Child Care Consultancy Service) (1998b) *Dangerous Care: Working to Protect Children*. London: The Bridge.

Briere, J. (1984) The long-term effects of childhood sexual abuse: defining a post-sexual-abuse syndrome. Paper presented at the Third National Conference on the Sexual Victimization of Children, Washington, DC.

Briggs, L. and Joyce, P. (1997) What determines post-traumatic stress disorder symptomatology for survivors of child sexual abuse, *Child Abuse & Neglect*, 21: 575–82.

Brilleslijper-Kater, S., Friedrich, W. and Corwin, D. (2004) Sexual knowledge and emotional reaction as indicators of sexual abuse in young children: theory and research challenges, *Child Abuse & Neglect*, 28: 1007–17.

British Medical Journal (2005) Russia's youth faces worst crisis of homelessness and substance misuse since Second World War, *British Medical Journal*, 330(1348): 3.

Bronfenbrenner, U. (1979) *The Ecology of Human Development: Experiments by Nature and Design*. Cambridge, MA: Harvard University Press.

Brown, C. (1986) *Child Abuse Parents Speaking: Parents' Impressions of Social Workers and the Social Work Process*, working paper. Bristol: Bristol School of Applied and Urban Studies.

Brown, T. and Waters, J. (1985) *Parental Participation at Case Conferences*. Rochdale: British Association for the Prevention of Cruelty and Neglect.

Browne, A. and Finkelhor, D. (1986) Initial and long-term effects: a review of the research, in D. Finkelhor et al. (eds) *A Sourcebook on Child Sexual Abuse*. Beverly Hills, CA: Sage.

Browne, K. and Saqi, S. (1988) Approaches to screening for Child Abuse & Neglect, in K. Browne, C. Davies and P. Stratton (eds) *Early Prediction and Prevention of Child Abuse*. Chichester: Wiley.

Bryson, B. (2011) *At Home: A Short History of Private Life*. New York: Doubleday.

Buckley, H. (2003) *Child Protection Work: Beyond the Rhetoric*. London: Jessica Kingsley.

Burke, J., Chandy, J., Dannerbeck, A. and Watt, J. (1998) The parental environment cluster model of child neglect: an integrative conceptual model, *Child Welfare*, 77: 389–406.

Burnett, B. (1993) The psychological abuse of latency age children: a survey, *Child Abuse & Neglect*, 17: 441–54.

Burns, B. J., Mustillo, S. A., Farmer, E. M. Z., McCrae, J., Kolko, D. J., Libby, A. M. and Webb, M. B. (2009) Caregiver depression, mental health service use, and child outcomes, in M. B. Webb, K. Dowd, B. J. Harden, J. Landsverk and M. Testa (eds) *Child Welfare and Child Well-being: New Perspectives from the National Survey of Child and Adolescent Well-being*, pp. 351–79. New York: Oxford University Press.

Butler-Sloss, Lord Justice E. (1988) *Report of the Inquiry into Child Abuse in Cleveland 1987*, Cmnd 412. London: HMSO.

Calam, R. and Franchi, C. (1987) *Child Abuse and its Consequences.* Cambridge: Cambridge University Press.

Calam, R., Horn, L., Glasgow, D. and Cox, A. (1998) Psychological disturbance and child sexual abuse: a follow-up study, *Child Abuse & Neglect*, 22: 901–13.

Calder, M. (ed.) (2004) *Child Sexual Abuse and the Internet: Tackling the New Frontier.* Lyme Regis: Russell House.

Campbell, B. (1988) *Unofficial Secrets.* London: Virago.

Campbell, M. (1991) Children at risk: how different are children on child abuse registers? *British Journal of Social Work*, 21: 259–75.

Camras, L. and Rappaport, S. (1993) Conflict behaviors of maltreated and nonmaltreated children, *Child Abuse & Neglect*, 17: 455–64.

Carlson, E. A. (1998) A prospective longitudinal study of attachment disorganization/disorientation, *Child Development*, 69: 1107–28.

Carmen, E., Rieker, P. and Mills, T. (1984) Victims of violence and psychiatric illness, *American Journal of Psychiatry*, 141: 378–83.

Carr, A. (2009) The effectiveness of family therapy and systemic interventions for adult-focused problems, *Journal of Family Therapy*, 31: 46–74.

Cassidy, J. and Shaver, P. R. (2008) *Handbook of Attachment: Theory, Research and Clinical Applications*, 2nd edn. New York: The Guilford Press.

Cawson, P., Wattam, C., Brooker, S. and Kelly, G. (2000) *Child Maltreatment in the United Kingdom.* London: NSPCC.

Ceci, S. J., and Bruck, M. (1995) *Jeopardy in the Courtroom: A Scientific Analysis of Children's Testimony.* Washington, DC: American Psychological Association.

Cemlyn, S. and Briskman, L. (2003) Asylum, children's rights and social work, *Child & Family Social Work*, 8: 163–78.

Chaffin, M. (2004) Is it time to re-think healthy start/healthy families? *Child Abuse & Neglect*, 28: 589–95.

Chand, A. (2000) The over-representation of black children in the child protection system: possible causes, consequences and solutions, *Child & Family Social Work*, 5(1): 67–77.

Chand, A. and Thoburn, J. (2005) Research review: child and family support services with minority ethnic families – what can we learn from research? *Child & Family Social Work*, 10: 169–78.

Cheeta, S., Drummond, C., Oyefeso, A., Phillips, T., Deluca, P., Perryman, K. and Coulton, S. (2008) Low identification of alcohol use disorders in general practice in England, *Addiction*, 103(5): 766–73.

Chen, J., Dunne, M. P. and Han, P. (2004) Child sexual abuse in China: a study of adolescents in four provinces, *Child Abuse & Neglect*, 28: 1171–86.

Chen, J., Dunne, M. P. and Han, P. (2007) Prevention of child sexual abuse in China: knowledge, attitudes, and communication practices of parents of elementary school children, *Child Abuse & Neglect*, 31: 747–55.

Chester D. L., Jose R. M., Aldlyami E., King H. and Moiemen N. S. (2006) Non-accidental burns in children – are we neglecting neglect? *Burns*, 32: 222–8.

China View (2007) China working to prevent child abuse, available at: http://news.xinhuanet.com/english/2007-10/11/content_6862247.htm.

Ching-Tung, W. and Holton, J. (2007) *Total Estimated Cost of Child Abuse & Neglect in the United States.* Chicago: Prevent Child Abuse America.

Churches' Child Protection Advisory Service (2010) *Good Practice for Working With Faith Communities and Places of Worship – Spirit Possession and Abuse*, available at: http://www.ccpas.co.uk/Documents/faith%20communities%20guidance.doc.

Cicchetti, D. and Carlson, V. (eds) (1989) *Child Maltreatment: Theory and Research on the Causes and Consequences of Child Abuse & Neglect*. Cambridge: Cambridge University Press.

Cicchetti, D. and Curtis, W. J. (2006) The developing brain and neural plasticity: implications for normality, psychopathology, and resilience, in D. Cicchetti and D. J. Cohen (eds) *Developmental Psychopathology: Vol. 2, Developmental Neuroscience*, 2nd edn. New York: Wiley.

Cicchetti, D., Rogosch, F. A. and Sturge-Apple, M. (2007) Interactions of child maltreatment and serotonin transporter and monoamine oxidase-A polymorphisms: depressive symptomatology among adolescents from low socioeconomic status backgrounds, *Development and Psychopathology*, 19(4): 1161–80.

Cicchetti, D., Rogosch, F. A., Sturge-Apple, M. and Toth, S. L. (2010) Interaction of child maltreatment and 5-HTT polymorphisms: suicidal ideation among children from low-SES backgrounds, *Journal of Pediatric Psychology*, 35(5): 536–46.

Cleaver, H. and Freeman, P. (1995) *Parental Perspectives in Cases of Suspected Child Abuse*. London: HMSO.

Cleaver, H. and Walker, S. (2004) From policy to practice: the implementation of a new framework for social work assessments of children and families, *Child & Family Social Work*, 9: 81–91.

Cleaver, H., Unell, I. and Aldgate, J. (1999) *Children's Needs – Parenting Capacity: The Impact of Parental Mental Illness, Problem Alcohol and Drug Use and Domestic Violence on Children's Development*. London: The Stationery Office.

Clyde, Lord (1992) *Report of the Inquiry into the Removal of Children from Orkney in February 1991*, HC 195. London: HMSO.

Coates, D. (2010) Impact of childhood abuse: biopsychosocial pathways through which adult mental health is compromised, *Australian Social Work*, 63(4): 391–403.

Cohen, F. and Densen-Gerber, J. (1982) A study of the relationship between child abuse and drug addiction in 178 parents: preliminary results, *Child Abuse & Neglect*, 6: 383–7.

Cohen, J. A., Mannarino, A. P. and Deblinger, E. (2006) *Treating Trauma and Traumatic Grief in Children and Adolescents*. New York: The Guilford Press.

Cohn, A. and Daro, D. (1987) Is treatment too late? What ten years of evaluative research tell us, *Child Abuse & Neglect*, 11: 433–42.

Coleman, K., Jansson, K., Kaiza, P. and Reed, E. (2007) *Homicides, Firearm Offences and Intimate Violence 2005/2006*: supplementary volume 1 to *Crime in England and Wales 2005/2006*. London: Home Office Research, Development and Statistics Directorate.

Colman, R. and Widom, C. (2004) Childhood abuse and neglect and adult intimate relationships: a prospective study, *Child Abuse & Neglect*, 28: 1133–51.

Colton, M. and Vanstone, M. (1996) *Betrayal of Trust: Sexual Abuse by Men who Work with Children – In Their Own Words*. London: Free Association Books.

Conte, J. and Schuerman, J. (1987) Factors associated with an increased impact of child sexual abuse, *Child Abuse & Neglect*, 11: 201–11.

Conway, E. E. (1998) Non-accidental head injury in infants: the shaken baby syndrome revisited, *Paediatric Annals*, 27(10): 677–90.

Conway, E. E., Alexander, R. C. and Smith, W. L. (1998) Shaken baby syndrome, *Infants and Young Children*, 10(3): 1–9.

Coohey, C. (1996) Child maltreatment: testing the social isolation hypothesis, *Child Abuse & Neglect*, 20: 241–54.

Coohey, C. and Braun, N. (1997) Toward an integrated framework for understanding child physical abuse, *Child Abuse & Neglect*, 21: 1081–94.

Corby, B. (1987) *Working with Child Abuse*. Buckingham: Open University Press.

Corby, B. (1990) Making use of child protection statistics, *Children and Society*, 4: 304–14.

Corby, B. (1996) Risk assessment in child protection work, in H. Kemshall and J. Pritchard (eds) *Good Practice in Risk Assessment and Risk Management*. London: Jessica Kingsley.

Corby, B. (1998) *Managing Child Sexual Abuse Cases*. London: Jessica Kingsley.

Corby, B. (2003a) Supporting families and protecting children – assisting child care professionals in initial decision-making and review of cases, *Journal of Social Work*, 3: 195–210.

Corby, B. (2003b) Towards a new means of inquiry into child abuse cases, *Journal of Social Welfare and Family Law*, 25: 229–41.

Corby, B. and Cox, P. (1998) The 'new witch-hunters'?, *NOTA News*, 26: 30–2.

Corby, B. and Millar, M. (1997) A parents' view of partnership, in J. Bates, R. Pugh and N. Thompson (eds) *Protecting Children: Challenges and Change*. Aldershot: Avebury Press.

Corby, B. and Mills, C. (1986) Child abuse: risks and resources, *British Journal of Social Work*, 16: 531–42.

Corby, B., Millar, M. and Young, L. (1996) Parental participation in child protection work: rethinking the rhetoric, *British Journal of Social Work*, 26: 475–92.

Corby, B., Doig, A. and Roberts, V. (1998) Inquiries into child abuse, *Journal of Social Welfare and Family Law*, 20: 377–95.

Corby, B., Doig, A. and Roberts, V. (2001) *Public Inquiries into the Abuse of Children in Residential Care*. London: Jessica Kingsley.

Corby, B., Millar, M. and Pope, A. (2002) Assessing children in need assessments: a parental perspective, *Practice*, 14: 5–15.

Corsaro, W. (2004) *The Sociology of Childhood*. Thousand Oaks, CA: Pine Forge Press.

Cox, P., Kershaw, S. and Trotter, J. (2001) (eds) *Child Sexual Assault: Feminist Perspectives*. Basingstoke: Palgrave.

Crawford, C. and Krebs, D. (2008) *Foundations of Evolutionary Psychology*. New York: Lawrence Erlbaum Associates.

Crawford, M. (2003) *The Little Princesses: The Story of the Queen's Childhood by Her Nanny*. London: Orion.

Cree, V. (2003) Worries and problems of young carers: issues for mental health, *Child & Family Social Work*, 8: 301–9.

Creighton, S. (1984) *Trends in Child Abuse*. London: NSPCC.

Creighton, S. (1985, 1986) *Initial Findings from NSPCC Register Research 1984, 1985, 1986*. London: NSPCC.

Creighton, S. (2004) *Prevalence and Incidence of Child Abuse*. London: NSPCC.

Creighton, S. and Noyes, P. (1989) *Child Abuse Trends in England and Wales 1983–1987*. London: NSPCC.

Crittenden, P. M. (2008) *Raising Parents: Attachment, Parenting and Child Safety*. Portland, OR: Willan.

Crittenden, P. and Ainsworth, M. (1989) Child maltreatment and attachment theory, in D. Cicchetti and V. Carlson (eds) *Child Maltreatment: Theory and Research into the Causes and Consequences of Child Abuse and Neglect*. Cambridge: Cambridge University Press.

Cunningham, H. (1991) *Children of the Poor*. Oxford: Blackwell.

Cunningham, H. (2005) *Children and Childhood in Western Society since 1500*, 2nd edn. Harlow: Pearson.

Cunningham, S. and Tomlinson, J. (2005) 'Starve them out': does every child really matter? A commentary on Section 9 of the Asylum and Immigration (Treatment of Claimants, etc.) Act, 2004, *Critical Social Policy*, 25: 253–75.

Curtis, Dame M. (1946) *Report of the Care of Children Committee*. London: HMSO.

Curtis, P. and McCullough, C. (1993) The impact of alcohol and other drugs on the child welfare system, *Child Welfare*, 72: 533–42.

Cusick, L. (2002) Youth prostitution: a literature review, *Child Abuse Review*, 11: 230–51.

Dale, P., Morrison, T., Davies, M., Noyes, P. and Roberts, W. (1983) A family therapy approach to child abuse: countering resistance, *Journal of Family Therapy*, 5: 117–43.

Dale, P., Davies, M., Morrison, T. and Waters, J. (1986) *Dangerous Families: Assessment and Treatment of Child Abuse*. London: Tavistock.

Dallos, R. and Draper, R. (2005) *Introduction to Systemic Family Therapy*, 2nd edn. Maidenhead: Open University Press.

Daly, M. and Wilson, M. I. (1985) Child abuse and other risks of not living with both parents, *Ethology & Sociobiology*, 6: 197–210.

Daly, M. and Wilson, M. (2005a) The 'Cinderella effect' is no fairy tale, *Trends in Cognitive Sciences*, 9: 507–8.

Daly, M. and Wilson, M. (2005b) Reply to David Buller, available at: http://psych.mcmaster.ca/dalywilson/research.html.

Daniel, B. and Taylor, J. (2006) Gender and child neglect: theory, research and policy, *Critical Social Policy*, 26: 426–39.

Davies, C. (2011) *The Ghost of Lily Painter*. London: Hutchinson.

Davies, C. and Ward, H. (2011) Safeguarding children across services: messages from research on identifying and responding to child maltreatment, pp. 163–4, available at: http://www.mars.stir.ac.uk/resources/2011/05/davies-c-ward-h-2011-safeguarding-children-across-services-messages-from-research-on-identifying-and-responding-to-child-maltreatment/.

Davin, A. (1990) The precocity of poverty, in *The Proceedings of the Conference on Historical Perspectives on Childhood*, University of Trondheim.

Davis, R. (2010) How some African cultural beliefs can lead to child abuse: social workers' role in identifying child protection risks where witchcraft beliefs are present, available at: http://www.communitycare.co.uk/Articles/12/01/2010/113531/the-challenge-of-witchcraft-to-child-protection-social-services.htm.

Dawkins, R. (1976) *The Selfish Gene*. Oxford: Oxford University Press.

de Mause, L. (ed.) (1976) *The History of Childhood*. London: Souvenir Press.

de Shazer, S. (2005) *More Than Miracles: The State of the Art of Solution-focused Therapy*. Binghamton, NY: Haworth Press.

Deacon, L. and Gocke, B. (1999) *Understanding Perpetrators, Protecting Children: A Practitioner's Guide to Working Effectively with Child Sexual Abusers*. London: Whiting & Birch.

Dearden, C. and Becker, S. (2001) Young carers: needs, rights and assessments, in J. Horwath (ed.) *The Child's World: Assessing Children in Need*. London: Jessica Kingsley.

Deblinger, E., McLeer, S., Atkins, M., Ralphe, M. and Foa, E. (1989) Posttraumatic stress in sexually abused, physically abused and non-abused children, *Child Abuse & Neglect*, 13: 403–8.

Deblinger, E., Steer, R. and Lippmann, J. (1999) Two-year follow-up of cognitive-behavioral therapy for sexually abused children suffering post-traumatic stress symptoms, *Child Abuse & Neglect*, 23: 1371–8.

Deklyen, M. and Greenberg, M. T. (2008) Attachment and psychopathology in childhood, in J. Cassidy and P. R. Shaver (eds) *Handbook of Attachment: Theory, Research and Clinical Applications*, 2nd edn. New York: Guilford.

Demos, J. (1986) *Past, Present and Personal*. Oxford: Oxford University Press.

Denicola, J. and Sandier, J. (1980) Training abusive parents in child management and self-control skills, *Behavior Therapy*, 11: 263–70.

Department for Children, Schools and Families (2007, 2008a, 2009a) *Referrals, Assessments and Children and Young People on Child Protection Registers, England – Year Ending 31 March 2007, 2008 and 2009*. London: DCSF.

Department for Children, Schools and Families (2008b) *Safeguarding Children in Whom Illness is Fabricated or Induced*. London: DCSF.

Department for Children, Schools and Families (2009b) *The Protection of Children in England: Action Plan – The Government's Response to Lord Laming.* London: DCSF.

Department for Children, Schools and Families (2009c) *Safeguarding Children and Young People from Sexual Exploitation.* London: DCSF.

Department for Children, Schools and Families (2009d) *Safeguarding Disabled Children: Practice Guidance.* London: DCSF.

Department for Children, Schools and Families/Home Office (2010) *Safeguarding Children and Young People Who May Have Been Affected by Gang Activity.* London: The Stationery Office.

Department for Education (2010) *Referrals, Assessments and Children and Young People on Child Protection Registers, England – Year Ending 31 March 2010.* London: DfE.

Department for Education (2011) *A Child-centred System. The Government's Response to the Munro Review of Child Protection.* London: DfE.

Department for Education and Skills (2004a, 2005, 2006) *Referrals, Assessments and Children and Young People on Child Protection Registers, England – Year Ending 31 March 2004, 2005 and 2006.* London: DfES.

Department for Education and Skills (2004b) Local Authority Social Services Letter (2004) 4, Female Genital Mutilation Act 2003. London: DfES.

Department for Education and Skills (2004c) *Identifying and Maintaining Contact with Children Missing, or at Risk of Going Missing, from Education.* London: DfES.

Department for Education and Skills (2007a) *Every Parent Matters.* London: DfES.

Department for Education and Skills (2007b) *Safeguarding Children from Abuse Linked to a Belief in Spirit Possession.* London: DfES.

Department for Work and Pensions (2002) *Family Resources Survey 2000/01.* London: HMSO.

Department for Work and Pensions/Department for Education (2011) *A New Approach to Child Poverty: Tackling the Causes of Disadvantage and Transforming Families' Lives.* London: HM Government.

Department of Health (1988) *Protecting Children: A Guide for Social Workers Undertaking a Comprehensive Assessment.* London: HMSO.

Department of Health (1989, 1990, 1991c, 1992, 1993, 1996, 2000b, 2003a) *Survey of Children and Young Persons on Child Protection Registers, Year Ending 31 March 1988, 1989, 1990, 1991, 1992, 1995, 1999, 2000, 2002, England.* London: HMSO.

Department of Health (1991a) *Child Abuse: A Study of Inquiry Reports 1980–1989.* London: HMSO.

Department of Health (1991b) *Working Together under the Children Act 1989: A Guide to Arrangements for Inter-agency Cooperation for the Protection of Children from Abuse.* London: HMSO.

Department of Health (1995) *Child Protection: Messages from Research.* London: HMSO.

Department of Health (1998b) *The Quality Protects Programme: Transforming Children's Services,* LAC(98)26. London: DH.

Department of Health (1999) *Working Together to Safeguard Children: A Guide to Inter-agency Working to Safeguard and Promote the Welfare of Children.* London: HMSO.

Department of Health (2000a) *Framework for the Assessment of Children in Need and Their Families: The Child's World.* London: The Stationery Office.

Department of Health (2000c) *Quality Protects: Disabled Children Numbers and Categories and Families.* London: DH.

Department of Health (2001) *The Children Act Now: Messages from Research – Studies in Evaluating the Children Act 1989.* London: The Stationery Office.

Department of Health (2003b) *Every Child Matters,* Cm 5860. London: The Stationery Office.

Department of Health (2005) *Responding to Domestic Violence: A Handbook for Health Professionals*. London: HMSO.

Department of Health (2006) *Working Together to Safeguard Children: A Guide to Inter-agency Working to Safeguard and Promote the Welfare of Children*. London: The Stationery Office.

Department of Health (2010) *Working Together to Safeguard Children: A Guide to Inter-agency Working to Safeguard and Promote the Welfare of Children*. London: The Stationery Office.

Department of Health/Department for Education and Skills (2007) *Good Practice Guidance on Working with Parents with a Learning Disability*. London: HM Government.

Department of Health/Department for Children, Schools and Families/Department for Business, Innovation and Skills (2010) *Building a Safe and Confident Future: Implementing the Recommendations of the Social Work Task Force*. London: HMSO.

Department of Health/Home Office/Department of Education and Employment/National Assembly for Wales (2000) *Safeguarding Children Involved in Prostitution: Supplementary Guidance to Working Together to Safeguard Children*. London: The Stationery Office.

Department of Health/NHS Executive (2000) *The Protection of Children Act 1999: A Practical Guide to the Act for all Organizations Working with Children*. London: DH.

Department of Health and Social Security (1974) *Report of the Committee of Inquiry into the Care and Supervision Provided in Relation to Maria Colwell*. London: HMSO.

Department of Health and Social Security (1975) *Report of the Committee of Inquiry into the Provision of Services to the Family of John George Auckland*. London: HMSO.

Department of Health and Social Security (1978) *Report of the Social Work Service of the DHSS into Certain Aspects of the Management of the Case of Stephen Menheniott*. London: HMSO.

Department of Health and Social Security (1979) *The Report of the Committee of Inquiry into the Actions of the Authorities and Agencies Relating to Darryn James Clarke*, Cmnd 7739. London: HMSO.

Department of Health and Social Security (1980) *Child Abuse: Central Register Systems*, LASSL (80)4. London: HMSO.

Department of Health and Social Security (1982) *Child Abuse: A Study of Inquiry Reports 1973–1981*. London: HMSO.

Department of Health and Social Security (1985a) *Social Work Decisions in Child Care: Recent Research Findings and Their Implications*. London: HMSO.

Department of Health and Social Security (1985b) *Review of Child Care Law: Report to Ministers of an Interdepartmental Working Party*. London: HMSO.

Department of Health and Social Security (1986) *Child Abuse – Working Together: A Draft Guide to Arrangements for Inter-agency Cooperation for the Protection of Children*. London: HMSO.

Department of Health and Social Security (1988) *Working Together: A Guide to Inter-agency Cooperation for the Protection of Children from Abuse*. London: HMSO.

Devaney, J. (2009) Chronic child abuse: the characteristics and careers of children caught in the child protection system, *British Journal of Social Work*, 39: 24–45.

Devaney, M. (2004) Relating outcomes to objectives in child protection, *Child & Family Social Work*, 9: 27–38.

Dibble, J. and Straus, M. (1980) Some structural determinants of inconsistency between attitudes and behavior: the case of family violence, *Journal of Marriage and the Family*, 42: 71–82.

Dickens, J. (1993) Assessment and control of social work: an analysis of the reasons for the non-use of the child assessment order, *Journal of Social Welfare and Family Law*, 15: 88–100.

Diggins, M. (2009) *Think Child, Think Parent, Think Family: A Guide to Parental Mental Health and Child Welfare. Parental Mental Health and Child Welfare: A Guide for Adult and Children's Health and Social Care Services*. London: SCIE, available at: http://www.scie.org.uk/publications/guides/guide30/

Dingwall, R. (1989) Some problems about predicting child abuse and neglect, in O. Stevenson (ed.) *Child Abuse: Public Policy and Professional Practice.* Hemel Hempstead: Harvester Wheatsheaf.

Dingwall, R., Eekelaar, J. and Murray, T. (1983) *The Protection of Children: State Intervention and Family Life.* Oxford: Blackwell.

Dingwall, R., Eekelaar, J. and Murray, T. (1984) Childhood as a social problem: a survey of the history of legal regulation, *Journal of Law and Society*, 11: 207–32.

Dixon, L., Hamilton-Giachritsis, C. and Browne, K. (2005) Attributions and behaviours of parents abused as children: a mediational analysis of the intergenerational continuity of child maltreatment (Part II), *Journal of Child Psychology and Psychiatry and Allied Disciplines*, 46(1): 58–68.

Dobash, R. and Dobash, R. (1992) *Women, Violence and Social Change.* London: Routledge.

Dominelli, L. (1986) Father-daughter incest: patriarchy's shameful secret, *Critical Social Policy*, 16: 8–22.

Dore, M., Doris, J. and Wright, P. (1995) Identifying substance abuse in maltreating families: a child welfare challenge, *Child Abuse & Neglect*, 19: 531–43.

Dozier, M., Chase Stovall-McClough, K. and Albus, K. E. (2008) Attachment and psychopathy in adulthood, in J. Cassidy and P. R. Shaver (eds) *Handbook of Attachment.* New York: Guilford.

Driver, E. and Droisen, A. (eds) (1989) *Child Sexual Abuse: Feminist Perspectives.* London: Macmillan.

Dubanoski, R., Evans, I. and Higuchi, A. (1978) Analysis and treatment of child abuse: a set of behavioral propositions, *Child Abuse & Neglect*, 2: 153–72.

Dufour, S., Lavergne, C., Larrivee, M. and Trocme, N. (2008) Who are these parents involved in child neglect? A differential analysis of parent gender and family structure, *Children and Youth Services Review*, 30: 141–56.

Duggan, A., Macfarlane, E., Fuddy, L., Burrell, L., Higman, S., Windham, A. and Sia, C. (2004) Randomized trial of a statewide home visiting program: impact in preventing child abuse and neglect, *Child Abuse & Neglect*, 28: 597–622.

Dunne, M. P., Chen, J. Q. and Choo, W. Y. (2008) The evolving evidence base for child protection in Chinese societies, *Asia-Pacific Journal of Public Health*, 20(4): 267–76.

Durrant, J. (1999) Evaluating the success of Sweden's corporal punishment ban, *Child Abuse & Neglect*, 23: 435–48.

Edleson, L. (1999) The overlap between child maltreatment and woman battering, *Violence Against Women*, 5: 134–54.

Egeland, B. and Vaughan, B. (1981) Failure of bond formation as a cause of abuse, neglect and maltreatment, *American Journal of Orthopsychiatry*, 51: 78–84.

Egeland, B., Sroufe, L. and Erickson, M. (1983) Developmental consequences of different patterns of maltreatment, *Child Abuse & Neglect*, 7: 459–69.

Elliot, M. (2002) *Bullying: A Practical Guide to Coping for Schools.* Harlow: Pearson Education.

Elmer, E. (1977) *Fragile Families, Troubled Children.* Pittsburgh, PA: University of Pittsburgh Press.

Elwell, M. and Ephloss, P. (1987) Initial reactions of sexually abused children, *Social Casework*, 68: 109–16.

English, D., Thompson, R., Graham, J. and Briggs, E. (2005) Towards a definition of neglect in young children, *Child Abuse & Neglect*, 29: 19–29.

Ennew, J. (1986) *The Sexual Exploitation of Children.* Cambridge: Polity Press.

Erickson, M. and Egeland, B. (1996) Child neglect, in J. Briere, L. Berliner, J. Bulkley, C. Jenny and T. Reid (eds) *The APSAC Handbook on Child Maltreatment.* Thousand Oaks, CA: Sage.

Erickson, M., Egeland, B. and Pianta, R. (1989) Effects of maltreatment on the development of young children, in D. Cicchetti and V. Carlson (eds) *Child Maltreatment: Theory and Research on the Causes and Consequences of Child Abuse and Neglect*. Cambridge: Cambridge University Press.

Erooga, M. and Masson, H. (1999) *Children and Young People Who Sexually Abuse Others: Challenges and Responses*. London: Routledge.

Evans, S., Davies, C. and DeLillo, D. (2008) Exposure to domestic violence: a meta-analysis of child and adolescent outcomes, *Aggression and Violent Behavior*, 13: 131–40.

Everson, M. and Boat, B. (1994) Putting the anatomical doll controversy in perspective: an examination of the major uses and criticisms of the dolls in child sexual abuse evaluations, *Child Abuse & Neglect*, 18: 113–29.

Faller, K. (1989) Why sexual abuse? An exploration of the intergenerational hypothesis, *Child Abuse & Neglect*, 13: 543–8.

Farmer, E. (1992) Restoring children on court orders to their families: lessons for practice, *Adoption and Fostering*, 16: 7–15.

Farmer, E. and Owen, M. (1995) *Child Protection Practice: Private Risks and Public Remedies – A Study of Decision-making, Intervention and Outcome in Child Protection Work*. London: HMSO.

Farmer, E. and Pollock, S. (2003) Managing sexually abused and/or abusing children in substitute care, *Child & Family Social Work*, 8: 101–12.

Fauth, R., Jelicic, H., Hart, D., Burton, S., Shemmings, D., Bergeron, C., White, K. and Morris, M. (2010) *Effective Practice to Protect Children Living in 'Highly Resistant' Families*. London: Centre for Excellence and Outcomes in Children and Young People's Services.

Featherstone, B. (1997) What has gender got to do with it? Exploring physically abusive behaviour towards children, *British Journal of Social Work*, 27: 419–33.

Featherstone, B. (2004) Fathers matter: a research review, *Children & Society*, 18: 312–19.

Featherstone, B. (2007) What difference does outreach make to family support? in P. Avis et al. (eds) *Supporting Children and Families: Lessons from Sure Start*. London: Jessica Kingsley.

Featherstone, B. and Lancaster, E. (1997) Contemplating the unthinkable: men who sexually abuse children, *Critical Social Policy*, 17: 51–68.

Featherstone, B. and Trinder, L. (1997) Familiar subjects? Domestic violence and child welfare, *Child & Family Social Work*, 2: 147–59.

Featherstone, B., Hooper, C-A., Scourfield, J. and Taylor, J. (eds) (2010) *Gender and Child Welfare in Society*. Oxford, Wiley-Blackwell.

Feder, A., Alonso, A., Tang, M., Warner, V., Barranco, E., Wang, Y., Pilowsky, D., Verdeli, H., Wickramaratne, P. and Weissman, M. M. (2009) Children of low-income depressed mothers: psychiatric disorders and social adjustment, *Depression and Anxiety*, 26(6): 513–20.

Fehrenbach, P., Smith, W., Monastersky, C. and Deister, R. (1986) Adolescent sex offenders: offender and offense characteristics, *American Journal of Orthopsychiatry*, 56: 225–33.

Ferguson, D. and Lynsky, M. (1996) Physical punishment/maltreatment during childhood and adjustment in young adulthood, *Child Abuse & Neglect*, 20: 617–30.

Ferguson, H. (1990) Rethinking child protection practices: a case for history, in The Violence against Children Study Group, *Taking Child Abuse Seriously*. London: Unwin Hyman.

Ferguson, H. (2004) *Protecting Children in Time: Child Abuse, Child Protection and the Consequences of Modernity*. Basingstoke: Palgrave Macmillan.

Ferguson, H. (2011) *Child Protection Practice*. Basingstoke: Palgrave Macmillan.

Field, F. (2010) *The Foundation Years: Preventing Poor Children Becoming Poor Adults*. London: HM Government.

Finkelhor, D. (1979) *Sexually Victimized Children*. New York: Free Press.

Finkelhor, D. (1993) Epidemiological factors in the clinical identification of child sexual abuse, *Child Abuse & Neglect*, 17: 67–70.

Finkelhor, D. (1994) Current information on the scope and nature of child sexual abuse, *The Future of Children*, 4(2): 31, 46–8.

Finkelhor, D. (2008) *Child Victimization: Violence, Crime, and Abuse in the Lives of Young People*. New York: Oxford University Press.

Finkelhor, D. and Baron, L. (1986) High risk children, in D. Finkelhor et al. (eds) *A Sourcebook on Child Sexual Abuse*. Newbury Park, CA: Sage.

Finkelhor, D. and Jones, L. (2004) Explanations for decline in sexual abuse cases, *Juvenile Justice Bulletin*, January 2004. Washington: Office of Juvenile Justice and Delinquency Prevention.

Finkelhor, D. and Korbin, J. (1988) Child abuse as an international issue, *Child Abuse & Neglect*, 12: 3–23.

Finkelhor, D. with Araji, S. et al. (eds) (1986) *A Sourcebook on Child Sexual Abuse*. Newbury Park, CA: Sage.

Finkelhor, D., Hotaling, G., Lewis, I. and Smith, C. (1990) Sexual abuse in a national survey of adult men and women: prevalence characteristics and risk factors, *Child Abuse & Neglect*, 14: 19–28.

Finkelhor, D., Asdigan, N. and Dziuba-Leatherman, J. (1995) The effectiveness of victimization prevention instruction: an evaluation of children's responses to actual threats and assaults, *Child Abuse & Neglect*, 19: 141–53.

Fischer, D. and Macdonald, W. (1998) Characteristics of intrafamilial and extrafamilial child sexual abuse, *Child Abuse & Neglect*, 22: 915–29.

Fonagy, P. and Target, M. (2005) Bridging the transmission gap: an end to an important mystery of attachment research? *Attachment and Human Development*, 7: 333–43.

Fook, J. (2002) *Social Work: Critical Theory and Practice*. London: Sage.

Forrester, D., Kershaw, S., Moss, H. and Hughes, L. (2008a) Communication skills in child protection: how do social workers talk to parents? *Child and Family Social Work*, 13(1): 41–51.

Forrester, D., McCambridge, J., Waissbein, C. and Rollnick, S. (2008b) How do child and family social workers talk to parents about child welfare concerns? *Child Abuse Review*, 17(1): 23–35.

Fox-Harding, L. (1991) *Perspectives in Child Care Policy*. London: Longman.

Fraser, S., Lewis, V., Ding, S., Kellet, M. and Robinson, C. (2004) *Doing Research with Children and Young People*. London: Sage.

Freeman, M. (1983) *The Rights and Wrongs of Children*. London: Pinter.

Freeman, M. (ed.) (2000) *Overcoming Child Abuse: A Window on A World Problem*. Dartmouth: Ashgate.

Freeman, P. and Hunt, J. (1998) *Parental Perspectives on Care Proceedings*. London: The Stationery Office.

Frenken, J. (1994) Treatment of incest perpetrators: a five-phase model, *Child Abuse & Neglect*, 18: 357–65.

Friedrich, W., Urquiza, A. and Beilke, R. (1986) Behaviour problems in sexually abused young children, *Journal of Pediatric Psychology*, 11: 47–57.

Frodi, A. and Lamb, M. (1980) Child abusers' response to infant smiles and cries, *Child Development*, 51: 238–41.

Frodi, A. and Smetana, J. (1984) Abused, neglected and non-maltreated preschoolers' ability to discriminate emotion in others: the effects of IQ, *Child Abuse & Neglect*, 8: 459–65.

Frost, N. and Stein, M. (1989) *The Politics of Child Welfare: Inequality, Power and Change*. Hemel Hempstead: Harvester Wheatsheaf.

Furby, L., Weinrott, W. and Blackshaw, L. (1989) Sex offender recidivism: a review, *Psychological Bulletin*, 105: 3–30.

Furniss, T. (1991) *The Multi-professional Handbook of Child Sexual Abuse: Integrated Management, Therapy and Legal Intervention*. London: Routledge.

Gagnon, J. and Parker, R. (1995) *Conceiving Sexuality: Approaches to Sex Research in the Modern World*. London: Routledge.

Garbarino, J. (1977) The human ecology of child maltreatment: a conceptual model for research, *Journal of Marriage and the Family*, 39: 721–35.

Garbarino, J. (1982) *Children and Families in Their Social Environment*. New York: Aldine.

Garbarino, J. and Crouter, A. (1978) Defining the community context for parent-child relations: the correlates of child mistreatment, *Child Development*, 49: 604–16.

Garbarino, J. and Vondra, J. (1987) Psychological maltreatment: issues and perspectives, in M. Brassard, R. Germain and S. Hart (eds) *Psychological Maltreatment of Children and Youth*. Oxford: Pergamon Press.

Gaughan, K. and Kalyniak, S. (2011) The centrality of relationships, in S. Goodman and I. Trowler (eds) *Reclaiming Social Work*, pp. 94–110. London: Jessica Kingsley.

Gazmararian, J., Petersen, R., Spitz, A., Goodwin, M., Saltzman, L. and Marks, J. (2000) Violence and reproductive health: current knowledge and future research directions, *Maternal and Child Health Journal*, 4: 79–84.

Gelles, R. (1982) Towards better research on child abuse and neglect: a response to Besharov, *Child Abuse & Neglect*, 6: 495–6.

Germain, C. and Gitterman, A. (1980) *The Life Model of Social Work Practice*. Cambridge, MA: Harvard University Press.

Ghate, D. (2001) Community-based evaluations in the UK: scientific concerns and practical constraints, *Children & Society*, 15: 23–32.

Ghate, D., Shaw, C. and Hazel, N. (2000) *Fathers and Family Centres: Engaging Fathers in Preventive Strategies*. York: Joseph Rowntree Foundation.

Giaretto, H. (1981) A comprehensive child sexual abuse treatment program, in P. Mrazek and C. Kempe (eds) *Sexually Abused Children and Their Families*. New York: Pergamon Press.

Giaretto, H., Giaretto, A. and Sgroi, S. (1978) Co-ordinated community treatment of incest, in A. Burgess, A. Groth, L. Holmstrom and S. Sgroi (eds) *Sexual Assault of Children and Adolescents*. Lexington, MA: Lexington Books.

Gibbons, J., Conroy, S. and Bell, C. (1995a) *Operating the Child Protection System: A Study of Child Protection Practices in English Local Authorities*. London: HMSO.

Gibbons, J., Gallagher, B., Bell, C. and Gordon, D. (1995b) *Development after Physical Abuse in Early Childhood: A Follow-up Study of Children on Child Protection Registers*. London: HMSO.

Gil, D. (1970) *Violence Against Children*. Cambridge, MA: Harvard University Press.

Gil, D. (1975) Unravelling child abuse, *American Journal of Orthopsychiatry*, 45: 346–56.

Gil, D. (1978) Societal violence and violence in families, in J. Eekelaar and S. Katz (eds) *Family Violence*. Toronto: Butterworth.

Gillham, B. (1991) *The Facts about Sexual Abuse*. London: Cassell.

Giovannoni, J. and Becerra, R. (1979) *Defining Child Abuse*. New York: Free Press.

Glaser, D. (2000) Child abuse and neglect and the brain: a review, *Journal of Child Psychology and Psychiatry*, 41: 97–116.

Glaser, D. (2002) Emotional abuse and neglect (psychological maltreatment): a conceptual framework, *Child Abuse & Neglect*, 26: 697–714.

Glaser, D. and Frosh, S. (1988) *Child Sexual Abuse*. London: Macmillan.

Gold, S., Hughes, D. and Swingle, J. (1996) Characteristics of childhood sexual abuse among female survivors in therapy, *Child Abuse & Neglect*, 20: 323–36.

Gomes-Schwartz, B., Horowitz, J. and Cardarelli, A. (1990) *Child Sexual Abuse: The Initial Effects*. Beverly Hills, CA: Sage.

Goodman, S. and Brumley, H. E. (1990) Schizophrenic and depressed mothers: relational deficits in parenting, *Developmental Psychology*, 26: 31–39.

Goodman, S. and Trowler, I. (2011) *Reclaiming Social Work*. London: Jessica Kingsley.

Gordon, D., Parker, R. and Loughran, F. (2000) *Disabled Children in Britain: A Re-analysis of the OPCS Disability Surveys*. London: TSO.

Gordon, L. (1989) *Heroes of Their Own Lives: The Politics and History of Family Violence, Boston 1880–1960*. London: Virago.

Gorham, D. (1978) The maiden tribute of Babylon re-examined: child prostitution and the idea of childhood in late-Victorian England, *Victorian Studies*, 21: 354–79.

Gough, D. (1993) *Child Abuse Interventions: A Review of the Research Literature*. London: HMSO.

Gough, D. (1996) Defining the problem, *Child Abuse & Neglect*, 20: 993–1002.

Graham-Bermann, S. A., Cutler, S. E., Litzenberger, B. W. and Schwartz, W. E. (1994) Perceived sibling violence and emotional adjustment during childhood and adolescence, *Journal of Family Psychology*, 8: 85–97.

Greenland, C. (1958) Incest, *British Journal of Delinquency*, 9: 62–5.

Greenland, C. (1987) *Preventing CAN Deaths: An International Study of Deaths Due to Child Abuse & Neglect*. London: Tavistock.

Greenwalt, B., Sklare, G. and Fortes, P. (1998) The therapeutic treatment provided in cases involving physical child abuse: a description of current practices, *Child Abuse & Neglect*, 22: 71–8.

Greenwich (London Borough of) (1987) *A Child in Mind: The Protection of Children in a Responsible Society – Report of the Commission of Inquiry into the Circumstances Surrounding the Death of Kimberley Carlile*. London: London Borough of Greenwich.

Griffiths, D. and Moynihan, F. (1963) Multiple epiphyseal injuries in babies ('battered baby syndrome'), *British Medical Journal*, 5372: 1558–61.

Guardian (2009) We all hate OFSTED, right?, 23 November.

Gunby, C. and Woodhams, J. (2010) Sexually deviant juveniles: comparisons between the offender and offence characteristics of 'child abusers' and 'peer abusers', *Pyschology, Crime and Law*, 16: 47–64.

Hall, G. (1995) Sexual offender recidivism revisited: a meta-analysis of recent treatment studies, *Journal of Consulting and Clinical Psychology*, 63: 802–9.

Hallett, C. and Stevenson, O. (1980) *Child Abuse: Aspects of Inter-professional Cooperation*. London: Allen & Unwin.

Halston, A. and Richards, D. (1982) Behind closed doors, *Social Work Today*, 14: 7–11.

Hanawalt, B. (1977) Childrearing among the lower classes of late medieval England, *Journal of Interdisciplinary History*, 8: 1–22.

Hanawalt, B. (1995) *Growing Up in Medieval London*. New York: Oxford University Press.

Hanson, R. and Morton-Bourgon, K. (2005) The characteristics of persistent sexual offenders: a meta-analysis of recidivism studies, *Journal of Consulting and Clinical Pyschology*, 73: 1154–63.

Haringey (London Borough of) (2008) *Haringey Local Safeguarding Children Board Serious Case Review 'Child A'*. London: Department for Education.

Harris, J. (1995) Where is the child's environment? A group socialization theory of development, *Psychological Review*, 102: 458–89.

Harris, J. (1998) *The Nurture Assumption*. New York: Free Press.

Harris, R. (1995) Child protection, child care and child welfare, in J. Wilson and A. James (eds) *The Child Protection Handbook*. London: Baillière Tindall.

Harrow (Area Child Protection Committee) (1999) *Part 8 Summary Report*. Harrow: Harrow ACPC.

Hearn, J. (1990) Child abuse and men's violence, in The Violence against Children Study Group, *Taking Child Abuse Seriously*. London: Unwin Hyman.

Heim, C., Young, L. J., Newport, D. J., Mletzko, T., Miller, A. H. and Nemeroff, C. B. (2009) Lower CSF oxytocin concentrations in women with a history of childhood abuse, *Molecular Psychiatry*, 14(10): 954–8.

Heller, S. S., Larrieu, J. A., D'Imperiod, R. and Boris, N. W. (1999) Research on resilience to child maltreatment: empirical considerations, *Child Abuse & Neglect*, 23(4): 321–38.

Hendrick, H. (1994) *Child Welfare: England 1872–1989*. London: Routledge.

Herman, J. (1981) *Father-Daughter Incest*. Cambridge, MA: Harvard University Press.

Hester, M. et al. (2009) 'Girls' and boys' experiences and perceptions of parental discipline and punishment while growing up in China and England, *Child Abuse Review*, 18: 401–13.

Heywood, C. (2001) *A History of Childhood: Children and Childhood in the West from Medieval to Modern Times*. Cambridge: Polity Press.

Hicks, J. and Allen, G. (1999) *A Century of Change: Trends in UK Statistics since 1900*. London: House of Commons Library.

Hicks, L. and Stein, M. (2010) *Neglect Matters: A Multiagency Guide for Professionals Working Together on Behalf of Teenagers*. London: The Stationery Office.

Hildyard, K. and Wolfe, D. (2002) Child neglect: developmental issues and outcomes, *Child Abuse & Neglect*, 26: 679–95.

Hillingdon (London Borough of) (1986) *Report of the Review Panel into the Death of Heidi Koseda*. London: London Borough of Hillingdon.

Hingley-Jones, H. and Mandin, P. (2007) Getting to the root of problems: the role of systems ideas in helping social work students to develop relationship-based practice, *Journal of Social Work Practice*, 21(2): 177–91.

Hobbs, C. and Wynne, J. (1986) Buggery in childhood: a common syndrome of child abuse, *The Lancet*, 8510: 792–6.

Holland, S. (2000) The assessment relationship: interactions between social workers and parents in child protection assessments, *British Journal of Social Work*, 30: 149–63.

Holman, B. (1988) *Putting Families First: Prevention and Child Care*. London: Macmillan.

Holmes, L., Munro, E. and Soper, J. (2010) *Calculating the Cost and Capacity Implications for Local Authorities Implementing the Laming (2009) Recommendations*. Report to the Local Government Association. Loughborough: Centre for Child and Family Research. Loughborough University.

Holt, J. (1974) *Escape from Childhood*. Harmondsworth: Penguin.

Home Office (1923) *Report of the Work of the Children's Branch*. London: HMSO.

Home Office (1945) *Report by Sir Walter Monckton on the Circumstances which led to the Boarding-out of Dennis and Terence O'Neill at Bank Farm, Minsterley and the Steps Taken to Supervise their Welfare*, Cmd 6636. London: HMSO.

Home Office (1950) *Children Neglected or Ill-treated in their Own Homes*. Joint Circular with the Ministry of Health and Ministry of Education. London: HMSO.

Home Office/Department of Health (1992) *Memorandum of Good Practice on Video-recorded Interviews with Child Witnesses for Criminal Proceedings*. London: HMSO.

Hooper, C-A. and Koprowska, J. (2004) The vulnerabilities of children whose parents have been sexually abused in childhood: towards a new framework, *British Journal of Social Work*, 34: 165–80.

Horwath, J. and Calder, M. (1998) Working together to protect children on the child protection register: myth or reality, *British Journal of Social Work*, 28: 879–95.

Hotaling, G. T., Straus, M. A. and Lincoln, A. J. (1990) Intrafamily violence and crime and violence outside the family, in M. A. Straus and R. J. Gelles (eds) *Physical Violence in American Families*, pp. 431–70. New Brunswick, NJ: Transaction Books.

Housden, L. (1955) *The Prevention of Cruelty to Children*. London: Cape.

House of Commons (1984) *Children in Care: Volume 1, Second Report from the Social Services Committee: Session 1983–4*. London: HMSO.

Howe, D. (1991) Knowledge, power and the shape of social work practice, in M. Davies (ed.) *The Sociology of Social Work*. London: Routledge.

Howe, D. (1995) *Attachment Theory for Social Work Practice*. London: Macmillan.

Howe, D. (2005) *Child Abuse and Neglect: Attachment, Development and Intervention*. Basingstoke: Palgrave Macmillan.

Howe, D. (2011) *Attachment across the Lifecourse*. Basingstoke: Palgrave Macmillan.

Hoyle, D. (2008) Problematizing *Every Child Matters, The Encyclopaedia of Informal Education*, available at: www.infed.org/socialwork/every_child_matters_a_critique.htm.

Hrdy, S. (1977) *The Langurs of Abu*. Cambridge, MA: Harvard University Press.

Hrdy, S. B. (2009) *Mothers and Others: The Evolutionary Origins of Mutual Understanding*. Cambridge, MA: Harvard University Press.

Huber, J. and Stanig, P. (2009) *Individual Income and Voting for Redisribution Across Democracies*, available at: http://www.columbia.edu/~jdh39/Site/Research_files/huber_stanig_voting.pdf.

Huddersfield Daily Examiner (2008) Over half UK's sniffer dogs used in search for Shannon, 12 March.

Human Rights Watch, *Death By Default: A Policy of Fatal Neglect in China's State Orphanages*, 1 January 1996, 1-56432-163-0, available at: http://www.unhcr.org/refworld/docid/3ae6a85a0.html, accessed 28 May 2012.

Humphreys, C. (1995) Whatever happened on the way to counselling? Hurdles in the inter-agency environment, *Child Abuse & Neglect*, 19: 801–9.

Humphreys, C. (2006) *Research and Practice Briefings: Domestic Violence and Child Abuse*, available at: http://www.uea.ac.uk/menu/acad_depts/swk/MRC_web/public_html/files/qpb14.pdf.

Humphreys, C. and Stanley, N. (2006) *Domestic Violence and Child Protection: Directions for Good Practice*. London: Jessica Kingsley.

Humphreys, C., Atkar, S. and Baldwin, N. (1999) Discrimination in child protection work: recurring themes in work with Asian families, *Child & Family Social Work*, 4: 283–91.

Hunt, P. (1994) *Report of the Independent Inquiry into Multiple Abuse in Nursery Classes in Newcastle-upon-Tyne*. Newcastle upon Tyne: City Council of Newcastle upon Tyne.

Hunter, R. and Kilstrom, N. (1979) Breaking the cycle in abusive families, *American Journal of Psychiatry*, 136: 1320–2.

Ingleby, Viscount (1960) *Report of the Committee on Children and Young Persons*, Cmnd 1191. London: HMSO.

Irfan, S. and Cowburn, M. (2004) Disciplining, chastisement and physical abuse: perceptions and attitudes of the British Pakistani community, *Journal of Muslim Minority Affairs*, 24: 89–98.

Itzin, C. (1997) Pornography and the organisation of intrafamilial and extrafamilial child sexual abuse: developing a conceptual model, *Child Abuse Review*, 6: 94–106.

Iwaniec, D. and Sneddon, H. (2001) Attachment style in adults who failed to thrive as children: outcomes of a 20 year follow-up study of factors influencing maintenance or change in attachment style, *British Journal of Social Work*, 31: 179–95.

Iwaniec, D., Herbert, M. and McNeish, A. (1985) Social work with failure to thrive children and their families, part II: behavioural social work intervention, *British Journal of Social Work*, 15: 375–89.

Iwaniec, D., Larkin, E. and Higgins, S. (2006) Research review: risk and resilience in cases of emotional abuse, *Child and Family Social Work*, 11(1): 73–82.

Jack, G. (2000) Ecological influences on parenting and child development, *British Journal of Social Work*, 30: 703–20.

Jackowski, A. P., de Araújo, C. M., de Lacerda, A. L. T., de Jesus, M. J. and Kaufman, J. (2009) Neurostructural imaging findings in children with post-traumatic stress disorder: brief review, *Psychiatry and Clinical Neurosciences*, 63(1): 1–8.

Jackson, S. (1996) Educational success for looked-after children: the social worker's responsibility, *Practice*, 10: 47–56.

Jaffe, A. (2011) Failure to thrive: current clinical concepts, *Pediatrics in Review*, 32: 100–8.

Jaffee, S. R. and Maikovich-Fong, A. K. (2011) Effects of chronic maltreatment and maltreatment timing on children's behavior and cognitive abilities, *Journal of Child Psychology and Psychiatry*, 52(2): 184–94.

Jahoda, M. (1977) *Freud and the Dilemmas of Psychology*. London: Hogarth Press.

Jampole, L. and Weber, M. (1987) An assessment of the behaviour of sexually abused and nonsexually abused children with anatomically correct dolls, *Child Abuse & Neglect*, 11: 187–92.

Jaser, S. S., Langrock, A. M., Keller, G., Merchant, M. J., Benson, M. A., Reeslund, K., Champion, J. E. and Compas, B. E. (2005) Coping with the stress of parental depression II: adolescent and parent reports of coping and adjustment, *Journal of Child and Adolescent Psychology*, 34: 193–205.

Jaudes, P. and Diamond, L. (1985) The handicapped child and child abuse, *Child Abuse & Neglect*, 9: 341–7.

Jaudes, P. and Morris, M. (1990) Child sexual abuse: who goes home?, *Child Abuse & Neglect*, 14: 61–8.

Jenkins, H. and Asen, K. (1992) Family therapy without the family: a framework for systemic practice, *Journal of Family Therapy*, 14: 1–14.

Johnson, T. (1989) Female child perpetrators: children who molest other children, *Child Abuse & Neglect*, 13: 571–86.

Jones, D. (1987) The unbeatable family, *Child Abuse & Neglect*, 11: 409–20

Jonker, F. and Jonker-Bakker, I. (1997) Effects of ritual abuse: the results of three surveys in the Netherlands, *Child Abuse & Neglect*, 21: 541–56.

Jordanova, L. (1989) Children in history: concepts of nature and society, in G. Scarre (ed.) *Children, Parents and Politics*. Cambridge: Cambridge University Press.

Joseph, Sir Keith (1972) The next ten years, *New Society*, 5 October, pp. 8–9.

Juffer, F., Bakermans-Kranenburg, M. J. and Van IJzendoorn, M. H. (eds) (2008) *Promoting Positive Parenting: An Attachment-based Intervention*. New York: Lawrence Erlbaum/Taylor & Francis.

Kadushin, A. and Martin, J. (1981) *Child Abuse: An Interactional Event*. New York: Columbia University Press.

Kajese, T., Nguyen, L., Pham, G., Pham, V., Melhorn, K. and Kallall, K. (2011) Characteristics of child abuse homicides in the state of Kansas from 1994 to 2007, *Child Abuse & Neglect*, 35: 147–54.

Kaplan, S. J., Labruna, V., Pecovitz, D. and Salzinger, S. (1999) Physically abused adolescents: behavior problems, functional impairment, and comparison of informants, *Pediatrics*, 104(1): 43–9.

Kaufman, D. and Widom, C. (1999) Childhood victimisation, running away and delinquency, *Journal of Research in Delinquency and Crime*, 36: 347–70.

Kaufman, J. and Zigler, E. (1989) The intergenerational transmission of child abuse, in D. Cicchetti and V. Carlson (eds) *Child Maltreatment: Theory and Research on the Causes and Consequences of Child Abuse and Neglect*. Cambridge: Cambridge University Press.

Kearney, P., Levin, E., Rosen, G. and Sainsbury, M. (2003) *Families that have Alcohol and Mental Health Problems: A Template for Partnership Working*. London: SCIE, available at: http://www.scie.org.uk/publications/guides/guide02/index.asp.

Keen, J. and Alison, L. (2001) Drug misusing parents: key points for health professionals, *Archives of Disease in Childhood*, 85: 296–9.

Kelly, L., Regan, L. and Burton, S. (1991) *An Exploratory Study of the Prevalence of Sexual Abuse in a Sample of 16–21 Year Olds*. London: Child Abuse Studies Unit, University of North London.

Kelly, P. and Koh, J. (2006) Sexually transmitted infections in alleged sexual abuse of children and adolescents, *Journal of Paediatrics and Child Health*, 42(7–8): 434–40.

Kelly, P., Koh, J. and Thompson, J. M. (2006) Diagnostic findings in alleged sexual abuse: symptoms have no predictive value, *Journal of Paediatrics and Child Health*, 42(3): 112–17.

Kempe, C., Silverman, P., Steele, B., Droegemueller, W. and Silver, H. (1962) The battered child syndrome, *Journal of the American Medical Association*, 181: 17–24.

Kempe, R. and Kempe, C. (1978) *Child Abuse*. London: Fontana.

Kendall-Tackett, K. and Eckenrode, J. (1996) The effects of neglect on academic achievement and disciplinary problems: a developmental perspective, *Child Abuse & Neglect*, 20: 161–9.

Kendall-Tackett, R., Lyon, T., Taliaferro, G. and Little, L. (2005) Why child maltreatment researchers should include children's disability status in their maltreatment studies, *Child Abuse & Neglect*, 29: 147–51.

Kershaw, C., Nicholas, S. and Walker, A. (2008) *Crime in England and Wales 2007/8*. London: The Stationery Office.

Kessler, M., White, M. and Nelson, B. (2003) Group treatments for women sexually abused as children: a review of the literature and recommendations for future outcome research, *Child Abuse & Neglect*, 27: 1045–61.

Kilgallon, W. (1995) *Report of the Independent Review into Allegations of Abuse at Meadowdale Children's Home and Related Matters*. Morpeth: Northumberland County Council.

Kim, M. J. and Cicchetti, D. (2010) Longitudinal pathways linking child maltreatment, emotion regulation, peer relations, and psychopathology, *Journal of Child Psychology and Psychiatry*, 51(6): 706–16.

Kim, M. J., Tajima, E. A., Herrenkohl, T. I. and Huang, B. (2009) Early child maltreatment, runaway youths, and risk of delinquency and victimization in adolescence: a mediational model, *Social Work Research*, 33(1): 19–28.

Kinard, E. (1998) Methodological issues in assessing resilience in maltreated children, *Child Abuse & Neglect*, 22: 669–80.

Kline, P. (1981) *Fact and Fantasy in Freudian Theory*. London: Methuen.

Kneebone, R.L. (2009) Practice, rehearsal, and performance: an approach for simulation-based surgical and procedure training, *Journal of the American Medical Association*, 302: 1336–8.

Knutson, J.F. and Schartz, H.A. (1997) Physical abuse and neglect of children, in T. A. Widiger, A. J. Frances, H. A. Pincus, R. Ross, M. B. First and W. Davis (eds) *DSM-IV Sourcebook*, vol. 3, pp. 713–803. Washington, DC: American Psychiatric Association.

Koposov, R. A., Ruchkin, V. V., Eisemann, M. and Sidorov, P. I. (2005) Alcohol abuse in Russian delinquent adolescents: associations with comorbid psychopathology, personality and parenting, *European Child & Adolescent Psychiatry*, 14(5): 254–61.

Korbin, J. (ed.) (1981) *Child Abuse and Neglect: Cross Cultural Perspectives*. Berkeley, CA: University of California Press.

Korbin, J., Coulton, C., Lindstrom-Ufuti, H. and Spilsbury, J. (2000) Neighborhood views on the definition and etiology of child maltreatment, *Child Abuse & Neglect*, 24: 1509–27.

Koreola, C., Pound, J., Heger, A. and Lyttle, C. (1993) Relationship of child sexual abuse to depression, *Child Abuse & Neglect*, 17: 393–400.

Korkman, J., Pekka, J. and Sandnabba, K. (2006) Dynamics of verbal interaction between interviewer and child in interviews with alleged victims of child sexual abuse, *Scandinavian Journal of Psychology*, 47: 109–19.

Krähenbühl, S. J. and Blades, M. (2006) The effect of question repetition within interviews on young children's eyewitness recall, *Journal of Experimental Child Psychology*, 94: 57–67.

Kroll, B. (2004) Living with an elephant: growing up with parental substance misuse, *Child & Family Social Work*, 9: 129–44.

Kroll, B. and Taylor, A. (2003) Parental *Substance Misuse and Child Welfare*. London: Jessica Kingsley.

Krug, R. (1989) Adult male report of childhood sexual abuse by mothers: case descriptions, motivations and long-term consequences, *Child Abuse & Neglect*, 13: 111–19.

Krugman, R. (1998) Keynote address: it's time to broaden the agenda, *Child Abuse & Neglect*, 22: 475–9.

Kumar, V. (1993) *Poverty and Inequality in the UK: The Effects on Children*. London: National Children's Bureau.

La Fontaine, J. (1990) *Child Sexual Abuse*. Cambridge: Polity Press.

La Fontaine, J. (1994) *The Extent and Nature of Organised and Ritual Abuse: Research Findings.* London: HMSO.

La Fontaine, J. (1998) *Speak of the Devil: Tales of Satanic Abuse in Contemporary England.* Cambridge: Cambridge University Press.

Lakatos, K., Toth, I., Nemoda, Z., Ney, K., Sasvari- Szekely, M. and Gervai, J. (2000) Dopamine D4 receptor (DRD4) gene polymorphism is associated with attachment disorganization in infants, *Molecular Psychiatry*, 5: 633–7.

Lakatos, K., Nemoda, Z., Toth, I. et al. (2002) Further evidence for the role of the dopamine D4 receptor (DRD4) gene in attachment disorganization: interaction of the exon III 48-bp repeat and the 521 C/T promoter polymorphisms, *Molecular Psychiatry*, 7: 27–31.

Lambeth (London Borough of) (1987) *Whose Child? The Report of the Public Inquiry into the Death of Tyra Henry*. London: London Borough of Lambeth.

Lambeth, Lewisham and Southwark (London Boroughs of) (1989) *The Doreen Aston Report.* London: Lambeth, Lewisham and Southwark Area Review Committee.

Laming, Lord (2003) *The Victoria Climbié Inquiry: Report of an Inquiry by Lord Laming*, Cm 5730. London: The Stationery Office.

Laming, Lord (2009) *The Protection of Children in England: A Progress Report*. London: The Stationery Office.

Lamont, A. (2011) Child abuse and neglect statistics, *Australian Institute of Family Studies*, available at: http:////www.aifs.gov.au/nch/pubs/sheets/rs1/rs1.html.

Lamphear, V. (1985) The impact of maltreatment on children's psychosocial adjustment: a review of the research, *Child Abuse & Neglect*, 9: 251–63.

Langer, W. (1974) Infanticide: a historical survey, *History of Childhood Quarterly*, 1: 353–65.

Larrance, D. and Twentyman, C. (1983) Maternal attribution and child abuse, *Journal of Abnormal Psychology*, 92: 449–57.

Lasky-Su J. et al. (2008) Family-based association analysis of a statistically derived quantitative traits for ADHD reveal an association in DRD4 with inattentive symptoms in ADHD individuals, *American Journal of Medical Genetics Part B: Neuropsychiatric Genetics*, 147B(1):100–6.

Lazenbatt, A. (2010) *The Impact of Abuse and Neglect on the Health and Mental Health of Children and Young People*. London: NSPCC.

Le Grand, J. (2007) *Consistent Care Matters: Exploring the Potential of Social Work Practices.* London: DfES.

Leach, P. (1999) *The Physical Punishment of Children: Some Input from Recent Research.* London: NSPCC.

Lealman, C., Haigh, D., Phillips, J., Stone, J. and Ord-Smith, C. (1983) Prediction and prevention of child abuse – an empty hope?, *The Lancet*, 8339: 1423–4.

Lee, M. and O'Brien, R. (1995) *The Game's Up: Redefining Child Prostitution.* London: The Children's Society.

Leicestershire (County Council) (1993) *The Leicestershire Inquiry.* Leicester: Leicestershire County Council.

Letourneau, C. (1981) Empathy and stress: how they affect parental aggression, *Social Work*, 26: 383–90.

Leventhal, J. (2001) The prevention of child abuse and neglect: successfully out of the blocks, *Child Abuse & Neglect*, 25: 431–9.

Leventhal, J. (2003) The field of child maltreatment enters its fifth decade, *Child Abuse & Neglect*, 27: 1–4.

Lewis, D., Mallouh, C. and Webb, V. (1989) Child abuse, delinquency and violent criminality, in D. Cicchetti and V. Carlson (eds) *Child Maltreatment: Theory and Research on the Causes and Consequences of Child Abuse and Neglect.* Cambridge: Cambridge University Press.

Lewis, M. and Schaeffer, S. (1981) Peer behaviour and mother-infant interaction, in M. Lewis and S. Schaeffer (eds) *The Uncommon Child.* New York: Plenum Press.

Lewisham (London Borough of) (1985) *The Leeways Inquiry Report.* London: London Borough of Lewisham.

Liebenberg, L. and Ungar, M. (eds) (2009) *Researching Resilience.* Toronto, ON: University of Toronto Press.

Lindberg, F. and Distad, L. (1985) Survival reponses to incest: adolescents in crisis, *Child Abuse & Neglect*, 9: 413–15.

Lindon, J. and Nourse, C. (1994) A multi-dimensional model of group-work for adolescent girls who have been sexually abused, *Child Abuse & Neglect*, 18: 341–8.

Liotti, G. (2004) Trauma, dissociation and disorganised attachment: three strands of a single braid, *Psychotherapy: Theory, Research, Practice, Training*, 41: 472–86.

Littell, J. H. et al. (2005) *Multisystemic Therapy for Social, Emotional, and Behavioural Problems in Youth aged 10–17*, Cochrane Review, available at: www2.cochrane.org.reviews.

Loftus, E. and Ketcham, K. (1994) *The Myth of Repressed Memory: False Memories and Allegations of Sexual Abuse.* New York: St Martin's Press.

Lovell, E. (2001) *Megan's Law: Does it Protect Children? A Review of Evidence on the Impact of Community Notification as Legislated for through Megan's Law in the United States – Recommendations for Policy Makers in the United Kingdom.* London: NSPCC.

Lowe, N. (1989) The role of wardship in child care cases, *Family Law*, 19: 38–45.

Lownsbrough, H. and O'Leary, D. (2005) *The Leadership Imperative: Reforming Children's Services from the Ground Up.* London: Demos.

Lusk, R. and Waterman, J. (1986) Effects of sexual abuse on children, in K. Macfarlane and J. Waterman (eds) *The Sexual Abuse of Young Children.* New York: Holt, Rinehart & Winston.

Luyten, P., Kempke, S. and Van Houdenhove, B. (2009) Stressonderzoek in de psychiatrie: een complex verhaal [Stress research in psychiatry: a complex story], *Tijdschrift voor Psychiatrie Journal of Psychiatry*, 51: 611–18.

Lynch, M. and Roberts, J. (1982) *The Consequences of Child Abuse.* London: Academic Press.

Lyon, C. (1989) Legal developments following the Cleveland report in England: a consideration of some aspects of the Children Bill, *Journal of Social Welfare Law*, 11: 200–6.

Lyon, C. (1997) Children abused within the care system: do current representation procedures offer the child protection and the family support?, in N. Parton (ed.) *Child Protection and Family Support: Tensions, Contradictions and Possibilities*. London: Routledge.

Lyon, C. (2003) *Child Abuse*, 3rd edn. Bristol: Jordan Publishing.

Lyons, J. S., Anderson, R. L. and Larson, D. B. (1993) The use and effects of physical punishment in the home: a systematic review. Paper presented at the meeting of the American Academy of Pediatrics, Washington, DC.

Lyons-Ruth, K. and Jacobvitz, D. (2008) Attachment disorganisation: genetic factors, parenting contexts, and developmental transformation from infancy to adulthood, in J. Cassidy and P. R. Shaver (eds) *Handbook of Attachment: Theory, Research and Clinical Applications*, 2nd edn, pp. 666–97. New York: Guilford.

Lyons-Ruth, K., Lyubchik, A., Wolfe, R. and Bronfman, E. (2002) Parental depression and child attachment: hostile and helpless profiles of parent and child behavior among families at risk, in S. H. Goodman and I. H. Gotlib (eds) *Children of Depressed Parents: Mechanisms of Risk and Implications for Treatment*, pp. 89–120. Washington, DC: American Psychological Association.

MacDonald, G. (2001) *Effective Interventions for Child Abuse and Neglect*. Chichester: Wiley.

Macfarlane, A. (1970) *The Family Life of Ralph Josselin*. Cambridge: Cambridge University Press.

Macfarlane, A. (1979) Review of 'The family, sex and marriage in England 1500–1800' by Lawrence Stone, *History and Theory*, 18: 103–26.

Macfarlane, K. and Waterman, J. (1986) *The Sexual Abuse of Young Children*. New York: Holt, Rinehart & Winston.

Mackenzie, T., Collins, N. and Popkin, M. (1982) A case of fetal abuse? *American Journal of Orthopsychiatry*, 52: 699–703.

Macleod, M. and Saraga, E. (1988) Challenging the orthodoxy: towards a feminist theory and practice, *Feminist Review*, 28: 15–55.

MacMillan, H.L. (2010) *Interventions to Prevent Child Maltreatment*. PreVAiL: Preventing Violence Across the Lifespan Research Network, available at: www.uwo.ca/fims/prevail/docs.

MacMillan, H.L. et al. (2009) Interventions to prevent child maltreatment and associated impairment, *The Lancet*, 373(9659): 250–66.

Madigan, S., Bakermans-Kranenburg, M. J., Van IJzendoorn, M. H., Moran, G., Pederson, D. R. and Benoit, D. (2006) Unresolved states of mind, anomalous parenting behaviour, and disorganized attachment: a review and meta-analysis of a transmission gap, *Attachment and Human Development*, 8: 89–111.

Maestripieri, D. (2010) Neurobiology of social behavior, in M. Platt and A. Ghazanfar (eds) *Primate Neuroethology*. Oxford: Oxford University Press.

Maestripieri, D., Wallen, K. and Carroll, K. (1997) Infant abuse runs in families of group-living pigtail macaques, *Child Abuse & Neglect*, 21: 465–71.

Main, N. and Goldwyn, R. (1984) Predicting rejection of her infant from mother's representation of her own experience: implications for the abused-abusing intergenerational cycle, *Child Abuse & Neglect*, 8: 203–17.

Main, M. and Solomon, J. (1990) Procedures for identifying infants as disorganized/disoriented during the Ainsworth Strange Situation, in M. T. Greenberg, D. Cicchetti and E. M. Cummings (eds) *Attachment in the Preschool Years: Theory, Research, and Intervention* (The John D. and Catherine T. MacArthur Foundation series on mental health and development, pp. 121–60). Chicago, IL: The University of Chicago Press.

Manion, K. (2002) Trafficking in women and children for sexual purposes: a growing threat in Europe, *Social Work in Europe*, 9: 14–22.

Margolin, L. (1992) Sexual abuse by grandparents, *Child Abuse & Neglect*, 16: 735–41.

Margolin, L. (1994) Child sexual abuse by uncles: a risk assessment, *Child Abuse & Neglect*, 18: 215–24.

Marneffe, C. (1996) Child abuse treatment: a fallow land, *Child Abuse & Neglect*, 20: 379–84.

Marr, N. and Field, T. (2001) *Bullycide: Death at Play-time*. Didcot: Success Unlimited.

Marsh, P. and Crowe, G. (1998) *Family Group Conferences in Child Welfare*. Oxford: Blackwell.

Martin, G., Bergen, H., Richardson, A., Roeger, L. and Allison, S. (2004) Sexual abuse and suicidality: gender differences in a large community sample of adolescents, *Child Abuse & Neglect*, 28: 491–503.

Martin, J. and Elmer, E. (1992) Battered children grown up: a follow-up study of individuals severely maltreated as children, *Child Abuse & Neglect*, 16: 75–87.

Masson, H. and Erooga, M. (1999) Children and young people who sexually abuse others: incidence, characteristics, causation, in M. Erooga and H. Masson (eds) *Children and Young People who Sexually Abuse Others: Challenges and Responses*. London: Routledge.

Masson, H. and O'Byrne, P. (1990) The family system approach: a help or hindrance?, in The Violence against Children Study Group, *Taking Child Abuse Seriously*. London: Unwin Hyman.

Masson, J. (1984) *Freud: The Assault on Truth*. London: Faber & Faber.

Masson, J., Pearce. J. and Bader, O. (2008) *Care Profiling Study*. London: Ministry of Justice.

Masten, A., Best, K. and Garmezy, N. (1990) Resilience and development: contributions from the study of children who overcome adversity, *Development and Psychopathology*, 2: 425–44.

May-Chahal, C. and Cawson, P. (2005) Measuring child maltreatment in the United Kingdom: a study of the prevalence of child abuse and neglect, *Child Abuse & Neglect*, 29(9): 969–84.

McCafferty, S. (2011) Behavioural-based interventions: social learning theory, in S. Goodman and I. Trowler (eds) *Social Work Reclaimed*, pp. 34–56. London: Jessica Kingsley.

McCloskey, K. and Raphael, D. (2005) Adult perpetrator gender asymmetries in child sexual assault victim selection: results from the 2000 National Incident-Based Reporting System, *Journal of Child Sexual Abuse*, 14: 1–24.

McClure, R. (1981) *Coram's Children: The London Foundling Hospital in the Eighteenth Century*. New Haven, CT: Yale University Press.

McClure, R. J., Davis, P. M., Meadow, S. R. and Sibert, J. R. (1996) Epidemiology of Munchausen syndrome by proxy, non-accidental poisoning, and non-accidental suffocation, *Archives of Disease in Childhood*, 75, 57–61.

McCluskey, U. (2005) *To Be Met as a Person: The Dynamics of Attachment in Professional Encounters*. London: Karnac.

McConnell, D. and Llewellyn, G. (2000) Disability and discrimination in statutory child protection proceedings, *Disability and Society*, 15: 883–95.

McCord, J. (1983) A 40 year perspective on the effects of child abuse and neglect, *Child Abuse & Neglect*, 7: 265–70.

McCrory, E., De Brito, S. A. and Viding, E. (2010) Research review: the neurobiology and genetics of maltreatment and adversity, *Journal of Child Psychology and Psychiatry*, doi: 10.1111/j.1469-7610.2010.02271.x, accessed February 2010.

Meadow, R. (1977) Munchausen syndrome by proxy: the hinterland of child abuse, *The Lancet*, 57: 92–8.

Meadow, R. (1997) *The ABC of Child Abuse*. London: British Medical Association.

Meiselman, K. (1978) *Incest*. San Francisco, CA: Jossey Bass.

Melton, G. and Flood, M. (1994) Research policy and child maltreatment: developing the scientific foundation for effective protection of children, *Child Abuse & Neglect*, 18 (supplement 1): 1–28.

Mennen, F. E., Kim, K., Sang, J. and Trickett, P. K. (2010) Child neglect: definition and identification of youth's experiences in official reports of maltreatment, *Child Abuse & Neglect*, 34: 647–58.

Messing, J. (2011) The social control of family violence, *Journal of Women and Social Work*, 26: 154–68.

Michenbaum, D. (1977) *Cognitive Behavior Modification: An Integrative Approach*. New York: Plenum Press.

Mikulincer, M. and Shaver, P. R. (2007) *Attachment in Adulthood: Structure, Dynamics and Change*. New York: Guilford Press.

Millar, M. and Corby, B. (2006) The framework for assessing the needs of children and their families: a basis for a 'therapeutic' encounter?, *British Journal of Social Work*, 36(6): 887–99.

Miller, A. (1985) *Thou Shalt Not Be Aware*. London: Pluto Press.

Miller, D. (2002) *Disabled Children and Abuse*, available at: http://www.nspcc.org.uk/inform/research/briefings/disabledchildrenandabuse_wda48224.html.

Miller, W. R. and Rollnick, S. (2002) *Motivational Interviewing: Preparing People to Change*, 2nd edn. New York: Guilford Press.

Ministry of Justice (2011) *Achieving Best Evidence in Criminal Proceedings: Guidance on Interviewing Victims and Witnesses, and Guidance on Using Special Measures*. London: Ministry of Justice.

Minuchin, S. (1974) *Families and Family Therapy*. Cambridge, MA: Harvard University Press.

Mitchell, J. (1974) *Psychoanalysis and Feminism*. London: Allen Lane.

Montagu, A. (1980) *Sociobiology Reexamined*. Oxford: Oxford University Press.

Montgomery, P. et al. (2009) *Systematic Reviews of Interventions Following Physical Abuse: Helping Practitioners and Expert Witnesses Improve the Outcomes of Child Abuse*, available at: www.education.gov.uk/research.

Montgomery, S. (1982) Problems in the perinatal prediction of child abuse, *British Journal of Social Work*, 12: 189–96.

Morrison, T., Erooga, M. and Beckett, R. (1994) *Sexual Offending Against Children: Assessment and Treatment of Male Abusers*. London: Routledge.

Morton, N. and Browne, K. (1998) Theory and observation of attachment and its relation to child maltreatment: a review, *Child Abuse & Neglect*, 22: 1093–104.

Mrazek, P. and Mrazek, D. (1987) Resilience in child maltreatment victims: a conceptual exploration, *Child Abuse & Neglect*, 11: 357–66.

Mueller, E. and Silverman, N. (1989) Peer relations in maltreated children, in D. Cicchetti and V. Carlson (eds) *Child Maltreatment: Theory and Research on the Causes and Consequences of Child Abuse and Neglect*. Cambridge: Cambridge University Press.

Mullender, A. and Morley, R. (1994) *Children Living with Domestic Violence: Putting Men's Abuse of Women on the Child Care Agenda*. London: Whiting & Birch.

Munir, A. and Yasin, S. (1997) Commercial sexual exploitation, *Child Abuse Review*, 6: 147–53.

Munro, E. (2002) *Effective Child Protection*. London: Sage.

Munro, E. (2008) *Effective Child Protection*, 2nd edn. London: Sage.

Munro, E. (2010) *The Munro Review of Child Protection – Part One: A Systems Analysis*. London: The Stationery Office.

Munro, E. (2011a) *The Munro Review of Child Protection – Interim Report: The Child's Journey*. London: The Stationery Office.

Munro, E. (2011b) *The Munro Review of Child Protection: Final Report*. London: The Stationery Office.

Munro, E. R., Brown, R. and Manful, E. (2011a) *Safeguarding Children Statistics: The Availability and Comparability of Data in the UK*. London: Childhood Wellbeing Research Centre.

Munro, E. R., Brown, R., Sempick, J., Ward, H. and Owen, C. (2011b) *Scoping Review to Draw Together Data on Child Injury and Safeguarding and to Compare the Position of England with that in Other Countries*. London: Childhood Wellbeing Research Centre.

Murphy-Beaman, V. (1994) A conceptual framework for thinking about risk assessment and case management in child protective services, *Child Abuse & Neglect*, 18: 193–201.

Mustillo, S., Dorsey, S., Conover, K. and Burns, B. (2011) Parental depression and child outcomes: the mediating effects of abuse and neglect, *Journal of Marriage and Family*, 73: 164–80.

National Center on Child Abuse and Neglect (1988) *Study Findings: Study of National Incidence and Prevalence of Child Abuse and Neglect* (Contract no. 105-85-1702). Washington, DC: Administration for Children, Youth and Families.

National Institute of Alcohol Abuse and Alcoholism (1993) *Eighth Special Report to U.S. Congress on Alcohol and Health*. Washington, DC: US Government Printing Office.

National Research Council and Institute of Medicine (2009) *Depression in Parents, Parenting, and Children: Opportunities to Improve Identification, Treatment, and Prevention*. Washington, DC: National Academies Press.

National Scientific Council on the Developing Child (2005) Excessive stress disrupts the architecture of the developing brain, working paper no. 3. Cambridge, MA: Center on the Developing Child, Harvard University, available at: http://developingchild.harvard.edu/library/reports_and_working_papers/wp3/, accessed 4 December 2009.

National Scientific Council on the Developing Child (2009) *Excessive Stress Disrupts the Architecture of the Developing Brain*, working paper 3. Cambridge, MA: Center on the Developing Child, Harvard University, available at: http://developingchild.harvard.edu/library/reports_and_working_papers/wp3/.

Nelson, B. (1984) *Making an Issue of Child Abuse: Political Agenda Setting for Social Problems*. Chicago: University of Chicago Press.

Nelson, S. (1987) *Incest: Fact and Myth*. Edinburgh: Strathmullion.

Neursten, L., Goldering, J. and Carpenter, S. (1984) Non-sexual transmission of sexually transmitted diseases: an infrequent occurrence, *Pediatrics*, 74: 67–76.

Newberger, C. and White, K. (1989) Cognitive foundations for parental care, in D. Cicchetti and V. Carlson (eds) *Child Maltreatment: Theory and Research on the Causes and Consequences of Child Abuse and Neglect*. Cambridge: Cambridge University Press.

Newham Area Child Protection Committee (2002) *Ainlee*. London Borough of Newham: Newham ACPC.

Ney, P., Fung, T. and Wickett, A. (1994) The worst combinations of child abuse and neglect, *Child Abuse & Neglect*, 18: 705–14.

Nobes, G. and Smith, M. (1997) Physical punishment of children in two parent families, *Clinical Child Psychology and Psychiatry*, 2: 271–81.

Nolan, M., Carr, A., O'Flaherty, A., Keary, K., Turner, R., O'Shea, D., Smyth, P. and Tobin, G. (2002) A comparison of two programmes for victims of child sexual abuse: a treatment outcome study, *Child Abuse Review*, 11: 103–23.

Oates, R., Forrest, D. and Peacock, A. (1985) Self-esteem of abused children, *Child Abuse & Neglect*, 9: 159–63.

O'Brien, N. and Moules T. (2011) *The Impact of Cyber-bullying on Young People's Mental Health*. Chelmsford: Department of Community and Family Studies, Faculty of Health and Social Care, Anglia Ruskin University.

Observer (2009) Baby P: born into a nightmare of abuse, violence and despair, he never stood a chance, 16 August.

Observer (2010) Female circumcision growing in Britain despite being illegal, 25 July.

Office for National Statistics (2001a) *Census 2001*. Cardiff: ONS.

Office for National Statistics (2001b) *Pyschaitric Morbidity Report*. London: ONS.

Office for National Statistics (2009) *Divorces in England and Wales, 2009*. Cardiff: ONS.

Ofsted (2009) *The Exclusion from School of Children Aged Four to Seven*. London: Office for Standards in Education, Children's Services and Skills.

O'Hagan, K. and Dillenberger, K. (1995) *The Abuse of Women in Childcare Work*. Buckingham: Open University Press.

Olds, D. et al. (1997) Long-term effects of home visitation on maternal life course and child abuse and neglect: fifteen-year follow-up of a randomized trial, *Journal of the American Medical Association*, 278: 637–43.

Oliver, C. and Candappa, M. (2003) *Tackling Bullying: Listening to the Views of Children and Young People*. London: DfES.

Oliver, J. (1985) Successive generations of child maltreatment, *British Journal of Psychiatry*, 147: 484–90.

Ong, B. (1985) The paradox of 'wonderful children': the case of child abuse, *Early Child Development and Care*, 21: 91–106.

Out, D., Bakermans-Kranenburg, M. J. and Van IJzendoorn, M. H. (2009) The role of disconnected and extremely insensitive parenting in the development of disorganized attachment: the validation of a new measure, *Attachment and Human Development*, 11: 419–43.

Owen, R. and Sweeting, A. (2007) *Hoodie or Goodie? The Link Between Violent Victimsation and Offending in Young People: A Research Report*. London: British Market Research Bureau.

Packman, J. (1975) *The Child's Generation: Child Care Policy from Curtis to Houghton*. Oxford: Blackwell.

Packman, J. (1986) *Who Needs Care?* Oxford: Blackwell.

Panter-Brick, C. (2002) Street children, human rights and public health: a critique and future directions, *Annual Review of Anthropology*, 31: 147–71.

Papadopoulos, L. (2010) *Sexualisation of Young People Review*, available at: http://webarchive. nationalarchives.gov.uk/20100418065544/http:/homeoffice.gov.uk/documents/Sexualisation-of-young-people.html.

Parker, H. and Parker, S. (1986) Father-daughter sexual abuse: an emerging perspective, *American Journal of Orthopsychiatry*, 56: 531–49.

Parker, H. J., Bakx, K. and Newcombe, R. (1988) *Living with Heroin: The Impact of a Drugs Epidemic on an English Community*. Milton Keynes: Open University Press.

Parton, N. (1979) The natural history of child abuse: a study in social problem definition, *British Journal of Social Work*, 9: 431–51.

Parton, N. (1981) Child abuse, social anxiety and welfare, *British Journal of Social Work*, 11: 391–414.

Parton, N. (1985) *The Politics of Child Abuse*. London: Macmillan.

Parton, N. (1990) Taking child abuse seriously, in The Violence Against Children Study Group, *Taking Child Abuse Seriously*. London: Unwin Hyman.

Parton, N. (1991) *Governing the Family: Child Care, Child Protection and the State*. London: Macmillan.

Parton, N. (2005) *Safeguarding Childhood: Early Intervention and Surveillance in Late Modern Society*. London: Palgrave Macmillan.

Parton, N. (2007) Safeguarding children: a socio-historical analysis, in K. Wilson and A. James (eds) *The Child Protection Handbook*. Oxford: Baillière Tindall.

Parton, N. and O'Byrne, P. (2000) *Constructive Social Work: Towards a New Practice*. Basingstoke: Macmillan.

Parton, N., Thorpe, D. and Wattam, C. (1996) *Child Protection, Risk and the Moral Order*. London: Macmillan.

Patterson, G. R. (1982) *Coercive Family Process*. Eugene, OR: Castalia Press.

Pavlov, I. (1927) *Conditioned Reflexes: An Investigation of the Physiological Activity of the Cerebral Cortex*. Oxford: Oxford University Press.

Pearl, J. (2009) Causal inference in statistics: an overview, *Statistics Surveys*, 3: 96–146.

Pelton, L. (1978) Child abuse and neglect: the myth of classlessness, *American Journal of Orthopsychiatry*, 48: 608–17.

Perrin, S., Smith, P. and Yule, W. (1999) Practitioner review: the assessment and treatment of post-traumatic stress disorder in children and adolescents, *Journal of Child Psychology and Psychiatry*, 41: 277–89.

Perry, B. (2002) Childhood experience and the expression of genetic potential: what childhood neglect tells us about nature and nurture, *Brain and Mind*, 3: 79–100.

Peters, R. and Barlow, J. (2003) Systematic review of instruments designed to predict child maltreatment during the antenatal and postnatal periods, *Child Abuse Review*, 12: 416–39.

Pfohl, S. (1977) The 'discovery' of child abuse, *Social Problems*, 24: 310–23.

Pierce, R. and Pierce, L. (1985) The sexually abused child: a comparison of male and female victims, *Child Abuse & Neglect*, 9: 191–9.

Pincus, A. and Minahan, A. (1973) *Social Work Practice: Models and Methods*. Itasca, IL: Peacock.

Pinker, S. (2002) *The Blank Slate: The Modern Denial of Human Nature*. New York: Viking Press.

Pithouse, A. and Holland, S. (1999) Open access family centres and their users: positive results, some doubts and new departures, *Children and Society*, 13: 167–78.

Platt, D. (2001) Refocusing children's services: evaluation of an initial assessment process, *Child and Family Social Work*, 6: 139–48.

Polansky, N., Chalmers, M., Buttenweiser, E. and Williams, D. (1985) *Damaged Parents: An Anatomy of Child Neglect*. Chicago: University of Chicago Press.

Pollock, L. (1983) *Forgotten Children: Parent-Child Relations from 1500 to 1900*. Cambridge: Cambridge University Press.

Porter, C., Lawson, J. and Bigler, E. (2005) Child neuropsychology, *Neuropsychology, Development and Cognition: Section C*, 11(2): 203–20.

Porter, R. (ed.) (1984) *Child Sexual Abuse within the Family*. London: Tavistock.

Prabhat, J., Kumar, R., Vasa, P., Dhingra, N., Thiruchelvam, D. and Moineddin, R. (2006) Low male-to-female sex ratio of children born in India: national survey of 1.1 million households, *The Lancet*, 367: 211–18.

Prevent Child Abuse America (2005) *Fact Sheet: Emotional Child Abuse*. Chicago: Prevent Child Abuse America.

Pringle, K. (1995) *Men, Masculinities and Social Welfare*. London: UCL Press.

Pringle, K. (1998) *Children and Social Welfare in Europe*. Buckingham: Open University Press.

Pritchard, C. (2004) *The Child Abusers: Research and Controversy*. Maidenhead: Open University Press.

Radford, L., Corral, S., Bradley, C., Fisher, H., Bassett, C., Howat, N. and Collishaw, S. (2011) *Child Abuse and Neglect in the UK Today*. London: NSPCC.

Ramchandani, P. and Jones, D. (2003) Treating psychological symptoms in sexually abused children, *British Journal of Psychiatry*, 183: 484–490.

Ravallion, M. and Chen, S. (2007) China's (uneven) progress against poverty, *Journal of Development Economics*, 82(1): 1–42.

Read, J. (1998) Child abuse and severity of disturbance among adult psychiatric patients, *Child Abuse & Neglect*, 22: 359–68.

Reavley, W. and Gilbert, M. (1979) The analysis and treatment of child abuse by behavioural psychotherapy, *Child Abuse & Neglect*, 3: 509–14.

Reder, P. and Duncan, S. (1998) A proposed system for reviewing child deaths, *Child Abuse Review*, 7: 280–86.

Reder, P., Duncan, S. and Gray, M. (1993) *Beyond Blame: Child Abuse Tragedies Revisited*. London: Routledge.

Rees, G. (1993) *Hidden Truths: Young People's Experiences of Running Away*. London: The Children's Society.

Rees, G. and Smeaton, M. (2001) *Child Runaways: Under 11s Running away in the UK*. London: The Children's Society.

Reite, M. (1987) Infant abuse and neglect: lessons from the laboratory, *Child Abuse & Neglect*, 11: 347–55.

Richardson, S. and Bacon, H. (2001) *Creative Responses to Child Sexual Abuse: Challenges and Dilemmas*. London: Jessica Kingsley.

Roberts, J. and Taylor, C. (1993) Sexually abused children and young people speak out, in L. Waterhouse (ed.) *Child Abuse and Child Abusers: Protection and Prevention*. London: Jessica Kingsley.

Roberts, J., Lynch, M. and Golding, J. (1980) Postneonatal mortality in children from abusing families, *British Medical Journal*, 281: 102–4.

Rorty, M., Yager, J. and Rossotto, E. (1995) Aspects of childhood physical punishment and family environmental correlates in bulimia nervosa, *Child Abuse & Neglect*, 19: 659–67.

Rose, L. (1986) *The Massacre of the Innocents*. London: Routledge & Kegan Paul.

Rose, L. (1991) *The Erosion of Childhood: Child Oppression in Britain 1860–1918*. London: Routledge.

Ross, G. and O'Carroll, P. (2004) Cognitive behavioural psychotherapy intervention in childhood sexual abuse: identifying new directions from the literature, *Child Abuse Review*, 13: 51–64.

Roudik, P. (2011) Children's rights: Russian Federation, available at: http://www.loc.gov/law/help/child-rights/russia.php.

Rowe, J. and Lambert, L. (1973) *Children Who Wait*. London: Association of British Agencies for Fostering and Adoption.

Royal College of Paediatrics and Child Health (2009) *Fabricated or Induced Illness by Carers (FII): A Practical Guide for Paediatricians*, available at: http://www.rcpch.ac.uk/sites/default/files/Fabricated%20or%20Induced%20Illness%20by%20Carers%20A%20Practical%20Guide%20for%20Paediatricians%202009.pdf.

Ruch, G., Turney, D. and Ward, A. (2010) *Relationship-based Social Work: Getting to the Heart of Practice*. London: Jessica Kingsley.

Rush, F. (1980) *The Best Kept Secret*. Englewood Cliffs, NJ: Prentice Hall.

Russell, D. (1986) *The Secret Trauma: Incest in the Lives of Girls and Women*. New York: Basic Books.

Rutter, M. (1978) *Maternal Deprivation Reassessed*. Harmondsworth: Penguin.

Rutter, M. (1985) Resilience in the face of adversity: protective factors and resistance to psychiatric disorder, *British Journal of Psychiatry*, 147: 598–611.

Rutter, M. (1993) Resilience: some conceptual considerations, *Journal of Adolescent Health*, 14: 626–31.

Ryan, G. (2002) Victims who go on to victimize others: no simple explanations, *Child Abuse & Neglect*, 26: 891–2.

Sack, W., Mason, R. and Higgins, J. (1985) The single-parent family and abusive child punishment, *American Journal of Orthopsychiatry*, 55: 253–9.

Samayam, P., Chander, R. and Reddy, S. (2011) An unusual case of failure to thrive in a child, *The National Medical Journal of India*, 24: 86–7.

Sanders, M., Cann, W. and Markie-Dadds, C. (2003) Why a universal population-level approach to the prevention of child abuse is essential, *Child Abuse Review*, 12: 145–54.

Scarre, G. (1980) Children and paternalism, *Philosophy*, 55: 117–24.

Schore, A.N. (2000) Attachment and the regulation of the right brain, *Attachment & Human Development*, 2(1): 23–47.

Schore, A.N. (2001) Effects of a secure attachment relationship on right brain development, affect regulation and infant mental health, *Journal of Infant Mental Health*, 22: 7–66.

Schwartz, M., O'Leary, S. G. and Kendziora, K. T. (1997) Dating aggression among high school students, *Journal of Violence and Victims*, 12: 295–305.

Schweppe, K. (2002) Child protection in Europe: different systems, common challenges, *German Law Journal*, available at: http://www.germanlawjournal.com/index.php?pageID=11&artID=196.

SCIE (2003) *Families that Have alcohol and Mental Health Problems: A Template for Partnership Working*. London: SCIE.

Scott, M. (1989) *A Cognitive-behavioural Approach to Clients' Problems*. London: Tavistock.

Scourfield, J. (2001) Constructing women in child protection work, *Child and Family Social Work*, 6: 77–87.

Scourfield, J. (2003) *Gender and Child Protection*. Basingstoke: Palgrave Macmillan.

Scourfield, J., Roen, K. and McDermott, E. (2011) The non-display of authentic distress: public-private dualism in young people's discursive construction of self-harm, *Sociology of Health and Illness*, 33(5): 777–91.

Seagull, E. (1987) Social support and child maltreatment: a review of the evidence, *Child Abuse & Neglect*, 11: 41–52.

Searing, H. (2003) The continuing relevance of casework ideas to long-term child protection work, *Child and Family Social Work*, 8: 311–20.

Sedlak, A. J. and Broadhurst, D. (1996) *Executive Summary of the Third National Incidence Study of Child Abuse and Neglect (NIS-3)*. Washington, DC: US Department of Health and Human Services, US Government Printing Office.

Sedlak, A. J., Mettenburg, J., Basena, M., Petta, I., McPherson, K., Greene, A. and Li, S. (2010) *Fourth National Incidence Study of Child Abuse and Neglect (NIS–4): Report to Congress, Executive Summary*. Washington, DC: US Department of Health and Human Services, Administration for Children and Families.

Seebohm, F. (1968) *Report of the Committee on Local Authority and Allied Personal Social Services*, Cmnd 3703. London: HMSO.

Seeley, K., Tombari, M. L., Bennett, L. J. and Dunkle, J. B. (2009) Peer victimization in schools: a set of quantitative and qualitative studies of the connections among peer victimization, school engagement, truancy, school achievement, and other outcomes, *National Center for School Engagement*, 1: 13–46.

Seng, J. S., Low, L. K., Sperlich, M., Ronis, D. L. and Liberzon, I. (2011) Post-traumatic stress disorder, child abuse history, birthweight and gestational age: a prospective cohort study, *BJOG: An International Journal of Obstetrics & Gynaecology*, 118(11): 1329–39.

Serious Organised Crime Agency (2011) *Making Every Child Matter . . . Everywhere*. London: Child Exploitation and Online Protection Centre.

Shahar, S. (1990) *Childhood in the Middle Ages*. London: Routledge.

Shapiro Gonzalez, L., Waterman, J., Kelly, R., McCord, J. and Oliver, M. (1993) Children's patterns of disclosure and recantations of sexual and ritualistic abuse allegations in psychotherapy, *Child Abuse & Neglect*, 17: 281–9.

Sharland, E., Seal, H., Croucher, M., Aldgate, J. and Jones, D. (1996) *Professional Intervention in Child Sexual Abuse*. London: HMSO.

Sharpe, J. (1984) *Crime in Early Modern England 1550–1750*. London: Longman.

Shaw, I. and Butler, I. (1998) Understanding young people and prostitution: a foundation for practice?, *British Journal of Social Work*, 28: 177–96.

Shaw, I., Bell, M., Sinclair, I., Sloper, P., Mitchell, W., Dyson, P., Clayden, J. and Rafferty, J. (2009) An exemplary scheme? An evaluation of the Integrated Children's System, *British Journal of Social Work*, 39(4): 613–26.

Shemmings, D. (ed.) (1999) *Involving Children in Family Support and Child Protection*. London: The Stationery Office.

Shemmings, D. (2000) Professionals' attitudes to children's participation in decision-making: dichotomous positions and doctrinal contests, *Child and Family Social Work*, 5(3): 235–44.

Shemmings, D. and Shemmings. Y. (2011) *Understanding Disorganised Attachment: Theory and Practice for Working with Children and Adults*. London: Jessica Kingsley.

Shemmings, D. Shemmings, Y. and Cook, A. (2012) Gaining the trust of 'highly resistant' families: insights from attachment theory and research, *Child & Family Social Work*, 17(2): 130–7.

Sheppard, M. (2003) The significance of past abuse to current intervention strategies with depressed mothers in child and family care, *British Journal of Social Work*, 33: 769–86.

Sher, L. and Hackman, N. (2002) Abandoned babies – abandoned issue, *Counselling Psychology Quarterly*, 15: 153–9.

Shin, S., Edwards, E. and Heeren, T. (2009) Child abuse and neglect: relations to adolescent binge drinking in the national longitudinal study of adolescent health (AddHealth) Study, *Addictive Behaviors*, 34: 277–80.

Shorter, E. (1976) *The Making of the Modern Family*. London: Collins.

Shumba, A. (2002) The nature, extent and effects of emotional abuse on primary school pupils by teachers in Zimbabwe, *Child Abuse & Neglect*, 26: 783–91.

Sidebotham, P. and Heron, J. (2006) Child maltreatment in the 'Children of the Nineties': a cohort study of risk factors, *Child Abuse & Neglect*, 30: 497–522.

Silbert, M. and Pines, A. (1981) Sexual child abuse as an antecedent to prostitution, *Child Abuse & Neglect*, 10: 283–91.

Silva, R. R., Alpert, M., Munoz, D. M. and Singh, S. (2000) Stress and vulnerability to post traumatic stress disorder in children and adolescents, *American Journal of Psychiatry*, 157(8): 1229–35.

Silverstein, M., Augustyn, M., Young, R., and Zuckerman, B. (2009) The relationship between maternal depression, in-home violence and use of physical punishment: what is the role of child behaviour? *Archives of Disease in Childhood*, 94: 138–43.

Simons, D., Wurtele, S. and Durham, R. (2008) Developmental experiences of child sexual abusers and rapists, *Child Abuse & Neglect*, 32: 549–60.

Sinclair, I. and Gibbs, I. (1998) *Children's Homes: A Study in Diversity*. Chichester: Wiley.

Sivan, A., Schor, D., Koeppi, G. and Noble, L. (1988) Interaction of normal children with anatomical dolls, *Child Abuse & Neglect*, 12: 295–304.

Sivarajasingam, J., Wells, S., Moore, P., Morgan., P. and Shepherd, J. (2010) *Violence in England and Wales in 2010: An Accident and Emergency Perspective*. Cardiff: University of Cardiff.

Skinner, A. (1992) *Another Kind of Home: A Review of Residential Child Care*. Edinburgh: HMSO.

Skinner, B. (1953) *Science and Human Behaviour*. Basingstoke: Collier Macmillan.

Slack, K., Berger, L., DuMont, K., Yang, M., Kim, B., Ehrhard-Dietzel, S. and Holl, J. (2011) Risk and protective factors for child neglect during early childhood: a cross-study comparison, *Children and Youth Services Review*, 33: 1354–63.

Slade, A. (2008) Working with parents in child psychotherapy: engaging the reflective function, in F. N. Busch (ed.) *Mentalisation: Theoretical Considerations, Research Findings and Clinical Implications*. New York: Taylor & Francis.

Smart, S., Neale, B. and Wade, A. (2001) *The Changing Experience of Childhood: Families and Divorce*. Cambridge: Polity.

Smith, J. (1984) Non-accidental injury to children 1: a review of behavioural intervention, *Behaviour Research and Therapy*, 22: 331–47.

Smith, J. and Rachman, S. (1984) Non-accidental injury to children II: a controlled evaluation of a behavioural management programme, *Behaviour Research and Therapy*, 22: 349–66.

Smith, M. and Prader, L. (1980) *Michelle Remembers*. New York: Congdon & Lattes.

Smith, P. (1991) The child's voice, *Children and Society*, 5: 58–66.

Smith, P. K. and Shu, S. (2000) What good schools can do about bullying: findings from a survey in English schools after a decade of research and action, *Childhood*, 7: 193–212.

Smolin, D. (2006) Overcoming religious objections to the Convention on the Rights of the Child, *Emory International Law Review*, 20(1): 81–110.

Social Services Inspectorate (1999) *Inspection of Services to Support Disabled Adults in their Parenting Role*. Bristol: Department of Health.

Social Services Inspectorate, Wales, and Social Information Systems (1991) *Accommodating Children: A Review of Children's Homes in Wales*. Cardiff: Welsh Office.

Social Work Task Force (2009) *Building a Safe, Confident Future*. London: DH/DCSF.

Social Work Task Force (2010) *Building a Safe and Confident Future: One Year On – Detailed Proposals from the Social Work Reform Board*. London: DfE.

Somerset Area Review Committee (1977) *Report of the Review Panel Appointed by Somerset Area Review Committee to Consider the Case of Wayne Brewer*. Taunton: Somerset Area Review Committee.

Sommerville, J. (1982) *The Rise and Fall of Childhood*. Beverly Hills, CA: Sage.

Spangler, G. and Zimmermann, P. (2007) Genetic contribution to attachment and temperament, paper presented at the biennial meeting of the Society for Research in Child Development, Boston, MA, 29 March–1 April.

Sparks, J. and Duncan, B. (2004) The ethics and science of medicating children, *Ethical Human Psychology and Psychiatry*, 6: 25–39.

Spencer, J. (1989) *Suffer the Child*. New York: Simon & Schuster.

Spratt, T. (2001) The influence of child protection orientation on child welfare practice, *British Journal of Social Work*, 31: 933–54.

Spratt, T. and Callan, J. (2004) Parents' views on social work interventions in child welfare cases, *British Journal of Social Work*, 34: 199–224.

Sroufe, L. A., Egeland, B., Carlson, E. and Collins, W. A. (2005) Placing early attachment experiences in developmental context, in K. E. Grossmann, K. Grossmann and E. Waters (eds) *The Power of Longitudinal Attachment Research: From Infancy and Childhood to Adulthood*. New York: Guilford.

Sroufe, L. A., Egeland, B., Carlson. W. and Collins, A (2009) *The Development of the Person: The Minnesota Study of Risk and Adaptation from Birth to Adulthood*. New York: Guilford Press.

Staffordshire County Council (1991) *The Pindown Experience and the Protection of Children: The Report of the Staffordshire Child Care Inquiry 1990*. Stafford: Staffordshire County Council.

Stalker, C. and Fry, R. (1999) A comparison of short-term group and individual therapy for sexually abused women, *Canadian Journal of Psychiatry*, 44: 168–74.

Stanley, N., Penhale, B., Riordan, D., Barbour, S. and Holden, S. (2003) *Child Protection and Mental Health Services: Inter-professional Responses to the Needs of Mothers*. Bristol: Polity Press.

Statham, J. and Holtermann, S. (2004) Familes on the brink: the effectiveness of family support services, *Child and Family Social Work*, 9: 153–66.

Steele, B. (1986) Notes on the lasting effects of early child abuse throughout the life cycle, *Child Abuse & Neglect*, 10: 283–91.

Steele, B. and Pollock, C. (1974) A psychiatric study of parents who abuse infants and small children, in R. Heifer and C. Kempe (eds) *The Battered Child*, 2nd edn. Chicago: University of Chicago Press.

Steen, K. and Hunskaar, S. (2004) Gender and physical violence, *Social Science and Medicine*, 59: 567–71.

Stephenson, P. (1997) *The Causes of Institutionalisation in Romania*. Bucharest: UNICEF.

Stevenson, J. and Cook, C. (1977) *The Slump: Society and Politics During the Depression*. London: Jonathan Cape.

Stevenson, O. (1998) *Neglected Children: Issues and Dilemmas*. Oxford: Blackwell.

Stith, S., Ting Liu, L., Davies, C., Boykin, E., Alder, M., Harris, J., Som, A., McPherson, M. and Dees, J. (2009) Risk factors in child maltreatment: a meta-analytic review of the literature, *Aggression and Violent Behaviour*, 14: 13–29.

Stobart, E. (2006) *Child Abuse Linked to Accusations of 'Possession' and 'Witchcraft'*. London: DfES.

Stoltenborgh, M. et al. (2011) A global perspective on child sexual abuse: meta-analysis of prevalence around the world, *Child Maltreatment*, 16(2): 79–101.

Stone, L. (1977) *The Family, Sex and Marriage in England 1500–1800*. London: Weidenfeld & Nicolson.

Stop It Now (2007) *Do Children Sexually Abuse Other Children? Preventing Sexual Abuse Among Children and Youth*. Brandon, VT: Safer Society Press.

Straus, M. (1979) Family patterns and child abuse in a nationally representative sample, *Child Abuse & Neglect*, 3: 213–25.

Straus, M. (1994) *Beating the Devil Out of Them: Corporal Punishment in American Families*. New York: Lexington Books.

Straus, M. and Gelles, R. (1986) Societal change and change in family violence from 1975 to 1985 as revealed by two national surveys, *Journal of Marriage and the Family*, 48: 465–79.

Straus, M. and Kantor, G. (2005) Definition and measurement of neglectful behavior: some principles and guidelines, *Child Abuse & Neglect*, 29: 19–29.

Straus, M. and Stewart, J. (1999) Corporal punishment by American parents: national data on prevalence, chronicity, severity and duration in relation to child and family characteristics, *Clinical Child and Family Psychology Review*, 2: 55–70.

Street, K., Harrington, J., Chiang, W., Cairns, P. and Ellis, M. (2003) How great is the risk of abuse in infants born to drug-using mothers? *Child: Care, Health & Development*, 30: 325–30.

Sullivan, J., Beech, A., Craig, L. and Gannon, T. (2011) comparing intra-familial and extra-familial child sexual abusers with professionals who have sexually abused children with whom they work, *International Journal of Offender Therapy and Comparative Criminology*, 55: 56–74.

Sullivan, P. and Knutson, J. (2000a) Maltreatment and disabilities: a population-based epidemiological study, *Child Abuse & Neglect*, 23: 1257–73.

Sullivan, P. and Knutson, J. (2000b) The prevalence of disabilities and maltreatment among runaway children, *Child Abuse & Neglect*, 23: 1275–88.

Swann, S. (1998) *Whose Daughter Next?* Essex: Barnardo's.

Swanston, H., Plunkett, A., O'Toole, B., Shrimpton, S., Parkinson, P. and Gates, R. (2003) Nine years after child sexual abuse, *Child Abuse & Neglect*, 27: 967–84.

Sydie, R. (1987) *Natural Women, Cultured Men*. Milton Keynes: Open University Press.

Tajima, E. A., Herrenkohl, T. I., Moylan, C. A. and Derr, A. S. (2011) Moderating the effects of childhood exposure to intimate partner violence: the roles of parenting characteristics and adolescent peer support, *Journal of Research on Adolescence*, 21(2): 376–94.

Tang, C. S. (1998) The rate of physical child abuse in Chinese families: a community survey in Hong Kong, *Child Abuse & Neglect*, 22(5): 381–91.

Testa, M., Hoffman, J. and Livingston, J. (2011) Intergenerational transmission of sexual victimization vulnerability as medicated via parenting, *Child Abuse & Neglect*, 35: 363–71.

The China Post (2010) Reports of child abuse increasing significantly, available at: http://www.chinapost.com.tw/taiwan/national/national-news/2010/04/03/250970/Reports-of.htm.

The Daily Telegraph (2011) Human traffickers could target Olympics, Home Secretary warns, available at: www.telegraph.co.uk/news/uknews/immigration/8647246/Human-traffickers-could-target-Olympics-Home-Secretary-warns.html.

Thoburn, J., Lewis, A. and Shemmings, D. (1995) *Paternalism or Partnership? Family Involvement in the Child Protection Process*. London: HMSO.

Thoburn, J., Wilding, J. and Watson, J. (2000) *Family Support in Cases of Emotional Maltreatment and Neglect*. London: The Stationery Office.

Thompson, A. (1995) Running out of time, *Community Care*, 7–13 December, pp. 14–15.

Thorpe, D. (1994) *Evaluating Child Protection*. Buckingham: Open University Press.

Thyen, U., Thiessen, R. and Heisohn-Krug, M. (1995) Secondary prevention: serving families at risk, *Child Abuse & Neglect*, 19: 1337–47.

Tickell, C. (2011) *The Early Years: Foundations for Life, Health and Learning*, available at: http://www.education.gov.uk/tickellreview.

Tilly, L., Fuchs, R., Kertzer, D. and Ransel, D. (1992) Child abandonment in European history: a symposium, *Journal of Family History*, 17: 1–22.

Tingus, K., Heger, A., Foy, D. and Leskin, G. (1996) Factors associated with entry into therapy for children evaluated for sexual abuse, *Child Abuse & Neglect*, 20: 63–8.

Tiurukanova, E. and the Institute for Urban Economics (2006) *Human Trafficking in the Russian Federation: Inventory and Analysis of the Current Situation and Responses*. Moscow: UNICEF/ILO/CIDA.

Tomak, S., Weschler, F., Ghahramanlou-Holloway, M., Virden, T. and Nademin, M. (2009) An empirical study of the personality characteristics of internet sex offenders, *Journal of Sexual Aggression*, 15: 139–48.

Tong, L., Gates, K. and McDowell, M. (1987) Personality development following sexual abuse, *Child Abuse & Neglect*, 11: 371–83.

Tooley, G. A., Karakis, M., Stokes, M. and Ozannesmith, J. (2006) Generalising the Cinderella effect to unintentional childhood fatalities, *Evolution and Human Behavior*, 27: 224–30.

Toth, S., Cicchetti, D., Macfie, J. and Emde, R. (1997) Representations of self and other in the narratives of neglected, physically abused and sexually abused pre-schoolers, *Development and Psychopathology*, 9(4): 781–96.

Trickey, D. and Black, D. (2009) Child trauma, in M. Gelder et al. (eds) *New Oxford Textbook of Psychiatry*, 2nd edn. Oxford: Oxford University Press.

Trowell, J., Kelvin, L., Weeramanthri, T., Sadowski, H., Berelowitz, D., Glasser, D. and Leitch, I. (2002) Psychotherapy for sexually abused girls: psychopathological outcome findings and patterns of change, *British Journal of Psychiatry*, 180: 234–47.

Tunstill, J. and Aldgate, J. (2000) *Services for Children in Need: From Policy to Practice*. London: The Stationery Office.

Turic, D., Swanson, J. and Sonuga-Barke, E. (2010) DRD4 and DAT1 in ADHD: functional neurobiology to pharmacogenetics, *Pharmacogenomics and Personalized Medicine*, 3: 61–78.

Turnell, A. (2009) *Of Houses, Wizards and Fairies: Involving Children in Child Protection Casework*. Perth: Resolutions Consultancy.

UNICEF (1997) *The Progress of Nations*. New York: UNICEF.

UNICEF (2003) *Guide to the Optional Protocol on the Involvement of Children in Armed Conflict*. New York: UNICEF.

UNICEF (2008) *Handbook on Legislative Reform: Realising Children's Rights*. New York: UNICEF.

UNICEF (2011) *The State of the World's Children*. New York: UNICEF.

United Nations (2000) *Protocol to Prevent, Suppress and Punish Trafficking Persons, Especially Women and Children, Supplementing the UN Convention Against Transnational Organisational Crime*. New York: Office of the United Nations High Commissioner for Human Rights.

US Department of Health and Human Services, Administration on Children, Youth and Families (2007a, 2008, 2009) *Child Maltreatment 2005, 2006, 2007*. Washington, DC: US Government Printing Office.

US Department of Health and Human Services, Administration on Children, Youth and Families (2007b) *National Child Abuse and Neglect Data System*. Washington, DC: US Government Printing Office.

US Department of Health and Human Services, Administration for Children and Families, Administration on Children, Youth and Families, Children's Bureau (2010a, 2010b) *Child Maltreatment 2009, 2010*, available at: http://www.acf.hhs.gov/programs/cb/stats_research/index.htm@n and http://www.acf.hhs.gov/programs/cb/stats_research/index.htm@n.

Utting, Sir W. (1991) *Children in the Public Care: A Review of Residential Child Care*. London: HMSO.

Utting, Sir W. (1997) *People Like Us: The Report of the Review of the Safeguards for Children Living Away from Home*. London: HMSO.

Utting, D., Monteiro, H. and Ghate, D. (2007) *Interventions for Children at Risk of Developing Antisocial Personality Disorder*. London: PRB/Department of Health/Cabinet Office.

Uzodike, E. (2000) Child abuse: the Nigerian perspective, in M. Freeman (ed.) *Overcoming Child Abuse: A Window on a World Problem*. Dartmouth: Ashgate.

Van IJzendoorn, M. H. and Bakermans-Kranenburg, M. J. (2003) Attachment disorders and disorganised attachment: same or different? *Attachment & Human Development*, 5(3): 313–20.

Veltman, M. W. and Browne, K. D. (2001) Three decades of child maltreatment research: implications for the school years, *Trauma, Violence, and Abuse*, 2(3): 215–39.

Verduyn, C. and Calam, R. (1999) Cognitive behavioral interventions with maltreated children and adolescents, *Child Abuse & Neglect*, 23: 197–207.

Vinchon, M., Defoort-Dhellemmes, S., Desurmont, M. and Dhellemmes, P. (2005) Accidental and non-accidental head injuries in infants: a prospective study, *Journal of Neurosurgery*, 102: 380–4.

von Mandach, U. (2005) Drug use in pregnancy, *Ther Umsch*, 62: 29–35.

Wald, M. (1982) State intervention on behalf of endangered children: a proposed legal response, *Child Abuse & Neglect*, 6: 3–45.

Wald, M. and Wolverton, M. (1990) Risk assessment: the emperor's new clothes?, *Child Welfare*, 69: 483–511.

Waller, G. (1994) Childhood sexual abuse and borderline personality disorder in eating disorders, *Child Abuse & Neglect*, 18: 97–102.

Wandsworth (London Borough of) (1990) *Report of the Inquiry into the Death of Stephanie Fox.* London: London Borough of Wandsworth.

Wardhaugh, J. and Wilding, P. (1993) Towards an explanation of the corruption of care, *Critical Social Policy*, 37: 4–31.

Warner, N. (1992) *Choosing with Care: The Report of the Committee of Inquiry into the Selection, Development and Management of Staff in Children's Homes.* London: HMSO.

Wastell, D., Peckover, S., White, S., Broadhurst, K., Hall, C. and Pithouse, A. (2011) Work in the laboratory: using microworlds for practice research, *British Journal of Social Work*, 41: 744–60.

Waterhouse, L. and Carnie, J. (1992) Assessing child protection risk, *British Journal of Social Work*, 22: 47–60.

Waterhouse, Sir R. (2000) *Lost in Care: The Report of the Tribunal of Inquiry into the Abuse of Children in Care in the Former County Council Areas of Gwynedd and Clwyd since 1974*, HC 201. London: The Stationery Office.

Webb, E., Maddocks, A. and Bongilli, J. (2002) Effectively protecting black and minority children from harm: overcoming barriers to the child protection process, *Child Abuse Review*, 11: 394–410.

Webster, R. (2005) *Why Freud was Wrong: Sin, Science and Psychoanalysis.* Oxford: Orwell Press.

Webster-Stratton, C. and Reid, J. M. (2005) *Adapting the Incredible Years Child Dinosaur: Social, Emotional, and Problem-solving Intervention to Address Co-morbid Diagnoses and Family Risk Factors.* Seattle, WA: University of Washington.

Welch, S. and Fairburn, C. (1996) Childhood sexual and physical abuse as risk factors for the development of bulimia nervosa: a community-based case control study, *Child Abuse & Neglect*, 20: 633–42.

Wellbourne, P. (2002) Videotaped evidence of children: application and implications of the *Memorandum of Good Practice*, *British Journal of Social Work*, 32: 553–71.

West, A. (2005) *Hubs and Centres for Developing Children's Participation and Child Protection in China.* Beijing: Save the Children.

West, D. and Farrington, D. (1977) *The Delinquent Way of Life: Third Report of the Cambridge Study in Delinquent Development.* London: Heinemann.

Westcott, H. and Kynan, S. (2006) Interviewer practice in investigative interviews for suspected child sexual abuse, *Psychology, Crime and Law*, 12: 367–82.

Westcott, H. and Page, M. (2002) Cross-examination, sexual abuse and child witness identity, *Child Abuse Review*, 11: 137–52.

Westcott, H., Kynan, S. and Few, C. (2006) Improving the quality of investigative interviews for suspected child abuse: a case study, *Psychology, Crime and Law*, 12: 77–96.

Whitaker, D., Le, B., Hanson, K., Baker, C., McMahon, P., Ryan, G., Klein, A. and Rice, D. (2008) Risk factors for the perpetration of child sexual abuse: a review and meta-analysis, *Child Abuse & Neglect*, 32: 529–48.

White, I. and Hart, K. (1995) *Report of the Management of Child Care in the London Borough of Islington.* London: London Borough of Islington.

White, S. (1997) Beyond retroduction? Hermeneutics, reflexivity and social work practice, *British Journal of Social Work*, 27(5): 739–53.

White, S., Hall, C. and Peckover, S. (2009) The descriptive tyranny of the Common Assessment Framework: technologies of categorisation and professional practice in child welfare, *British Journal of Social Work*, 39(7): 1197–217.

White, S., Wastell, D. G., Broadhurst, K. and Hall, C. (2010) When policy o'erleaps itself: the tragic tale of the Integrated Children's System, *Critical Social Policy*, 30(3): 405–29.

Whitmore, E., Kramer, J. and Knutson, J. (1993) The association between punitive childhood experiences and hyperactivity, *Child Abuse & Neglect*, 17: 357–66.

Widom, C. (2000) Childhood victimization: early adversity, later psychopathology, *National Institute of Justice Journal*, available at: www.communitycare.co.uk/Articles/2007/10/31/106309/research-children-with-antisocial-personality-disorders.htm.

Widom, C. and Hiller-Sturmhofel, S. (2001) Alcohol abuse as a risk factor for and consequence of child abuse, *Alcohol Research and Health*, 25: 52–7.

Widom, C., Raphael, K. and Dumont, K. (2004) The case for prospective longitudinal studies in child maltreatment research: commentary on Dube, Williamson, Thompson, Felitti and Anda (2004), *Child Abuse & Neglect*, 28: 715–22.

Wiedemann, T. (1989) *Adults and Children in the Roman Empire* London: Routledge.

Wiehe, V. (1989) Child abuse: an ecological perspective, *Early Child Development and Care*, 42: 141–5.

Wiehe, V. (1991) *Perilous Rivalry: When Siblings Become Abusive*. San Francisco: Lexington Books.

Wilkinson, R. and Pickett, K. (2010) *The Spirit Level*. London: Penguin.

Wilsnack, S., Vogeltanz, N., Klassen, A. and Harris, T. (1997) Childhood sexual abuse and women's substance abuse: national survey findings, *Journal of Studies on Alcohol*, 58: 264–71.

Wilson, E. (1975) *Sociobiology: The New Synthesis*. Cambridge, MA: Harvard University Press.

Wilson, S. (1984) The myth of motherhood: the historical view of European child rearing, *Social History*, 9: 181–98.

Wohl, A. (1978) Sex and the single room: incest among the Victorian working classes, in A. Wohl (ed.) *The Victorian Family*. London: Croom Helm.

Wolak, J., Finkelhor, D., Mitchell, D. and Jones, L. (2011) Arrests for child pornography production: data at two time points from a national sample of US law enforcement agencies, *Child Maltreatment*, 16: 184–95.

Wolfe, D. (1985) Child-abusive parents: an empirical review and analysis, *Psychological Bulletin*, 97: 462–82.

Wolfe, D., Sandier, J. and Kaufman, K. (1981) A competency-based parent training program for child abusers, *Journal of Consulting and Clinical Psychology*, 49: 633–40.

Wolock, L. and Horowitz, B. (1984) Child maltreatment as a social problem: the neglect of neglect, *American Journal of Orthopsychiatry*, 54: 530–43.

Woodhead, M. and Montgomery, H. (2003) *Understanding Childhood: An Interdisciplinary approach*. Chichester: Wiley.

Wurr, C. and Partridge, I. (1996) The prevalence of a history of childhood sexual abuse in an acute adult inpatient population, *Child Abuse & Neglect*, 20: 867–72.

Yampolsky L., Lev-Wiesel, R. and Ben-Zion, I. Z. (2010) Child sexual abuse: is it a risk factor for pregnancy? *Journal of Advanced Nursing*, 66(9): 2025–37.

Yelloly, M. (1980) *Social Work Theory and Psychoanalysis*. New York: Van Nostrand Reinhold.

Yorkshire Evening Post (2008a) Police quiz 1,500 drivers in hunt for missing Shannon, 28 February.

Yorkshire Evening Post (2008b) Search for Shannon: 3,000 homes to be searched, 5 March.

Index

**CONDUCTING THE HOME VISIT
IN CHILD PROTECTION**

Joanna Nicolas

9780335245277 (Paperback)
May 2012

eBook also available

Conducting a home visit is a fundamental part of a social worker's role, but in practical terms many key issues are overlooked during social work training.

Part of a new Social Work Pocketbooks series, this is a practical guide to conducting home visits, a task which many feel unprepared for and is fraught with difficulties.

Key features:

- Real case examples
- Realistic solutions to the everyday difficulties you face
- Examples of what to say

OPEN UNIVERSITY PRESS
McGraw - Hill Education

www.openup.co.uk

**SAFEGUARDING BABIES
AND YOUNG CHILDREN**
A Guide for Early Years Professionals
John Powell and Elaine Uppal

9780335234080 (Paperback)
2012

eBook also available

This practical and challenging book focuses on the relationship that early years professionals have with babies, young children and their families/carers. Powell and Uppal reprioritize practice in safeguarding and child protection, and emphasizing the importance of focusing on the skills needed to work successfully in this arena.

Key features:

- Highly practical discussion about safeguarding babies and young children
- A brief history and overview of a number of issues and their relevance for practice
- Case studies allowing the reader to rehearse their possible approaches to a particular scenario

www.openup.co.uk

OPEN UNIVERSITY PRESS
McGraw - Hill Education

SAFEGUARDING AND CHILD PROTECTION FOR NURSES, MIDWIVES AND HEALTH VISITORS
A Practical Guide

Catherine Powell

9780335236145 (Paperback)
2011

eBook also available

"All nurses have a duty to inform and alert appropriate personnel if they suspect a child has been abused, and to know where they can seek expert advice and support if they have concerns. This comprehensive text providing the link between legislation, policy, research and practice will enable students and practitioners to expand their knowledge and understanding of the key issues involved in safeguarding children and young people."
Fiona Smith, Adviser in Children and Young People's Nursing, Royal College of Nursing, UK

Key features:

- Includes realistic case scenarios, examples and reflective points throughout
- Covers the biggest safeguarding 'category' - physical, sexual and emotional abuse, as well as neglect
- Includes crucial chapters on integrated working and supervision and support in safeguarding

OPEN UNIVERSITY PRESS
McGraw · Hill Education

www.openup.co.uk

**WORKING WITH DENIED
CHILD ABUSE**
The Resolutions Approach

Andrew Turnell and Susie Essex

9780335216574 (Paperback)
2006

eBook also available

Working with 'Denied' Child Abuse presents an innovative, safety-focused, partnership-based, model called Resolutions, which provides an alternative approach for responding rigorously and creatively to such cases. It describes each stage of this practical model and demonstrates the approach through many case examples from therapists, statutory social workers and other professionals working in Europe, North America and Australasia.

Key features:

- How professionals can build constructive relationships with families where the parents dispute professional allegations of serious child abuse
- How meaningful safety for children can be created in these families
- How professionals can work together constructively in such cases

www.openup.co.uk

OPEN UNIVERSITY PRESS
McGraw - Hill Education